The BIG BOOK of HOCKEY TRIVIA

by DON WEEKES

GREYSTONE BOOKS
Vancouver / Toronto / Berkeley

To the game, and fans everywhere.

05 06 07 08 09 5 4 3 2

Greystone Books
A division of Douglas & McIntyre Ltd.
2323 Quebec Street, Suite 201
Vancouver, British Columbia
Canada V5T 4S7
www.greystonebooks.com

Library and Archives Canada Cataloguing in Publication
Weekes, Don
The big book of hockey trivia / Don Weekes
ISBN-13 978-1-55365-119-2
ISBN-10 1-55365-119-7
1. Hockey—Miscellanea 2. National Hockey League—Miscellanea I. Title.
GV847.W355 2005 796.962'64 C2005-903701-6

Library of Congress information is available upon request

Editing by Anne Rose
Cover design by Peter Cocking & Jessica Sullivan
Cover photo by Jessica Sullivan
Interior design and typesetting by Lisa Hemingway
Printed and bound in Canada by Friesens
Distributed in the U.S. by Publishers Group West

We gratefully acknowledge the financial support of the Canada Council for the Arts, the British Columbia Arts Council, and the Government of Canada through the Book Publishing Industry Development Program (BPIDP) for our publishing activities.

DON WEEKES *is an award-winning television producer at* CTV *in Montreal. He has written numerous hockey trivia books, including co-authoring the* Unofficial Guide *series.*

Contents

Introduction

After 14 years, 21 books, 300 puzzles and more than 4,200 trivia questions, we've finally gotten around to producing a "best of" book from our popular *Hockey Trivia* series. So what took so long? Frankly, I couldn't wrap my head around defining what made a trivia question "the best." Did it have to be especially hard? Really interesting? Truly unusual? I'd like to think those were our standards when we began writing trivia and making puzzles in 1991. Each question should spark debate; every puzzle should be a brainteaser, we thought. Still, let's face it, some of our trivia *is* more challenging because we deliberately taunt hockey fans with a variety of questions that all ages can sharpen their game skills on.

So how did we cull from the thousands of trivia questions we've written over the years to create an All-Star collection of anecdotes and quotes called *The Big Book of Hockey Trivia*? Well, it was a little easier than I thought it would be. We stuck with those "fun" qualities in the trivia that brought out the kid in us, stuff that made us say "Huh! I didn't know that" or "Yeah, that one's easy!" With that settled, our selection became a conscious choice of what questions best hit the mark on the NHL's most celebrated and least recognized exploits, innovations and opinions.

Through it all we dug up hundreds of new and forgotten treasures, such as little-known goalie Dave Gatherum's 100 minutes of shutout netminding, the longest such stretch from a career start; or the reason why Maurice Richard chose to wear his famous No. 9 on his jersey. We retold some classics, including tough guy Lou Fontinato's devastating blunder in fighting Gordie Howe, and Bronco Horvath's season-long battle with Bobby Hull that saw Horvath lose his place in history as an NHL scoring leader by one heartbreaking point.

We also discovered some minutiae: obscure connections in the careers of Doug Jarvis and Bob Bourne, and Mike Ramsey and Craig Ramsay; all the hockey faces that appeared on the cover of *Time* magazine; destiny's snub of Ted Lindsay and his drive to become the NHL's first 1,000-game man; and the multitude of number fours strangely linked to Bobby Orr's famous Cup-winner of 1970.

Hockey trivia is never static. *The Big Book of Hockey Trivia* has also been an opportunity for us to update our hockey facts, feats and firsts with current records and stories that make the game more relevant to today's enthusiasts. For example, what was once the mark for most shots faced by a goalie in one season is now a footnote thanks to Roberto Luongo, who smashed the old record with his 2,303-shot season in 2003–04.

More than a revision or review of past material, *Big Book* has also allowed us to present a large volume of trivia material with a fresh perspective. Our *Hockey Trivia* series evolved during an era of great change in the sport, between 1991 and 2005. There was always much to write about, but sometimes not enough of the right material presented itself to compile a decent set of trivia questions in our interactive chapter format. With new questions added, we hope this book is more comprehensive on those themes.

The Big Book of Hockey Trivia happened because of publisher Rob Sanders, who thought we could present some of our best trivia in a really big edition at a reasonable price to hockey fans. In the year of the nuclear winter of 2004–05, when the NHL went dark, it certainly felt appropriate to give a little more to our ailing game.

Our *Hockey Trivia* series has always been about those big and small events that define the game; those stories that appeal to its fans—from the pond hockey players to the midnight beer leaguers. Hopefully, *The Big Book of Hockey Trivia* will help keep alive that little kid in all of us.

Don Weekes
June 2005

1

Showtime

MOST HOCKEY PLAYERS are superstitious. Before each game they follow a closely scripted routine for dressing, lacing up and hitting the ice, and sometimes they can get quite inventive in their search for good-luck charms. So when Montreal Canadiens captain Vincent Damphousse glided to centre ice for the ceremonial faceoff against the Tampa Bay Lightning in March 1998, he knew exactly what he was about to do. After the puck was dropped by pop diva Celine Dion, Damphousse planted a kiss on the lady's cheek. "I wanted some of her talent to rub off on me," Damphousse said. It worked, considering he went on to score a hat trick in the Habs' 8–2 romp over the Lightning. In this opening faceoff on general hockey trivia, may Lady Luck sprinkle a little success over your game plan, too.

Answers are on page 12

1.1 Which NHL city hosted the largest crowd ever at a league game?

A. Detroit
B. Edmonton
C. Toronto
D. Miami

1.2 Which NHL city is known as Hockeytown?

A. Toronto
B. Philadelphia
C. New York
D. Detroit

1.3 What does hockey's legendary number 544 represent?

A. Maurice Richard's NHL career goal-scoring total
B. Phil Esposito's NHL record for most shots on goal
C. Wayne Gretzky's NHL career playoff-point total
D. Dave Schultz's NHL record for most penalty minutes

1.4 Even though Wayne Gretzky is famous for his playmaking behind opponents' nets, he wasn't the first to use this tactic. Who was?

A. Bryan Trottier
B. Bobby Clarke
C. Ken Hodge
D. Jacques Lemaire

1.5 Which excuse did legendary goalie Glenn Hall use to avoid training camp each fall?

A. He was painting his barn
B. He had a groin pull
C. He was writing his memoirs
D. He was being fitted for new pads

1.6 What significant event took place on October 5, 1965?

A. Gordie Howe became the NHL's first 20-year player
B. Long-time NHL president Clarence Campbell retired
C. Mario Lemieux and Patrick Roy were born
D. The NHL announced expansion plans for a second six-team division

1.7 What do baseball great Hank Aaron and hockey broadcaster Don Cherry have in common?

A. Both have the same birthdate
B. Both set league records in their respective sports
C. Both wear flamboyant suits with high-collared shirts
D. Both were the last players to play all positions in one game in their respective sports

1.8 In 1999–2000, hockey fanatic Taylor Railton visited every NHL arena to see each of the league's teams play a home game. How did he travel?

A. By car
B. By plane
C. By train
D. By bicycle

1.9 How long was the longest uninterrupted road trip made by an NHL team in league history?

A. 10 days on the road
B. 14 days on the road
C. 18 days on the road
D. 22 days on the road

1.10 How long was it before Gordie Howe's parents saw their son play in an NHL game?

A. One season
B. Three seasons
C. 13 seasons
D. Howe's parents never saw him play in the NHL

1.11 How long did Charlie Hodge play backup goaltender with the Montreal Canadiens before he became their number one man between the pipes?

A. One playoff game
B. One season
C. Three seasons
D. Nine seasons

1.12 What is the greatest number of games ever played by an NHLer during one regular season?

A. 86 games
B. 87 games
C. 88 games
D. 89 games

1.13 Steve Larmer was how many games short of breaking Doug Jarvis's ironman mark (963 consecutive games) when his streak ended in 1993–94?

A. Less than 50 games
B. 50 to 75 games
C. 76 to 100 games
D. More than 100 games

1.14 How many more games did Detroit great Ted Lindsay need to play to become the NHL's first 1,000-game man when he retired after the 1959–60 season?

A. One game
B. Three games
C. Six games
D. Nine games

1.15 Who was the last Original Six player to skate in NHL action?

A. Serge Savard
B. Carol Vadnais
C. Phil Esposito
D. Wayne Cashman

1.16 Who holds the record for the fastest hat trick in NHL history?

A. Max Bentley
B. Bobby Hull
C. Bill Mosienko
D. Jean Béliveau

1.17 What is the greatest number of consecutive game-winning goals scored by a player from the start of his career?

A. Two straight game-winners
B. Three straight game-winners
C. Four straight game-winners
D. Five straight game-winners

1.18 What is the most consecutive goals scored by one team in an NHL game?

A. Seven straight goals
B. 10 straight goals
C. 12 straight goals
D. 15 straight goals

1.19 What is the highest plus-minus recorded by a player in one game?

A. Plus six
B. Plus eight
C. Plus 10
D. Plus 12

1.20 What is the unofficial NHL record for the worst plus-minus by a player in one season?

A. Less than minus 40
B. Between minus 40 and minus 60
C. Between minus 60 and minus 80
D. More than minus 80

1.21 What is the most penalty-free seasons played by an NHL skater?

A. One season
B. Three seasons
C. Five seasons
D. Seven seasons

1.22 What is considered the top winning percentage attainable by faceoff specialists in the NHL?

A. Between 50 and 60 per cent
B. Between 60 and 70 per cent
C. Between 70 and 80 per cent
D. Between 80 and 90 per cent

1.23 Which NHL coach owns the dubious distinction of playing the most league games from the start of a career without scoring a goal?

A. Larry Robinson
B. Pat Quinn
C. Joel Quenneville
D. Terry Murray

1.24 What is the longest career of an NHLer who never scored a point?

A. 31 games
B. 41 games
C. 51 games
D. 61 games

1.25 In 1959–60, which little-known player battled the great Bobby Hull for the NHL scoring race and lost the Art Ross Trophy by one assist?

A. Bronco Horvath of the Boston Bruins
B. Tod Sloan of the Chicago Blackhawks
C. Andy Hebenton of the New York Rangers
D. Gary Aldcorn of the Detroit Red Wings

1.26 Who recorded the highest average ice time among forwards since the statistic was introduced in 1998–99?

A. Pavel Bure
B. Jaromir Jagr
C. Joe Sakic
D. Ilya Kovalchuk

1.27 Which NHLer has played in the most regular-season wins during his career?

A. Ray Bourque
B. Scott Stevens
C. Mark Messier
D. Larry Robinson

1.28 Who was the first NHLer to appear in more than 300 games with three different teams?

A. Bill Gadsby
B. Dave Babych
C. Joe Mullen
D. No NHLer has ever played 300 games with three different teams

1.29 Who has the puck that Paul Henderson used to score the winning goal in the 1972 Canada–Russia Summit Series?

A. The Hockey Hall of Fame
B. Team Canada member Paul Henderson
C. A Soviet Ice Hockey Federation official
D. A Team Canada member other than Paul Henderson

1.30 Which NHL general manager was ridiculed on a Web site devoted to getting him fired in 2003–04?

A. Glen Sather of the New York Rangers
B. Jim Rutherford of the Carolina Hurricanes
C. George McPhee of the Washington Capitals
D. Mike Milbury of the New York Islanders

1.31 What is the NHL record for the most man-games lost to injury by one team in a season?

A. 329 man-games lost
B. 429 man-games lost
C. 529 man-games lost
D. 629 man-games lost

1.32 Who wrote "Bettman sucks" across the front of his helmet during training camp in October 1994?

A. The Canadiens' Mathieu Schneider
B. The Blues' Brett Hull
C. The Blackhawks' Chris Chelios
D. The Maple Leafs' Doug Gilmour

1.33 According to the NHL Players Association, which arena has the best ice conditions?

A. Pengrowth Saddledome in Calgary
B. Wachovia Center in Philadelphia
C. The Bell Centre in Montreal
D. Edmonton's Rexall Place

1.34 In his last season in Boston, 1999–2000, Ray Bourque played with rookie goalie John Grahame. How was Grahame's father, Ron Grahame, connected to Bourque years earlier?

A. Ron Grahame was traded by Boston for Ray Bourque
B. Ron Grahame was Ray Bourque's first defense partner
C. Ron Grahame was Calder Trophy runner-up to Ray Bourque
D. Ron Grahame was Ray Bourque's first NHL coach

1.35 One of hockey's most enduring images is of Tiger Williams riding his stick between his legs—like a witch on a broom—after scoring a big goal. How often does Williams claim he performed the ritual in his career?

A. Only once
B. After every first goal of a new season
C. After every regular-season goal
D. After every playoff goal

1.36 What inspired hockey's three-star selection?

A. The name of a sponsor's product
B. A Gordie Howe hat trick in 1948
C. Dwindling attendance during third periods
D. A newspaper's promotional gimmick

1.37 Which 1960s player first made waving to the crowd at centre ice popular after receiving a star of the game?

A. Jean Béliveau
B. Johnny Bower
C. Eddie Shack
D. Gump Worsley

1.38 How did retired great Bryan Trottier respond when asked if he missed playing hockey?

A. "It's time to pass the torch."
B. "Only when my knees don't hurt."
C. "Six Cups is plenty for one fella."
D. "Only every day."

1.39 What tough guy helped New York capture its first Stanley Cup in 54 years in 1994, and later helped Detroit break a 42-year drought when it won the Cup in 1997?

A. Mike Peluso
B. Jay Wells
C. Joey Kocur
D. Kirk Maltby

1.40 Why do Detroit fans throw octopi on the ice during the playoffs?

A. Octopi, with their sucker-lined tentacles, are tossed at slimy on-ice officials after bad calls
B. In memory of Wings goalie Terry Sawchuk, whose legs and arms were likened to those of an octopus
C. The eight-legged octopus represented a playoff sweep during the six-team era
D. The octopus, a cephalopod native to Lake Michigan, is in season during the playoffs

Answers

1.1 B. Edmonton

The Heritage Classic at Edmonton's Commonwealth Stadium on November 22, 2003, established a few league marks, including the first outdoor game, the coldest match ever played and the largest attendance. Huddled in thick winter coats, hats, scarfs, mitts and even snowmobile suits, the crowd of 57,167 more than doubled the previous NHL high of 27,227 fans who watched Florida beat Tampa Bay 2–0 in the warmer confines of St. Petersburg's Thunderdome on October 9, 1993. In Edmonton, on chippy ice, Montreal beat the Oilers 4–3. The largest crowd ever assembled to watch a game happened on October 6, 2001, when the Michigan State Spartans and Michigan Wolverines university hockey teams played to a 3–3 tie outdoors on an artificial ice rink set on a football field at Spartan Stadium in front of 74,554 fans. It surpassed the 55,000 who watched Sweden defeat the USSR 3–2 at the 1957 World Championships in Moscow.

1.2 D. Detroit

If the Red Wings had their way, Detroit wouldn't be called the "Motor City" or "Motown." Instead, it would be Welcome to "Hockeytown," the nickname coined to launch a five-year marketing campaign by the Wings in 1996 to "a region full of hockey fans." After the 1996–97 season, Hockeytown had a lot to cheer about, boasting three champion hockey teams. In addition to the Stanley Cup-winning Red Wings, the Detroit Vipers won the IHL's Turner Cup and the Plymouth Whalers claimed the OHL junior title. Hockey-crazy Detroit also plays host to numerous college and minor hockey programs.

1.3 A. Maurice Richard's NHL career goal-scoring total

They called him the Rocket and claimed he was the best player from the blue line in. On most nights, few would argue with that assessment. Darting into his opponents' zone, Richard drove to the net with an intensity that struck fear into every goalie he faced. His glowing eyes widened to the size of chunks of black coal when he went in for the kill. Around the net, Richard was possessed. A pure goal scorer, he never tallied enough assists to win a scoring championship. But in Catholic Quebec, his homeland, where Richard was worshipped like a god, that didn't matter. Registering five-goal games, winning Stanley Cups on overtime goals and causing street riots in Montreal, he became the sniper others set their standards by. Richard recorded the NHL's first 50-in-50 season and reached the 500-goal plateau before anyone else. When he retired in 1960, he set the bar at 544 goals.

1.4 B. Bobby Clarke

According to Gretzky, Clarke was the first NHLer to play behind an opposing team's net, using it to set up his slot man or deking out either end to make a pass or score on a wraparound. Gretzky first tried it when he was 14 and playing against 19-year-olds in Junior B. Seeing the way Gretzky was being slammed around in front of the net, coach Gene Popeil suggested he play behind it, just like Clarke. Gretzky discovered that the net functioned almost like another player to protect him. Bryan Trottier also played with great effectiveness behind his opponents' net.

1.5 A. He was painting his barn

For years Hall had a reputation for missing training camp, claiming he had to stay home in Stoney Plain, Alberta, and paint his barn. One fall, Scotty Bowman, coach of the St. Louis Blues, visited Hall to have him sign a contract. Dick Irvin's *In the Crease* picks up Bowman's story: "We arrived and he (Hall) was sitting on the front step drinking a beer. We looked around for the famous barn but there wasn't one. We never did see one. As far as I know, he didn't have a barn."

1.6 C. Mario Lemieux and Patrick Roy were born

Were the planetary axes aligned in vertical positions resembling goalposts to deliver this cosmic hockey kapow, or what? The big bang happened on October 5, 1965, when two of hockey's future stars were born: Roy in Quebec City and Lemieux in Montreal.

1.7 A. Both have the same birthdate

Hank Aaron and Don Cherry were born on the same date, February 5, 1934. But although both are Aquarians, there is very little else these sports giants have in common, especially in their fields of play. Aaron hit a major-league-record 755 home runs in his career; Cherry scored no goals in his one NHL start. Aaron comes from Mobile, Alabama; Cherry from Kingston, Ontario.

1.8 A. By car

It was the road trip of a lifetime. Taylor Railton, a 67-year-old Philadelphia native, completed his eight-week, 18,000-mile cross-country odyssey in a 1995 Ford Taurus. The $6,000 trip began in Philadelphia on January 1, and before it was over on February 24, Railton had been profiled on television and in newspapers and had met many hockey legends, including Phil Esposito, Denis Potvin and Bryan Trottier. His Taurus went through three oil changes and plenty of Celine Dion tapes (to help him "relax" out on the road). The best hot dogs? Montreal. The worst? New Jersey ("the bun was cold").

1.9 C. 18 days on the road

It's the unofficial record for the longest stretch of away games in league history; or as San Jose Sharks assistant coach Bernie Nicholls put it, "the road trip from hell." For 18 days, from

February 3 to 21, 1999, the Sharks lived out of their suitcases as they played 10 road games in nine cities over four time zones. San Jose travelled from the dry heat of Phoenix on the west coast to the deep freeze of Chicago, then on to balmy Florida and Washington, north for more cold weather in Detroit and finally home to the warmth of San Jose. Only the Calgary Flames played a longer string of road games—11 in 1987–88 during the Winter Olympics in Calgary—but they returned home for the NHL All-Star break after three games. The Sharks' 10-game exile from San Jose Arena was partially self-inflicted; the franchise leased the building to a tennis tournament and the *Disney on Ice* show during February. The Sharks completed the gruelling road trip with a 4–5–1 record, closing with three straight defeats to Detroit, Buffalo and Washington. Those losses ruined San Jose's chances to become the first team to finish better than .500 on a road trip of nine or more games.

1.10 C. 13 seasons

According to Gordie Howe, his dad never saw him play more than 10 times. The first occasion was for "Gordie Howe Night" in Detroit, March 3, 1959. Before game time, Howe received a new car. To his surprise, sitting in the back seat were his parents, Catherine and Ab, who had travelled from Saskatchewan for the ceremony. It was Howe's 13th season—more than twice the average length of an NHL career.

1.11 D. Nine seasons

With regulars Plante, Bower, Hall, Sawchuk and Worsley filling NHL puckstopping positions during much of the six-team era, job prospects for other netminders were, at best, slim. Some goalies waited, played a few NHL games, bussed around the minors and then, maybe, bought a lucky break somehow. Such was the sorry journey of Jacques Plante's backup, Charlie Hodge, who, over nine seasons with the Montreal franchise beginning in 1952–53, played just 59 NHL games. Some years

Hodge never joined the big team at all, putting in time in the AHL, EPHL, QHL, QSHL and WHL. But that changed after Plante was dealt to New York in 1963, when Hodge's patience paid off. In 1963–64, his skills never sharper (and his new defense awesome), Hodge worked 62 games, recorded eight shutouts for a 2.26 goals-against average and won the Vezina Trophy as top goalie for fewest goals-against.

1.12 A. 86 games

The only way to play more games than in a regular-season schedule is through a trade, moving midseason from a team ahead in games played to a club behind in the schedule. Over the years, many traded NHLers have outplayed the schedules by a game, but only two have played two extra matches during the NHL's 84-game schedules. Jimmy Carson dressed for 86 games in 1992–93, playing 52 for Detroit and 34 for the Kings; Bob Kudelski split his 1993–94 season between Ottawa (42) and Florida (44).

1.13 C. 76 to 100 games

Larmer, with 884 consecutive games played in 11 complete seasons, was 81 games shy of breaking Jarvis's streak before a dispute with Chicago management ended his ironman run at the start of 1993–94. A player of principle, Larmer chose to give up his hard-earned streak rather than settle for his new role and the new direction the club had taken under first-year head coach Darryl Sutter. Instead, he cast his fate to the trade winds, which blew him to New York and a Stanley Cup with Mike Keenan's Rangers.

1.14 A. One game

When Lindsay retired after the 1959–60 season, he had scored more goals than any other left-winger (365) and accumulated more penalty minutes (1,635) and played in more regular-season games than any other player (999). Strangely, he called it quits despite needing only one more game to become the

NHL's first 1,000-game man. On November 26, 1961, Howe eclipsed Lindsay's mark and became the first to skate in 1,000 games. In 1964–65, after four years of retirement, Lindsay returned to play one more season with the Detroit Red Wings, adding 69 games to his aggregate. And, just to prove he hadn't gone soft, the 39-year-old warhorse registered 173 penalty minutes, the second-highest total of his career, and only four minutes behind the NHL's penalty-minute leader that year, Carl Brewer.

1.15 D. Wayne Cashman

A 17-year Bruin, Cashman outdistanced Vadnais and Savard as the last player from the six-team era to see action by mere playoff games alone. All began their careers prior to league expansion in 1967 and retired in 1982–83. Vadnais's career ended in the regular season when New Jersey failed to make the playoffs; Savard's career concluded after three 1983 playoff games with Winnipeg; Cashman's career finished in the 1983 Conference finals after eight postseason games. Esposito quit in 1980–81.

1.16 C. Bill Mosienko

The Blackhawks played ugly for much of the 1951–52 season (17–44–9), until their last game on March 23, 1952, when Mosienko pumped in three rapid-fire goals in 21 seconds on New York rookie goalie Lorne Anderson. The miracle hat trick came at 6:09, 6:20 and 6:30 of the third period with both teams at full strength and Chicago down 6–2. Mosienko's centre, Gus Bodnar, won three successive faceoffs and passed for three assists to establish the historic trio of goals. The game meant little, but the inspired play of Mosienko gave a bit of lustre to the dismal season while producing a 7–6 win. It also spelled the end for Anderson, who never backstopped in the NHL again. Mosienko's hat trick broke Carl Liscombe's record, set in 1938 when the Detroit rookie scored three goals in 1:52. The second-fastest hat trick is 44 seconds, scored by Jean Béliveau on November 5, 1955.

1.17 C. Four straight game-winners

An odd distinction to be sure. Even weirder, it was not until Artem Chubarov's third season that he notched a goal that wasn't a game-winner. The Russian rookie scored once in 49 games with the Canucks in 1999–2000. He played only one game in his second year, then potted three more consecutive game-winners in 2001–02 before the string ended.

1.18 D. 15 straight goals

It's been called "the most lopsided game in NHL history." No team scored more consecutive goals in one game than Detroit, which on January 23, 1944, whipped the hapless Rangers 15–0. Victimized in the onslaught was New York goalie Ken McAuley, who faced a sea of red sweaters and a barrage of 58 shots on goal. In fact, the Rangers didn't win another game all season. Detroit's 15-goal record stands today; as does McAuley's NHL record 6.20 goals-against average (30 or more games).

1.19 C. Plus 10

Tom Bladon's lengthy but unspectacular 696-game NHL career would not raise an eyebrow today were it not for one night against the Cleveland Barons: December 11, 1977. Bladon's four goals and four assists bumped him ahead of Bobby Orr's single-game seven-point defenseman record and earned the Philadelphia rearguard a whopping plus 10, a statistic unmatched today. The Flyers beat the Barons 11–1.

1.20 D. More than minus 80

Forgotten Bill Mikkelson's claim to fame is his plus-minus record, the worst in NHL history at minus 82. He earned the record in 1974–75 with the Washington Capitals, a team so bad it finished with only eight wins and five ties while suffering through 67 losses. The 1974–75 Caps also belong in the books, with the mark for the fewest points (21) in a 70-game schedule and the lowest winning percentage (.131) ever. Through it all, or at least for 59 games that season, Mikkelson suffered along with the Capitals—and feels his record is rock-solid. "It will be a hard one to beat, and why would you want to beat it?" he said in a 2000 *National Post* story. Away from hockey, Mikkelson later worked in Edmonton as an executive for IBM.

1.21 C. Five seasons

In 820 games over 13 NHL seasons, Val Fonteyne sat in the cooler for just 26 minutes. That's an average of a two-minute infraction once every year. The Detroit, New York and Pittsburgh winger recorded an amazing five penalty-clean seasons between 1959–60 and 1971–72, and never earned more than four penalty minutes in a year. To put Fonteyne's box time in perspective, choirboy Dave Keon played like a thug during his 18-year career, totalling 117 minutes of penalties—almost four times Fonteyne's numbers.

1.22 B. Between 60 and 70 per cent

When the NHL started publishing faceoff stats in the late 1990s, it became clear that the highest winning percentage among the best in the circle is in the mid-60-per-cent range. In 1999–2000, Yanic Perreault led the NHL by winning more than 62 per cent of his faceoffs. "To be over 60 per cent is pretty hard," said Perreault in a *Hockey News* story on faceoff battles. "You have to be strong on your stick and you have to be strong on your skates. And you have to try to remember how you've had success against the guys you come up against." Perreault places his bottom hand down low almost to the blade, his top hand halfway down the shaft—so that he's positioned squarely over the blade of the stick. Does he cheat? "Every centre cheats," said Perreault. "You watch the linesman's hand and you try to get the jump. If you see the other centre cheating, you try to cheat first."

1.23 D. Terry Murray

No NHL player has gone longer without scoring a goal in league action than one-time defenseman-turned-NHL-coach

Terry Murray, who played 218 goal-less games between 1972–73 (as a member of the California Golden Seals) and 1980–81, when he scored his first—of only four career goals—as a Philadelphia Flyer. It's an accomplishment few remember or will attribute to Murray. Likewise for others in this category, such as tough guy Tony Twist (181 games) and Carolina's Steve Halko, who went 155 NHL games without scoring a single goal. "A couple of times," Halko claimed, "I fired shots that were going into empty nets, but guys tipped them." Sure thing, Steve.

1.24 D. 61 games

The longest career without scoring a point belongs to Detroit defenseman Gord Strate, who played 61 games and never registered a point in three seasons, 1956–57 to 1958–59. In fact, most of the 13 NHLers who have played 20 or more games without scoring a point are rearguards, with skills just below NHL calibre.

1.25 A. Bronco Horvath of the Boston Bruins

Joseph "Bronco" Horvath came out of nowhere, exploded onto the NHL scoring sheets and, almost overnight, disappeared. After five years in the minors and two unimpressive NHL seasons, Boston coach Milt Schmidt combined Horvath with Johnny Bucyk and Vic Stasiuk on the Bruins' Uke Line. In 1957–58, they racked up 174 points, with Horvath scoring 30 goals and 36 assists. But Horvath's best season came in 1959–60, when he battled Hull for the scoring title. The race was a nail-biter, eventually coming down to the season's final match between Chicago and Boston, with Horvath ahead of Hull by one point (a goal). In the first period, Horvath left the game and was taken to hospital after a puck hit his face. Hull, with room to breathe, turned it on and scored a goal and an assist to gain a one-point advantage. Horvath heroically returned for the last period of the season, but no matter how many plays his teammates set up or how loud the Bruins fans roared, he couldn't put one behind Glenn Hall. Tied with 39 goals each, Hull won the Art Ross by one assist; Bronco, it was later revealed, set an NHL record for scoring in 22 successive regular-season games. Final season point total: Hull 81 points, Horvath 80 points. Horvath scored an impressive 326 career points in 434 NHL games, but never lived up to the superstar potential he displayed during the season he lost the scoring race by one point to Bobby Hull.

1.26 A. Pavel Bure

"Energizer Bunny" defensemen such as Chris Pronger and Nicklas Lidstrom routinely average 27 minutes per game, but ice time among forwards is usually less, Bure being an exception with 26:52 for the Panthers in 2000–01. The only other 25-minute men are Jagr, who logged 25:51 in 1998–99; Sakic, with 25:35 in 1998–99; and Bure, again, with 25:00 in 2001–02.

1.27 B. Scott Stevens

Player performance is never evaluated on the number of team wins, but the statistics are fascinating. Stevens has been on the winning end of more regular-season games than anyone else in league history. Larry Robinson has the best winning percentage, a 59 per cent rate. The only forward among the top five in the team-wins category is Mark Messier.

Most Regular-Season Wins by a Player*

PLAYER	TEAMS	GP	TEAM WINS
Scott Stevens	Wash, St. L., N.J.	1,635	879
Mark Messier	Edm, NYR, Van	1,756	865
Ray Bourque	Bos, Col	1,612	832
Larry Robinson	Mtl, L.A.	1,384	815
Larry Murphy	L.A., Wash, Min, Pit, Tor, Det	1,615	814

**Courtesy the* Hockey News; *current to 2004–05*

1.28 A. Bill Gadsby

As of 2004–05, only seven players—Bill Gadsby, Dave Babych, Larry Murphy, Joe Mullen, Ron Francis, Chris Chelios and Vincent Damphousse—have played 300 or more games with three different teams. Gadsby was the first, playing 20 seasons in the NHL: with Chicago for 468 games, then with New York for 457 matches and finally with Detroit for 323 games. Gadsby was one of hockey's best defensemen, either on the rush, as a shot-blocker or as a playmaker. And during his era, from 1946–47 to 1965–66, he proved invaluable to the Blackhawks, the Rangers and the Red Wings, earning multiple All-Star appearances for his stellar play on the blue line. He was precisely what lowly Chicago and New York needed to anchor their game against the league's elite teams. In Chicago, he captained the Hawks; in New York, he was voted Norris Trophy runner-up three times to Doug Harvey and Tom Johnson. But it wasn't until Detroit traded for him in 1961–62 that he got his chance to play for a successful team. Unfortunately, the Red Wings appeared in three Stanley Cup finals but lost them all before Gadsby retired in 1965–66. Gadsby became the first NHLer to play 300 games on three different teams on February 5, 1966, picking up an assist in a 2–2 tie in Montreal.

1.29 D. A Team Canada member other than Paul Henderson

For many Canadians, Henderson's 1972 Summit Series goal stands as hockey's greatest moment. The Canada–Soviet Union hockey series was the first true test between hockey's two superpowers. It was Canada defending its national sport, indeed, its pride, and as 15 million of Canada's 20 million people looked on, Henderson scored in the dying seconds of the final game in Moscow. He was mobbed by the entire team after the goal, but whatever happened to the puck? The speculation ended in 1997 when Team Canada defenseman Pat Stapleton revealed its whereabouts in a story published in the *Globe and Mail*. As his teammates were celebrating Henderson's goal, Stapleton apparently scooped up the puck.

"The truth is, it's in a box with a lot of other pucks," he told reporter David Shoalts. "It was stored away about 20 years ago, and it's still there." But Stapleton, who made a habit out of saving pucks from important games, is able to identify it. "It's just plain black, but it's marked." Rather than sell or donate it to the Hockey Hall of Fame, he plans to return it to the game's roots. "What I want to do is skate with it with my grandchildren on the pond. What we'll do is skate around for a while and then shoot it into a snowbank. And that'll be it."

1.30 A. Glen Sather of the New York Rangers

New York fans are not to be trifled with, especially when one of their beloved sports teams, such as the Rangers, stink. In other words, it can get real ugly when things go wrong at Madison Square Garden. Just ask Sather, who was brought aboard in June 2000 to turn the club into a winner, but ended up being chased from his self-appointed coaching position by chants of "Fire Sather! Fire Sather!" at MSG in 2003–04. Disgruntled fans, who had not seen their team in playoff form for six, going on seven, seasons, also masterminded www.glensathersucks.com, a devastatingly clever Web site dedicated to ousting Sather from his New York job that listed, in excruciating detail, his failures as both coach and GM. The site boasted a petition to have Sather fired, a message board ("Glen Sather is an idiot. Discuss.") and an audio file of an actual "Fire Sather" chant from the Garden. Most damning was the meticulously researched list of personnel moves made during his tenure that depleted "the Rangers' organization of quality young prospects through trades for older veteran players."

1.31 D. 629 man-games lost

No team has ever been as badly hurt in every skating position, both up front and on the blue line, as Los Angeles in 2003–04. Injuries cost the club an NHL-record 629 man-games. Concussions sidelined Jason Allison and Adam Deadmarsh, two of the Kings' best scorers, for the entire year (that's

164 games right there). Then, Ziggy Palffy blew out his shoulder midseason, Aaron Miller suffered a pinched nerve in his neck after plowing face first into the boards, Lubomir Visnovsky had a freak fall into the boards and was carried off on a stretcher and Martin Straka got hit on two different occasions (the prognosis: two tears in the cartilage of his knee). The Injury Reserve List also saw Ian Laperrière for a spell. The enigmatic Roman Cechmanek might as well have been in the witness protection program for the number of nights he failed to show up to backstop the Kings. Thankfully, the league's most injury-riddled team had Peter Demers, its trainer for 32 years and more than 2,500 games—probably another NHL record.

1.32 A. The Canadiens' Mathieu Schneider

Schneider's crude helmet graffiti raised such an uproar, the former Canadiens defenseman apologized to both NHL commissioner Gary Bettman and Canadiens boss Serge Savard. Bettman responded by saying that the lockout was not personal, but business. There was also a promise by the commish to buy Schneider a beer once everything was settled. (No word on whether they ever did suck back the suds.)

1.33 D. Edmonton's Rexall Place

Long considered a league-wide problem, excellent ice conditions exist at only a few arenas. The best, according to most of the NHL players surveyed in 1998–99, is at Skyreach Centre, now Rexall Place, where the ice is made as hard and as thin as possible without it being brittle. (Thin ice is harder because the cooling agents in the floor are closer to the ice surface.) Hard ice means less friction, which produces greater speed, crisp passing and more responsive skating. Another reason the ice is superior in Edmonton is because of the Zamboni blades used. They are sharpened twice a week (compared to once a month in other buildings) to give a fine and fast ice finish. Elsewhere, league representatives inspect arenas and work with staff to try and improve their ice, but some facilities, such as New York's Madison Square Garden and the Continental Airlines Arena in New Jersey, still have terrible playing surfaces.

1.34 A. Ron Grahame was traded by Boston for Ray Bourque

If you stick around long enough in hockey there is no telling who you'll cross paths with. In a game against Toronto on October 4, 1999, Bourque played in front of Boston rookie netminder John Grahame, the son of Ron Grahame. Ron Grahame signed as a free agent with the Bruins in 1977, then two years later was traded to Los Angeles for the Kings' first-round pick in 1979's NHL draft. Who did Boston choose with that pick? Ray Bourque.

1.35 A. Only once

Sports has witnessed many memorable post-score celebrations. In the initial euphoria, fists are pumped, balls spiked, crowds saluted, sticks raised and struts performed. It's the dance of high-five glory—showboating. But particularly well-remembered by hockey fans is Tiger Williams's wild stick ride after he scored the winning goal in 1998's old-timers All-Star game. Williams, the game's most incarcerated player (almost 4,000 career penalty minutes) and a long-time Toronto fan favourite, was making his first appearance back at Maple Leaf Gardens after his trade to Vancouver. In his moment of ecstasy, Williams spontaneously turned, tucked his stick between his legs, squatted and rode the shaft around the rink—to the jubilation of thousands. His act of on-ice ingenuity was seared into the brains of kids across the country, who watched it on TV replays. "Everybody... thinks that this happened hundreds and hundreds of times," Williams told the *National Post*. "But I only did it once. That's the greatest thing about it. When you do something and it's unique, it sticks in the memory for a long time."

1.36 A. The name of a sponsor's product

The tradition of naming three stars at the end of NHL games originated in 1936 on *The Hot Stove League*, a radio program broadcast across North America and sponsored by Imperial Oil, which wanted to pump up sales of its Three Stars brand of gasoline. Old-time greats such as Syl Apps and Joe Primeau originally chose the three stars.

1.37 B. Johnny Bower

Hockey's long-standing tradition of the three-star selection and skate to centre ice by those stars after the game took on an added twist when Johnny Bower began waving to fans each time he received a game star in the 1960s. Bower admitted the gesture was originally intended for his wife's mother, but later for all the grandmothers watching him play. On one occasion, after receiving a star he felt undeserving of, Bower did not perform his usual wave. As a result, the Toronto netminder was flooded with letters from furious grannies, scolding him for not waving to them from centre ice.

1.38 D. "Only every day."

Trottier squeezed every last game out of his tired legs before he quit his 18-year NHL career in 1993–94. Even then he was just hanging on, a shadow of his former self during his glory years as scoring ace and inspirational leader of the 1980s Islanders' four-in-a-row championship teams. "He had nice soft hands, but he could also knock over a moose," former Islanders GM Bill Torrey once said. Trottier had a lot to miss. He was NHL rookie of the year in 1976, once led the NHL in scoring, twice led in assists, twice led the playoffs in scoring, was league MVP in 1978–79 and playoff MVP the next year. He scored 524 goals and 1,425 points in 1,279 games. He also won six Stanley Cups between the Islanders and Pittsburgh Penguins, and was elected to the Hockey Hall of Fame in 1997, his first year of eligibility.

1.39 C. Joey Kocur

Every team needs a scrapper with a head on his shoulders come playoff time, and Joey Kocur fit the bill perfectly during the 1990s. With Kocur in the lineups of New York and Detroit—the two teams with the longest Cup-less streaks—the Rangers snapped 54 years of frustration with their 1994 Cup victory and, later, in 1997 and 1998, the Red Wings won championships after a 42-year drought. Kocur is one of the very few NHLers who claimed as many as three Stanley Cups during the 1990s. (Larry Murphy had four in that decade.)

1.40 C. The eight-legged octopus represented a playoff sweep during the six-team era

The throwing of octopi was a Red Wings tradition that started during the 1952 finals between Montreal and Detroit. Fans at the Olympia began tossing the eight-legged creatures onto the ice to represent the eight games Detroit needed to sweep the two-round playoffs that year. The Red Wings never repeated the feat in their two subsequent successful trips to the championships (1954 and 1955), but the octopus gimmick caught on and continues today, despite the impossibility of an eight-game sweep in the post-expansion four-round playoff format.

GAME 1

Strange Starts

BEFORE BRETT HULL became the NHL's leading goal scorer of the 1990s with St. Louis and Dallas, he played 57 games for another team that traded him to the Blues. So which unlucky club gave up on Brett? The answer is included below. Match the player with his first-year club.

Solutions are on page 560

PART 1

1. _____ St. Louis' Brett Hull	A. New York Rangers
2. _____ Boston's Cam Neely	B. Montreal Canadiens
3. _____ Philadelphia's Reggie Leach	C. Los Angeles Kings
4. _____ New York Islanders' Billy Smith	D. Calgary Flames
5. _____ Chicago's Tony Esposito	E. Toronto Maple Leafs
6. _____ Boston's Rick Middleton	F. Boston Bruins
7. _____ Winnipeg's Randy Carlyle	G. Vancouver Canucks

PART 2

1. _____ Buffalo's Dominik Hasek	A. Quebec Nordiques
2. _____ Toronto's Eddie Shack	B. Chicago Blackhawks
3. _____ Pittsburgh's Rick Kehoe	C. Detroit Red Wings
4. _____ Philadelphia's Bernie Parent	D. Winnipeg Jets
5. _____ Toronto's Mats Sundin	E. Toronto Maple Leafs
6. _____ Anaheim's Teemu Selanne	F. Boston Bruins
7. _____ Los Angeles' Marcel Dionne	G. New York Rangers

2

Shooting the Light Fantastic

BOBBY HULL'S SLAP SHOT was a fearsome weapon. Johnny Bower said that stopping one of the Golden Jet's screamers was "like being slugged with a sledgehammer." Not only did Hull's shot have tremendous velocity, his curved blade often made the puck curve and dip. It's no accident that after Hull joined the league, goalies began wearing masks. In this chapter, we put the radar gun on blasts of every description.

Answers are on page 37

2.1 Bobby Hull's slap shot is generally considered the fastest of his era. How fast was it?

A. 100 mph
B. 106 mph
C. 112 mph
D. 118 mph

2.2 Who has the hardest recorded slap shot in the modern-day NHL?

A. Glen Murray
B. Al Iafrate
C. Al MacInnis
D. Rob Blake

2.3 Who is the first NHLer to win both the hardest-shot and the fastest-skater categories at an All-Star skills competition?

A. Sergei Fedorov
B. Pavel Bure
C. Peter Bondra
D. Bill Guerin

2.4 Which Original Six sniper popularized the slap shot?

A. Bernie Geoffrion
B. Stan Mikita
C. Phil Esposito
D. Bobby Hull

2.5 A shot from which NHL scoring star finally drove Jacques Plante to don hockey's first regularly worn goalie mask?

A. Detroit's Ted Lindsay
B. Montreal's Maurice Richard
C. Chicago's Bobby Hull
D. New York's Andy Bathgate

2.6 Who blasted a shot so hard that it shattered Dominik Hasek's helmet during the 1998 Olympics?

A. Team Canada's Steve Yzerman
B. Team U.S.A.'s Brett Hull
C. Team Russia's Pavel Bure
D. Team Czech Republic's Jaromir Jagr

2.7 Maurice Richard shot left-handed. What position did he play with the Montreal Canadiens?

A. Centre
B. Right wing
C. Left wing
D. All three forward positions, depending on his linemates

2.8 Which NHLer scored a goal in every possible way in one game?

A. Mario Lemieux
B. Bryan Trottier
C. Gordie Howe
D. Syl Apps

2.9 Who surpassed Mario Lemieux as the NHL's all-time leader in penalty shots in 2001–02?

A. Steve Yzerman
B. Theo Fleury
C. Pavel Bure
D. Mats Sundin

2.10 Which old-timer was the first NHLer to score two penalty-shot goals in one season?

A. Charlie Conacher of the Toronto Maple Leafs
B. Sid Abel of the Detroit Red Wings
C. Pat Egan of the Brooklyn Americans
D. Maurice Richard of the Montreal Canadiens

2.11 Who set a new NHL record by scoring three penalty-shot goals in 1997–98?

A. Vancouver's Pavel Bure
B. Chicago's Tony Amonte
C. Calgary's Theo Fleury
D. St. Louis' Pierre Turgeon

2.12 How many players have scored their first NHL goal on a penalty shot?

A. Only one, Reggie Savage in 1992
B. Two players
C. Three players
D. Four players

2.13 Who became the youngest player in NHL history to score on a penalty shot in 2003–04?

A. Nathan Horton of the Florida Panthers
B. Michael Ryder of the Montreal Canadiens
C. Trent Hunter of the New York Islanders
D. Tuomo Ruutu of the Chicago Blackhawks

2.14 Who was the first NHLer to have a penalty shot in overtime in the regular season? It happened in 1989.

A. Steve Larmer
B. Kirk Muller
C. Mike Foligno
D. Luc Robitaille

2.15 Which NHLer owns the career record for most overtime penalty shots?

A. Patrik Elias of the New Jersey Devils
B. Pavel Bure of the New York Rangers
C. Markus Naslund of the Vancouver Canucks
D. Peter Forsberg of the Colorado Avalanche

2.16 What is the NHL record for fewest days between penalty-shot goals?

A. One day
B. Eight days
C. 16 days
D. 32 days

2.17 What is the highest career-penalty-shot count by a player who failed to score a goal?

A. Three penalty shots
B. Four penalty shots
C. Five penalty shots
D. Six penalty shots

2.18 What is the greatest number of penalty shots awarded in one NHL season?

A. 27 penalty shots
B. 37 penalty shots
C. 47 penalty shots
D. 57 penalty shots

2.19 What is the greatest number of penalty-shot goals awarded in one season?

A. 14 penalty-shot goals
B. 18 penalty-shot goals
C. 22 penalty-shot goals
D. 26 penalty-shot goals

2.20 What is the record for most penalty shots faced by a goalie in one season?

A. Four penalty shots
B. Five penalty shots
C. Six penalty shots
D. Seven penalty shots

2.21 Which goalie faced the most shots in one season?

A. Curtis Joseph of the St. Louis Blues in 1993–94
B. Felix Potvin of the Toronto Maple Leafs in 1996–97
C. Dominik Hasek of the Buffalo Sabres in 1997–98
D. Roberto Luongo of the Florida Panthers in 2003–04

2.22 Who was the first NHL goalie on record to face more than 2,000 shots in a season?

A. St. Louis' Mike Liut
B. Hartford's Greg Millen
C. Edmonton's Grant Fuhr
D. Philadelphia's Pelle Lindbergh

2.23 What is the highest number of shots faced by a goalie in an NHL game in 60 minutes of regulation time?

A. Between 50 and 60 shots on goal
B. Between 60 and 70 shots on goal
C. Between 70 and 80 shots on goal
D. More than 80 shots on goal

2.24 Which modern-day goalie faced the most shots in 60 minutes of regulation time in a game without losing?

A. Mike Richter of the New York Rangers
B. Ron Tugnutt of the Quebec Nordiques
C. Craig Billington of the Ottawa Senators
D. Mike Liut of the St. Louis Blues

2.25 What is the highest number of shots faced by a goalie in a game that included overtime (in regular-season or playoff action)?

A. Between 60 and 80 shots on goal
B. Between 80 and 100 shots on goal
C. Between 100 and 120 shots on goal
D. More than 120 shots on goal

2.26 How many shots did New York goalie Ken "Tubby" McAuley face in a record 15–0 loss to Detroit on January 23, 1944?

A. 28 shots on goal
B. 38 shots on goal
C. 48 shots on goal
D. 58 shots on goal

2.27 What is the greatest number of shots on goal by two teams in one NHL game?

A. Between 125 and 150 shots on goal
B. Between 150 and 175 shots on goal
C. Between 175 and 200 shots on goal
D. More than 200 shots on goal

2.28 What is the most number of shots faced by a modern-day goalie in his playoff debut?

A. 44 shots on goal
B. 54 shots on goal
C. 64 shots on goal
D. 74 shots on goal

2.29 What is the greatest shot count by a player in one game?

A. 10 shots
B. 13 shots
C. 16 shots
D. 19 shots

2.30 On February 2, 1977, Toronto's Ian Turnbull established the single-game goal record for NHL defensemen by scoring five times in a 9–1 win over Detroit. How many shots did Turnbull take to score those five goals?

A. Five shots
B. Seven shots
C. Nine shots
D. 11 shots

2.31 Which NHL sniper holds the record for the most shots on goal during a single season?

A. Bobby Hull in 1968–69
B. Phil Esposito in 1970–71
C. Phil Esposito in 1971–72
D. Paul Kariya in 1998–99

2.32 Phil Esposito's record 550-shot count produced a league-high 76 goals in 1970–71. How many shots did Wayne Gretzky need in 1981–82 to score 77 goals and break Espo's goal-scoring record?

A. 300 shots on goal
B. 400 shots on goal
C. 500 shots on goal
D. 600 shots on goal

2.33 How many shots on net did Wayne Gretzky take during his NHL-record 92-goal season in 1981–82?

A. 319 shots on goal
B. 369 shots on goal
C. 419 shots on goal
D. 469 shots on goal

2.34 What is the fewest number of shots on goal recorded by an NHL scoring champion (minimum 70 games)?

A. 166 shots on goal
B. 186 shots on goal
C. 206 shots on goal
D. 226 shots on goal

2.35 What is the most number of shots taken by a defenseman in a single season?

A. 353 shots on goal
B. 383 shots on goal
C. 413 shots on goal
D. 443 shots on goal

2.36 What star forward originated a shot he called the "wrist slap shot" during the 1950s?

A. Gordie Howe
B. Frank Mahovlich
C. Dickie Moore
D. Andy Bathgate

2.37 A player from which position has recorded the most career shots on net in NHL history?

A. Centre
B. Right wing
C. Left wing
D. Defense

2.38 During the 1967 Toronto–Chicago semifinals, Bobby Hull fired an errant slap shot over the glass at Maple Leaf Gardens, breaking the nose of a spectator. Who was the unlucky victim?

A. Player-agent Alan Eagleson
B. Maple Leafs owner Harold Ballard
C. NHL president Clarence Campbell
D. Canadian prime minister Pierre Trudeau

Answers

2.1 D. 118 mph

Although less reliable than today's timing devices, speed guns in Hull's era reportedly clocked his shot at 118.3 mph. Ken Dryden and Jacques Plante figured that, at that speed, a Hull slap shot from the blue line, aimed at the glove-side upper corner, would be impossible to stop. That's because a puck blasted at 118 mph would blaze from stick to net (60 feet) in less than half a second (.346 second), too quick to catch if a goalie's glove hand is two feet below the puck entry point. If you blinked on a Hull slap shot, Plante admitted, you would see only a black blur before the puck entered the net or hit you.

2.2 B. Al Iafrate

Despite the numbers registered in the hardest-shot events at the annual NHL All-Star game, the question of who has the hardest boomer in game situations is far from settled. Goalies around the league are convinced that some players hold back (raise your sticks Brett Hull and Al MacInnis), not wanting to reveal just how fast their shots really are. In the absence of full representation, the prize goes to master blaster Al Iafrate, who holds the NHL record after discharging a 105.2-mph lightning bolt at the 1993 All-Star game in Montreal. Shawn Heins of

San Jose's American League team in Kentucky recorded two blasts of 105.5 mph and 106.1 mph in 1998–99; and, as mentioned previously, during the late 1960s, the great Bobby Hull reportedly fired slappers clocked at 118 mph.

2.3 A. Sergei Fedorov

They say that speed kills. In that case Fedorov qualifies as a serial killer. The Detroit Red Wings centre, who had won the fastest-skater category at the All-Star skills competition in 1992 and 1994, added another notch to his stick by winning the hardest-shot category at the 2002 All-Star shindig. The talented Russian registered a 101.5 mph howler to become the first player to capture both events.

2.4 A. Bernie Geoffrion

This answer may be as controversial as the man himself. Geoffrion never shied away from making noise. His fierce temper and loud opinions often got him into referee trouble, but that wasn't what earned him the nickname "Boom-Boom" in the 1950s. At practice one day, reporters remarked on the thundering noise of Geoffrion's shots as they banged off the boards, echoing across the rink. The description personified the player and his explosive shots, which became harder and more accurate as he practised his unique golf-swing windups. The Boomer was perfecting the slap shot, the novel shooting technique that soon became standard weaponry in the sniper's scoring arsenal.

2.5 D. New York's Andy Bathgate

Before Plante revolutionized hockey by regularly wearing hockey's "first" mask on November 1, 1959, goalies routinely had their faces carved up by pucks and sticks and required hundreds of stitches. (Before donning his mask, Plante himself had 200 stitches, four broken noses, a fractured jaw and cheekbones and a hairline fracture.) Facial injuries were considered an occupational hazard, and masks the devices that impaired eyesight and implied weakness. But the shot that ended

Plante's barefaced days was a Bathgate backhand that, according to the Rangers forward, was a "get-even" shot aimed deliberately at the Canadiens goalie's face. Plante had levelled Bathgate earlier in the game, sending him crashing into the boards. Bathgate retaliated with a short backhand that struck Plante on the nose and right cheekbone, cutting him badly. Plante left the ice bloodied, received the necessary stitch work and returned with his crude face guard in place and a resolve never to go maskless again.

2.6 C. Team Russia's Pavel Bure

During the first Czech Republic–Russia game at the Olympics, Hasek had his helmet shattered by a Pavel Bure slap shot. "I don't care if it's my head that stops the puck," Hasek said. "It's part of my body. If I see the puck coming at my head, I don't move my head. I can make a save with my head also." Hasek wears the old-style wire cage and helmet instead of the modern NHL wraparound mask sported by such netminders as Patrick Roy and Ed Belfour. After his helmet was smashed, Hasek used an older Buffalo Sabres wire-cage mask.

2.7 B. Right wing

Although Richard shot left-handed, he played right wing. The Rocket's scoring skills were maximized when Paul Haynes, coach of the Senior Amateur Canadiens, moved Richard to his "wrong wing." The new position gave him more net to shoot at, and he developed a devastating backhand shot. The skill proved invaluable, launching Richard on an 18-year tear through the NHL, in the course of which he racked up a record 544 goals—including the first 50-in-50, in 1944–45.

2.8 A. Mario Lemieux

On December 31, 1988, Lemieux conducted a clinic in goal scoring, recording goals in every conceivable fashion: at even strength on a pass from Rob Brown; shorthanded on a slap shot above the left faceoff circle; on the power play with a shot that dribbled through New Jersey goalie Bob Sauve's legs; on a penalty shot against Chris Terreri, who had replaced Sauve; and into an empty net. It's the only time a player has scored in every manner possible in one game. The Penguins whipped the Devils 8–6.

2.9 C. Pavel Bure

Who else, but the Breakaway Kid? The speedy Russian was awarded the eighth and ninth penalty shots of his career in 2001–02 with the Florida Panthers, surpassing Mario Lemieux as the NHL's all-time leader in the category. In a bizarre twist, not only did Bure not score on either attempt, he didn't even register a shot on net. In the first case, on January 25, 2002, Bure lost control of the puck on a bad patch of ice while skating in on Carolina Hurricanes netminder Arturs Irbe, then tripped while trying to dig it out of his skates and slid into the end-boards. On his record-setting ninth penalty shot, taken against Boston Bruins goalie Byron Dafoe on February 9, 2002, the Russian Rocket lost the handle while trying a backhand deke and wound up ringing the puck off the outside of the post. A frustrated Bure said after the game: "That's the way it is. If I scored on every breakaway I had this year I'd have 90 goals." All told, Bure scored on five of his nine attempts, while Lemieux has been successful on six of his eight.

2.10 C. Pat Egan of the Brooklyn Americans

Last-place Brooklyn piled up the losses in 1941–42, but they didn't get pushed around, not with rugged rearguard Pat Egan and his league-leading 124 penalty minutes. Egan scored only eight goals, but 25 per cent came from two penalty-shot goals, one against Montreal's Bert Gardiner on November 16, 1941, the other against Chicago's Sam LoPresti on March 5, 1942.

2.11 A. Vancouver's Pavel Bure

The Russian Rocket set an NHL record on February 28, 1998, when he wristed the puck past Ottawa Senators goalie Damian Rhodes to count his third penalty-shot goal of the season.

Bure's other two penalty-shot markers came against the Coyotes' Nikolai Khabibulin on January 26, 1998, and the Sharks' Mike Vernon on November 12, 1997. The last player to have three penalty-shot attempts in a single season was Joe Mullen of the Calgary Flames in 1986–87. Mullen scored on all three shots, but one was disallowed because it was ruled that he had used an illegal stick.

2.12 D. Four players

Since the rule was instituted in 1934, only four NHLers have potted their first goals mano-a-mano.

Players with First Career Goals on Penalty Shots*

PLAYER	TEAM	SEASON	OPPOSING GOALIE
Ralph Bowman	St. Louis	1934–35	Alex Connell
Phil Hoene	Los Angeles	1973–74	Cesare Maniago
Ilkka Sinisalo	Philadelphia	1981–82	Paul Harrison
Reggie Savage	Washington	1990–91	Jon Casey

**Current to 2004–05*

2.13 A. Nathan Horton of the Florida Panthers

After being taken down by Philadelphia's John LeClair, Horton was awarded a penalty shot and, according to Florida coach Rick Dudley, "did what good penalty-shot people do." The rookie centre waited until goalie Jeff Hackett made a move, then tacked it top shelf. "It happened so fast, I didn't have enough time to think about the shot," said Horton. "If I had more time, I might have been more nervous. I was either going to go high or go to my backhand. The top shelf was there, so I went up and it went in." Horton's goal came at 3:38 of the second period on January 8, 2004. He was 18 years, 224 days old, only 38 days younger than Toronto's Jack Hamilton, who established the record on February 19, 1944.

2.14 D. Luc Robitaille

After being hauled down on a breakaway on February 2, 1989, Luc Robitaille was awarded the NHL's first penalty shot in regular-season overtime. But a rolling puck on bad ice forced the Kings sniper to shoot quickly, missing the Devils' half-open net and hitting a flopping Sean Burke on the shoulder.

2.15 A. Patrik Elias of the New Jersey Devils

Few players have ever been awarded penalty shots in overtime, but Elias has two—both unsuccessful and both against the New York Islanders. He missed his first shot in a scoreless tie on December 1, 2000, against John Vanbiesbrouck; his record-setting second opportunity in an extra period came opposite Garth Snow on December 10, 2003, in a 1–0 win. As of 2004–05, Elias had one other penalty shot, a goal against Damian Rhodes in a 9–0 win on March 10, 2000.

2.16 B. Eight days

A few NHLers have had penalty shot opportunities in less time than Milan Hejduk, but no one has capitalized with fewer nights between goals. In 1967–68, Toronto's Mike Walton had penalty shots in successive nights but failed to score on his second attempt. Joe Nieuwendyk got two freebies four days apart in 1988–89 and scored once. Then, rookie Esa Pirnes was thwarted twice on October 10 and 12, 2003. Hejduk's NHL mark was set five games and eight days apart—January 11 and January 19, 2004—on penalty shot goals against Chicago's Michael Leighton and Nikolai Khabibulin of Tampa Bay. Both goals were scored with wrist shots high on the glove in 5–4 wins by Colorado. The goal against Leighton came in the second period and trimmed the Blackhawks' lead to 3–2. But Hejduk's goal on Khabibulin was particularly outstanding, a game-winning goal in overtime and only the third overtime game-winner in NHL history. After waiting six years for a penalty shot chance, Hejduk connected on two, little more than a week apart.

2.17 C. Five penalty shots

Vancouver's Greg Adams had a knack for earning penalty shots, he just couldn't capitalize on his one-on-one opportunities. Interestingly, all his shots came early in his 17-year career. After five consecutive misses he probably went out of his way to avoid further embarrassment. Adams played from 1984–85 to 2000–01.

2.18 D. 57 penalty shots

While penalty shot calls have risen, scoring mano-a-mano has dropped in frequency. Players once routinely potted goals on two of every five shots. In 2001–02 they managed just one goal in four attempts, connecting only 11 times on 46 blasts. That same year, more shots were stopped (39) than in any other year in league history—except for 2003–04, when goalies again blocked 39 of the record 57 penalty shots awarded. Shooters scored just 18 times.

2.19 B. 18 penalty-shot goals

Referees not only awarded a record number of penalty shots (57) in 2003–04, shooters also produced their best totals that year, scoring a league-high 18 goals. Interestingly, the goal-impaired Minnesota Wild, among the NHL's lowest scoring teams, surprisingly netted the greatest number of goals on penalty shots awarded: four goals on six attempts, reversing a league-wide trend. While all NHL shooters scored only 31 per cent of the time in 2003–04, Minnesota's blasters doubled that figure with a 66 per cent accuracy.

2.20 C. Six penalty shots

Curtis Joseph set the single-season mark for one-on-one shots among modern-day goalies, with five, when he backstopped Toronto in 2001–02. Cujo stonewalled four of five shooters, another present-day record (shared with Alan Bester) for most penalty shots stopped. But George Hainsworth holds the all-time records in both categories: six shooters up and six shot down, all in 1934–35, when the rule for penalty shots required a player to shoot from 38 feet out.

2.21 D. Roberto Luongo of the Florida Panthers in 2003–04

Never mind being named Florida's most valuable player, Luongo would have been a strong candidate for the Hart Trophy as league MVP had the Panthers reached the playoffs. He was a warrior through 72 games, battling 2,475 shots to establish a new NHL record and break Felix Potvin's old mark of 2,438 in 1996–97. Luongo also set a new league record with 2,303 saves, allowing only 172 goals for a .931 save percentage, third best in the league during 2003–04. He recorded seven shutouts on the 24th-place-overall Panthers. His most impressive work may have come in the three games in which he faced 50 shots. Luongo won two and was 7–7–5 in games with 40 or more shots. It is hard to imagine how bad Florida would have been without him.

2.22 B. Hartford's Greg Millen

The first 2,000-shot goalie on record is Greg Millen, who faced 2,056 shots while backstopping 60 Whalers games in 1982–83, the first year shots were officially recorded. Millen averaged 34.3 shots per game—or five shots more each match—than that season's league average of 29.1. A pretty good goalie who had the misfortune of playing behind a feeble defense, Millen went 14–38–6 and produced a dreadful 4.81 goals-against average. Hartford finished the year tied at 45 points with Pittsburgh in the NHL cellar, 65 points behind the league-leading Boston Bruins.

2.23 D. More than 80 shots on goal

On March 4, 1941, Chicago goalie Sam LoPresti stepped between the pipes and faced a league-record 83 shots. But despite stopping 80 shots against Boston marksmen, LoPresti still lost the game, as his lacklustre teammates failed to score more than two goals in the 3–2 Bruins win.

2.24 B. Ron Tugnutt of the Quebec Nordiques

Fifty years after Chicago's Sam LoPresti was peppered with a record 83 shots in a 3–2 Bruins victory in March 1941, Quebec's Ron Tugnutt faced 73 shots to become the second-busiest goalie in one night of NHL hockey. In Tugnutt's case the struggling Nordiques knotted the Bruins 3–3, providing Tugnutt with the distinction of not losing a game with the greatest shots-against. Perhaps Tugnutt's best save came with eight seconds remaining in overtime, off a Ray Bourque slap shot. With Cam Neely in Tugnutt's face at the edge of the crease, Tugnutt did the splits and snatched the rising slapper to preserve the tie. Both Bruin stars skated away shaking their heads. After the game, in an unusual gesture for regular-season play, several Boston players skated across the ice to shake Tugnutt's hand. The game, played on March 21, 1991, was held at Boston Garden, which saw LoPresti's historic loss a half-century earlier.

2.25 C. Between 100 and 120 shots on goal

No other goalie in NHL history faced as many shots in one game as Boston netminder Tiny Thompson. On April 3 and 4, 1933, Thompson stood on his head and faced a mind-boggling 114 shots from Toronto Maple Leaf snipers in a contest of endurance that went almost nine complete periods. Unfortunately for Thompson, the 114th shot produced a Toronto goal and sent the Maple Leafs to the next round, the Stanley Cup finals (which they lost to New York). Thompson is the only NHL goalie to break the triple-digit barrier in shots on net.

2.26 D. 58 shots on goal

It wasn't the most shots a goalie faced in a game, but McAuley, who saw Detroit red all night, still produced an NHL record, or, more precisely, *allowed* the Red Wings a record: most consecutive goals by one team in one game (15). The rookie Ranger goalie was blitzed with 58 shots but stopped 43—a great performance under most circumstances. If McAuley's pals on defense disappeared, his New York offense (an oxymoron) shouldn't have bothered dressing. The team directed only nine shots on Detroit goalie Connie Dion in the entire game. Counting assists, every Red Wing player figured in the scoring except Dion and defenseman Cully Simon. Detroit players accounted for 35 individual points.

2.27 D. More than 200 shots on goal

Although the NHL's longest game, a March 1936 Montreal Maroons–Detroit Red Wings playoff tilt, didn't produce the most shots in league history, the second-longest match ever did—a record 207 shots fired by Toronto and Boston shooters on April 3 and 4, 1933. The Maple Leafs' Lorne Chabot blocked 93 blasts and the Bruins' Tiny Thompson handled 113 before Leaf winger Ken Doraty finally scored on Toronto's next shot, the game's 207th shot on net. It came in the sixth overtime period after 163 minutes and 46 seconds of shutout hockey.

2.28 C. 64 shots on goal

In a sports story that drew David and Goliath parallels, seventh-place Anaheim beat the heavily favoured defending Stanley Cup champion Detroit Red Wings in four straight games during the 2003 Conference quarterfinals. In Game 1, Jean-Sébastien Giguère performed his impression of a wall and stopped a record 63 of 64 shots in the 2–1 triple-overtime victory on April 10, 2003. "It was a great learning experience for me," Giguère said later, without a trace of conceit. The turning point of the series was Game 1's first overtime period, when Detroit outshot Anaheim 20–4 but failed to score. "If we lose that game, I bet you they crush us," said Ducks coach Mike Babcock. The all-time record for shots on goal by a playoff rookie is held by Normie Smith, who blocked 90 shots in a 1–0 Detroit victory on March 24 and 25, 1936.

2.29 D. 19 shots

It's an unofficial record, but Boston's Ray Bourque holds top spot with 19 shots on net in a 3–3 tie against the Quebec Nordiques on March 21, 1991. The Bruins fired a record 73 shots; Bourque scored one goal, on his 14th shot. Some sources claim Gordie Howe shares this mark with his own 19-shot effort on January 27, 1955. Howe outshot the entire New York team, which fired just 18 times compared to Detroit's 31 in the 3–3 tie.

2.30 A. Five shots

Turnbull was the first (and to date the only) rearguard to score five goals in a single NHL game and is one of the few five-goal scorers in league history to score five times on just five shots—two against the Red Wings' Eddie Giacomin and three against backup Jim Rutherford.

2.31 B. Phil Esposito in 1970–71

The NHL had never witnessed a performance like the Phil Esposito show of 1970–71, when he blasted home a record 76 goals on 550 shots. His 76-goal and 550-shot counts smashed Bobby Hull's mark of 58 goals on 414 shots in 1968–69.

2.32 A. 300 shots on goal

Wayne Gretzky broke Espo's 11-year-old record of 76 goals on his 300th shot, firing goal number 77 of the 1981–82 season against Buffalo's Don Edwards on February 24, 1982.

2.33 B. 369 shots on goal

To establish his NHL goal-scoring record of 92 goals in 1981–82, the Great One directed 369 shots on net in 80 games, an average of 4.6 shots per game or, incredibly, almost a goal on every fourth shot.

2.34 A. 166 shots on goal

Since shot counts became available in 1967–68, only one player had won the scoring race with a shot total below 200: Bryan Trottier. Few expected anyone to break Trottier's record low of 187 shots in 1978–79, especially considering scoring leaders average about 322 shots to win the title. But in 2002–03, Peter Forsberg led the loop with 106 points and set a new mark, potting 29 goals on 166 shots—almost half the average shot count by scoring champions. Forsberg's low total may be because he doesn't shoot enough, the only knock against hockey's best all-round player. Or it may be, as Calgary coach Darryl Sutter says, that Forsberg is "an old-time player." Only twice in more than a half-century of hockey has a scoring leader had fewer goals than Forsberg. Ted Lindsay won the crown with 23 goals in 1949–50 and Stan Mikita had 28 goals in 1964–65.

2.35 C. 413 shots on goal

It doesn't take a rocket scientist to figure out which defenseman owns this record. Trailing super snipers Phil Esposito (550 and 426 shots in 1970–71 and 1971–72), Paul Kariya (429 shots in 1998–99) and Bobby Hull (414 shots in 1968–69) by just one shot on goal, Bobby Orr fired an astounding 413 shots in 1969–70, the most ever by an NHL rearguard. Orr scored 33 goals and 87 assists for 120 points to become the first and only defenseman to win the NHL scoring race. The next-best shots-on-goal count by a D-man also belongs to Orr, who had 392 in 1970–71. Ray Bourque had 390 shots in 1995–96.

2.36 A. Gordie Howe

While players in the late 1950s attempted to master the slap shot, Gordie Howe was reinventing that haphazard drive into a more controllable shot—the wrist slap shot. According to Howe: "The blade of the stick should come back waist high or higher on the backswing and should hit the puck clearly off the heel. I snap my wrists as I hit the puck." Howe's new shot worked so well that in 1962–63 he won the NHL scoring race and MVP status. Remarkably, he was in his 17th season and often recording 40 minutes of ice time per game—almost twice that of most NHL forwards—and still outshooting and outskating players a decade younger.

2.37 D. Defense

In NHL history no one has blasted more shots on goalies than Ray Bourque. Bourque had an awesome career count of 6,206 shots on net—compared to Wayne Gretzky's career 5,089 shots, Brett Hull's 4,868, Phil Esposito's 4,595 (which does not count his shot totals for four seasons prior to 1967–68, when shot stats were first available) and Paul Coffey's 4,385. Bourque managed those unreal numbers with offensive skills that equal those of the game's best forwards. He had the touch and vision of a sniper, shooting heavy shots from the point, mid-range snap shots or in-close wrist shots, both down low and top shelf to either corner (as he has demonstrated so accurately at All-Star game skills competitions). Bourque played only 60 or fewer games in a season twice (and one was the lockout year of 1994–95) during 22 NHL years, and routinely logged 25 to 28 minutes of quality ice time per game.

2.38 B. Maple Leafs owner Harold Ballard

The Hawks were engaged in a pre-game shooting drill when Bobby Hull let loose a wicked drive that rose over the glass and smashed into Harold Ballard's private booth, 40 feet above the ice. The puck ripped through a program that Ballard was reading, shattering his spectacles and squashing his nose like a ripe tomato. Despite the injury, Ballard didn't hold a grudge. Just before the next game he grabbed a photographer and hailed Hull as the Hawks made their way to the ice. "Bobby, over here!" he hollered, lifting his dented face in profile. "Let's show the world what you've done. Make a helluva photo." It would have, too, but Chicago coach Billy Reay interceded and chased Ballard off.

GAME 2

Hockey Crossword

Solutions are on page 560

ACROSS

1. Anaheim team
8. Broadcaster Dick _____
10. 1980s Boston tough guy Chris _____
12 Philadelphia's John _____ Clair
13 Full name of Russian sniper with Atlanta (initials "I.K.")
17. Crowd or _____ the goalie
18. _____ Belfour
19. Best pro hockey league
20. Montreal university, site of very first hockey game
22. Coast-_____-coast
24. Goalie Garth _____
26. _____ your words
28. 2000 Devil Cup-winner Jason _____
29. Mark on face
30. _____ Nedved
32. _____ Modano
33. Put the puck _____ _____ _____
35. Oiler GM Kevin _____
38. Emergency Room, abbrv.
39. _____-timers game
41. Pittsburgh Cup-winner Peter _____
42. Edmonton's _____ Smyth
44. Toronto's Owen _____
45. Montreal 1986 Cup-winner Stephane _____

DOWN

1. _____ Wild
2. Long-time Hurricane Martin _____
3. Full name of long-time Chicago sniper (initials "T.A.")
4. Montreal old-timer _____ Moore
5. Los Angeles D-man Joe _____
6. Veteran centre with 10 teams, Columbus in 2002–03, Mike _____
7. Television, abbrv.
9. Philadelphia sniper Mark _____
11. & 20. Full name of St. Louis D-man with hardest shot
14. Old-time Ranger from 1930s and 1940s, Ott _____
15. 1970s goalie _____ Dryden
21. Home of the Kings, abbrv.
23. Long-time Bruin Terry _____
24. Vancouver D-man Brent _____

25. Hometown of the Senators
27. 1970s and 1980s Islander sniper Bryan _____
31. Dallas forward _____ Lehtinen
34. Brother of the Rocket, _____ Richard
37. Bruin old-timer from 1940, Pat _____
39. Bobby _____
40. Predators D-man _____ Hamhuis
43. Number, abbrv.

3

War of Words

AFTER PASSING JEAN BÉLIVEAU with his 508th career goal to move into 25th place on the NHL all-time goal-scoring list, Detroit's Pat Verbeek said of the Canadiens great: "It's kind of a crime because he was such an elegant player. The way he scored goals was beautiful. The way I score goals is ugly." The hard-working, crease-crashing Verbeek hammered home number 508 on January 4, 2001. In this chapter on deep thoughts and cheap shots we check out what's good, bad and ugly in hockey's war of words.

Answers are on page 61

3.1 Who said to Bobby Orr: "Kid, I don't know what the f@!# they're paying you, but it's not enough"?

A. Toronto owner Harold Ballard
B. Boston veteran Ted Green
C. Boston teammate Phil Esposito
D. Boston head scout Wren Blair

3.2 During the 2003 playoffs, New Jersey Devils fans chanted "Marty's better! Marty's better!" Which opposition goalie were New Jersey fans slighting in their comparison to Martin Brodeur?

A. Jeff Hackett of the Boston Bruins
B. Nikolai Khabibulin of the Tampa Bay Lightning
C. Patrick Lalime of the Ottawa Senators
D. Jean-Sébastien Giguère of the Anaheim Mighty Ducks

3.3 Who was Adam Oates referring to when he paid Joé Juneau this compliment: "He can't hold Joey's jockstrap"?

A. Eric Lindros
B. Felix Potvin
C. Teemu Selanne
D. Boston equipment manager Ken Fleger

3.4 In 1998, who said "Vincent Lecavalier is the Michael Jordan of hockey"?

A. Tampa Bay owner Art Williams
B. Tampa Bay president Phil Esposito
C. Tampa Bay coach Jacques Demers
D. Tampa Bay linemate Fredrik Modin

3.5 Who bellowed, "Let's get something straight—I wouldn't trade Ian Turnbull for God"?

A. Maple Leafs owner Harold Ballard
B. Kings GM George Maguire
C. Colorado coach Don Cherry
D. Maple Leafs coach Roger Neilson

3.6 In a 1923 Stanley Cup finals game, Ottawa Senators goalie Clint Benedict told his defenseman King Clancy, "Here kid. Take care of this place till I get back." Where was "this place"?

A. The goal net
B. The penalty box
C. The trainer's massage table
D. A bar stool in the lounge car on a train

3.7 Who said, "Even if I wanted to go straight, I said to myself, I couldn't: There are too many enforcers around the league looking to take me on and prove they are number one"?

A. Dave Schultz
B. Bob Probert
C. Paul Holmgren
D. Dave Williams

3.8 Which Montreal player said of Canadiens coach Al MacNeil during the 1971 Stanley Cup finals: "Al MacNeil is the worst coach that I have ever known"?

A. Jean Béliveau
B. Pete Mahovlich
C. John Ferguson
D. Henri Richard

3.9 Which team's logo did broadcaster Don Cherry derisively describe as looking like "a condom package"?

A. The New York Islanders'
B. The Ottawa Senators'
C. The Colorado Avalanche's
D. The Los Angeles Kings'

3.10 When Jeremy Roenick said, "I'm surprised he wasn't in the toilet when I went to the bathroom," who was he talking about?

A. His 1993 playoff shadow, St. Louis Blues centre Bob Bassen
B. Ex-Chicago GM Mike Keenan
C. NHL referee Don Koharski
D. St. Louis Blues goaltender Curtis Joseph

3.11 During the 2002 Winter Olympics, who was American goalie Mike Richter speaking of when he confessed: "He's sneaky... it was a beautiful play"?

A. Joe Sakic
B. Jaromir Jagr
C. Mario Lemieux
D. Mike Modano

3.12 Which NHL team's dressing room is graced with the inscription, "You play for the emblem on the front, not the name on the back"?

A. The Philadelphia Flyers'
B. The Los Angeles Kings'

C. The Vancouver Canucks'
D. The Buffalo Sabres'

3.13 Which enforcer said, "It's not often a plumber gets to go to a grand ball" after being invited to the 1992–93 All-Star weekend?

A. Mike Peluso
B. Stu Grimson
C. Kelly Buchberger
D. Bob Probert

3.14 When Conn Smythe said, "I'm not a drinking man, but I know if you pour too much water in your whiskey, the whiskey gets weaker," what was he referring to?

A. NHL expansion
B. Longer regular-season schedules
C. Million-dollar player salaries
D. Prolonged play stoppages for TV commercials

3.15 Before Alexander Mogilny defected in 1989, a fellow Soviet player told him: "*Vsevo khoroshevo.*" What does it mean?

A. "Meet lots of American girls."
B. "All good things."
C. "Watch your back."
D. "Live long and prosper."

3.16 Who said, "I don't want to get into a war of words, but if he wants one, I've got more lines than he has teeth. And he hits like a butterfly, anyway"?

A. Bob Probert
B. Gino Odjick
C. Tie Domi
D. Todd Ewen

3.17 Which two players was long-time Boston GM Harry Sinden referring to when he said, "If I'm down a goal late in the game, I want _____ on the ice. If I'm up a goal late in the game, _____'s the one I want out there"?

A. Phil Esposito and Bobby Orr
B. Bobby Orr and Ray Bourque
C. Ray Bourque and Cam Neely
D. Cam Neely and Phil Esposito

3.18 Who posted, "To you from failing hands we throw the torch; be yours to hold it high" in the Montreal Canadiens' dressing room?

A. Coach Dick Irvin
B. Manager Frank Selke
C. Manager Sam Pollock
D. Coach Toe Blake

3.19 Who was NHL commissioner Gary Bettman talking about when he said, "I open (my newspaper) every day, wondering what he said this time"?

A. Brett Hull
B. Bobby Clarke
C. Chris Chelios
D. Mike Keenan

3.20 Which referee quit his NHL officiating job after being publicly criticized by league president Clarence Campbell?

A. Frank Udvari
B. Red Storey
C. Eddie Powers
D. Bill Chadwick

3.21 Which goalie did Phil Esposito call "a thieving giraffe" in the 1970s?

A. Philadelphia's Bernie Parent
B. Montreal's Ken Dryden

C. The Soviet Union's Vladislav Tretiak
D. Chicago's Tony Esposito

3.22 Which Montreal Canadiens goalie predicted that Guy Lafleur would put Wayne Gretzky "in his back pocket"?
A. Patrick Roy
B. Rogatien Vachon
C. Richard Sevigny
D. Ken Dryden

3.23 Which NHL coach criticized Wayne Gretzky, when he said, "You have to expect your best players to carry the team, and that's not happening"?
A. Glen Sather
B. Larry Robinson
C. Mike Keenan
D. Barry Melrose

3.24 When asked who he thought was the NHL's dirtiest player, who responded "Can I vote for myself"?
A. Ulf Samuelsson
B. Mike Peluso
C. Chris Chelios
D. Bryan Marchment

3.25 Which goalie made headlines by calling the Maple Leafs "undeserving" Stanley Cup contenders in the playoff finals of 1947?
A. The Canadiens' Bill Durnan
B. The Bruins' Frank Brimsek
C. The Red Wings' Harry Lumley
D. The Maple Leafs' Turk Broda

3.26 When Jaromir Jagr apologized to Wayne Gretzky by saying, "I didn't mean to do that," during No. 99's last game in April 1999, what was the Pittsburgh Penguin referring to?

A. A goal
B. A bodycheck
C. A fight
D. A comment on national television

3.27 When asked why he didn't wear a mask, which old-time puck stopper replied, "My face is my mask"?

A. Johnny Bower
B. Glenn Hall
C. Turk Broda
D. Gump Worsley

3.28 Which goalie was Ron Hextall talking about when he said: "It's hard to beat this guy. This guy doesn't know what he's going to do"?

A. Mike Richter
B. Dominik Hasek
C. Martin Brodeur
D. Hextall was talking about himself

3.29 Who threatened: "If I was Gary Bettman, I'd be worried about my family, about my well-being right now"?

A. Chris Chelios
B. Marty McSorley
C. Jeremy Roenick
D. Bob Goodenow

3.30 Who was the first NHLer to publicly state that many players "would vote to accept" an agreement, at a time when negotiations had broken down between the league and the NHL Players Association in 1994?

A. Mark Messier
B. Pat Verbeek

C. Ray Bourque
D. Stephane Richer

3.31 In 1953, managing director Frank Selke said: "All I did was open the Forum vault and say, "Help yourself Jean." How much money was, in fact, Jean Béliveau's first Montreal Canadiens contract worth? And for how long?

A. Three years; $25,000; no signing bonus
B. Three years; $50,000; $5,000 signing bonus
C. Four years; $50,000; $10,000 signing bonus
D. Five years; $100,000; $20,000 signing bonus

3.32 Who said, "Around here, the 'C' stands for 'See ya later' "?

A. Chicago's Tony Amonte
B. Toronto's Wendel Clark
C. Montreal's Mike Keane
D. St. Louis' Brett Hull

3.33 According to New Jersey's Claude Lemieux, during the 2000 Eastern Conference finals, what did the "C" on Eric Desjardins's Flyers sweater stand for?

A. "Selfish"
B. "Coward"
C. "Cop-out"
D. "Klutz"

3.34 Which Boston Bruins tough guy was involved in what TV commentator Don Cherry called the "greatest fight I've ever seen"?

A. Jay Miller
B. John Wensink
C. Stan Jonathan
D. Terry O'Reilly

3.35 What was Philadelphia goalie Bernie Parent referring to when he said before Game 3 of the 1975 Stanley Cup finals: "I wouldn't take my boat out in these conditions"?

A. A low-lying fog on the ice
B. A rash of injuries plaguing his Flyer teammates
C. Plastic cups thrown on the ice by unhappy fans
D. Ice coolant seeping up through the rink surface from a broken pipe

3.36 Which Canadiens star said to his bride: "Someday, I'll score more goals than your father did"?

A. Jean Béliveau
B. Bernie Geoffrion
C. Ralph Backstrom
D. Henri Richard

3.37 Which NHL coach publicly criticized Mario Lemieux in 2000–01, saying, "I'm going to make a comeback," after Lemieux complained about all the clutching and grabbing?

A. Larry Robinson
B. Mike Keenan
C. Ken Hitchcock
D. Jacques Lemaire

3.38 Who was the Dallas crowd taunting when they chanted "Eddie's better" during the 2000 Western Conference finals?

A. Patrick Roy
B. Curtis Joseph
C. Martin Brodeur
D. Ron Tugnutt

3.39 In November 2003, *Hockey Night in Canada* announcer Don Cherry called which Canadian junior star a "hot dog" because of the way he celebrated scoring a goal?

A. Corey Locke of the Ottawa 67s
B. Jeremy Williams of the Swift Current Broncos

C. Sidney Crosby of the Rimouski Océanic
D. Corey Perry of the London Knights

3.40 Which defenseman said of his chances to win the top defenseman award in 2003–04: "The only Norris I know is Chuck"?

A. Bryan McCabe of the Toronto Maple Leafs
B. Wade Redden of the Ottawa Senators
C. Kim Johnsson of the Philadelphia Flyers
D. Sheldon Souray of the Montreal Canadiens

3.41 Which Stanley Cup–losing coach said: "If I had shaken hands, I wouldn't have meant it, and I refuse to be a hypocrite"?

A. The Maple Leafs' Punch Imlach
B. The Blackhawks' Billy Reay
C. The Canadiens' Dick Irvin
D. The Bruins' Milt Schmidt

Answers

3.1 B. Boston veteran Ted Green

After being deked out of his drawers on several occasions at Orr's first Bruins practice, bruising All-Star defenseman Ted Green looked ready to go nose-to-nose with the deft rookie who had turned him into a pretzel on the ice. Instead, Green—who knew greatness when he saw it—paid Orr this compliment. It was more appropriate than Green may have realized, considering Orr's landmark contract had made him the NHL's highest-paid rookie. And indeed, whatever Orr got, it was not enough.

3.2 D. Jean-Sébastien Giguère of the Anaheim Mighty Ducks

Giguère was *the* story of the 2003 playoffs. Everyone believed it except New Jersey fans, who goaded the Anaheim netminder with chants of "Marty's better! Marty's better!" during Game 2 as the Mighty Ducks lost their second straight finals game 3–0. In Anaheim, fans weren't so clever, taunting Brodeur with "Mar-ty, Mar-ty."

3.3 C. Teemu Selanne

If rookies were rated by the publicity they generate, Eric Lindros would have won the 1993 Calder—and every other award handed out by the NHL. But who can argue that Selanne didn't deserve *his* press coverage, considering his dazzling 76-goal rookie season? Joé Juneau's linemate Adam Oates, for one. Oates scoffed at the European's "one-dimensional" play compared to Juneau's "complete game" and plus-minus skills. "Everywhere you go, people are talking about Selanne. It's not fair for Joey," fumed Oates. In any other year, Juneau, with 102 points and plus 23, might have taken the Calder, but how do you win a rookie race against Lindros, anointed the Next One; Felix Potvin with a 2.50 GAA in 48 games; and a Finn who explodes for 76 goals? It's obvious who carried the athletic support in Calder balloting in 1992–93: Selanne, with his startling 132 points and plus eight.

3.4 A. Tampa Bay owner Art Williams

Art Williams, a man with more money than hockey brains, probably meant well, but Wayne Gretzky is still the only hockey icon on par with Michael Jordan, who many consider basketball's greatest player ever. "My owner was excited about getting the number one player in the 1998 draft, but I don't think he realized that hockey players take a while to get established," said coach Jacques Demers, after reminding everyone that Lecavalier was just 18 years old.

3.5 A. Maple Leafs owner Harold Ballard

After being pressed by coach Neilson to trade Turnbull, a stubborn Ballard made it clear that his favourite defenseman was untouchable, even if the Almighty Himself were available. One clever soul piped back: "How about God and a fourth-round draft choice?"

3.6 A. The goal net

Clancy is the only NHLer to play every position—including goalie—in one Stanley Cup game. In Game 2 of the 1923 Ottawa–Edmonton Cup finals, Clancy, a second-year D-man, subbed for Ottawa's injured defensive stars George Boucher and Eddie Gerard, winded centre Frank Nighbor, bruised left-winger Cy Denneny and exhausted right-winger Punch Broadbent. With only 10 minutes remaining in the game, Senators goalie Benedict drew a penalty and was forced to serve it in the box, as was the custom in old-time hockey. Out skated Clancy again, met by Benedict, who handed him his stick and the famous line about taking care of "this place."

3.7 A. Dave Schultz

They didn't call him the Hammer for nothing. In the 1970s, Schultz was the baddest Broad Street Bully, racking up misconducts and fighting majors faster than you could say, "Philadelphia, City of Brotherly Love." He did have one 20-goal season, but Schultz was hockey's reigning goon, defending his title every game. In a four-year span from 1972–73 to 1975–76, Schultz amassed 1,386 penalty minutes and accounted for almost 20 per cent of all time in the box by the Flyers, the most penalized team in hockey, with 7,455 minutes. Schultz's 1974–75 record for most penalty minutes (472) in one season remains unbeaten.

3.8 D. Henri Richard

Richard had many eventful series over his lengthy playoff career, but none more dramatic than the 1971 finals against Chicago, when he publicly admonished coach Al MacNeil after his Game 5 benching. The incident turned into a French–English issue, and by the next game MacNeil had plainclothes policemen protecting him behind the bench. Richard apologized and then settled the score his own way. In Game 7, down two goals and with the Cup on the line, he brought Montreal back by scoring two goals, including the Stanley Cup winner.

3.9 B. The Ottawa Senators'

In adopting the name the Senators, Ottawa was tipping its hat to tradition. The original Ottawa Senators won nine Stanley Cups between 1903 and 1927, before relocating to St. Louis in 1934. Still, the choice of a helmeted Roman centurion for the team's emblem was peculiar, as it had little in common with either the original Senators or Roman statesmen. In typical bombastic fashion, Don Cherry used his soapbox on CBC's *Hockey Night in Canada* to compare the Senators' new logo to "a condom package." Presumably, Grapes was referring to Trojan-brand prophylactics.

3.10 A. His 1993 playoff shadow, St. Louis Blues centre Bob Bassen

Chicago won the 1992–93 divisional title but was stoned four straight in the first playoff round by the rejuvenated St. Louis Blues, who had finished the regular season 21 points back of the Hawks. Give credit to Curtis Joseph's 174-minute shutout streak and Bob Bassen's scrappy checking, which held 50-goal man Roenick to just one point until he got a goal and an assist in the final game. Afterwards, a frustrated Roenick quipped: "They kept throwing [Bassen] back out there, throwing him back at me. Every time I turned around, he had a stick in my face. I'm surprised he wasn't in the toilet when I went to the bathroom."

3.11 C. Mario Lemieux

Among the many spectacular offensive plays witnessed in men's hockey at the 2002 Olympics, one of the most memorable was an inspired Mario Lemieux move that led to Canada's first goal in the gold-medal game against the U.S.A. Behind 1–0 to the Americans late in the first period, Chris Pronger appeared to feed a pass to a streaking Lemieux. But the Canadian captain let the puck go through his legs to Paul Kariya, who had the open net, to tie the game. Mike Richter was sensational in net for the U.S.A. He viewed the play this way: "I can see them both there, and the pass goes practically to Mario's stick. He doesn't just not play it, he actually puts his stick there to play it, then moves his stick. It was a beautiful play, and a play you have to honour as a goalie. Obviously I honoured it a bit too much," said Richter.

3.12 A. The Philadelphia Flyers'

"Money doesn't live forever. But great moments do." The late coach Fred Shero was never at a loss for words or quotes, especially those inspirational messages he scribbled on a player's locker or on the Flyers' blackboard before each game. His best became Philadelphia's motto in perpetuity: "As a Flyer, you play for the emblem on the front, not the name on the back."

3.13 B. Stu Grimson

Grimson's heavy shot landed him a spot among the NHL's elite scorers in the skills competition during the 1993 All-Star weekend. The Hawks enforcer, who totalled two points and 193 minutes in 78 games in 1992–93, gunned a 97.7 mph blast that earned him the distinction as the fourth-hardest shooter in the old Campbell Conference.

3.14 A. NHL expansion

Although improved rules and equipment have brought great changes to hockey, nothing has had more impact on the game in recent decades than expansion. In just seven years

(1967–68 to 1973–74), North American pro hockey exploded from the "Original Six" into a 32-franchise operation with two pro leagues. As owners scrambled to discover and sign the best players, the talent pool was depleted. Scoring records were broken, salary scales went through the roof and physical intimidation reached the goon stage. Smythe's whiskey analogy was right on—at the time. In the 1990s, expansion was considered crucial to the NHL's future success in the U.S. Intrastate rivalries in Sun Belt states such as California and Florida and the rebirth of the Stars in Texas made the footprint of pro hockey in the U.S. significant enough to attract major network coverage and national advertising revenues. And Smythe probably never imagined his six-team "old boys league" drafting 18-year-olds from Valkeakoski, Finland. Today, more than 17 per cent of NHLers come from Europe, blending in to fortify the "whiskey" Smythe so carefully guarded.

3.15 B. "All good things."

At the 1989 World Championships in Stockholm, Mogilny asked teammate Sergei Fedorov to defect with him. Fedorov declined, stating he couldn't leave his family, but said to Mogilny: "You go, Alex. *Vsevo khoroshevo.* Best of luck to you in your new life." Within two years, Fedorov and Pavel Bure signed NHL contracts. In Russian hockey circles, Bure–Fedorov–Mogilny were considered the successors to the famed KLM line of Krutov–Larionov–Makarov. Could they have resurrected Russian dominance in international hockey? As it was, their defections dealt another blow to the once-awesome Soviet hockey machine. As famed Soviet coach Anatoli Tarasov said, "We have no hockey players left—they're all working in Canada."

3.16 C. Tie Domi

It was a war of words for two seasons. Probert called Domi a goon and a dummy, then Domi spouted on about Probert "hitting like a butterfly." But the showdown match on December 2,

1992, proved who could really sting when the gloves were dropped. Just 37 seconds into the game, Rangers coach Roger Neilson sent Domi, who hadn't played in three games, out to line up against Probert. The inevitable happened. In the 30-second fight a flurry of 59 punches were thrown, with Probert connecting on more than half of his. Here's the punch count.

Tie Domi–Bob Probert Heavyweight Title Match	PROBERT	DOMI
PUNCHES THROWN	38	21
PUNCHES LANDED	22	7
PER CENT LANDED	58%	33%

3.17 B. Bobby Orr and Ray Bourque

Harry Sinden, the Bruins' long-time general manager and Stanley Cup–winning coach, once said, "If I'm down a goal late in the game, I want Orr on the ice. If I'm up a goal late in the game, Bourque's the one I want out there." Sinden should know, having been around long enough to have had the privilege of utilizing two of hockey's greatest offensive defensemen. Orr could always be counted on to score the big ones when Boston needed it most, and Bourque was the Bruins' most dependable defender.

3.18 A. Coach Dick Irvin

If, as the saying goes, hockey is a religion in Quebec and the Montreal Forum its cathedral, then Irvin's homily about holding high the torch has proven not only inspirational but a cross to bear for the players who have followed such immortal Canadiens as Maurice Richard, Howie Morenz, Jacques Plante, Jean Béliveau and Guy Lafleur. These demigods of the famous CH are honoured along a stretch of dressing-room wall above poet John McCrae's famous words from *In Flanders Fields*, which coach Irvin borrowed and inscribed, in French and English.

3.19 A. Brett Hull

No one, but no one, in the NHL talks the talk better than Brett Hull. And with 18 NHL seasons and 741 goals (and counting), people listen. But when Hull, the self-described "laziest man alive" and the only superstar "who comes complete with love handles," says that Mario Lemieux shouldn't have come out of retirement or that today's NHL is boring or that he could walk away from the game without a day's regret, those same people also wonder. "I actually care," Hull said in a Fort Worth *Star-Telegram* story. "If you don't care, you aren't going to say anything. That's what drives me nuts. I get in shit about caring." So what's an NHL commissioner to do? Suspensions work for stick fouls, but what to slap hockey's All-Star mouth with? "I open (my newspaper) every day, wondering what he said this time," said Gary Bettman.

3.20 B. Red Storey

Storey's resignation as an NHL referee was front-page news in 1959. After being criticized by Campbell for "freezing" on an alleged trip by Montreal's Junior Langlois on Bobby Hull, Storey whistled the public denunciation as unfair and resigned, firing back: "When your decisions are not backed up by your boss, it's time to quit." According to Storey, Langlois hit Hull with a "beautiful hip check." The hometown Chicago crowd, smarting from an earlier non-call that resulted in a Montreal goal during the very important playoff game, descended on Storey in a rage, throwing beer in his face and littering the ice with debris. The match was delayed for 25 minutes, and at one point the Canadiens' Doug Harvey had to rescue Storey after fans jumped him from behind. Montreal won the game (and the series), while Storey fought his way to the dressing room, fending off attacking fans with a borrowed stick. Campbell, who later regretted his "chat" with the press, claimed some of his comments had been taken out of context.

3.21 B. Montreal's Ken Dryden

No one player was more responsible for stealing the Stanley Cup from the heavily favoured Boston Bruins in 1971 than the Canadiens' Ken Dryden. Not yet a rookie (just six NHL games to his credit), Dryden came out of nowhere and burned Phil Esposito, Bobby Orr and the first-place Bruins in the quarter-finals, staging one of the greatest heists in playoff history. Similar to today's Dominik Hasek, Dryden was a "sprawler," with a nimble, acrobatic style that defied the awkwardness of his six-foot-four frame. He lunged after and smothered pucks; along the ice his stick and catching glove became extensions of his swooping torso and gangly arms and legs. A frustrated Esposito called Dryden "a thieving giraffe" during the 1971 upset.

3.22 C. Richard Sevigny

Richard Sevigny's quotation came during the 1981 playoffs, when Guy Lafleur and Wayne Gretzky met in their first post-season. Lafleur, the game's most exciting player in six previous seasons, had reached his peak, while Gretzky, after a 164-point scoring binge that season, seemed poised to assume the Flower's place. In the first game, Gretzky scored a playoff-record five assists in a 6–3 Oilers win over Montreal. After the sixth goal, Gretzky skated past the Canadiens' net and patted his rear end, a jab at Sevigny and his "back-pocket" line. Gretzky dominated the best-of-five series, playing in a different class from even Lafleur, as the Oilers swept Montreal in three games.

3.23 C. Mike Keenan

During the 1996 Detroit–St. Louis Western Conference semi-finals, Mike Keenan publicly questioned Wayne Gretzky's performance, saying, among other things, "If he's not injured, then something must be bothering him." Keenan also berated the Great One in front of his teammates, which prompted Oilers general manager Glen Sather to muse: "I think [Keenan] should have his head examined. As far as I'm concerned, he must be touched by the wind or something to be critical of a guy like Wayne Gretzky." Later, Keenan apologized to No. 99, saying he might have "overstepped" himself in his comments.

3.24 A. Ulf Samuelsson

In a 1995 issue of *Sports Illustrated,* 56 anonymous NHL veterans were asked to select the dirtiest player in the league. Samuelsson collected 26 votes as Public Enemy No. 1. Bryan Marchment was a distant second with nine. As is evident by his quote, Samuelsson doesn't mind the label. Universally loathed by opposition players and fans alike, the Swedish D-man was known as a cheap-shot artist and unabashed coward when the gloves came off. It was a Samuelsson knee that put Boston forward Cam Neely out of action for a year in 1991 and later ended his career. Yet, despite his villainous reputation, Samuelsson was suspended just twice, first in February 1993 for one game for his role in a multi-player brawl; and again, three weeks later, for a stick-swinging incident with Mark Messier. Both players were given match penalties, suspended for three off-days and fined $500. Samuelsson lost $8,697 and Messier $25,545. Samuelsson retired in February 2001 at age 36. At the time, he ranked 18th on the NHL's all-time penalty-minutes list.

3.25 A. The Canadiens' Bill Durnan

Flush from victory after whipping a young Toronto team 6–0 in Game 1 of the 1947 finals, a confident Durnan quipped to reporters: "How did these guys ever make the playoffs?" Coach Hap Day flashed Durnan's reckless remarks around Toronto's dressing room and the return fire stunned Montreal. The Habs went down in four of the next five games to surrender to the youngest Stanley Cup winners ever. The lesson learned: Never underestimate your rivals, especially out loud.

3.26 A. A goal

Wayne Gretzky lost his last NHL game, a 2–1 New York Rangers defeat to the Pittsburgh Penguins, when Jaromir Jagr scored the overtime winner. According to Gretzky, "Maybe it was only fitting that the best young player in the game scored the goal in overtime. Everyone talks about passing torches. Well, he caught it." And did the finest one-on-one player in the game apologize? "Yeah," Gretzky commented, "he said, 'I didn't mean to do that.' 'That's what I used to say,' I told him."

3.27 D. Gump Worsley

Gump was as quick with a quip as he was with his catching glove. Despite receiving facial cuts requiring more than 200 stitches, Worsley resisted donning a mask until 1973–74, the final season of his 21-year career.

3.28 B. Dominik Hasek

The Sabres netminder mesmerized opposition shooters (and apparently Hextall) with his unorthodox style in 1996–97. Hextall's quote about Hasek came after a frustrating 3–2 Flyers loss to the Sabres on March 11, 1997. "It's hard to tell how to beat this guy. This guy doesn't know what he's going to do. So, therefore, neither does the shooter. He has no pattern to the way he stops the puck. A guy on a breakaway has no clue what Hasek will do. Most goalies stick to a style. Not this guy. He's on his back, he's flipping over. You have to shoot high on him. He covers low very well."

3.29 A. Chris Chelios

Bettman, who withstood a lot of heat from players during the lockout, was not amused by Chelios's outburst. His silly and dangerous remarks earned the Chicago D-man a 45-minute appointment at the commissioner's office in New York, after which Chelios was forced to sign a written apology.

3.30 D. Stephane Richer

The first player to break union solidarity and publicly admit that "the guys are fed up with losing money" and "the season would start tomorrow" if a vote were held was Richer, who made the comments during the lockout's darkest days, when stalled talks halted full-scale negotiating between Gary Bettman and Bob Goodenow. Although Goodenow and the union's bargaining committee rebuked Richer, his quotes were seen as "a small crack" in player solidarity. Within four weeks a deal would be struck.

3.31 D. Five years; $100,000; $20,000 signing bonus

Selke's quote to the press at Béliveau's contract signing, about opening "the Forum vault," was literally true. For two years Selke tried to woo Béliveau away from the Quebec Senior League, but it wasn't until the Canadiens bought the entire league and turned it professional that Le Gros Bill jumped to the big club. Under tremendous pressure to sign the province's second most popular player (after Maurice Richard), Selke offered Béliveau whatever he wanted. In 1953, $100,000 was a lot of cash, but the rookie was worth every penny. Overnight, Béliveau developed into the star the Canadiens imagined he would and one of the league's highest-paid players.

3.32 C. Montreal's Mike Keane

Prophetically, Keane made this quip when he was named captain of the Montreal Canadiens in April 1995. Eight months later, Keane was dealt to Colorado in the Patrick Roy deal. He was the fourth consecutive Canadiens captain to be traded in a six-year period. The others sent packing were Chris Chelios, Guy Carbonneau and Kirk Muller. Once considered a badge of honour and a sign of stability, the Montreal "C" has come to represent something else entirely—a bull's-eye.

3.33 A. "Selfish"

Except for his 19 playoff game-winners (third only behind Wayne Gretzky and Brett Hull, each with 24 goals respectively) in the NHL record book, no other statistic can demonstrate

Claude Lemieux's true postseason contributions, particularly as hockey's greatest pest. Throwing his opponents off their game with his on-ice, off-ice shenanigans is part of Lemieux's act, which reached new heights of mischief during the 2000 Eastern finals when he said to Philadelphia captain Eric Desjardins: "What's the 'C' stand for—selfish?" Obviously, Lemieux never scored any points in spelling class.

3.34 C. Stan Jonathan

At five foot eight and 175 pounds, Jonathan was no heavyweight, but he hit like one. Nicknamed Bulldog because of his chunky build and tenacity, Jonathan rarely, if ever, lost a fight. During the fourth game of the 1978 finals, Jonathan tangled with Montreal's Pierre Bouchard, who stood six foot two and weighed 230 pounds. Bruins coach Don Cherry called it the greatest fight he'd ever seen. "Boy, does Pierre start off great. He is lifting Stan off the ice and throwing him around. I'm on the bench and I say, 'Uh-oh, Stan looks like he's bitten off more than he can chew.' All of a sudden, Stan switches hands, from a righty to a lefty. This is tough for Pierre and it catches him off balance. Stan landed a heavy left and Pierre started to go down, but as he's falling, Stan pours about three more on him, then the *coup de grâce,* as they say, was just as Pierre hit the ice. The blood was everywhere, even on linesman John D'Amico."

3.35 A. A low-lying fog on the ice

Who knows what caused it? High humidity, poor air circulation or angry hockey gods, it could have been any of the three. The result was a billowing broth that brought Game 3 of the Stanley Cup finals at Buffalo's Memorial Auditorium to a shuddering halt a dozen times on May 20, 1975. During the delays, the Philadelphia Flyers and Buffalo Sabres players skated in circles and rink attendants waved towels in an attempt to dissipate the mist. Buffalo finally won the game on Rene Robert's slap shot in overtime. Flyers goalie Bernie Parent could honestly claim he never saw it.

3.36 B. Bernie Geoffrion

Ten years after Geoffrion married Howie Morenz's daughter, Marlene, Geoffrion's prediction came true. On December 7, 1960, the Boomer blasted home his 270th and 271st NHL goals, which equalled and passed the career goal totals of his father-in-law, the legendary Morenz.

3.37 D. Jacques Lemaire

After a 4–2 upset loss against the first-year Minnesota Wild on February 11, 2001, Mario Lemieux said the Wild's defensive style of play "was not what we're trying to sell"—referring to the expansion team's offense-stifling neutral-zone trap. Wild coach Jacques Lemaire fired back: "If we're not allowed to hit and not allowed to check, I'm going to make a comeback. I'm going to play in the league if nobody touches me..." In the rematch between the two teams, Lemieux made his point, this time on the ice, scoring twice in the third period for a 2–1 Pittsburgh victory.

3.38 A. Patrick Roy

The 2000 Western Conference finals between heavyweights Dallas and Colorado featured hockey's two premier goaltenders in a classic showdown of battling egos: Patrick Roy against Ed Belfour. In the winner-take-all seventh game for the West's Stanley Cup finalist, Belfour and Roy duelled through 60 minutes to a 2–2 deadlock. During the match, Dallas fans began chanting "Ed-die's better! Ed-die's better!" at Roy, often regarded as the game's best money goalie. Then, at 12:10 in sudden-death overtime, Joe Nieuwendyk scored the series winner, sending the fans into pandemonium and Roy to the links to lick his wounds.

3.39 C. Sidney Crosby of the Rimouski Océanic

After calling premium prospect Sidney Crosby a "hot dog" for his enthusiastic goal-scoring celebrations, Cherry got lots of ink for riding the 16-year-old kid with the "Next One" label. Perhaps the best observation was made by Jack Todd of the *Gazette* in Montreal, who wrote: "Are we missing something here? Don Cherry is the guy who made himself rich and famous by dressing like a cross between Liberace and Superfly—and he's calling the kid a hot dog?" After hearing Cherry's comment, Crosby, defying his tender age, coolly said, "When I score a goal, I'm going to be happy." Months later, at the 2004 World Junior Championships, the scoring phenom had occasion to pump it up again after becoming the youngest Canadian to score at the World Juniors, in a 7–2 win against Switzerland on December 28, 2003.

3.40 D. Sheldon Souray of the Montreal Canadiens

After breaking Montreal's team record for single-game points by a defenseman in an 8–0 whitewash against the anemic Pittsburgh Penguins on January 10, 2004, Souray kept scoring points with his self-deprecating sense of humour during the post-game interviews. Besides his Norris wisecrack, Souray, who scored once and added five assists to break the Canadiens record of five points held by the great Doug Harvey and Lyle Odelein, also quipped: "The only Harvey they've ever associated me with is the place you build your own burger."

3.41 C. The Canadiens' Dick Irvin

The most bitter rivalry in hockey during the 1950s was between the league's two powerhouses, the Red Wings and Canadiens. So intense was their mutual dislike that when sharing trains between back-to-back games the players refused to acknowledge one another as they made their way to the dining car. Fights even broke out on occasion. The Montreal–Detroit battles were most fierce in the playoffs, particularly between 1952 and 1956. During those five years, four Stanley Cup finals were played out at the Olympia and the Forum, two series going the maximum seven games. Game 7 of the 1954 showdown was a classic. The largest crowd in Detroit history witnessed a see-saw clash that went deadlocked 1–1 into overtime, thanks to brilliant goaltending by Terry Sawchuk and Gerry McNeil. But a fluke goal by Tony Leswick ended the thriller. It came on a shift change as Leswick flipped the puck at the Montreal net. Doug Harvey reached for it, but the puck bounced off his glove and behind McNeil to score. The Olympia shook and the shocked Canadiens stormed off the ice without congratulating their victorious rivals. Later, a disheartened Irvin could only say he would have been a hypocrite for shaking hands.

GAME 3

Captains of Time

STEVE YZERMAN PLAYED three seasons with Detroit before being named team captain in 1986–87. He has proudly worn the "C" on his Red Wings jersey ever since, a record 18 seasons, to 2004–05. No other captain in NHL history has come close to his length of service, including all of the long-time captains in the column on the left, below. Match them with the teams they led.

Solutions are on page 561

1. _____	Johnny Bucyk	A. Washington Capitals
2. _____	George Armstrong	B. Montreal Canadiens, 1960s
3. _____	Pierre Pilote	C. Boston Bruins, 1990s
4. _____	Alex Delvecchio	D. Toronto Maple Leafs, 1960s
5. _____	Jean Béliveau	E. New York Rangers
6. _____	Bob Gainey	F. St. Louis Blues
7. _____	Bill Cook	G. Toronto Maple Leafs, 1930s
8. _____	Brian Sutter	H. Montreal Canadiens, 1980s
9. _____	Hap Day	I. Detroit Red Wings
10. _____	Stan Smyl	J. Chicago Blackhawks
11. _____	Rod Langway	K. Boston Bruins, 1970s
12. _____	Ray Bourque	L. Vancouver Canucks

4

So Much for Technology, Eh?

AT THE 2003 ALL-STAR GAME, the hardest-shot competition was won by a player using a wooden stick. True or False? In this chapter, some simple truths about the game, including the old master blaster himself, Al MacInnis, who won the hardest-shooter event at the NHL SuperSkills for a seventh time in 2003, with a 98.9-mph screamer. One of the few NHLers to resist the new composite metal sticks, MacInnis fired his bullet with a Sher-Wood woodie. In characteristic Canadian style, MacInnis later said: "So much for technology, eh?"

Answers are on page 87

4.1 On average, how many pucks are used in a game?
- A. Less than five pucks
- B. Between five and 10 pucks
- C. Between 10 and 20 pucks
- D. More than 20 pucks

4.2 How many pucks per game are prevented from going into the crowd because of rink netting?
- A. Six pucks
- B. 10 pucks
- C. 14 pucks
- D. 18 pucks

4.3 In what decade did team logos first appear on NHL pucks?
- A. In the 1940s
- B. In the 1950s
- C. In the 1960s
- D. In the 1970s

4.4 Which NHL coach publicly complained during the 1998 playoffs about the Foxtrax puck?

A. Washington's Ron Wilson
B. Buffalo's Lindy Ruff
C. Detroit's Scotty Bowman
D. Dallas' Ken Hitchcock

4.5 Why did the NHL conduct an investigation into goalie nets in 1957?

A. To determine the best method for anchoring nets
B. To verify standard net dimensions
C. To prove the netting was puck proof
D. To correct crease size

4.6 In what NHL season did a goalie first place his water bottle on the top of his net?

A. 1964–65
B. 1974–75
C. 1984–85
D. 1994–95

4.7 Which major hockey league first used the Marsh Flexible Goal Peg, now a standard device used by all hockey leagues to keep the goal net anchored to the ice during play?

A. The National Hockey League
B. The American Hockey League
C. The Ontario Hockey League
D. The Western Hockey League

4.8 After retiring from hockey in 2003, what suggestion did Patrick Roy have for increasing goal scoring?

A. Increase the size of the nets
B. Play five men per side
C. Reduce the size of goalie equipment
D. Eliminate the trap

4.9 Who invented the curved stick blade?

A. An NHL player
B. An NHL executive
C. A hockey stick manufacturer
D. The 10-year-old son of a Stanley Cup-winning coach

4.10 In what year were aluminum sticks approved for NHL use?

A. 1962
B. 1972
C. 1982
D. 1992

4.11 Which company introduced a revolutionary high-tech hockey stick called Synergy in 2000–01?

A. Koho
B. Easton
C. Bauer
D. Cooper

4.12 How many hockey sticks are purchased each year in North America?

A. 500,000
B. One million
C. Three million
D. Five million

4.13 In what season did Jacques Plante first wear his mask in an NHL game?

A. 1956–57
B. 1957–58
C. 1958–59
D. 1959–60

4.14 In 1995–96, which French-Canadian goalie donned a new mask, with artwork that paid tribute to Jacques Plante?

A. Guy Hebert
B. Patrick Roy
C. Martin Brodeur
D. Jocelyn Thibault

4.15 What did ex-Phoenix Coyotes netminder Sean Burke have painted on his mask?

A. Images of rock guitarists
B. Images of fighter pilots
C. Images of rattlesnakes
D. Images of Roman gladiators

4.16 What symbol did Pittsburgh rookie Marc-Andre Fleury paint on his mask to represent Canada at the 2004 World Junior Hockey Championships in Helsinki?

A. A red maple leaf
B. A flying puck and stick
C. An igloo and penguins
D. A Canadian one-dollar coin, a.k.a. a lucky loonie

4.17 What piece of goalie equipment did Canadian netminder Martin Brodeur decorate to honour his father Denis Brodeur's bronze-medal win in hockey at the 1956 Olympics?

A. His mask
B. His leg pads
C. His stick
D. His sweater

4.18 How many protective cups does goalie Manny Legace wear in NHL games?

A. None, Legace goes alfresco
B. One player's cup
C. One goalie's cup
D. Two cups

4.19 What piece of equipment, used by more than a dozen NHL goalies, was made illegal after the 2000–01 season?

A. An extra piece of webbing on the trapper
B. The air-filled chest protector
C. The hanging throat guard
D. A small secondary skate blade

4.20 Which old-time netminder invented the goaltender's trapper glove?

A. Toronto's Turk Broda
B. Chicago's Emile Francis
C. Detroit's Harry Lumley
D. Montreal's Jacques Plante

4.21 In 1998–99, the NHL standardized the goaltender's catching glove to 50 inches. What did the league reduce or increase that measurement to the following season, 1999–2000?

A. 46 inches
B. 48 inches
C. 52 inches
D. 54 inches

4.22 In what decade was the first Crouch Collar invented?

A. The 1950s
B. The 1960s
C. The 1970s
D. The 1980s

4.23 Which sport inspired hockey's goalie pads?

A. Shinty
B. Field hockey
C. Cricket
D. Hurley

4.24 Who is considered the first goalie to extend his career by switching from regular leg pads to synthetic pads?

A. Bob Sauve
B. Reggie Lemelin
C. Billy Smith
D. Denis Herron

4.25 Which NHL team first experimented with long pants for their uniforms?

A. The New York Islanders
B. The Chicago Blackhawks
C. The Hartford Whalers
D. The Philadelphia Flyers

4.26 In what season did an NHLer first win the scoring title wearing a visor?

A. 1992–93
B. 1994–95
C. 1996–97
D. 1998–99

4.27 Which professional hockey league was the first to mandate the use of protective visors for all of its players?

A. The American Hockey League
B. The East Coast Hockey League
C. The United Hockey League
D. The Central Hockey League

4.28 At the time of Bryan Berard's horrific eye injury in March 2000, how many teams had no players wearing face shields?

A. None, every team had at least one player wearing a shield
B. Only one team
C. Three teams
D. Five teams

4.29 Barring a rule change, in which season did the NHL's last helmet-less player score a goal?

A. 1994–95
B. 1995–96
C. 1996–97
D. 1997–98

4.30 While every Soviet player in the 1972 Summit Series wore a helmet, few, if any, players for Team Canada did. How many?

A. None
B. Only one, Paul Henderson
C. Two players
D. Three players

4.31 Which NHL club first painted its gloves to match its uniform colours?

A. The Toronto Maple Leafs
B. The Detroit Red Wings
C. The New York Rangers
D. The Montreal Canadiens

4.32 In 2000–01, which team became the first to use a video device called XOS Sketch as a strategic tool on the bench during games?

A. The Atlanta Thrashers
B. The Washington Capitals

C. The Vancouver Canucks
D. The Los Angeles Kings

4.33 In what year was the Zamboni introduced to hockey?
A. 1939–40
B. 1944–45
C. 1949–50
D. 1954–55

4.34 In what season did the NHL require the ice surfaces in all arenas to be painted white?
A. 1944–45
B. 1949–50
C. 1954–55
D. 1959–60

4.35 In what year did advertising first appear on NHL arena rink-boards?
A. 1972
B. 1975
C. 1979
D. 1981

4.36 What 1963 incident led NHL arenas to install separate penalty boxes for each team?
A. A sellout crowd
B. A peanut vendor's heart attack
C. A player fight
D. A coach's dismissal

4.37 What was the last undersized NHL arena?
A. Boston Garden
B. Chicago Stadium
C. The War Memorial Auditorium in Buffalo
D. The Tampa Bay Lightning's first arena, Expo Hall

4.38 Which NHL team's scoreboard crashed to the ice prior to a game in 1996–97?

A. The San Jose Sharks'
B. The Buffalo Sabres'
C. The Calgary Flames'
D. The Washington Capitals'

4.39 Which NHL arena hosted the first National Football League championship game?

A. Boston Garden
B. Chicago Stadium
C. Detroit Olympia
D. New York's Madison Square Garden

4.40 Which Colorado player celebrated his team's Stanley Cup triumph in 2001 by wearing his hockey equipment for 25 hours?

A. Dan Hinote
B. Milan Hejduk
C. Shjon Podein
D. Chris Dingman

4.41 During the Stanley Cup playoffs, two sets of caps and T-shirts are produced, each set declaring one finalist as the Cup champion. What happens to the merchandise for the team that doesn't win the Cup?

A. It gets burned
B. It gets auctioned off
C. It goes to the losing team
D. It goes on sale at the Hockey Hall of Fame

Answers

4.1 D. More than 20 pucks

Pucks usually have a game existence measured in minutes, or even seconds. According to the NHL, between 20 and 40 pucks are used for three periods of play. Has any puck ever survived an entire game? Only in one documented case during the league's modern era. On November 10, 1979, the Minnesota North Stars and the Los Angeles Kings played to a 6–6 tie at the Great Western Forum, and only one puck was used during the match. Such longevity is rare, considering pucks are either lost to the crowd or replaced by the referee once they thaw. (Pucks are kept frozen for swifter movement and truer bounce during games.)

4.2 B. 10 pucks

On average, 10 pucks are saved every game because of the protective netting above the glass behind each goal. Rink netting was first installed in all NHL arenas in 2002–03, after a teenage fan was hit in the head by a deflected shot from Columbus centre Espen Knutsen during a March 16, 2002, game between the Blue Jackets and the Calgary Flames at Nationwide Arena in Columbus. The fan, 13-year-old Brittanie Cecil, died two days later in hospital. It was the first such fatality in the NHL's 85-year history. In a related story, while most teams went with black netting in the end zones, Philadelphia was the first club to switch to a clear mesh, a move that was criticized at first. Detractors claimed the mesh refracted light and distorted the view.

4.3 B. In the 1950s

The simple black puck has been decorated in many ways since it was first introduced during the late 1800s. Originally, it was a square-shaped piece of wood. Then, in 1886, the rubber puck became hockey's official disk (three inches in diameter, one inch thick and weighing six ounces); it remained a basic black until the early 1950s, when team logos began to grace its smooth surface. The World Hockey Association, the NHL's rival league in the 1970s, then upped the ante and introduced red, blue and other coloured pucks into their game. But the coloured disks were soon scrapped, as were two later innovations: the Minnesota North Stars' so-called "fire puck" (used only in practices) and its successor, the loathsome Foxtrax puck, which emitted streaks of red-and-blue light to help the American TV audience follow the play.

4.4 C. Detroit's Scotty Bowman

Bowman became the NHL's most successful coach because he knew how to work not only his bench but the media, too. During the 1998 Conference finals against Dallas, the Red Wings bench boss ranted to the press about the glowing puck used on the FOX telecasts, complaining that the pucks (with the computer chip inside) bounced too much and made for ugly hockey (because they can't be frozen). "I never saw a puck bounce so much. I hope the NHL is researching this puck," fumed Bowman. "If it's only to make a blue streak in the puck, if that's going to make the NHL live for the next 20 years, I've got to be happy. I have a pension coming." NHL senior vice-president Brian Burke shrugged off Bowman's criticism, saying, "If it wasn't that, it would have been something else."

4.5 B. To verify standard net dimensions

Everyone thought Jacques Plante had finally lost it when he said nets varied in size—until measurements were taken. Even though all NHL clubs used official goal nets, Plante believed the nets in Chicago, Boston and New York were lower than the four-foot regulation height. He was soon proven correct. The three NHL rinks had welded the two-inch crossbar to the sides of the posts rather than to the tops, shortening the nets by two inches. Plante noticed the irregularity because the crossbars at these three rinks hit his back in a different place than the crossbars at other rinks.

4.6 C. 1984–85

No exact date is on record, but the water bottle first appeared on top of the net in 1984–85, when the Flyers duo of Bob Froese and Pelle Lindbergh began using the green plastic containers during game action. The idea probably originated in the U.S. college ranks. In the pro system, Froese first brought the water bottle out—stuck on top of the net with Velcro. Since no rules were broken, few objected, except Edmonton coach Glen Sather. Smarting after a 4–1 loss to the Flyers in Game 1 of the 1985 Stanley Cup finals, Sather snapped, "What are they going to want up there next, a bucket of chicken?"

4.7 D. The Western Hockey League

It's a simple, remarkable, long-overdue invention. Before the Marsh Flexible Goal Peg came along in 1991–92, the NHL used at least two different systems to anchor goal nets to the ice: foot-long steel pegs that made nets virtually immovable, then magnets. Neither method was ideal. The unforgiving pegs injured many NHLers who collided with them, and their successor, the magnet, gave way too easily, often shifted by desperate goalies or defensemen under siege. Fred Marsh, an arena manager and ice-maker in Kitimat, B.C., came up with the flexible peg of rubber and plastic that now holds a net in place until a significant force (such as a flying player) pops it out of its steel case—embedded in the ice. But the NHL needed convincing at first. The first league to buy into Marsh's pegs was the WHL in 1987. After glowing reviews and further inspection by NHL executives, the NHL adopted the plastic pegs league-wide in 1991–92. The Marsh system is now used in every NHL and AHL arena and the three major-junior leagues in Canada, and is approved by the International Ice Hockey Federation.

4.8 C. Reduce the size of goalie equipment

After hanging up the pads, the goalie with the most wins decided the best way to save the game (and, presumably, his career records) was to shrink goalie gear, to help increase scoring. "I'm not going to have a lot of friends with the goalies, but we have to cut their pads back to 10 inches from 12," Roy said at the 2004 NHL All-Star game. Now an owner of the Quebec Remparts, Roy wants more scoring. "I know all my fans went home happy after seeing a 7–7 junior game with my Remparts. I didn't like seeing the seven on my guy, but scoring seven goals? Yeah, I liked that," said Roy.

4.9 A. An NHL player

Most often credited with the curved stick are three players: Andy Bathgate, Stan Mikita and Bobby Hull, who in the late 1950s began experimenting with bent blades and the weird flight patterns they produced when firing a puck. Bathgate began experimenting with curved sticks before he turned pro and later refined his technique in the NHL. "I would heat up the blades with hot water, bend them, then put them in the toilet-stall door jam and leave them overnight. The next day they would have a hook in them," Bathgate once revealed to an interviewer. Quite accidentally, Mikita began blasting shots with a bent blade during practice and discovered his shots jumped and dipped in flight. After experimenting, Mikita and teammate Bobby Hull used a simple steaming method to curve their blades and, through trial and error, discovered the optimum curvature for adding velocity and accuracy to their blasts. All three players deserve credit for an innovation that changed hockey forever: Bathgate was the first to use a bent blade on a consistent basis, but Hull and Mikita popularized its use.

4.10 C. 1982

Long before Wayne Gretzky took his aluminum-shafted Easton and turned the hockey world on edge, Brad Park was quietly experimenting with the game's first aluminum stick. The blade was wood, but it slid into a metal shaft that had been developed by the famous Quebec stickmaker, Sher-Wood. Park began using it during practices as early as 1979, then, after league approval, regularly in 1982. At that time only a few other players, including Stan Johnathan and Dave Christian, followed Park's lead and abandoned the traditional wooden stick.

4.11 B. Easton

Midway through the 2001–02 season about 180 NHLers were using the Easton Synergy, a one-piece stick made of carbon graphite and Kevlar. At 16 ounces, it's one-third lighter than most wooden models yet is still strong and flexible. The Synergy can supposedly increase the velocity of an NHLer's shot by as much as 10 per cent, and, because the manufacturing process produces a consistent curve, players no longer have to spend hours fine-tuning their blades. Other companies rushed to join the composite revolution, leading some to suggest that this new breed of stick could swing the balance back in favour of shooters after a long period of dominance by goalies. The masked men are worried. As Detroit Red Wings netminder Manny Legace once noted, "A guy like Al MacInnis could be up there around a buck twenty [120 mph] if he starts using these new sticks. That's getting scary."

4.12 D. Five million

It's estimated that the global stick market is worth U.S.$100 million annually—about five million pieces a year—according to figures from Bruce Dowbiggin's book, *The Stick*. And among elite players, composite or graphite sticks are slowly being favoured over wood-based sticks. But because of the cost differential between the two kinds of sticks, wood or fibreglass still dominate the public market. The cost of a graphite stick is still too much for many consumers.

4.13 D. 1959–60

Perhaps the greatest shots Plante faced during his magnificent and unusual career came from his critics, those managers, coaches and even fellow goalies who targeted him as a rebel and a coward for his face mask. Plante challenged them all after he stepped into the line of fire at Madison Square Garden on November 1, 1959, a blistering Andy Bathgate backhand that turned his nose to pulp. Plante retreated to the medical clinic, bloodied but not intimidated. The four-time Vezina Trophy winner pulled out his self-styled mask and stood up to coach Toe Blake and the other skeptics. Blake reluctantly agreed to allow the mask, and Plante put a new face on the future of goaltending.

4.14 D. Jocelyn Thibault

Thibault's mask in 1995–96 sported an illustrated reproduction of the front of one of Jacques Plante's early goalie masks. The idea of honouring the former Montreal great came not from Thibault but from artist Michel Lefebvre, to whom Thibault gave carte blanche to design the mask. As Lefebvre noted: "It's about time someone paid tribute to Plante and what he did for goalies."

4.15 A. Images of rock guitarists

An avid guitarist himself, Burke has adorned his masks with portraits of several rock legends, including Jimi Hendrix, Jimmy Page, Eddie Van Halen and Slash, the lead guitarist from the band Guns N' Roses. Burke says that the images on their masks are an expression of a goalie's personality. "It's not like every other position, where everybody's wearing the same thing. Masks are a lot cooler now. It's an art form."

4.16 D. A Canadian one-dollar coin, a.k.a. a lucky loonie

Although it brought gold to Canada's teams three times in international competition previously, the loonie lost some of its lustre at the World Juniors in 2004. Fleury's mask was decorated with each side of the coin—a loon and a portrait of Queen Elizabeth. But maybe the obvious tempted fate too much. Canada saw a 3–1 lead in the third period evaporate on three weird goals by Team U.S.A., including the tournament winner, which came when a routine clearing pass by Fleury bounced off teammate Braydon Coburn, flipped back into the Canadian crease and dribbled slowly over the goal line. Fleury belly-flopped into his net, desperate to stop the fluke goal. Despite some big stops, the loonie-laden Fleury was clearly the team goat. And he knew it. "The first one hit my shoulder and went in the net. The second one hit my stick, bounced over my head and went in the net. The third one, I chipped off my 'D' and it went in again," said Fleury. Bad luck can't be blamed for blowing a 3–1 lead and losing the gold, but it could be some time before another Canadian goalie sports headgear with a loonie design. Fleury's mask motif was conceived by 18-year-old Tanner Klassen of Campbell River, B.C., who submitted the winning design in a Hockey Canada contest.

4.17 A. His mask

Although some goaltenders wore their own NHL masks (such as Mike Richter, who donned his New York Rangers Lady Liberty mask), Canada's Martin Brodeur commissioned a new mask to celebrate his participation in the 2002 Olympics. Painted with red and orange streaking flames, Brodeur's mask featured a neck protector engraved with the words: "Cortina d'Ampezzo 1956" and "Salt Lake City 2002." At the 1956 Games in Cortina, Italy, Martin's father, Denis, won a bronze medal as goalie for Canada's Kitchener-Waterloo Dutchmen. Martin and Denis Brodeur are the only father-and-son goaltenders to win Olympic hockey medals.

4.18 D. Two cups

Prior to the 1994 Olympics in Lillehammer, Canadian goalie Manny Legace took a shot in a sensitive area at practice. "Oh yeah, I took a slap shot right in the balls," Legace told the *National Post*. "Oh yeah. Kept me out for a week and a half. That's when I went to two cups. Oh yeah. Slap shot from like four or five feet away, I just went down... I wear two. A player's cup and a regular goalie cup." Legace recovered in time for the Olympics, and continued to sport two cups in his NHL career.

4.19 D. A small secondary skate blade

The device, a small piece of sharpened metal that attaches to the bottom of a goalie's skate boot to improve traction, had been used by NHL netminders since 1996–97. The blade gave goalies greater mobility because they could use it to push off while on their knees—even when their main skate blade was off the ice. NHL general managers banned the blade after the 2000–01 season, ruling it was a performance-enhancing device rather than a protective piece of equipment.

4.20 B. Chicago's Emile Francis

Remarkable as it may seem, it wasn't until 1946–47 that the netminding fraternity could boast a suitable catching glove. Until then, goalies wore a regular hockey glove with a piece of leather sewn between the thumb and forefinger on the catching hand. Francis, who played local baseball in Saskatchewan during the off-season, took a Rawlings George McGuinn-model three-finger first-baseman's mitt and sewed on a hockey glove gauntlet cuff. His hybrid became the game's first trapper. Soon other netminders followed Francis's lead, adding a completely new dimension to the position.

4.21 B. 48 inches

In an effort to increase scoring in 1999–2000, the NHL implemented new restrictions governing catching gloves, which they downsized by two inches to 48 inches. Some goalies felt more susceptible to injury with less catching glove. "There's no margin for error anymore," Toronto's Curtis Joseph told the *National Post*. "If you close your hand too fast and catch a shot on the end of your glove, you're in trouble." The evidence backed up Joseph's claim. In a one-week stretch in December 1999, four goalies—Phoenix's Sean Burke, Chris Osgood of Detroit, Los Angeles' Stephane Fiset and Jocelyn Thibault of Chicago—were all out of action with hand injuries. With shots coming harder than ever, Joseph began putting his trapper only halfway on his hand and taping it in place.

4.22 C. The 1970s

The Crouch Collar dates to 1975, when Kim Crouch, an 18-year-old goalie in the Ontario Junior A league, nearly bled to death on-ice after a skate blade severed his jugular vein. The six-inch gash in Crouch's neck took 40 stitches to close. Motivated by the near fatal accident, Crouch's father, Ed, a firefighter in Whitby, Ontario, invented the Crouch Collar. Made of ballistic nylon, the 1½-inch-high collar has a small protective bib that covers the area just below the neck. The first model was patented in Canada in 1976.

4.23 C. Cricket

The origins of hockey can be traced back to older games like shinty, field hockey and hurley, but cricket gave us the goalie pad. In an 1896 Stanley Cup game, spectators and players were flabbergasted when Winnipeg goalie George Merritt stepped onto the ice wearing white cricket pads. After some discussion over their legality, the game began and Merritt proved their worth by posting the first shutout in Cup history.

4.24 B. Reggie Lemelin

In 1986–87, Calgary Flames netminder Reggie Lemelin tried out a pair of synthetic leg pads (made by inventor Jim Lowson) that weighed one-third the weight of his conventional pads.

As a result, Lemelin's back problems eased and his career was revitalized. Other netminders also benefited from Lowson's Aeroflex pads, but Lemelin is credited as being the first to wear them.

4.25 D. The Philadelphia Flyers

In the early 1980s, some hockey manufacturers began designing uniforms that replaced traditional short pants and stockings with a heavily padded girdle and long shell pants that extended from the waist to the skates. The Flyers, and later the Whalers, both experimented with long pants but, after much criticism, returned to the usual hockey uniform.

4.26 B. 1994–95

In the lockout-shortened season of 1994–95, Jaromir Jagr collected 70 points in the 48-game schedule to become the first European-trained player to win the scoring championship and the first NHLer to win the title wearing a face shield. Neither Mario Lemieux nor Wayne Gretzky, hockey's other scoring leaders between 1981 and 2000, wore visors.

4.27 B. The East Coast Hockey League

The ECHL pioneered pro hockey's first visor rule in 2003–04. The 31-team class-AA league, which has affiliations with 21 NHL clubs, may eventually change the face of hockey, but their motivation came in part from ECHL teams trying to keep an eye on insurance premiums. Wayne Gretzky endorsed the league's decision to mandate eye protection, which—in place decades ago throughout hockey—might have reduced the 1,914 hockey-related eye injuries reported between 1972–73 and 2001–02 if it had been reintroduced earlier. While the facts are chilling (311 players legally blinded in one eye; 302 of them because they weren't wearing visors), they still haven't changed the opinion of some players, such as Tyler Rennette. A 42-goal scorer and arguably the ECHL's top forward, Rennette goes through six half-shields per season. "I've always worn one, and I'm not taking it off," said Rennette in a Peoria *Journal Star* story. "But it's not right to tell pros they have to do this."

4.28 B. Only one team

In the wake of the horrific eye injury suffered by Toronto's Bryan Berard in March 2000, the *Hockey News* conducted a team-by-team survey of visor use in the NHL. The Edmonton Oilers were the only team in 1999–2000 without a player wearing a face shield. St. Louis had just one visor wearer, Pierre Turgeon. Two teams—the New Jersey Devils and the New York Rangers—led the pack with nine visor-wearing players. Among 644 NHLers in 1999–2000, only 133 players, or 21 per cent, wore visors. Further, almost half (49 per cent), or 65, of those visor wearers were European, a group that represents only 28 per cent of the NHL population. More than one-third of Europlayers donned visors compared to about one-seventh of North Americans.

4.29 C. 1996–97

The NHL's last bareheaded player, Craig MacTavish, scored his last goal on November 9, 1996, against Calgary's Rick Tabaracci in a 3–2 win over the Flames. A 17-year veteran, MacTavish played 50 games for the St. Louis Blues in 1996–97, his retirement year, picking up two goals and seven assists.

4.30 D. Three players

The only Team Canada players to wear helmets in the 1972 Summit Series were Stan Mikita, Red Berenson and Paul Henderson. Few NHLers wore helmets at the time, but it was fortunate for Canada that Henderson did. During the seventh game of the series, he whacked his head on the boards after taking a nasty spill. Without the helmet he likely would have suffered a concussion and been out of the lineup for game eight. As it was, Henderson played and scored the last-minute game-winner, considered by many to be the most famous goal in Canadian hockey history.

4.31 C. The New York Rangers

The Rangers led the shift to colour coordination, painting their neutral-coloured gloves red, white and blue to match their uniforms in 1957–58. The last fashion holdout was the Detroit Red Wings, who waited until 1967 before making the switch.

4.32 B. The Washington Capitals

One of the first computers used as a teaching tool on an NHL bench during games was the XOS Sketch, a U.S.$50,000 video system operated by using a stylus on a touch screen. Among those impressed with the system's quick feedback was Capitals winger Peter Bondra, who credited the device with helping him improve his performance on the power play. "You don't have to wait until the period is over," noted Bondra. "Right after a shift you can see what type of box opponents have and then adjust." After the introduction of the XOS Sketch, it was reported that the Capitals' power play rose from 21st overall in 1999–2000 to fourth best in the league in 2000–01.

4.33 D. 1954–55

Old records indicate that both Boston Garden and the Montreal Forum received Zambonis in 1954. However, the Forum is credited with using its Zamboni first, on March 10, 1955.

4.34 B. 1949–50

Prior to 1948, ice surfaces around the league were not tinted or painted, but had a drab grey look that came from the arenas' concrete floors. As the game wore on, the ice deteriorated with snow and cut marks, which made the puck harder to follow, especially after the advent of television.

4.35 C. 1979

The first time rink-boards were used as advertising space was during the 1979 Challenge Cup, a three-game series between Team NHL and the Soviet National Team at Madison Square Garden. The series, won by the Soviets two games to one, replaced the 1979 NHL All-Star game.

4.36 C. A player fight

Until the mid-1960s, NHL arenas had one penalty box for both teams. That changed soon after a fight between Montreal's Terry Harper and Toronto's Bob Pulford at Maple Leaf Gardens in Toronto, November 8, 1963. Pulford and Harper, already thrown off the ice for fisticuffs, couldn't contain themselves at such close striking distance and resumed their battle in the box. Soon, teams installed separate penalty box doors and, eventually, separate home and visitor penalty boxes. The Gardens was also the first hockey building to sport a four-sided clock (1932), Herculite glass (1947) and escalators (1955).

4.37 C. The War Memorial Auditorium in Buffalo

Sixty years after the NHL first adopted the regulation 200-by-85-foot ice surface in 1930, the league still had four undersized rinks in Boston (191 by 83 feet), Chicago (185 by 85 feet), Buffalo (193 by 84 feet) and Tampa Bay (192 by 85 feet). Those four arenas featured a smaller neutral zone, which was the only place clubs could shorten the rink without dramatically altering the play. In the Garden, the area between the blue lines was reduced from 58 to 49 feet, dimensions the Bruins believed still presented some advantages when drafting players and developing playing systems. As a result, so the theory goes, Boston liked bangers such as Terry O'Reilly, who could create tighter checking games by grinding down the forwards in the smaller neutral zone. The opening of Buffalo's Marine Midland Arena in 1996–97 spelled the end of the last undersized arena.

4.38 B. The Buffalo Sabres'

On November 16, 1996, a cable snapped as the $4.5-million, eight-sided scoreboard at Buffalo's new Marine Midland Arena was being lowered during a routine afternoon maintenance check, sending the four-ton structure crashing to the ice. Luckily, no one was on the rink at the time. The ice was not damaged, but the state-of-the-art scoreboard shattered on impact. The mishap forced the cancellation of that night's game between the Sabres and Boston Bruins.

4.39 B. Chicago Stadium

When a snowstorm struck the state of Illinois in December 1932, National Football League officials decided that it would be impossible to play its championship game between the Chicago Bears and the Portsmouth Spartans on an outdoor field. The solution was to stage the game at Chicago Stadium, home of the Blackhawks. Trucks dumped a layer of soil over the arena floor and crude line markings were painted over the surface. Because the field was only 80 yards long, every time a team crossed midfield, it was put back 20 yards. More than 11,000 fans turned out for the contest, which was played on December 18, 1932. The Bears won the historic encounter 9–0. Chicago Stadium remains the only NHL rink used for an NFL game.

4.40 C. Shjon Podein

Podein was still seated in the dressing room after his teammates had left for a restaurant to celebrate their Stanley Cup win, when one of the players' wives suggested that he wear his uniform to the party. Podein did just that, donning skate guards to soften his steps on the dance floor. At the party, former NHL coach Barry Melrose told Podein that he'd once seen another player wear his uniform for 24 hours in Adirondack. As the Avalanche winger later confessed, "That was the triple-dog dare right there. I had to do it." After the party, Podein and his wife went home to bed, where he slept in his gear with the family dog between them. "My dog didn't mind the smell, but my wife thought it was disgusting," said Podein, who met friends later that day for lunch outside Denver, then went to a tavern still wearing his sweaty duds. The stunt ended 25 hours after it began with Podein jumping into a creek at sunset. "My feet were pretty sore from wearing the skates," he conceded. "It was 20 per cent funny and 80 per cent dumb. It's something I'll always remember, though."

4.41 A. It gets burned

The NHL's consumer product division orders sets of hats and shirts for each finalist, but only one set of goods goes public—to the Cup champions when they skate around the ice with the Stanley Cup and celebrate in the dressing room. The Cup merchandise for the losing finalists gets incinerated at the manufacturer's plant. (The NHL does distribute some wrongly labelled clothes to charity, but only in non-hockey-playing countries.)

GAME 4

Bloodlines

THE GAME OF HOCKEY has produced more than 70 father-and-son combinations and at least 200 brothers have appeared in the NHL. Listed below are the first names of fathers, sons and brothers from 22 hockey families. Once you figure out their family names from their first-name combinations, find them in the puzzle by reading across, down or diagonally. Following our example of Chris and Sean **PRONGER**, connect the family names using letters no more than once. Start with the letters printed in heavy type.

Solutions are on page 561

Pavel/Valeri ________

Bobby/Brett ________

Phil/Tony ________

Kevin/Derian ________

Geoff/Russ ________

Dale/Dave ________

Eric/Brett ________

Neal/Aaron ________

Daniel/Henrik ________

Joe/Brian ________

Marcel/Gilbert ________

Frank/Pete ________

Max/Doug ________

Gordie/Mark ________

Scott/Rob ________

Maurice/Henri ________

Brian/Brent ________

Pierre/Sylvain ________

Ken/Dave ________

Wayne/Brent ________

Peter/Anton ________

Chris/Sean **PRONGER**

N											**E**
B	I	E	D	**M**	T	A	**H**	O	P	S	**B**
E	**T**	Y	A	E	C	H	S	**B**	R	**H**	U
N	U	E	H	R	**H**	I	E	O	U	O	R
T	L	R	O	M	O	E	T	R	L	E	T
E	G	**R**	A	V	T	W	R	L	R	**D**	E
O	I	Y	R	**P**	L	T	E	Y	L	Y	N
N	E	C	O	**S**	U	I	R	D	L	**D**	K
R	**S**	N	H	N	D	E	C	E	A	I	Z
L	T	I	A	R	G	L	N	H	N	O	T
I	A	D	E	**S**	E	N	L	R	T	N	E
N	S	T	S	**H**	U	O	U	U	**M**	N	R
D	R	O	N	Y	**C**	N	T	E	R	E	**G**

5

A Company of Superstars

IF WAYNE GRETZKY HADN'T played hockey, Brett Hull would hold the single-season record for goals scored (86) and Mario Lemieux would own the regular-season mark for points scored (199). But Gretzky *did* play hockey and established more milestones than anyone imagined possible. His accomplishments are staggering, especially considering the company of superstars he supersedes. In this chapter, we look at Misters Gretzky, Lemieux and Hull—but also at those not-so-greats, from the first- to the fourth-liners, who hold a measure of distinction for their scoring exploits.

Answers are on page 113

5.1 What was the number one hockey rule Walter Gretzky taught his son, Wayne?

A. Go where the puck's *going,* not where it's been
B. Practise, practise, practise
C. Don't get big-headed
D. When taking a pass, keep your head up

5.2 What is the record for the fastest two goals by one player in a game?

A. Three seconds
B. Four seconds
C. Five seconds
D. Six seconds

5.3 What is the highest number of goals scored by one player in one NHL game?

A. Six goals
B. Seven goals
C. Eight goals
D. Nine goals

5.4 Who holds the NHL record for most points in one game?

A. Mario Lemieux
B. Bryan Trottier
C. Wayne Gretzky
D. Darryl Sittler

5.5 At what age did an NHLer become the youngest player to score a hat trick?

A. 17 years old
B. 18 years old
C. 19 years old
D. 20 years old

5.6 If Mario Lemieux holds the NHL mark for most shorthanded goals in a season (13), what is the record for most shorthanded goals by an individual in one game?

A. No player has ever scored more than one shorthanded goal in a game
B. Two
C. Three
D. Four

5.7 What is the greatest number of shorthanded points scored by a player in one game?

A. Three
B. Four
C. Five
D. Six

5.8 Who is the youngest player to score five goals in an NHL game?

A. Mats Sundin
B. Wayne Gretzky
C. Don Murdoch
D. Bryan Trottier

5.9 Who is the only player in NHL history to record a five-goal game and score all of his team's goals in that game?

A. Pittsburgh's Mario Lemieux
B. Detroit's Sergei Fedorov
C. Edmonton's Wayne Gretzky
D. Montreal's Yvan Cournoyer

5.10 On January 14, 1922, Montreal Canadiens Sprague and Odie Cleghorn each scored four goals in the same game. When was the next time in NHL history that two teammates recorded a four-goal night together?

A. 1940–41
B. 1960–61
C. 1980–81
D. 2000–01

5.11 What is the greatest number of points scored by two teammates in one game?

A. 10 points
B. 12 points
C. 14 points
D. 16 points

5.12 Only two NHLers since expansion in 1967 have scored six goals in a game. Darryl Sittler is the last player to do it, in February 1976, but who also shares this feat?

A. Red Berenson
B. Mats Sundin

C. Don Murdoch
D. Dave Andreychuk

5.13 What is the greatest number of goals scored in two consecutive games by a modern-day player?

A. Six goals
B. Seven goals
C. Eight goals
D. Nine goals

5.14 What is the record for the longest consecutive goal-scoring streak in NHL history?

A. 12 games
B. 16 games
C. 20 games
D. 24 games

5.15 How many points did Wayne Gretzky score during his 51-game point-scoring streak in 1983–84?

A. Less than 125 points
B. Between 125 and 150 points
C. Between 150 and 175 points
D. More than 175 points

5.16 Which Flyer scored the most goals during Philadelphia's NHL-record 35-game unbeaten streak in 1979–80?

A. Brian Propp
B. Bill Barber
C. Rick MacLeish
D. Reggie Leach

5.17 Who owns the NHL record for most goals in a calendar month?

A. Wayne Gretzky
B. Teemu Selanne
C. Brett Hull
D. Mario Lemieux

5.18 Besides Wayne Gretzky, who is the only other teenager to register a 50-goal season?

A. Pierre Larouche
B. Mario Lemieux
C. Jimmy Carson
D. Dale Hawerchuk

5.19 Who is the oldest NHLer to score 50 goals in a season?

A. Johnny Bucyk
B. Joe Mullen
C. Phil Esposito
D. Marcel Dionne

5.20 Who is the only 50-goal scorer traded midseason to score at least 25 goals for each team during the season?

A. Craig Simpson, with Pittsburgh and Edmonton
B. Joe Mullen, with St. Louis and Calgary
C. Dave Andreychuk, with Buffalo and Toronto
D. Mike Gartner, with Minnesota and New York

5.21 What is the fewest number of NHL career goals scored by a player after he recorded a 50-goal season?

A. Less than 10 goals
B. Between 10 and 30 goals
C. Between 30 and 50 goals
D. More than 50 goals

5.22 Which NHLer scored the highest number of goals in his career without ever posting a 50-goal season?

A. Gordie Howe
B. Mark Messier
C. Mike Gartner
D. Marcel Dionne

5.23 Who holds the mark for scoring the fewest power-play goals during a season in which he notched 50 goals?

A. Reggie Leach of the Philadelphia Flyers
B. Mark Messier of the Edmonton Oilers
C. Joe Mullen of the Calgary Flames
D. Steve Yzerman of the Detroit Red Wings

5.24 What is the record for most goals in a season by a player who did not score a single power-play goal?

A. 21 goals
B. 26 goals
C. 31 goals
D. 36 goals

5.25 What is the NHL record for most goals scored in a season by a player who had no assists?

A. Seven goals
B. 10 goals
C. 13 goals
D. 16 goals

5.26 There are few NHL assist records that Wayne Gretzky doesn't own outright. One mark that No. 99 tied but could not top in the books is most assists in a game: seven. Which Detroit Red Wings forward set this record in 1947?

A. Sid Abel
B. Jim McFadden
C. Ted Lindsay
D. Billy Taylor

5.27 Who was the first NHLer to collect 100 assists in a season?

A. Bobby Orr
B. Stan Mikita
C. Marcel Dionne
D. Wayne Gretzky

5.28 Most players record more assists than goals, but for some snipers the reverse is true. Who holds the NHL mark for the largest goals-to-assists differential in a season?

A. Brett Hull
B. Pavel Bure
C. Cam Neely
D. Lanny McDonald

5.29 According to Brett Hull, from where on the ice does he score at least half his goals?

A. The point
B. The slot
C. The faceoff circles
D. In the crease

5.30 What is the highest percentage of goals that a modern-day player has scored of his team's total goals in a season?

A. 19.5 per cent
B. 24.5 per cent
C. 29.5 per cent
D. 34.5 per cent

5.31 The NHL's fastest 100 goals from the start of a career were scored in how many games?

A. Less than 120 games
B. Between 120 and 140 games
C. Between 140 and 160 games
D. More than 160 games

5.32 Who is the first player to score 100 goals against every other team in the league?

A. Maurice Richard
B. Gordie Howe
C. Bobby Hull
D. Jean Béliveau

5.33 Who is the youngest NHLer to score 100 points in a season?

A. Jimmy Carson
B. Dale Hawerchuk
C. Mario Lemieux
D. Wayne Gretzky

5.34 What is the most senior age at which an NHLer has recorded a 100-point season?

A. Less than 33 years old
B. 33 to 36 years old
C. 37 to 40 years old
D. More than 40 years old

5.35 The first NHLer to post a 100-point season was Canadian Phil Esposito. Which country trained the first non-Canadian 100-point player?

A. U.S.A.
B. Finland
C. Sweden
D. USSR

5.36 What is the highest point total by a runner-up in the NHL scoring race?

A. 78 points
B. 108 points
C. 138 points
D. 168 points

5.37 What is the most number of points scored by a player who played only one NHL season?

A. 48 points
B. 58 points
C. 68 points
D. 78 points

5.38 What is the NHL record for most points in a season by a player who collected zero minutes in penalties?

A. 34 points
B. 44 points
C. 54 points
D. 64 points

5.39 Who holds the record for collecting the most points in his final NHL season?

A. Mike Bossy
B. Bobby Clarke
C. Hakan Loob
D. Frank Mahovlich

5.40 Who broke Maurice Richard's 544-goal career record?

A. Montreal's Bernie Geoffrion
B. Chicago's Bobby Hull
C. Detroit's Gordie Howe
D. Boston's Phil Esposito

5.41 How many more games did Mario Lemieux take to score 600 goals than Wayne Gretzky?

A. Lemieux scored his 600th faster than Gretzky
B. One game
C. 66 games
D. 99 games

5.42 Who is the lone member of the NHL's 500-goal club with fewer than 1,000 career points?

A. Bobby Hull
B. Mike Bossy
C. Maurice Richard
D. Lanny McDonald

5.43 Which sniper led the NHL in goal scoring the most times?

A. Gordie Howe
B. Bobby Hull
C. Phil Esposito
D. Wayne Gretzky

Answers

5.1 A. Go where the puck's *going,* not where it's been

Wayne Gretzky's first and most important coach was his dad. The elder Gretzky taught his son about practising, avoiding overconfidence and keeping his head up, but his number one rule was this: Know where the play is heading and be there. A little something called anticipation.

5.2 B. Four seconds

It's hard to imagine scoring two goals faster than four seconds apart. Consider how much clock time it takes after scoring the first goal to win the faceoff, skate, maybe take a pass, shoot and score again. But it's happened twice, almost 64 years apart. The Montreal Maroons' Nels Stewart scored two goals in four seconds at 8:24 and 8:28 of the third period on January 3, 1931, in a 5–3 win. More recently, on December 15, 1995, Winnipeg's Deron Quint scored at 7:51 and 7:55 of the second period as the Jets defeated the Oilers 9–4.

5.3 B. Seven goals

On the bitterly cold night of January 31, 1920, Joe Malone of the Quebec Bulldogs stepped onto the ice in Quebec City and into the record books by scoring seven goals (including three in two minutes) against the Toronto St. Pats' Ivan Mitchell in a 10–6 romp. Because of the freezing temperatures, few fans were there to witness Malone's historic game, but no one has forgotten his NHL scoring record, still unbroken 85 years later. Many players have come close, however, most recently Darryl Sittler, who scored six goals for Toronto in 1976.

5.4 D. Darryl Sittler

Sittler smashed the single-game record on February 7, 1976, scoring 10 points on six goals and four assists in an 11–4 Toronto joyride over Boston. It was that kind of night: whenever the Leafs captain was on the ice, something happened, including a goal he scored from behind the net when his attempted pass struck the skates of two Bruins and bounced into the goal. Needless to say, Sittler owned the Bruins—and goalie Dave Reece, who never played another NHL game.

5.5 B. 18 years old

A handful of teenagers have registered hat tricks in NHL action, including Wayne Gretzky, who was just five days past his 19th birthday when he pegged his first on February 1, 1980, and Jaromir Jagr, who got his first three-goal night in a Penguins 6–2 win against Boston on February 2, 1991. Jagr, at 18, just 13 days shy of his 19th birthday, topped Gretzky in age but fell short of Jack Hamilton, a little-known Toronto centre who played only 102 career games during the 1940s. Hamilton was a war-time replacement for the Maple Leafs but earned everlasting fame on February 19, 1944, when he became the NHL's youngest trickster at age 18 years and 262 days, in a 10–4 Toronto win over the Bruins.

5.6 C. Three

On March 9, 1991, Calgary's Theo Fleury set a league record by notching an unprecedented three shorthanded goals against St. Louis in an 8–4 win. Curiously, the two Flames who were credited with assists on Fleury's first shorthanded goal, Frank Musil and Stephane Matteau, played a large part in Fleury's second and third shorthanders. Musil was the Calgary player penalized when Fleury scored his second shorthanded goal; Matteau was in the box for Fleury's historic third. The shorthanded hat trick, an NHL first, included Fleury's 42nd, 43rd and 44th goals of the season.

5.7 **B. Four**

In a 7–4 win against the Vancouver Canucks on April 7, 1995, Winnipeg Jets forward Keith Tkachuk scored a league-record four shorthanded points on two goals and two assists while the Jets were playing a man short. Tkachuk earned two shorthanded points from assists on goals by Nelson Emerson and Darrin Shannon while the Canucks' Brent Thompson was serving an instigator penalty for fighting with Gino Odjick. He later added shorthanded goals when Dave Manson was off for holding and Shannon was in the box for hooking.

5.8 **C. Don Murdoch**

The New York Rangers figured they had a budding superstar in Murdoch, especially after the rookie winger blitzed Minnesota North Stars goalie Gary Smith for five goals in a 10–4 rout on October 12, 1976. Murdoch was two weeks shy of turning 20 and in just his fourth NHL game. A midseason ankle injury cost him the rookie-of-the-year award, but he still finished with 32 goals and 56 points in 59 games. Then, after a sophomore season of 55 points in 66 games, Murdoch ran into trouble with the law. In the summer of 1978, a routine search by customs officers in Toronto led to the discovery of cocaine stashed in one of his socks and five marijuana joints inside a cigarette packet. Although Murdoch didn't get any jail time for the drug charge, he was suspended for the first 40 games of the 1978–79 season. Having all that idle time didn't help the youngster, who had a fondness for Manhattan's nightlife. When he returned to action, he had lost some of his spark. By 1982, Murdoch was playing in the minors and never made it back to the NHL.

5.9 B. Detroit's Sergei Fedorov

Forty-one players before him had recorded a five-goal game, but Sergei Fedorov was the first NHLer to fire home all five of his team's goals. On December 26, 1996, Fedorov notched the unusual NHL first, beating Washington's Jim Carey for five goals in Detroit's 5–4 win. In playoff action, five NHLers have recorded five-goal games, but Maurice Richard is the only player to score all of his team's goals as the Montreal Canadiens defeated Toronto 5–1 on March 23, 1944.

5.10 D. 2000–01

After Sprague and Odie Cleghorn blasted Hamilton goalie Howie Lockhart for four goals apiece in Montreal's 10–6 whipping of the Tigers in 1922, another 78 years passed before two other teammates duplicated the eight-goal performance in a single game. New Jersey's Randy McKay and John Madden repeated the scoring oddity on October 28, 2000, scoring four goals each against Pittsburgh's Garth Snow and Jean-Sébastien Aubin in the Devils' 9–0 lashing. After learning that McKay and Madden had become the league's first four-goals-apiece teammates since 1922, New Jersey coach Larry Robinson said: "Holy mackerel."

5.11 D. 16 points

On February 20, 1981, Peter and Anton Stastny both counted hat tricks for the Quebec Nordiques in a 9–3 romp over Vancouver. Two nights later, the Slovak duo ran wild against Washington, as Peter counted four goals and four assists and Anton added three goals and five assists in an 11–7 win. Not only did the Stastnys establish a new mark for most points by two brothers in a game, they set a new NHL record for most points by two teammates.

5.12 A. Red Berenson

Since the Quebec Bulldogs' Joe Malone set the NHL record for most goals in a game at seven in 1920, five old-timers have come close and recorded six-goal games. In modern times, two others have netted a half-dozen in a night: Darryl Sittler on February 7, 1976, and Red Berenson on November 7, 1968. But Sittler's achievement has always overshadowed Berenson's mark. One reason may be that Sittler played for the Maple Leafs and scored his six in Toronto, Canada's media capital, while Berenson fired his half-dozen on the road in Philadelphia against Doug Favell during an 8–0 win over the Flyers. Berenson remains the only NHLer ever to score six goals in a road game.

5.13 D. Nine goals

The highest goal-count in two consecutive games by one player was recorded on December 27 and 30, 1981, by Wayne Gretzky. The Great One scored four goals on December 27 and then registered his first five-goal game on December 30. The scoring outburst came in Gretzky's 38th and 39th games of 1981–82 and capped hockey's fastest 50-goal streak. No NHLer has ever scored consecutive five-goal games. Only a few players in NHL history have scored more than five goals in one match, and none have followed up (or preceded) it with another multiple-goal effort for a two-game total better than nine goals. A few players have scored eight goals in two games, including old-timers Newsy Lalonde and Joe Malone during the 1920s.

5.14 B. 16 games

Despite all the old records that have been broken by today's snipers, no one has ever matched the 84-year-old NHL mark of the 16-game goal-scoring streak. Still, a few players have come close: Mario Lemieux netted 18 goals in a 12-game stretch in 1992–93, and the Kings' Charlie Simmer scored 17 goals in his 13-game run in 1979–80. The unbreakable streak has stood since 1921–22, when Ottawa's Harry "Punch" Broadbent went on a 25-goal rampage in 16 straight games, from December 24, 1921, through February 15, 1922. Broadbent won the NHL scoring title that season with 32 goals in the 24-game schedule.

5.15 C. Between 150 and 175 points

Wayne Gretzky had seven streaks of 20 or more consecutive games with at least one point, but during his best streak, an NHL record 51-game span, he totalled an astonishing 61 goals and 92 assists for 153 points. The streak began on October 5, 1983, and continued uninterrupted for almost four months before Los Angeles Kings goalie Markus Mattsson finally shut down No. 99 on January 28, 1984.

5.16 D. Reggie Leach

The Flyers scored 154 goals and 240 assists for 394 points during their NHL-record 35-game unbeaten streak, October 14, 1979, to January 6, 1980. Philly's most prolific goal scorers were Leach (24–15–39), followed by Brian Propp (20–19–39), Bill Barber (20–17–37), Rick MacLeish (19–13–32), Ken Linseman (9–23–32), Paul Holmgren (9–9–18) and Bobby Clarke (6–28–34). The Flyers allowed 98 goals and played every NHL team (except Washington) during their 25–0–10 stretch. It is the longest undefeated streak of any team in the history of North American professional sports.

5.17 B. Teemu Selanne

Most hockey analysts predicted that Finnish rookie Teemu Selanne would have trouble adjusting to the NHL style of play in his first season. They were wrong. Selanne struck for a hat trick in his fifth game with the Winnipeg Jets in 1992–93, and never looked back. On March 2, 1993, Selanne scored his 54th goal of the season, breaking Mike Bossy's NHL record for most goals by a rookie. He celebrated by tossing one glove up in the air, then dropped to one knee and pointed his stick like a rifle as he pretended to shoot it out of the air. The Finnish Flash went on a wild tear in March, firing 20 goals, the most ever by an NHLer in one calendar month. Selanne ended the season with 76 goals, obliterating Bossy's rookie mark.

5.18 C. Jimmy Carson

Among the hot young snipers who have made their first NHL marks early in their careers, only Jimmy Carson has equalled Wayne Gretzky by turning in a 50-goal season before his 20th birthday. Gretzky was 19.2 years old when he passed the 50-goal mark in the 78th game of his first NHL season on April 2, 1980. Carson, at 19.8 years of age, was just six months older when he netted his 50th in the 77th game of his second season on March 26, 1988. Gretzky totalled 51 goals and Carson achieved 55 in those seasons.

5.19 A. Johnny Bucyk

Like fine wine, Bucyk seemed to improve with age. He enjoyed his best offensive campaign at age 35.10 years, in his 16th NHL season, when he compiled 51 goals and 116 points. The Boston left-winger continued to fill the net until age 42, when he retired with a career total of 556 goals. Only seven NHLers have recorded 50-goal seasons past the "advanced age" of 30. Next youngest among 50-goal men after Bucyk are Phil Esposito, who was 33 years old when he netted 61 goals in 1974–75; and Joe Mullen at age 32.1 in his 51-goal campaign in 1988–89.

5.20 C. Dave Andreychuk, with Buffalo and Toronto

Only two NHLers—Craig Simpson and Dave Andreychuk—have been traded midseason in a 50-goal year: Simpson was the first in 1987–88, when he posted a 56-goal season-split between Pittsburgh (13 goals in 21 games) and Edmonton (43 goals in 59 games). But Andreychuk scored at least 25 goals with each team during his 50-goal trade year. After he had netted 29 goals for the Sabres in 52 games in 1992–93, Buffalo dealt Andreychuk to Toronto, where he exploded for another 25 in his 31 remaining games for a career-high 54-goal season.

5.21 A. Less than 10 goals

After scoring 50 goals in 49 games in 1993–94, Cam Neely managed only 53 goals during his last two seasons; Mike Bossy scored just 38 more times after his 1985–86 68-goal effort; Mickey Redmond potted 26 goals after his 51-goal year in 1973–74. All three 50-goal men suffered injuries that curtailed their goal production dramatically, but that was not the case for Bobby Hull. Hull leads all 50-goal scorers with just six NHL goals. After his fifth 50-goal season in 1971–72, he joined the renegade WHA and only returned to the NHL in 1979–80, scoring six times with the Hartford Whalers before finally retiring.

5.22 A. Gordie Howe

In the 1950s the most commonly debated hockey question was: Who is the better player, Gordie Howe or Maurice Richard? Yet for all their success, both Richard and Howe suffered major disappointments in their careers. Richard, hockey's first 50-goal scorer, never won an NHL scoring championship; Howe, a four-time league scoring leader, failed to notch a 50-goal season despite scoring 801 goals. But both came agonizingly close to realizing their dreams: Richard missed the scoring title by one point in 1954–55; Howe totalled 49 goals in 1952–53.

5.23 A. Reggie Leach of the Philadelphia Flyers

Because he had such a wicked slap shot, Leach often played the point when the Flyers had the man-advantage, which may partly explain why he scored only five of his 50 goals in 1979–80 on the power play. Even so, it's a real eye-opener to see his name at the top of this list. Obviously, Leach was a major threat to score at even strength, a common trait among superior players. It's also a surprise to see Mike Bossy and Jari Kurri so high in the category. They both routinely posted double-digit goal totals on the power play.

Fewest Power-Play Goals by a 50-Goal Scorer*

PLAYER	TEAM	SEASON	G	PPG
Reggie Leach	Philadelphia	1979–80	50	5
Mike Bossy	N.Y. Islanders	1983–84	51	6
Jari Kurri	Edmonton	1986–87	54	7
Rick Martin	Buffalo	1973–74	52	8
Bobby Hull	Chicago	1971–72	50	8
Danny Gare	Buffalo	1975–76	50	8
Steve Shutt	Montreal	1976–77	60	8
Wayne Gretzky	Edmonton	1984–85	73	8

**Since 1967–68/current to 2004–05*

5.24 C. 31 goals

Reaching more than 30 goals in a season without counting a single goal on the power play is a rare achievement. In fact, it's happened only once in NHL history. The marksman was Winnipeg Jets left-winger Doug Smail, who tallied 31 goals in 1984–85. The 31-goal tally was a single-season high for the Moose Jaw native, who was usually employed in a checking role by the Jets. In fact, of the 210 goals Smail scored in his career, only eight came on the power play.

Most Goals in a Season Without Scoring a Power-Play Goal*

PLAYER	TEAM	SEASON	GOALS
Doug Smail	Winnipeg	1984–85	31
John Wensink	Boston	1978–79	28
Stan Jonathan	Boston	1977–78	27
Bob Errey	Pittsburgh	1988–89	26

**Since 1967–68/current to 2004–05*

5.25 C. 13 goals

It took a lot of digging to discover the owner of this oddball record. His name? John McKinnon of the Pittsburgh Pirates, 1926–27. Amazingly, McKinnon was a defenseman. Although NHL scorekeepers awarded fewer assists in the 1920s than they do today, it's still hard to imagine how a defenseman could register 13 goals without picking up a single assist. Judging by his career numbers—28 goals, 11 assists—McKinnon definitely preferred shooting to passing. The closest challenger to McKinnon that we could find was Mickey Roach, who scored 11 goals without an assist for the New York Americans in 1926–27.

5.26 D. Billy Taylor

Although Wayne Gretzky accomplished it three times, the first and only other seven-assist game in NHL history came courtesy of Billy "The Kid" Taylor. On March 16, 1947, Taylor caught fire, notching seven helpers in Detroit's 10–6 win over Chicago. Thanks to his playmaking skills, the slick Red Wing centre led the league in assists with 46 and finished third in the scoring race with 63 points. His most-assists-in-a-game record lasted for a remarkable 33 years until equalled by the Great One, first on February 15, 1980, and twice in the 1985–86 season.

5.27 A. Bobby Orr

Boston's fabled No. 4 bagged 102 assists in 1970–71 to become the first NHLer to reach the century mark. In doing so, Bobby Orr broke his own record for assists (87), set the previous year. The bowlegged kid from Parry Sound completely revolutionized the role of the defenseman with his stick play and end-to-end dashes. Before Orr established his mark, Pat Stapleton held the NHL record for assists by a defenseman, with 50. The only other players to break 100 assists in a season are Wayne Gretzky (11 times) and Mario Lemieux (once). Orr's 102-assist mark was snapped by Gretzky in 1980–81, when he notched 109 helpers.

5.28 A. Brett Hull

In his prime, Brett Hull was a goal-scoring machine. In 1990–91, with the St. Louis Blues, he notched 86 goals to go with 45 assists, by far the largest goals-to-assists differential in NHL history. In fact, the winger owns three of the top six rankings in the category. Hull was aided in 1990–91 by the precision passing of centre Adam Oates, who collected 90 assists, the most ever by a St. Louis player.

Largest Single-Season Goals-to-Assists Differentials*

PLAYER	TEAM	SEASON	G	A	DIF
Brett Hull	St. Louis	1990–91	86	45	41
Joe Malone	Montreal	1917–18	44	4	40
Lanny McDonald	Calgary	1982–83	66	32	34
Tim Kerr	Philadelphia	1986–87	58	26	32
Brett Hull	St. Louis	1989–90	72	41	31
Brett Hull	St. Louis	1991–92	70	39	31
Reggie Leach	Philadelphia	1975–76	61	30	31

**Since 1967–68/current to 2004–05*

5.29 B. The slot

When Brett Hull scored his 600th career goal on December 31, 1999, he did it in his 900th game—third-fastest in the NHL behind Wayne Gretzky (718th game) and Mario Lemieux (719th game). Hull achieved the feat on a typical play, a shot from the slot, while Dallas had the man-advantage. "I think I've scored maybe half my goals from that spot," said Hull, who became just the 12th NHLer to net 600 goals. Hull and his father, Bobby, are the first father-son duo in the 600-goal club.

5.30 C. 29.5 per cent

As often as it's been tried, few hockey managers have ever had success building a winning team with just one star player. Look at the Florida Panthers' experiment with Pavel Bure in 2000–01. Bure had too much finesse for the lunch pail crew that Panther GM Bryan Murray had assembled. The Russian Rocket broke numerous club records but couldn't get the Cats into the playoffs. Bure scored an NHL record 29.5 per cent of Florida's goals, blasting home 59 of the Panthers' 200 goals. The next-highest Panther scorer was Viktor Kozlov with 14 goals. Prior to Bure, Brett Hull owned the lead since 1990–91, when he potted 86 goals, or 27.7 per cent of St. Louis' 310-goal count. Other players to account for at least a quarter of their team's goals: Montreal's Maurice Richard in 1949–50, Washington's Peter Bondra in 1994–95 and Anaheim's Teemu Selanne in 1997–98.

5.31 B. Between 120 and 140 games

The Islanders' Mike Bossy is the fastest 100-goal scorer from the start of a career, notching goal number 100 during his 129th game in his second NHL season, 1978–79. Bossy scored 53 goals during his rookie campaign and then popped in his 47th of 1978–79 on February 19, 1979, for his 100th career goal. The next-fastest NHLer to score 100 goals is Teemu Selanne, who missed Bossy's record by just one game, scoring his 100th in game number 130 (January 12, 1994). Wayne Gretzky scored his 100th NHL goal into an empty net on March 7, 1981. It was Gretzky's 145th NHL match.

5.32 B. Gordie Howe

Yes, there were only six teams during Howe's prime, but even so this is quite a feat. Maurice Richard, for example, never popped 100 goals against all five opposition teams. Howe completed his historical sweep by notching his 100th against Montreal in a 6–0 Detroit whitewash on February 7, 1965. The goal came against Gump Worsley, the same netminder that Howe victimized for his 500th NHL goal, three years earlier.

5.33 B. Dale Hawerchuk

Dale Hawerchuk fulfilled all of the Winnipeg Jets' expectations as 1981's first overall draft pick, winning the Calder Trophy as top rookie and breaking the 100-point barrier when he was 18 years and 11 months old. Hawerchuk, who became the NHL's youngest 100-point man on March 24, 1982, beat Wayne Gretzky (19.2 years) in age by just three months. The only other two teenagers to hit the century mark are Mario Lemieux (19.6 years) and Jimmy Carson (19.8 years).

5.34 D. More than 40 years old

This mark could only belong to Mr. Hockey, Gordie Howe. During his remarkable NHL career, Howe scored 1,850 points but had just one century season. It came in 1968–69 when Howe was still in his prime, at age 41. He accumulated 103 points, but his most famous marker was his 700th goal (a league first), which he scored on December 4, 1968, in a 7–2 win over Pittsburgh.

5.35 C. Sweden

The old WHA endured many insults for its brand of game, but the rival league pioneered the European style of play into North American hockey. Kent Nilsson from Nynashamn, Sweden, delivered two 100-point seasons in the WHA before graduating to the NHL, where, unlike most former WHAers, he excelled, scoring 49 goals and 131 points in 1980–81 with the Calgary Flames. Nilsson's historic 100th point, the first by a non-Canadian NHLer, came on February 27, 1981, against Hartford. That season, Nilsson finished third in the scoring race, behind ex-WHAers Wayne Gretzky and Marcel Dionne. Another answer might be England, but native-born Ken Hodge moved to Canada long before he got his hockey legs or his 105 points of 1970–71.

5.36 D. 168 points

In Wayne Gretzky's first season in Los Angeles, the Great One amassed 168 points—a high number, but only good enough for second place to league leader Mario Lemieux's career year of 199 points in 1988–89. In fact, Lemieux made a career out of stealing thunder, outscoring the totals of the three runners-up in this category during his Art Ross years. Lemieux, with 161 points, bested Jaromir Jagr's 149 points in 1995–96; in 1987–88 he beat Gretzky's 149-point total with a 168-point year; and he captured the headlines in 1992–93 by amassing 160 points in just 60 games to top Pat LaFontaine's career best of 148 points.

5.37 A. 48 points

The NHL record book is dotted with hundreds of one-year washouts, most of whom never racked up more than a few games or points in their brief big-league careers. Washington's Milan Novy would be an exception among those castoffs. A three-time Czechoslovakian player of the year (1977, 1981 and 1982), Novy was drafted by the Capitals in 1982, played the 1982–83 season as a 31-year-old rookie and scored 18 goals and 48 points, a mark unequalled among one-year players. The following season he returned to his native country, never to skate in NHL action again.

5.38 C. 54 points

This mark is shared by teammates. In 1944–45, Bill Mosienko and Clint Smith of the Chicago Blackhawks both notched 54 points without making a single visit to the sin bin, a record high for unpenalized players. Mosienko won the Lady Byng Trophy for most gentlemanly player that year. Smith, who accumulated only 24 penalty minutes in 483 career games, had won the award on two previous occasions.

5.39 C. Hakan Loob

No player ever departed the NHL on a higher note than Hakan Loob. In his last season, in 1988–89, the 28-year-old winger amassed 85 points on 27 goals and 58 assists for the Calgary Flames and helped his club win the Stanley Cup. After the season, Loob returned home to Sweden, where he skated for seven more years in the Swedish Elite League and played for his country in two Olympics and two World Championships.

Most Points in Final NHL Season*

PLAYER	TEAM	SEASON	G	A	P
Hakan Loob	Calgary	1988–89	27	58	85
Frank Mahovlich	Montreal	1973–74	31	49	80
Jean Béliveau	Montreal	1970–71	25	51	76
Mike Bossy	N.Y. Islanders	1986–87	38	37	75
John McKenzie	Boston	1971–72	22	47	69

**Current to 2004–05 (at the time of this writing, some players were considering early retirement from NHL action due to 2004–05's player lockout; those players are not represented here)*

5.40 C. Detroit's Gordie Howe

Almost 11 years to the day after Richard broke Nels Stewart's 324-goal career record with his 325th goal on November 8, 1952, Howe topped the Rocket's record of 544 goals with his goal number 545, November 10, 1963. Both Howe's record-tying 544th and record-breaking 545th came against Richard's former team, the Canadiens. Number 545 was a shorthanded goal against Charlie Hodge in a 3–0 Detroit victory. The shutout was the 94th of goalie Terry Sawchuk's career, a milestone that equalled the all-time mark established by George Hainsworth in 1937. Ironically, Hainsworth played most of his career with Montreal.

5.41 B. One game

The crowd chanted "Mar-i-o, Mar-i-o, Mar-i-o" and threw hundreds of hats onto the ice as Lemieux acknowledged the standing ovation with a wave of his stick. Lemieux, before a hometown Pittsburgh crowd, had scored his 600th career goal. The historic marker, an empty-netter, came in the last minute of play against Vancouver in the Penguins' 6–4 win on February 4, 1997. It was Mario's 719th game, only one more match than it took Gretzky to score number 600, which happened in the Great One's 718th contest, on November 23, 1988.

5.42 C. Maurice Richard

The purest of goal scorers, Richard finished his career with 544 goals and 421 assists for 965 points. This is a remarkable ratio: 123 more goals than his assist total. As of 2004–05, no other player among the NHL's top 100 all-time point leaders has posted 100 more goals than assists with the exception of Peter Bondra, who has 115 more goals in a 477–362–839 career. In the playoffs, Richard was even more of a goal-scoring specialist, recording nearly twice as many goals as assists: 82 to 44. Bondra's ratio in postseason play wasn't as dramatic: 30 goals and 26 assists.

5.43 B. Bobby Hull

One of the NHL's most famous No. 9s, Bobby Hull was not only among the league's speediest skaters, he also possessed the hardest shot in the game. Unlike Wayne Gretzky, who was relatively small and slight, Hull had a remarkable physique. His powerful legs and muscular torso were built to play hockey. His slap shot, unlike Gretzky's, was unrivalled (it was once clocked at a terrifying 118.3 miles per hour). And with his high-velocity slapper and first-rate stickhandling and checking skills, the Golden Jet was unstoppable, winning scoring crowns, MVP awards and the Lady Byng Trophy as most gentlemanly player—the same accolades that No. 99 attained. But Hull was a pure scorer and Gretzky, first and foremost, a playmaker who could also score. In the days before the Great One, few players matched Hull's superstar status. He leads all NHLers with seven goal-scoring titles.

The NHL's Top Goal-Scoring Champs*

PLAYER	TEAM	TITLES
Bobby Hull	Chicago	7
Phil Esposito	Boston	6
Wayne Gretzky	Edmonton	5
Maurice Richard	Montreal	5
Charlie Conacher	Toronto	5
Gordie Howe	Detroit	5

**Current to 2004–05*

GAME 5

What's in a Name?

TO MAKE IT IN THE NHL, they say you've got to have hockey in your blood. But some NHLers can also boast having the league's initials in their family names. Discover the hockey players, teams and terms with N-H-L roots by filling in the blanks in the left column using the clues given on the right.

Solutions are on page 562

1.	__N_ H___L__	Atlanta's 2002 Calder Trophy winner as top NHL rookie
2.	N__H___L_	City of 1998 expansion club
3.	__N _H_ ___L__	Hockey term: crash the net
4.	__N_H __L___	Famous old-time Toronto coach
5.	__N H____L_	The Flyers' 1987 playoff MVP goalie
6.	N___L__ _H________	2004 Stanley Cup-winning netminder
7.	__N_H-_L______ _____	Hockey term: team vs. team fight
8.	___N_____H_L__	The Kings' 70-goal sniper
9.	__N_H L___	Montreal's 1950s scoring trio
10.	___N___H__L___	Hall of Famer, "The Big M"
11.	_____N-____H___L	Hockey term: winner in overtime
12.	___N_ H__L__	NYR's 1994 Cup backup goalie
13.	______N _H____L_	Chicago goalie in 2003–04
14.	__N__ _H_ _L__	Hockey term: D-man in high-scoring position

6

Breaks and Scrapes

HOCKEY PLAYERS ARE RENOWNED for their ability to tolerate pain. In fact, their pain thresholds are higher than those of most athletes. But former Montreal Canadiens physician Doug Kinnear, who has witnessed every hockey player ailment and injury over his 30-plus-year career, will never forget his first patient: Claude Provost. The defensive forward needed stitch work to close a deep two-inch laceration on his forehead. Kinnear asked the nurse for a local anaesthetic before stitching the gash, but the team's physiotherapist, Bill Head, shook off the request, implying that cuts don't require freezing. So Kinnear breathed deeply, and, with needle and suture, sewed up the gaping wound. And Provost? He was back on the ice in time for his next shift—to Kinnear's amazement. In this chapter, we get bloodied but settle a few scores by staying in the game.

Answers are on page 140

6.1 Which old-time hockey roughneck was nicknamed "Scarface"?

A. Detroit's Ted Lindsay
B. Boston's Eddie Shore
C. Toronto's Red Horner
D. Detroit's Jimmy Orlando

6.2 Which NHL great sawed his own leg cast off so he could play in the Stanley Cup playoffs?

A. Bernie Geoffrion
B. Gordie Howe
C. Ted Lindsay
D. Stan Mikita

6.3 How many knee operations did Bobby Orr have during his career?

A. Seven operations
B. Nine operations
C. 11 operations
D. 13 operations

6.4 What incident suddenly ended the stellar NHL career of goalie Bernie Parent in 1979?

A. An eye injury
B. A botched knee operation
C. A broken foot after a fall on street ice
D. A shoulder separation during a fight with another goalie

6.5 Which NHLer occasionally celebrates scoring a goal by smashing himself into the rink glass?

A. Jordin Tootoo of the Nashville Predators
B. Georges Laraque of the Edmonton Oilers
C. Jonathan Cheechoo of the San Jose Sharks
D. Tie Domi of the Toronto Maple Leafs

6.6 How many times did defenseman Rod Langway break his nose during his career?

A. Never
B. Twice
C. Five times
D. 10 times

6.7 What is slew-footing?

A. A term used in contract negotiations
B. An on-ice act of violence
C. A method of moulding plastic skate boots
D. A practical joke played on rookies

6.8 How many times has gunner Al MacInnis hit an opposing shot-blocker in the face with his famed slap shot?

A. Never
B. Only once
C. Three times
D. Six times

6.9 How many stitches were sewn into Jacques Plante's face before the veteran donned his famous goalie mask?

A. 100 stitches
B. 200 stitches
C. 300 stitches
D. 400 stitches

6.10 Which Original Six netminder is considered to be the most scarred goalie?

A. Jacques Plante
B. Johnny Bower
C. Glenn Hall
D. Terry Sawchuk

6.11 How many games did Mario Lemieux miss after being diagnosed with cancer in 1992–93?

A. 24 games
B. 44 games
C. 64 games
D. The entire 84-game season

6.12 Which team's mascot had to be rescued after he fell into a pit of fire during pre-game ceremonies at the club's 1995–96 home opener?

A. The New Jersey Devils'
B. The Calgary Flames'
C. The Florida Panthers'
D. The Mighty Ducks of Anaheim's

6.13 Which Dallas Stars player hit his own coach, Ken Hitchcock, in the head with a puck during game action in February 1999?

A. Guy Carbonneau
B. Mike Modano
C. Mike Keane
D. Joe Nieuwendyk

6.14 What ailment ended Glenn Hall's consecutive-games record?

A. A back strain
B. A pulled groin
C. Ligament damage to his knee
D. Facial lacerations

6.15 How much money would Bryan Berard have received in disability insurance had he quit hockey after suffering an eye injury on March 11, 2000?

A. U.S.$4 million
B. U.S.$6 million
C. U.S.$8 million
D. U.S.$10 million

6.16 Who cross-checked Paul Kariya in the head during an NHL game, forcing him to miss the 1998 Olympics because of a concussion?

A. Chicago's Gary Suter
B. Washington's Dale Hunter
C. New York's Mike Keane
D. Philadelphia's Joel Otto

6.17 What helped cure Paul Kariya of his post-concussion symptoms in 1998?

A. Psychoanalysis
B. Acupuncture
C. Hypnosis
D. A hyperbaric chamber

6.18 Toronto Maple Leafs tough guy Tie Domi was hit with a U.S.$1,000 fine for doing what to a fan at a game in March 2001?

A. Swearing at him
B. Squirting water at him
C. Throwing a snowball at him
D. Hitting him with his stick

6.19 Which goalie once painted stitches on his mask to represent the injuries he might have received?

A. Gerry Cheevers
B. Don Edwards
C. Rogatien Vachon
D. Bob Sauve

6.20 What kind of injury forced Mark Messier to end his games-played streak as a Vancouver Canuck?

A. A charley horse
B. A concussion
C. A separated shoulder
D. A broken finger

6.21 What unusual event almost ended Arturs Irbe's career after his spectacular 1993–94 season with San Jose?

A. He sustained injuries mountain climbing
B. He was bitten by his dog
C. He suffered a concussion in a roller hockey match
D. He was diagnosed with a rare disease

6.22 Which defenseman sidelined Eric Lindros with his sixth concussion during the 2000 playoffs?

A. Chris Pronger
B. Scott Stevens
C. Ken Daneyko
D. Darius Kasparaitus

6.23 Eric Lindros suffered six concussions as a Philadelphia Flyer over how many years?

A. Between two and three years
B. Between three and four years
C. Between four and five years
D. Between five and six years

6.24 A fight with which old-time superstar earned Detroit Hall of Famer Sid Abel the nickname "Bootnose"?

A. Maurice Richard
B. Eddie Shore
C. Gordie Howe
D. Babe Pratt

6.25 In 1951–52, NHL goalies experienced one of their most injury-free seasons. How many starting goalies in the six-team NHL played the entire 70-game schedule?

A. Three goalies
B. Four goalies
C. Five goalies
D. Six goalies

6.26 Which player lost the most teeth in 2001–02?

A. Mike Ricci of the San Jose Sharks
B. Doug Weight of the St. Louis Blues
C. Ilya Kovalchuk of the Atlanta Thrashers
D. Martin Straka of the Pittsburgh Penguins

6.27 Former NHL goalie Eddie Johnston was the last goalie to play every minute of an NHL season. How many broken noses did he suffer in that perfect season, 1963–64?

A. None
B. One
C. Two
D. Four

6.28 According to Florida Panthers goalie Roberto Luongo, where does a netminder suffer the worst pain?

A. In the collarbone
B. In the groin
C. In the neck
D. In the catching hand

6.29 What is the most number of stitches that has been required to sew up a player's face after an on-ice injury?

A. Fewer than 100 stitches
B. Between 100 and 150 stitches
C. Between 150 and 200 stitches
D. More than 200 stitches

6.30 Which goaltender nearly died on the ice when his jugular vein was slashed by a skate blade?

A. Clint Malarchuk
B. Murray Bannerman
C. Gilles Meloche
D. Mike Palmateer

6.31 Which Calgary player scaled the glass partition behind the Flames bench in Edmonton on November 23, 1997, to get at a heckling fan?

A. Sasha Lakovic
B. Todd Simpson
C. Ron Stern
D. Cal Hulse

6.32 A photo of which goalie's scarred face was once featured in *Life* magazine to illustrate the perils of tending net in the maskless NHL?

A. Gump Worsley
B. Johnny Bower
C. Terry Sawchuk
D. Jacques Plante

6.33 Which NHL player made a miraculous return to action in 1996–97, only eight months after undergoing brain surgery?

A. Donald Audette
B. Kris Draper
C. Mike Ridley
D. Tony Granato

6.34 A vocal cord injury prevented which ex-NHL defenseman from hollering to his teammates on the ice?

A. Chris Pronger
B. Mark Tinordi
C. Dave Manson
D. Robert Svehla

6.35 Which former NHL enforcer fought an exhibition bout with heavyweight champion Muhammad Ali?

A. Dave Schultz
B. Tiger Williams
C. John Ferguson
D. Dave Semenko

6.36 How many stitches was the great Eddie Shore estimated to have acquired during his NHL career?

A. 600 stitches
B. 700 stitches
C. 800 stitches
D. 900 stitches

6.37 Hall of Famer Andy Bathgate delivered the backhand shot that led to Jacques Plante donning his mask, but which legend was responsible for forcing Clint Benedict to wear the NHL's first face protector in 1930?

A. Howie Morenz of the Montreal Canadiens
B. Charlie Conacher of the Toronto Maple Leafs

C. Dit Clapper of the Boston Bruins
D. Bill Cook of the New York Rangers

6.38 On December 1, 1996, the Canucks' Trevor Linden sprained his knee, ending his league-leading streak of 482 consecutive games. How many games was Linden short of Doug Jarvis's NHL ironman record?

A. Exactly one-quarter of Jarvis's total
B. Exactly half of Jarvis's total
C. Exactly three-quarters of Jarvis's total
D. Only one game short of Jarvis's total

6.39 Which player's career-ending injury brought about the NHL's first All-Star game?

A. Howie Morenz of the Montreal Canadiens
B. Bill Cook of the New York Rangers
C. Babe Siebert of the Montreal Maroons
D. Ace Bailey of the Toronto Maple Leafs

6.40 Which NHL owner accused his club's doctor of mistreating one of the team's star players and of conspiring to aid the team's opponents during the 1997 playoffs?

A. Philadelphia's Ed Snider
B. Chicago's Bill Wirtz
C. Detroit's Mike Ilitch
D. New Jersey's John McMullen

6.41 Which NHL tough guy had his nose broken and face smashed after foolishly challenging Gordie Howe to a heavyweight bout in 1958–59?

A. Boston's Fern Flaman
B. Toronto's Carl Brewer
C. The New York Rangers' Lou Fontinato
D. Chicago's Eric Nesterenko

6.42 How long was Brad May's suspension after slashing Steve Heinze in the face during 2000–01?

A. Five games
B. 10 games
C. 15 games
D. 20 games

6.43 As of 2002–03, what is the greatest number of concussions in one season?

A. 54 concussions
B. 74 concussions
C. 94 concussions
D. 114 concussions

Answers

6.1 A. Detroit's Ted Lindsay

Despite his small size (five foot eight and 160 pounds), Lindsay was a fearless player who battled all comers with his stick and his fists. Blood often ran freely when Terrible Ted was on the ice, including his own. Lindsay stopped counting his stitches after they reached 200, but there was no ignoring the toll on his facial features. Referee Red Storey described Lindsay as having "one of those faces that holds about three days of rain." Opposition players were less poetic. They called him Scarface.

6.2 A. Bernie Geoffrion

Don't try this at home. It's not something players would do today, but in Geoffrion's time there was a sixth straight Stanley Cup on the line. At least, that was Doug Harvey and Bernie Geoffrion's logic when they hacked into Geoffrion's leg cast on a train ride to Chicago with their Canadiens—winners of five straight Cups—facing elimination, down 3–2 in the 1961 semifinals against the Blackhawks. Geoffrion, who had torn the ligaments in his left knee, picks up the story in his bio *Boom-Boom:* "Doug got a knife from the train kitchen and the two of us sneaked into the ladies' washroom. With my leg up on a chair, I watched my captain saw away at the heavy plaster of Paris cast. He cut it lengthwise and, the way the train was bouncing around, it was a miracle I wasn't cut. It seemed to take hours to complete the job. The next morning... Doug was feeling like a surgeon, 'I didn't do it in record time but you have to take into consideration the rolling train,' he said." Coach Toe Blake was furious, but the Boomer's knee was frozen for the big game. He got to play sparingly on the power play, but with little reward. Montreal couldn't turn it around to become a six-time champion as Chicago went on to claim the Cup.

6.3 D. 13 operations

Between 1967 and 1980, Orr's left knee went under the knife 13 times to repair cartilage and ligament damage. Had Orr played in today's era of arthroscopic surgery, when such procedures are less intrusive, he might have had more career time than 915 games. The wear and tear on Orr's knees from the surgery alone, which meant removing the knee cap to do repair work each time, likely took several seasons off his Hall of Fame career.

6.4 A. An eye injury

On February 17, 1979, Philadelphia's Bernie Parent suffered a fluke eye injury when a stick blade pierced the unprotected eye space of his goalie mask in a game against the New York Rangers at the Spectrum. The injury—two small tears in the conjunctiva of his right eye—ended Parent's stellar career, which included two Vezina Trophies as top goalie, two Conn Smythes as playoff MVP and two Stanley Cups, all during the Flyers' heyday of the mid-1970s.

6.5 B. Georges Laraque of the Edmonton Oilers

It's called the Laraque Leap, and for anyone who hasn't witnessed this signature scoring celebration, watch out, especially if you're sitting in Section 132 or 134 in Rows 1, 2 or 3 at Edmonton's Rexall Place. Laraque doesn't just high-five, arm-pump or team hug, his form of celebration is pure smash-mouth hockey. After a big goal at home, almost always in the south-end net, the six-foot-three, 245-pound Laraque freight-trains it into the glass, jumping up with arms wide apart, his face in a grimace. His chest slams the glass with a thunderous wallop and his knees pound the dasher between the glass and the boards. "I hit it as hard as I can. It hurts like crazy," said Laraque in the *Edmonton Journal.* Why does he do it? "Because it [scoring goals] doesn't happen so often, I go crazy. I have so much adrenalin that I have to release it. This is my way to release it."

6.6 D. 10 times

In 15 seasons of stick whacks, sharp elbows and face-plants into the boards, Langway's beak has suffered its share of breaks. The first one, the All-Star blueliner proudly admits, was courtesy of Mr. Elbows himself, Gordie Howe.

6.7 B. An on-ice act of violence

Slew-footing entered the public's lexicon of hockey terms in the late 1990s, after a rash of on-ice incidents and subsequent suspensions gained media attention. In one particularly frightening episode, Ruslan Salei of Anaheim was given a five-game suspension for riding Phoenix's Daniel Briere into the boards while taking his feet out from underneath him. Briere went into convulsions and suffered a concussion. Slew-footing—kicking an opponent's skates out and forward while pushing his body backwards with an elbow or stick—renders an adversary defenseless in a backward freefall onto the ice. Even hockey's heavyweights consider it a dirty, loathsome play.

6.8 B. Only once

At last count, Al MacInnis had hit only one shot-blocker in the noggin. This, despite almost 20 years of firing his 100-mph blasts at opposing NHL netminders. "I've only hit one guy in the face and, luckily for everybody, it was a knuckleball where I hit my own guy, Pavol Demitra. The puck stood up on me," MacInnis said in an *Edmonton Journal* story in January 2001. But MacInnis has still "broken a lot of bones over the years"—though never intentionally. In fact, MacInnis will even pull up or step around if the shot-blocker is vulnerable, particularly with the "craziest shot-blocker" he's faced, Kelly Buchberger. "He'll go down in front of anything. I'd see him sliding... and I'd look up and think, 'What are you doing?'" Because MacInnis keeps his shots low, toes and feet are the most likely targets. In one game he hit Craig MacTavish three times in the same spot on the same foot within 30 seconds on the same penalty kill. "When Dallas Drake got here (St. Louis in 2000–01), he told me I'd broken his toe and Mike Sullivan's in the same game when we were playing Phoenix," MacInnis said.

6.9 B. 200 stitches

When Plante introduced his mask in 1959, pucks, sticks, elbows and skates had already carved up his face: his nose had been broken four times, his jaw and both cheekbones had been fractured and he had sustained a hairline skull fracture. Even so, critics, including members of his own brotherhood, called him puck-shy. At the time, facial injuries were considered normal, a trademark in an occupation full of hazards. But Plante, being the quintessential eccentric goalie, defied everyone. As Habs netminder Gerry McNeil once said: "If I'd worn one, they would have sent me home." The mask had arrived, thanks to Plante.

6.10 D. Terry Sawchuk

Because most goalies of the six-team era only donned masks in the 1960s (and some waited until the early 1970s), they often averaged upwards of 200 stitches on their faces by the time they retired. Terry Sawchuk may be the exception. Before he wore his first mask in 1962, Sawchuk had already had 400 stitches to sew up his face, including three in his right eyeball.

6.11 A. 24 games

It's one of the NHL's all-time great sports stories. Diagnosed with Hodgkin's disease after doctors removed an enlarged lymph node from his neck, Lemieux underwent seven weeks of radiation treatment—the last blast coming just 12 hours before his first game back on March 2, 1993. Lemieux played 21 minutes that night, netting a goal and an assist. And the magnitude of his comeback was epic. He missed only 24 games to cancer, and on his return roared past Pat LaFontaine to win the NHL scoring race with 69 goals and 160 points in just 60 games. His team, which had just suffered through an 11–11–2 record during his absence, eventually finished the 1992–93 season 35 games above .500 (56–21–7). Half the season's losses occurred in those 24 games Super Mario missed. After his comeback, he led the Penguins to 17 straight wins, an NHL record. Lemieux also claimed his second Hart Trophy as MVP and his first Masterton Trophy for perseverance and dedication.

6.12 D. The Mighty Ducks of Anaheim's

Wild Wing, Anaheim's web-footed mascot, was nearly barbecued prior to the team's 1995–96 home opener when he tried to bounce off a mini-trampoline to sail through fire, only to stumble and fall into a gas-powered wall of flames. The impromptu roasting was just one of the misfortunes that befell the Ducks' bumbling mascot in 1995–96. On another occasion, Wild Wing was left dangling helplessly midair when the rigging that lowers him to the ice during the pre-game show jammed.

6.13 C. Mike Keane

On February 15, 1999, Dallas coach Ken Hitchcock received 16 stitches after being struck in the head by a clearing shot from Mike Keane. At the time, Hitchcock was admonishing a player for making a blunder. Asked about Keane, Hitchcock replied, "We've asked him to make sure and check into condos in Tampa and see how he likes it there." Mike Modano noted, "Now he knows what it feels like to be a hockey player."

6.14 A. A back strain

Before the two-goalie system, clubs in the six-team NHL often counted on their goalies to play entire seasons without missing a game. Some netminders managed to complete the gruelling 70-game schedule, but no one matched the consistency of Hall—he played continuously for seven seasons from 1955–56 to 1961–62, a total of 502 straight games. Hall's astonishing ironman streak earned him rookie-of-the-year honours in 1956, the Stanley Cup in 1961 and six All-Star berths. But his stretch ended on November 7, 1962. He had strained his back at practice while fastening a toe strap. And the next night, midway through the first period, the pain was so severe that Hall removed himself from play.

6.15 B. U.S.$6 million

It was a terrific golden parachute, but Bryan Berard preferred his career over the settlement money. After doctors reached the conclusion that Berard couldn't make the 20/400 minimum vision requirement stipulated by the NHL, the Toronto defenseman spent the next 18 months in rehab to prove he could make a comeback. Although not nearly the player he was before being accidentally struck in the right eye by Ottawa Senator Marian Hossa's stick, Berard signed with the New York Rangers in October 2001 and passed up the U.S.$6-million disability payment.

6.16 A. Chicago's Gary Suter

Among hockey's elite, Kariya lost his chance to represent Canada at the 1998 Olympics after Suter cross-checked him in the jaw during an Anaheim–Chicago game on February 1, 1998. The dangerous hit, probably a reflex action, came late after Kariya had scored his second goal. "It was a wild scramble and I turned around and I saw a Duck and cross-checked him," Suter said. "He must have crouched down because I didn't hit him that high." Suter, who later received a four-game suspension, also knocked Wayne Gretzky out of the 1991 Canada Cup with a vicious hit from behind. "I was just trying to clear the net. Unfortunately, every time I hit somebody it turns out to be a superstar," said Suter.

6.17 B. Acupuncture

After being sidelined with a concussion for the last three months of the 1997–98 season and missing the Nagano Olympics, Kariya took Eric Lindros's advice and turned to acupuncture to help clear the fog. "I had needles all over me. I don't enjoy needles but these are very fine. And at that point I was for whatever helped." For the mightiest Duck, normal activities such as walking, or talking on the phone for any length of time, were impossible. But after a month of treatments two or three times a week, the fuzziness and other symptoms disappeared. On the ice, Kariya then followed Pat LaFontaine's recovery plan for post-concussion syndrome and began wearing a customized helmet, chin strap and mouth guard to absorb the shock of any blows to his head.

6.18 B. Squirting water at him

When fans began tossing garbage at Tie Domi after he entered the penalty box at Philadelphia's First Union Center on March 29, 2001, he responded by grabbing a water bottle and spraying them. This prompted Chris Falcone, a portly 36-year-old Flyers fan, to leap out of his seat and charge the penalty box.

When Falcone hit the Plexiglass it gave way, sending him tumbling into the box, where a mêlée ensued. After being fined U.S.$1,000 by the NHL for his actions, Domi confessed that he "shouldn't have lowered himself to squirt water, [but] that's our territory. Fans pay to watch the game, not get involved in the game. That's when it can get ugly."

6.19 A. Gerry Cheevers

Cheevers is considered the first NHL goalie to decorate his face mask. Although less artful than today's customized paint jobs, Cheevers's "fright-night" mask conveyed a simple but dramatic image of the battle-scarred warrior. The famous black stitch marks covering his mask date back to 1967–68, when Cheevers was hit by a Fred Stanfield shot at practice. As a joke the scratch on the mask was painted with stitches. By 1971, Cheevers had etched hundreds of stitches on three different masks. His zipper-like motif inspired a trend of self-expression as goalies began to decorate their masks, first with team logos and later with more stylized designs. As the mask evolved in construction to include greater protection to the sides and top of the head, an industry of mask makers and artists developed, producing both safer and more ornate mask designs for goal-tenders.

6.20 B. A concussion

The crash into the goal net was spectacular. Messier, on his second shift of a game against Calgary, December 22, 1998, smashed into the Flames' net in full flight, snapping his head back on one of the posts before slamming down on the ice. The impact sent a chill through the crowd. Messier, who scored on the play, was taken to the dressing room and didn't return. The next night he missed his first game since joining Vancouver—a streak of 113 consecutive contests.

6.21 B. He was bitten by his dog

The Sharks' impressive 58-point turnaround in 1993–94 and seven-game, first-round playoff victory over the heavily favoured Red Wings amounted to what was supposed to be Arturs Irbe's coming-out year as a top-flight NHL goalie. He was brilliant in goal and a bonafide sports celebrity in San Jose and the Bay area. But that summer, Irbe suffered severe damage to both hands after being mauled by his dog in his hometown of Riga, Latvia. While working out, Irbe knocked the sleeping hound by accident. The dog awoke and went wild, biting his startled owner's hands. After it was over, Irbe had cut tendons and nerve damage. "I was really worried. It was serious damage. I thought I might not play again," he later said. The dog was put down.

6.22 B. Scott Stevens

As of 2000–01, Eric Lindros had suffered six concussions—his sixth after a thundering hit from New Jersey's Scott Stevens during the 2000 playoffs. Lindros, with his head down, was cutting across the Devils' offensive blue line when Stevens steamed across the rink and put the full force of his shoulder into the Flyer superstar. The hit was clean, but Stevens remained unnerved by it: "I'm just trying to put the [hit] behind me. I don't want to talk about it," he said shortly afterwards. The play riveted the hockey world, setting the Flyers on their heels during the series and putting Lindros's future in doubt. When asked about Stevens a few days later, Lindros said: "Leave the guy alone. He was doing his job." Would Stevens do the same thing again given the circumstances? Stevens told the *New York Post:* "It depends on what time of year it would be. I mean, in the playoffs everything is at stake. So no matter what my personal feelings are, my obligation to myself and my teammates is to play to win."

6.23 A. Between two and three years

Eric Lindros suffered six concussions between March 7, 1998, and May 26, 2000, a 27-month period that saw his status fall as arguably hockey's best player to its most fragile; and, ultimately, its most unbankable.

6.24 A. Maurice Richard

Unlike today's snipers who get on-ice protection from designated team bad boys, old-time superstars used their hands for more than just goal scoring; on any given night they had to fight. Gordie Howe and Maurice Richard, hockey's two most famous No. 9s, were no exception. They battled for respect every night—and for every square inch of ice. Case in point: After a one-punch scrap that left Richard on the ice, Sid Abel skated by the Rocket and suggested that he shouldn't tangle with the Red Wings. Richard leaped to his feet and broke Abel's nose in three places. The mutilation earned Abel the uncomplimentary nickname "Bootnose." But Richard wasn't finished. Before the game was over, he extracted further revenge by cross-checking Ted Lindsay, high-sticking Glen Skov and running Red Kelly. And when Marcel Pronovost began jawing at him, the Rocket broke his jaw and knocked out six of his teeth.

6.25 C. Five goalies

New York's Chuck Rayner was the only goalie among all six starters in 1951–52 to suffer an injury severe enough to sideline him for an extended period; he played in 53 games before being replaced by Emile Francis. The five other regulars, Terry Sawchuk, Al Rollins, Gerry McNeil, Sugar Jim Henry and Harry Lumley, all completed their teams' 70-game schedules.

6.26 C. Ilya Kovalchuk of the Atlanta Thrashers

The 18-year-old Russian rookie lost nine of his teeth, but it wasn't the result of getting a stick in the face. Kovalchuk had four wisdom and five rotten teeth extracted. In Russia, the water is not treated with fluoride, and Kovalchuk clearly had not heeded the advice to brush three times a day, much to the chagrin of his mother, a dental hygienist. But Kovalchuk was unconcerned by the loss of his pearlies. "I have no problem," he said, through the aid of an interpreter. "The only difference is I know they are not there."

6.27 D. Four

Eddie Johnston played all 70 games in 1963–64, the last goalie with a perfect attendance record for every minute of every game in a season. But his pain threshold was tested time and again. Johnston suffered four broken noses—maybe an NHL record. His eyes would be so swollen from the bruising that, on two occasions, doctors applied leeches to suck the blood so he could see well enough to play. And play he did, for all 4,200 agonizing minutes.

6.28 B. In the groin

When asked by the *Miami Herald* to rank the worst three pains a goalie feels, Roberto Luongo said the nastiest hurt comes from a hit to the mid-body. "First is the worst, and you know where I'm talking about without me even having to tell you. Let's call it the jock-strap area. Second is when you get hit in the neck with a shot. And third is getting hit in the collar-bone. That feels like someone takes a baseball bat and swings it right at you as hard as they can. The pain can stay with you for weeks," said Luongo.

6.29 D. More than 200 stitches

There is no definitive proof, but the NHL record for most stitches to close a facial wound in an on-ice incident probably belongs to Toronto's Borje Salming, who required more than 200 stitches in his face after being accidentally cut by the skate of Detroit winger Gerard Gallant on November 26, 1986.

Salming's gash extended from his mouth, snaked up his right cheek to the inside of his right eye and up over his brow. The Leaf defenseman was lost to Toronto for 24 games in 1986–87.

6.30 A. Clint Malarchuk

It was one of the most horrific injuries in NHL history. On March 22, 1989, Buffalo Sabres goalie Clint Malarchuk was involved in a collision with St. Louis Blues rookie Steve Tuttle and Buffalo's Uwe Krupp. Tuttle's skate blade sliced a six-inch gash in Malarchuk's throat, and blood gushed from the wound. Aware he was in serious trouble, the Sabres goalie clutched his throat and skated frantically to the bench. "I thought I was dying," Malarchuk said. "I knew it was my jugular vein and I didn't have long to live." The team's trainer and doctor controlled the bleeding with pressure and gauze, then rushed the stricken goalie to the hospital. Incredibly, Malarchuk was back in the Sabres' net 11 days later, with 300 stitches.

6.31 A. Sasha Lakovic

In a spectacle reminiscent of the famous glass-climbing incident involving three Boston players at Madison Square Garden in the 1970s, Lakovic scaled the glass partition behind Calgary's bench at Edmonton's Northlands Coliseum in an attempt to reach a heckler who had dumped rum and coke and a bag of popcorn over the head of Flames assistant coach Guy Lapointe. Lakovic failed, but Lapointe, from a better position atop the glass, appeared to land a hard right. Lakovic received a $1,000 fine and two-game suspension. The drunken heckler, Raymond Howarth, 27, of Whitecourt, Alberta, pleaded guilty to mischief and was handed a 30-day jail sentence and fined $1,000. Howarth's lawyer called his client's action "an act of childish stupidity."

6.32 C. Terry Sawchuk

On March 4, 1966, *Life* magazine devoted a few pages to the exploits of NHL goaltenders. The most startling aspect of the layout was a nightmarish photo of Sawchuk's face. A makeup artist had retouched and highlighted his various facial scars to make them appear fresh. The grotesque patchwork of stapled tissue represented more than 200 stitches—all accumulated before Sawchuk donned a mask in 1962. The Winnipeg-born goalie battled injuries throughout his 21-year career. His ailments included a broken arm, severed wrist tendons, a fractured instep and several ruptured discs. Surgeons were also constantly removing bone chips from his battered left elbow. As a grisly reminder of his pain, Sawchuk used to keep the fragments in a jar that he displayed on his mantel.

6.33 D. Tony Granato

After sliding headfirst into the boards during a game against the Hartford Whalers on January 25, 1995, the Los Angeles Kings winger began experiencing severe headaches and loss of memory. Medical tests revealed that Granato needed brain surgery. And on February 14, 1995, he underwent a four-hour operation to remove an abnormal swelling on the left side of his brain. The surgery was successful. A few months later, Granato's doctors told him he could resume his career. He signed as a free agent with the San Jose Sharks in August and returned to action at the start of the 1996–97 season. In his second game, Granato scored a hat trick against his former team, the Kings.

6.34 C. Dave Manson

The saying "Speak softly and carry a big stick" accurately described Dave Manson. The rugged rearguard was one of the NHL's more intimidating players, but to hear Manson speak you had to stand close to him—his voice had been damaged after he was punched in the throat by Sergio Momesso during a 1991 fight. The blow crushed Manson's vocal cords, leaving him with a gravelly rasp. A 1994 operation failed to correct the problem, and Manson continued to play without being able to verbally communicate with his teammates on the ice.

6.35 D. Dave Semenko

Semenko climbed into the ring with Ali to fight a three-round exhibition in Edmonton in the 1980s. Semenko trained seriously for the bout. Too seriously, in fact. As he recalls in his book, *Looking Out for Number One,* during one training session a member of Ali's entourage came over to Semenko and said, "Listen, make sure you don't do something stupid like trying to take the champ's head off." Semenko got the message. Neither he nor Ali landed any serious blows during the bout.

6.36 D. 900 stitches

No one ever played hockey with more reckless abandon than Eddie Shore. During his 14-year NHL career, the hardrock Boston D-man antagonized fans, fought opponents, harassed officials and ignited countless controversies. A perpetual target of rival players, who would often gang up in twos and threes to nail him, Shore paid a heavy toll in injuries. His face and body were embroidered with more than 900 stitches and he suffered fractures to his hip, back and collarbone. His nose was broken 14 times, his jaw smashed five times and he had almost every tooth in his mouth knocked out. But nothing ever stopped Shore for long. Still brawling and banging at age 37, he led Boston to the Stanley Cup in 1939.

6.37 A. Howie Morenz of the Montreal Canadiens

The distinction of hockey's first mask falls to Clint Benedict, who wore his face protector after he was felled by a rising 25-foot blast from Howie Morenz on January 7, 1930. The shot smashed Benedict's nose and cheekbone. "I saw it at the last split second and lunged," Benedict said. "Wham, I was out like a light and woke up in the hospital." A reporter recalled that the puck "crushed the side of Benny's face like an eggshell." The injury later forced the Montreal Maroons netminder to use a crude leather mask, modified either from a football face mask or a boxer's sparring mask. But the contraption didn't work. "The nosepiece protruded too far and obscured my vision on low shots," Benedict said. After a 2–1 loss to Chicago, he threw out the mask and tried a wire-cage-type protector, "but the wires distracted me. That's when I gave up." Benedict continued to play maskless, but later that season another Morenz shot struck him in the throat, ending his career. He held no grudges against Morenz. "But you know, had we been able to perfect the mask I could have been a 20-year man." Benedict played 17 seasons and was inducted into the Hockey Hall of Fame in 1965.

6.38 B. Exactly half of Jarvis's total

An innocent-looking collision with John LeClair of the Flyers in December 1996 damaged the medial collateral ligament in Linden's left knee and ended his NHL-leading ironman streak. The Canucks captain had played 482 straight games, exactly half of Doug Jarvis's record total of 964. Amazingly, Jarvis didn't miss a game after making his NHL debut on October 8, 1975, until his retirement on October 10, 1987.

6.39 D. Ace Bailey of the Toronto Maple Leafs

The NHL's first All-Star game was a benefit match for Toronto's Ace Bailey, who had been seriously injured in a Bruins–Maple Leafs fight in 1934 when Boston's Eddie Shore, retaliating for a trip by King Clancy, mistook Bailey for Clancy and charged him from behind. Bailey struck the ice and fractured his skull, causing his body to twist and twitch in a seizure-like state. The Leafs' Red Horner then decked Shore, knocking him cold on the ice. Both teams stormed over the boards. The mêlée ended with Horner and Conacher holding off the Bruins with sticks raised bayonet-fashion. Near death for 10 days, Bailey recovered and was well enough to attend his benefit All-Star game and shake hands with Shore at centre ice. For the rest of the season, the Bruins wore helmets. Bailey never played another game.

6.40 B. Chicago's Bill Wirtz

As the Colorado Avalanche and Chicago Blackhawks duelled on the ice during the 1997 playoffs, a bizarre medical controversy erupted behind the scenes. The Hawks' team physician, Louis Kolb, resigned during Game 3 after he was berated by Wirtz, who was furious that Kolb had allowed Avalanche team physician Andrew Parker to perform surgery on the ankle of Hawks centre Alexei Zhamnov—without consulting management. Kolb said he asked Parker to perform the operation in Denver because he did not have the proper licence to do surgery in Colorado, but Wirtz accused Kolb of conspiring with the enemy. The Chicago owner also accused Kolb of misdiagnosing a Brent Sutter knee injury as a sprain, clearing the veteran centre to play with what was actually a torn ligament.

6.41 C. The New York Rangers' Lou Fontinato

During the 1950s, Leapin' Lou enjoyed a reputation as the NHL's resident bad boy and premier pugilist. In 1955–56, the Ranger defenseman compiled 202 penalty minutes in 70 games to break Red Horner's league record of 167 PIM (set in 1935–36's 48-game schedule). However, in February 1959, Fontinato made the mistake of challenging Gordie Howe. The big Red Wing shook off Fontinato's initial flurry of punches, grabbed the neck of his tormentor's jersey and began repeatedly driving his right hand into Fontinato's face. By the time Howe was done, Leapin' Lou's nose and cheekbone were mashed to a bloody pulp; plastic surgeons had to rearrange his face. The thumping ruined Fontinato. Some say it did the same to the Rangers, who slumped badly in the last half of the season and eventually missed the playoffs by one point.

6.42 D. 20 games

After being horribly slashed in the face by Brad May in November 2000, Columbus' Steve Heinze tersely instructed the Blue Jackets' trainers: "Stitch me up, boys, we're on a power play." Heinze was back out on the ensuing man-advantage and scored the power-play goal. May received a 20-game suspension.

6.43 C. 94 concussions

Measuring the severity of a concussion is as difficult as pinpointing the reasons for the injury's dramatic increase among NHL players. Since the reporting of head injuries began in the 1990s, the usual suspects—bigger players, modern equipment and harder glass—have been targeted, but studies suggest that a newfound respect for concussions has meant an increased awareness by players and doctors about their seriousness. This has meant an increase in concussions reported. In 2002–03, the NHL's injury analysis panel reported an all-time-record 94 concussions, a figure likely surpassed in 2003–04. (As of this writing, no newer numbers were available.) A concussion occurs when the brain smacks against the skull after a collision. And several players' careers have been cut short, including Pat LaFontaine's and Brett Lindros's, because of the repercussions.

GAME 6

Stanley's MVPs

ONLY ONE FORWARD IN NHL HISTORY has captured the Conn Smythe Trophy as playoff MVP while playing on a Stanley Cup-losing team. Unscramble the names of these other winners by placing each letter in the correct order in the boxes. (To help, each name starts with the bolded letter.) Next, unscramble the letters in the diamond-shaped boxes to spell out the first name of our secret MVP, then the circled boxes for his family name and then the square-shaped boxes for his team.

Solutions are on page 562

ICKA**S**

LUXIEME

R**O**R

LEX**H**ALT

ZY**G**KTER

FA**L**ERUL

NA**G**IYE

of the

7

True or False?

HOCKEY GREAT EDDIE SHORE was once asked to describe old-time hockey. "It was pretty much a 50–50 proposition," answered Shore. "You socked the other guy and the other guy socked you." This chapter is also a 50–50 proposition. Each statement is either true or false. There are no maybes. Be careful though, as good as these odds are, even the pros sometimes miss a wide-open net with the goalie down and out.

Answers are on page 163

7.1 **In 2003–04, the captains of the Edmonton Oilers and the Calgary Flames each hailed from their rival's hometown.** True or False?

7.2 **Wayne Gretzky is the first NHLer to record more assists in a season than anyone else had points.** True or False?

7.3 **The Vancouver Canucks franchise actually made money in 2002–03.** True or False?

7.4 **Despite being hockey's most successful pair of goaltending brothers, Ken and Dave Dryden never played opposite each other in the NHL.** True or False?

7.5 **During his career, Bobby Orr accumulated more penalty minutes than total points.** True or False?

7.6 **Red Kelly scored more goals on defense with Detroit than as a centre with Toronto.** True or False?

7.7 **Dave "Tiger" Williams was the last NHLer to log more than 400 penalty minutes in a season.** True or False?

7.8 **The centre-ice red line was always checkered (as opposed to one solid red stripe).** True or False?

7.9 **Trevor Kidd was chosen ahead of Martin Brodeur in the 1990 NHL Entry Draft.** True or False?

7.10 **Most goalies follow the same routine when dressing: left skate, right skate, left pad, right pad.** True or False?

7.11 **Glenn Hall's only game misconduct occurred during his first NHL game using a goalie mask?** True or False?

7.12 **Maurice Richard won only one NHL scoring title.** True or False?

7.13 **In 1947, the NHL initiated a rule whereby a scoring player must skate 30 feet with raised arms and stick to signal a goal. That little-known gem is still in the NHL's *Official Rules.*** True or False?

7.14 **Grace and Louis Sutter, parents of six NHL-playing Sutter brothers, actually have seven sons.** True or False?

7.15 **The Atlanta Thrashers' first NHL victory was against the New York Islanders, the same team that the original Atlanta team (the Flames) beat for its first franchise win 27 years earlier.** True or False?

7.16 **Defense great Larry Robinson never scored a hat trick in his 20-year career.** True or False?

7.17 Toronto tough guy Eddie Shack was the first player in All-Star history to be named game MVP. True or False?

7.18 When heavyweight bad boy Gino Odjick was obtained by the Montreal Canadiens in December 2000, he was given Hall of Famer Ken Dryden's old sweater, No. 29. True or False?

7.19 It is illegal to include bonuses for fighting in NHL player contracts. True or False?

7.20 The first hockey goaltender to don a mask during play was a woman. True or False?

7.21 Glenn Hall never played a single overtime playoff game during his 552 consecutive-game streak between 1955 and 1962. True or False?

7.22 Wayne Gretzky scored his first 50th goal the same night Guy Lafleur scored his last 50th. True or False?

7.23 Maple Leaf Gardens was built during the six-team era, 1942 to 1967. True or False?

7.24 Maurice Richard never saw a game at the Montreal Forum before he played there as a Canadiens rookie. True or False?

7.25 After Maurice Richard was nicknamed "Rocket" and Henri Richard "Pocket-Rocket," their younger brother was called "Vest-Pocket Rocket." True or False?

7.26 The Colorado Rockies had a different head coach in each of the club's six NHL seasons between 1976–77 and 1981–82. True or False?

7.27 **No coach has ever coached in all three major junior leagues in Canada.** True or False?

7.28 **No one in NHL history has ever played his first league game as team captain.** True or False?

7.29 **All six captains of Canadian NHL clubs at the start of 2000–01 were born outside Canada.** True or False?

7.30 **Columbus winger Steve Heinze wore No. 57 with the Blue Jackets in 2000–01.** True or False?

7.31 **Since goalie Pelle Lindbergh died in 1985, no member of the Philadelphia Flyers has worn his No. 31.** True or False?

7.32 **The regular-season record for points by a defenseman, set by Babe Pratt in 1943–44, lasted until Bobby Orr broke it after the six-team era ended in 1967.** True or False?

7.33 **No NHLer has ever scored a five-goal game in a losing cause.** True or False?

7.34 **Bobby Orr is the last player to win the NHL scoring title while racking up 100 or more penalty minutes.** True or False?

7.35 **The first NHL team to put a hockey stick on its crest was a team from St. Louis.** True or False?

7.36 **At one time in NHL history, all overtime games resulted in a winner.** True or False?

7.37 **The last player to score on his brother in an NHL game was Phil Esposito, who scored on his brother Tony in November 1980.** True or False?

7.38 **Gordie Howe never wore a helmet.** True or False?

7.39 **The only scoreless penalty-free game in NHL history actually had a goal that was called back.** True or False?

7.40 **Martin St. Louis, winner of the Art Ross Trophy as top scorer in 2003–04, was never drafted into the NHL.** True or False?

7.41 **At 2004's trade deadline, New York Ranger GM Glen Sather traded players to every Canadian team in the league except his former club, the Edmonton Oilers.** True or False?

7.42 **The Pittsburgh Penguins still held Alexei Kovalev Bobblehead Night at the Mellon Arena in March 2003, even though the Russian forward had been traded to the New York Rangers a month earlier.** True or False?

7.43 **Hockey was once part of the Summer Olympics.** True or False?

7.44 **Every captain of the Original Six teams in 1966–67 has been inducted into the Hockey Hall of Fame.** True or False?

7.45 **No player has ever won the NHL scoring title while averaging less than a point per game.** True or False?

7.46 **Frozen pucks slide better on ice than pucks that aren't frozen.** True or False?

7.47 **The name of coach Jacques Lemaire's pleasure boat is *The Trap.*** True or False?

7.48 **American coach Herb Brooks, who led Team U.S.A. to the 1980 Olympic Gold medal, was the final cut on the U.S. Olympic squad that won gold in 1960.** True or False?

7.49 **Since Montreal's Tom Johnson and Doug Harvey won Norris Trophies as best defenseman in 1959 and 1960 respectively, no other team has had back-to-back winners.** True or False?

7.50 **For many years during his NHL career, Ron Hextall had more goals than shutouts.** True or False?

7.51 **In 1998–99, the Detroit Red Wings paid Sergei Fedorov more than the Nashville Predators paid its entire roster.** True or False?

7.52 **Wayne Gretzky's highest career goal count against one team came against the same team he would later become managing partner of, the Phoenix Coyotes.** True or False?

7.53 **A shot on goal is counted when the puck hits the post.** True or False?

Answers

7.1 **True**

There's got to be something in the NHL rule book to stop this kind of thing: Jason Smith, captain of the 2003–04 Oilers, hails from Calgary; Jarome Iginla, captain of the Flames in 2003–04, is an Edmontonian.

7.2 False

A top playmaker in the Wayne Gretzky mould, Bill Cowley could see the whole ice. He recorded 45 assists with Boston in 1940–41, one point better than five runners-up in the NHL scoring race. The only other NHLer to match Cowley's feat was Gretzky himself, who amassed more assists than anybody else's point totals on three occasions: in 1982–83, 1985–86 and 1986–87.

7.3 True

After years of losing on the ice and at the box office, the Canucks finally produced a winning season and turned a small profit in 2002–03. The club finished seventh overall with 104 points and sold out 37 regular-season games. Eight home playoff games and the slide of the U.S. dollar also contributed to Vancouver's positive bottom line. According to the team's chief operating officer, Dave Cobb, a one-cent shift in the exchange rate means about Cdn$300,000 per year to the Canucks. The team also had a black bottom line in 2003–04.

7.4 False

Brother netminders are rare. In fact, the Drydens are the only siblings to play at the NHL level in more than 100 games each. Combined, the brothers worked 778 regular-season and playoff matches but only six times against each other. So when they faced each other as opposing goalies for the first time in a Montreal–Buffalo game at the Montreal Forum on March 20, 1971, it was a landmark occasion in league history. Both were backups in the game, but when Ken subbed for an injured Rogatien Vachon, Sabres coach Punch Imlach pulled Joe Daley to let Dave play opposite Ken. The Forum fans were thrilled. After the 5–2 Canadiens win, the two Drydens skated to centre ice and, in a regular-season oddity, shook hands. Dave and Ken played five more times against each other, including twice during the 1973 playoffs, another NHL first. For the record, Ken won three, lost one and tied two against his big brother.

7.5 True

Bobby Orr, the only defenseman in NHL history to lead the league in scoring and the only player besides Wayne Gretzky and Mario Lemieux to earn more than 100 assists in a season, amassed more minutes in the box than points on the scoreboard. Orr collected 915 points and 953 penalty minutes during his 12-year career.

7.6 True

No NHLer has ever had as much success moving to the opposite position as Red Kelly. Before Kelly was traded to the Maple Leafs, where he scored 119 goals as a centre in 7½ seasons, he spent 12½ years on Detroit's blue line, recording 162 goals, the most among all defensemen of his era.

7.7 False

Although he is the all-time NHL penalty-minute leader, Williams never topped the 400-PIM mark in any season. Only three NHL enforcers own the dubious distinction of collecting 400 minutes of box time: Dave Schultz, in 1974–75 and 1977–78; Paul Baxter, in 1981–82; and Mike Peluso, in 1991–92.

7.8 False

The red line was solid red until the late-1950s, when the league checkered it to distinguish the red and blue rink lines for black-and-white television.

7.9 True

Calgary might have made the most important draft swap of its franchise when it flipped first-round draft positions with New Jersey in 1990. The Flames moved to 11th overall and the Devils to 22nd. Both teams sought goaltenders but Calgary failed to capitalize on its improved position, grabbing Trevor Kidd instead of the player who would become New Jersey's later choice, Martin Brodeur. Brodeur led New Jersey to multiple

Stanley Cups, while Kidd played four mediocre seasons with the Flames before being traded to Carolina, Florida and Toronto.

7.10 True

Although no official survey substantiates this claim, it's considered a fact that most big-league goalies lace up their left skate and then their right, followed by their left and right pads.

7.11 True

The only time Hall was tossed from an NHL game was on November 13, 1968, the night the goalie marvel wore his first mask. Rarely at ease before any game, Hall was especially nervous on that critical evening. Almost immediately, the St. Louis netminder gave up a 60-footer to New York's Vic Hatfield. Then, after Blues defenseman Noel Picard was penalized, Hall flicked his glove at referee Vern Buffey in protest, connecting with the official's shoulder. After just two minutes of play the masked Hall was ejected, the only game misconduct in his 18-year NHL career. Afterwards, Hall joked, "Well, every time I wear a mask I get thrown out of the game."

7.12 False

The Rocket's biggest regret was never winning an Art Ross Trophy. But he came very close, twice. In 1946–47, Richard finished one point back of Max Bentley, 72 to 71 points; then, in 1954–55, he missed the scoring championship again by one point to Canadiens teammate Bernie Geoffrion, 75 to 74 points.

7.13 False

Although players had long celebrated a goal by raising their stick, in 1947 the NHL began enforcing the custom in order to more readily identify the scorer. Under the policy, the Canadiens' Billy Reay was the first. Later, in the same game, Toe Blake scored but forgot to raise his arms, and then Chicago's Roy Conacher did do it, only to have his goal called back. No wonder there is no such rule in the books today.

7.14 True

The six Sutter brothers—Brian, Duane, Darryl, Brent, Rick and Ron—have another brother, Gary, who never played hockey. But as Brent has said: "Gary would have made it, because when we were young he was the best of all of us."

7.15 True

Talk about a sense of history. First, the Thrashers invited Atlanta's first coach in 1972, Bernie Geoffrion, to drop the ceremonial first puck on October 2, 1999. Then, in another twist, the inaugural wins of both the Atlanta Flames and the Atlanta Thrashers turned out to be victories against the same team, the New York Islanders. The old Flames defeated the Isles 3–2 for their first win on October 7, 1972, and, 27 years later, the Thrashers captured their first victory by whitewashing New York 2–0 on October 14, 1999. It was the Thrashers' fourth NHL game and their first on the road. Let's hope the Flames and the Thrashers share nothing more than inaugural wins. Eight years after that first victory, the Flames moved to Calgary.

7.16 False

Twenty-year man Larry Robinson only scored one hat trick in his NHL career. It came on December 19, 1985, in a 5–4 Canadiens loss to the Quebec Nordiques.

7.17 True

He ran on his skates and generally acted like a buffoon, but Eddie "Clear the Track" Shack picked up the All-Star game's first MVP honour after scoring one goal in the 1962 event. The defending Stanley Cup champion, the Toronto Maple Leafs, defeated the NHL All-Stars 4–1.

7.18 True

The Montreal Canadiens would probably have to retire 25 per cent of the team's sweater numbers between Jacques Plante's No. 1 and Patrick Roy's No. 33 to honour all the outstanding players who served hockey's most storied franchise. The once-proud club has hit rock bottom several times in recent years, including its slide to last place in league standings in 2000–01, the sale of the team (and the monstrous Molson Centre) to an American and the final insult to its glorious past: giving away Ken Dryden's No. 29 to bruiser journeyman Gino Odjick. Besides Dryden's No. 29, other prominent Canadiens numbers not retired to date include Bernie Geoffrion's No. 5, Dickie Moore and Yvan Cournoyer's No. 12, Serge Savard's No. 18, Larry Robinson's No. 19, Bob Gainey's No. 23 and Jacques Lemaire's No. 25.

7.19 True

The Toronto Maple Leafs put blatant incentives for fighting in tough guy Ken Baumgartner's contract in 1995–96—$10,000 for 170 penalty minutes and $55,000 for 260 minutes. But both bonuses were rejected by NHL arbitrator George Nicolau. Other teams circumvent the rule by clever wording. For example, the Hartford Whalers agreed to pay Kelly Chase a $25,000 bonus if he led the league in any statistical category. Of course, the only statistical categories in which Chase would ever lead the NHL are box time or fighting majors.

7.20 True

Decades before Jacques Plante became hockey's first goalie to regularly wear a mask and three years before Clint Benedict tried a crude leather face mask for a few games in 1930, Queen's University goalie Elizabeth Graham wore a wire fencing mask during intercollegiate games, beginning in 1927. The *Montreal Star* reported: "The Queen's goalie gave the fans a surprise when she stepped into the nets and then donned a fencing mask. It was safety first with her and even at that she can't be blamed for her precautionary methods."

7.21 False

Since there was no regular-season overtime during Hall's era, the only occasion for extra periods was in playoff action. In

49 post-season games (during his 552-game streak), Hall played 65 minutes and 12 seconds of overtime, winning two of three games. In Detroit's 5–4 win over Toronto on March 24, 1956, Hall played 4:22 of overtime; in the March 26, 1960, Chicago 4–3 loss to Montreal, he went 8:38; and in the Blackhawks' 2–1 marathon victory against Montreal on March 26, 1961, Hall survived 52:12 of OT.

7.22 True

The torch was truly passed from a superstar in one era of hockey to the next generation's superstar on April 2, 1980, when Guy Lafleur and Wayne Gretzky each scored 50th goals. It was the sixth and final time Lafleur would score a 50th marker and the first of nine for the Great One. Amazingly, the goalie who gave up Gretzky's first 50th, Gary Edwards, was the same netminder that Lafleur scored his very first NHL goal against.

7.23 False

The Gardens was built in 1931 at the height of the Depression by the indomitable Conn Smythe, the driving force behind the Maple Leafs for almost half a century. When MLG opened to great fanfare on November 12, 1931, the league was an eight-game circuit.

7.24 True

Although Richard listened religiously to *La Soirée du Hockey au Canada (Hockey Night in Canada)* each Saturday evening on the radio when he was a boy, it wasn't until he graduated to the big club in 1942 that he saw the hallowed Montreal Forum in person.

7.25 True

To follow in the skate strides of the Rocket and the Pocket Rocket must have been difficult for brother Claude. Despite a tryout with the Canadiens, he's remembered only for his nickname: the Vest-Pocket Rocket.

7.26 True

Colorado's first go-round in the NHL was an unmitigated disaster. The Rockies' six-year run from 1975 to 1982 included seven coaches. First, Johnny Wilson was replaced by Pat Kelly, who was then blown out in favour of Aldo Guidolin; who was later fired to hire Don Cherry; who was exchanged a year later for Billy MacMillan; who was dropped to bring in Bert Marshall; who lasted mere months before Marshall Johnston got the nod and finally the heave-ho as the last Rockies coach—departures all tied to the team's dismal record. The Rockies failed to qualify for postseason play each and every year of their existence. The team won just 113 regular-season games in six seasons.

7.27 False

"Travellin'" Joe Canale may be the only person who has coached in all three Canadian major junior leagues, the OHL, QMJHL and WHL. Canale has been a bench boss with seven major junior teams across Canada, including the Medicine Hat Tigers of the WHL, the Sarnia Sting of the OHL and five teams (Sherbrooke, Laval, Chicoutimi, Beauport and Shawinigan) in the QMJHL. He also coached Canada's national junior team to two golds at the World Junior Championships in 1993 (as assistant coach) and 1994 (as head coach). Many future NHLers played under his tutelage, including Paul Kariya, Chris Pronger and Eric Daze.

7.28 False

It's not unusual for players to play their first NHL game as captain, but most of the time it happens with new franchises. The New York Rangers (Bill Cook), Chicago Blackhawks (Dick Irvin) and Detroit Red Wings (Art Duncan) were all captained by first-year NHL players. More recently, the Winnipeg Jets (Lars-Erik Sjoberg) and Edmonton Oilers (Ron Chipperfield) each entered the NHL with rookie captains, in 1979–80.

7.29 True

Markus Naslund (Vancouver), Daniel Alfredsson (Ottawa) and Mats Sundin (Toronto) are from Sweden; Saku Koivu (Montreal) is from Finland; Doug Weight (Edmonton) is American; and Steve Smith (Calgary) is Canadian-raised but was born in Scotland.

7.30 True

Before Columbus selected Steve Heinze at the NHL Expansion Draft in 2000, the Boston right-winger wore No. 23. When his nine-year career with the Bruins ended, Heinze chose No. 57, the number made famous by the popular food manufacturer of the same name.

7.31 True

Even though Pelle Lindbergh's No. 31 is still active (it has never been officially retired), Philadelphia has never assigned his jersey number to any other player. Lindbergh, the reigning Vezina Trophy winner as the NHL's top goalie, died on November 10, 1985, after crashing his Porsche 930 Turbo at high speed. The Flyer goalie had a blood-alcohol level of .24, a figure considerably higher than the .10 legal limit. He was 26 years old. On the 15th anniversary of Lindbergh's death, Flyer equipment manager Jim Evers said in the *Philadelphia Daily News:* "One guy, Neil Little, asked for it (Lindbergh's sweater number) when he first got here. He didn't know, and he was OK with it when I explained it to him."

7.32 False

In 1964–65, defenseman Pierre Pilote scored 59 points (14 goals, 45 assists) to break Babe Pratt's 21-year-old mark of 57 points, set in 1943–44. Pilote's record was in turn wiped out when Orr earned 64 points in 1968–69.

7.33 True

No NHLer has ever scored five times in a game and lost, but Winnipeg's Alexei Zhamnov's five-goal performance on April 1, 1995, was almost wasted (or seemed like a very bad April Fool's joke) as his Jets couldn't stem Los Angeles' attack in the 7–7 knot. Kelly Hrudey (3) and Grant Fuhr (2) of the Kings shared the blame in Zhamnov's five-goal output.

7.34 False

Orr, who compiled 101 PIM while winning the Art Ross Trophy in 1974–75, is not the last scoring champ to reach triple digits in box time. Mario Lemieux had exactly 100 PIM when he won the scoring title in 1988–89.

7.35 True

The stick has been the most common icon on NHL crests since expansion in 1967. At least 10 teams (Pittsburgh, Vancouver, Phoenix, the New York Islanders, Washington, Los Angeles, Atlanta, Columbus, Anaheim and San Jose) have used the stick symbol to market the game in new NHL cities. The idea wasn't unique prior to '67, either. When the old Ottawa Senators franchise moved to St. Louis in 1934 and called themselves the Eagles, their jerseys sported a bald eagle clutching a hockey stick.

7.36 True

In the NHL's first four years, 1917–18 to 1920–21, all games were played to a conclusion, no matter how long it took. But considering that the arenas weren't heated, there was an added incentive to get things wrapped up in regulation. As you might expect, this was not a defensive era.

7.37 False

As rare a commodity as goals are for Mathieu Biron, none has been sweeter than his marker on November 24, 2003, when the Florida defenseman scored the game-winner against his older brother, Martin, in a 2–1 victory over the Buffalo Sabres. Despite their three-year age difference, the siblings had never faced each other in junior or minor hockey. "It's something that you dream about," said Mathieu Biron in an Associated Press story. "It's something you get excited about. We are always chatting about that during the off-season. Even when I spoke with him yesterday about scoring against him, he said, 'You wish.' Tonight he won't be talking about that. That's for sure." The Birons' brother-on-brother goal was the first since Phil and Tony Esposito connected, while Phil was with the New York Rangers and Tony was in goal for the Chicago Blackhawks, on November 5, 1980.

7.38 False

In 32 years, Howe wore a helmet only once, in 1950–51. After sustaining a severe concussion in a dangerous collision with Toronto's Ted Kennedy late in 1949–50, Howe came back the following season wearing a leather helmet. As was once the custom, players only used helmets after a serious injury.

7.39 True

Officially, the game report for the Chicago–Toronto tilt on February 20, 1944, shows no goals and no penalties recorded, the only such match in league history. But at 9:16 of the second period, Chicago's Fido Purpur *had* slammed one past Paul Bibeault—only to have the play nullified when referee Bill Chadwick ruled the shot illegal. Apparently, Purpur scored the goal with his stick above his shoulders. The mild-mannered 0–0 draw was played in one hour and 55 minutes.

7.40 True

At least four inches shorter and 20 pounds lighter than the average NHLer, Martin St. Louis was never drafted by an NHL team because most scouts considered him too small to play in heavy traffic at the NHL level. St. Louis spent four years at the University of Vermont and one season putting up impressive numbers in the minors before getting a sniff from Calgary in 1998. The Flames signed him but he managed only four goals in 69 games. St. Louis was released and became a free agent again, signing with Tampa Bay in 2000. Among all players eligible for draft selection since 1969, St. Louis is the only NHL scoring champion who was never drafted.

7.41 False

In 2003–04 no GM in the NHL made more trades than Sather: 11 during the season, most coming during New York's fire sale leading up to the March 9 trade deadline. By the time he finished dismantling the mess he had made of the Rangers, Sather had worked a deal with every Canadian-based club. American teams also benefited, but not in proportion to their league representation. Sather's biggest deals included Martin Rucinsky to Vancouver; Greg de Vries to Ottawa; Brian Leetch to Toronto; Alexei Kovalev to Montreal; Chris Simon to Calgary; and Petr Nedved and Jussi Markkanen to his former team, Edmonton. Among U.S. clubs, Washington got Anson Carter, Colorado got Matthew Barnaby, and Philadelphia got Vladimir Malakhov. So ended Sather's grand experiment of an all-finesse team on Broadway. Instead he got a team of aging, overpaid underachievers who failed to live up to their talent or income because they didn't care enough about each other to win.

7.42 True

Despite the fact that Kovalev had been traded February 10 to the New York Rangers, the Penguins still gave out about 16,000 Alexei Kovalev bobblehead dolls at their March 6 match against Carolina. According to reports, the club did not want to disappoint their fans. Instead, how about a win to bring the fans back? The game was a sellout, but the Pens lost to the Hurricanes 4–0.

7.43 True

In 1920, the Winnipeg Falcons won the Allan Cup to become the amateur champions of Canada, an honour that earned them the right to represent their country when hockey was first admitted as a sport at the Antwerp Summer Olympics. It was the first and only time hockey was played at the Summer Games.

7.44 False

Five of six captains from the last year of the six-team era have Hall of Fame status. George Armstrong (Toronto), Johnny Bucyk (Boston), Pierre Pilote (Chicago), Alex Delvecchio (Detroit) and Jean Béliveau (Montreal) all gained Hall entry. The lone exception was Bob Nevin, captain of the New York Rangers from 1964–65 to 1970–71.

7.45 False

On four occasions players have won the NHL scoring title while averaging less than a point per game: Bill Cook, Ace Bailey, Sweeney Schriner (twice) and Toe Blake.

7.46 True

Whatever the physics are behind the phenomenon, it's a fact. Every kid who's played pond hockey knows that's why pucks are frozen solid for game use. Or look it up in the NHL rule book: Section 3, Rule 25, Paragraph B.

7.47 True

Lemaire, the often-credited inventor of hockey's dreaded trap system of defense, christened his pleasure yacht *The Trap.* Big sense of humour, that Lemaire.

7.48 True

Brooks's failure as a player to make the 1960 gold-medal team pushed him to succeed when he became a coach. Apparently, when the 1960 squad won gold without him, Brooks and his father were at home in Minnesota. "I guess they cut the right guy," the old man said, devastating the younger Brooks. That moment of humiliation drove Brooks to win three national championships as coach at the University of Minnesota and then, before a stunned hockey world, a gold medal for Team U.S.A. at the 1980 Olympics.

7.49 False

A number of teams have iced defensemen (Paul Coffey, Ray Bourque, Rod Langway) with consecutive Norris Trophies, but no club can claim back-to-back Norrises by two players, with the exception of Montreal and St. Louis. Exactly 40 years after Tom Johnson (1959) and Doug Harvey (1960) won their Norrises with the Canadiens, St. Louis became just the second team with Norris teammates in consecutive years: Al MacInnis in 1999 and Chris Pronger in 2000.

7.50 True

In his first five NHL seasons, Hextall's record stood at two goals and just one shutout.

7.51 True

Fedorov earned $14 million from Detroit—almost half a million more than the $13.6 million Nashville paid to ice its entire team in its first year of expansion, 1998–99.

7.52 True

During his 20-year NHL career, Wayne Gretzky scored at least one goal against all 27 teams he faced, but his easiest target was Edmonton and Los Angeles' conference rival, the Winnipeg Jets, the franchise that transferred to Phoenix in 1996–97. After Gretzky retired in 1999, he was offered a managing partnership with the club. Gretzky scored 79 regular-season goals against the Coyotes/Jets, his highest goal count against any NHL franchise.

7.53 False

A shot that hits the post is not considered a shot on goal as it has no chance of going directly into the net.

GAME 7

Frère Jacques (French 101)

IN 1909, OTTAWA BUSINESSMAN J. Ambrose O'Brien founded an "all French-Canadian team" he called "le Canadien," a nickname originally given to French explorers and settlers of Canada during the 1700s. The Montreal Canadiens became hockey's greatest dynasty, and French-speaking players proved to be among the most elite puck shooters and stoppers. Listed below are 12 NHLers with French names (including a few born outside of Quebec). Match the player's *nom de famille* and its literal English translation.

Solutions are on page 563

1. ______	Patrick Roy	A.	The Flower
2. ______	Pat LaFontaine	B.	Small
3. ______	Simon Gagné	C.	The Knight
4. ______	Eric Desjardins	D.	The Mayor
5. ______	Michel Petit	E.	King
6. ______	Guy Lafleur	F.	The Best
7. ______	Jacques Lemaire	G.	The Gardens
8. ______	Vincent Lecavalier	H.	Side
9. ______	Wilf Paiement	I.	Little Bit of Love
10. ______	Sylvain Côté	J.	The Fountain
11. ______	Rod Brind'Amour	K.	Payment
12. ______	Mario Lemieux	L.	Win

8

Moolah

AFTER STEPPING DOWN as long-time manager of the Boston Bruins in October 2000 to become club president, Harry Sinden was asked whether the Bruins would ever have a $10-million player. His reply: "Never. Seems to me it's pretty hard to put your face in front of a puck when you've got $40 million in the bank." In this chapter, we check out the biggest name in the game—money.

Answers are on page 188

8.1 In 1962, the Boston Bruins secured the cornerstone of a dynasty when they purchased the lifetime hockey rights to Bobby Orr. How much was the contract worth?

A. U.S.$2,800
B. U.S.$6,800
C. U.S.$24,800
D. U.S.$50,800

8.2 Which NHL rookie made more money than any established star in the league upon signing his contract?

A. Wayne Gretzky
B. Bobby Orr
C. Jean Béliveau
D. Paul Kariya

8.3 What was Bobby Hull's WHA contract with the Winnipeg Jets worth?

A. $750,000 over 10 years
B. $1.75 million over 10 years

C. $2.75 million over 10 years
D. $3.75 million over 10 years

8.4 How much did the World Hockey Association's Edmonton Oilers pay to acquire the rights to Wayne Gretzky in 1978?

A. Less than $1 million
B. $1 million
C. $2 million
D. $3 million

8.5 How did Toronto owner Conn Smythe raise money to obtain the great King Clancy from the old Ottawa Senators?

A. He sold the rights to Busher Jackson
B. He bet on a racehorse
C. He solicited donations at home games
D. He sold hockey pencils on street corners

8.6 Which Saskatchewan town made national headlines in 2002 with a novel attempt to raise money to save its community hockey rink?

A. Kelvington, Saskatchewan
B. Wapella, Saskatchewan
C. Bellegarde, Saskatchewan
D. Saskatoon, Saskatchewan

8.7 On the Canadian $5 bill there is a winter scene showing kids playing hockey on an outdoor pond. What hockey number is displayed prominently in the picture?

A. No. 1
B. No. 5
C. No. 9
D. No. 99

8.8 The NHL's first million-dollar contract was a multi-year deal signed by whom?

A. Phil Esposito
B. Bobby Orr
C. Derek Sanderson
D. Bobby Hull

8.9 Who earned the highest percentage of his team's payroll in 2002–03?

A. Pittsburgh's Mario Lemieux
B. The New York Islanders' Alexei Yashin
C. Anaheim's Paul Kariya
D. Washington's Jaromir Jagr

8.10 How much money did Philadelphia general manager Bobby Clarke pay centre Chris Gratton in his only complete season with the Flyers, 1997–98?

A. U.S.$4 million
B. U.S.$6 million
C. U.S.$8 million
D. U.S.$10 million

8.11 How much money did the Colorado Avalanche spend to re-sign Joe Sakic, Patrick Roy and Rob Blake to long-term contracts on June 30, 2001?

A. U.S.$85 million
B. U.S.$100 million
C. U.S.$115 million
D. U.S.$130 million

8.12 Which player was awarded the most money in NHL history in an arbitration case?

A. Phoenix's Keith Tkachuk
B. Calgary's Fred Brathwaite

C. Philadelphia's Mark Recchi
D. Philadelphia's John LeClair

8.13 When goalie Fred Brathwaite went to arbitration after his surprising 61-game performance for Calgary in 1999–2000, how much of a salary increase were the Flames ordered to pay Brathwaite in 2000–01?

A. A 53 per cent increase
B. A 103 per cent increase
C. A 153 per cent increase
D. A 203 per cent increase

8.14 Which NHL team was the first to lose a player to free agency rather than pay him his estimated worth via arbitration?

A. The Philadelphia Flyers
B. The Calgary Flames
C. The Boston Bruins
D. The Ottawa Senators

8.15 How much did Ottawa's Alexei Yashin forfeit in 1999–2000 by refusing to honour the final year of his contract with the Senators?

A. U.S.$2.6 million
B. U.S.$3.6 million
C. U.S.$4.6 million
D. U.S.$5.6 million

8.16 Detroit players gave which fellow Red Wing the nickname "Sam Jones" in 1997?

A. Sergei Fedorov
B. Darren McCarthy
C. Steve Yzerman
D. Nicklas Lidstrom

8.17 How much money did the Winnipeg Jets pay Keith Tkachuk in order to match the five-year deal he was offered by the Chicago Blackhawks in 1995?

A. U.S.$10.2 million
B. U.S.$13.2 million
C. U.S.$17.2 million
D. U.S.$20.2 million

8.18 How much did goalie Martin Brodeur earn (before his case went to arbitration and his Stanley Cup win) during 1995's lockout-shortened season?

A. Less than U.S.$100,000
B. U.S.$500,000
C. U.S.$1 million
D. U.S.$2 million

8.19 How much money was Boston Bruins minor pro goalie Jim "Ace" Carey guaranteed to make in two seasons with the AHL's Providence Bruins, 1998–99 and 1999–2000?

A. U.S.$250,000
B. U.S.$500,000
C. U.S.$1 million
D. U.S.$5 million

8.20 What was NHLer John MacLean's salary after he cleared waivers and the New York Rangers sent him to the IHL's Manitoba Moose?

A. U.S.$2,500
B. U.S.$25,000
C. U.S.$250,000
D. U.S.$2.5 million

8.21 Which NHL general manager demanded more money back from a player in a contract dispute during 2003–04?

A. Darryl Sutter of the Calgary Flames
B. Kevin Lowe of the Edmonton Oilers
C. Doug Wilson of the San Jose Sharks
D. David Poile of the Nashville Predators

8.22 Which NHL star goalie refused half of his salary in 2003–04?

A. Martin Brodeur of the New Jersey Devils
B. Miikka Kiprusoff of the Calgary Flames
C. Patrick Lalime of the Ottawa Senators
D. Dominik Hasek of the Detroit Red Wings

8.23 Which NHL club promised its season-ticket holders a refund if the team didn't make the playoffs in 2002–03?

A. The Nashville Predators
B. The Atlanta Thrashers
C. The Los Angeles Kings
D. The Calgary Flames

8.24 Which NHL team offered its fans free playoff tickets in 2003–04?

A. The Toronto Maple Leafs
B. The New York Islanders
C. The Nashville Predators
D. The Vancouver Canucks

8.25 Players often have incentive clauses in their contracts for goals or points scored in a season. How much bonus money was riding on St. Louis' Scott Young and his final shot on goal during the 1998–99 season?

A. U.S.$200,000
B. U.S.$400,000
C. U.S.$600,000
D. U.S.$800,000

8.26 How much did Toronto's Wendel Clark earn in regular-season bonus money in 1992–93?

A. U.S.$25,000
B. U.S.$125,000
C. U.S.$225,000
D. U.S.$325,000

8.27 Despite the NHL's rookie salary cap, how much did Atlanta's Ilya Kovalchuk and Dany Heatley make during 2001–02?

A. U.S.$1 million
B. U.S.$2 million
C. U.S.$3 million
D. U.S.$4 million

8.28 How much bonus money did Ottawa's Jason Spezza receive for reaching the 20-goal plateau in 2003–04?

A. Between U.S.$1 million and U.S.$2 million
B. Between U.S.$2 million and U.S.$3 million
C. Between U.S.$3 million and U.S.$4 million
D. More than U.S.$4 million

8.29 How much did Vancouver's Todd Bertuzzi lose in salary for sucker punching Steve Moore of the Colorado Avalanche in March 2004?

A. U.S.$402,000
B. U.S.$502,000
C. U.S.$602,000
D. U.S.$702,000

8.30 How much money did Sergei Fedorov lose after being suspended five games for slashing Zdeno Chara during the 1998–99 season?

A. Less than U.S.$100,000
B. Between U.S.$100,000 and U.S.$250,000

C. Between U.S.$250,000 and U.S.$400,000
D. More than U.S.$400,000

8.31 Philadelphia's Jeremy Roenick was fined almost U.S.$100,000 for throwing what object at a referee during a game in 2003–04?

A. A water bottle
B. A roll of tape
C. A stick
D. A helmet

8.32 Which NHL owner was fined U.S.$100,000 for scuffling with a disgruntled fan in January 2004?

A. Thomas Hicks of the Dallas Stars
B. Ted Leonsis of the Washington Capitals
C. Mario Lemieux of the Pittsburgh Penguins
D. Ed Snyder of the Philadelphia Flyers

8.33 How much money were Bryan McCabe, Darius Kasparaitis and Rick DiPietro each fined for diving in 2002–03?

A. U.S.$100
B. U.S.$500
C. U.S.$1,000
D. U.S.$5,000

8.34 How much money did Brad May forfeit after being suspended for 20 games for slashing Steve Heinze in November 2000?

A. U.S.$50,000 to $100,000
B. U.S.$100,000 to $150,000
C. U.S.$150,000 to $200,000
D. More than U.S.$200,000

8.35 What happens to the money collected as player fines?

A. The NHL contributes it to the Players Association's pension fund
B. The NHL puts it towards minor league hockey programs
C. The NHL turns it over to the Hockey Hall of Fame
D. The NHL uses it as an emergency fund for retired players and their families

8.36 What was the admission price to Wayne Gretzky's fantasy camp in 2003?

A. U.S.$3,999
B. U.S.$6,999
C. U.S.$9,999
D. U.S.$12,999

8.37 How much did a private bidder pay in 2003 for the puck that was used to score Team U.S.A.'s game-winning goal against the Soviets at the 1980 Olympics?

A. Between U.S.$1,000 and U.S.$4,000
B. Between U.S.$4,000 and U.S.$8,000
C. Between U.S.$8,000 and U.S.$12,000
D. More than U.S.$12,000

8.38 What item fetched the most money at the Maple Leaf Gardens auction in November 2000?

A. The Gardens' Zamboni
B. The Maple Leafs' 1967 Stanley Cup banner
C. The Gardens' home penalty box
D. The Gardens' nets

8.39 When the Montreal Forum closed its doors on March 11, 1996, the Canadiens held a charity auction that saw everything from rink scrapers to hot-dog grills go on the block. Which item attracted the highest bid?

A. Captain Pierre Turgeon's locker
B. The Canadiens' 1993 Stanley Cup banner

C. The Canadiens' dressing-room door
D. Ex-NHL president Clarence Campbell's seat

8.40 How much money was bid at a team charity auction in 2000 for dinner with Florida Panthers star Pavel Bure?

A. U.S.$2,500
B. U.S.$4,500
C. U.S.$6,500
D. U.S.$8,500

8.41 How much did Wayne Gretzky's Heritage Classic jersey sell for in an auction on eBay in December 2003?

A. U.S.$6,000
B. U.S.$16,000
C. U.S.$26,000
D. U.S.$36,000

8.42 Which player led the NHL in sweater sales in 2003–04?

A. Steve Yzerman
B. Mike Modano
C. Joe Sakic
D. Martin Brodeur

8.43 How many different sweater looks (third jerseys, etc.) were worn in the 30-team NHL in 2003–04?

A. 36 sweaters
B. 56 sweaters
C. 76 sweaters
D. 96 sweaters

Answers

8.1 A. U.S.$2,800

Originally, 14-year-old Bobby Orr signed the standard NHL "C" form, which gave the Boston Bruins his hockey rights for life in exchange for U.S.$2,800, a used car and the promise of a new wardrobe (though the Bruins never did deliver the wardrobe). But in 1966, when Orr tuned pro, agent Alan Eagleson negotiated a more lucrative deal, the largest rookie contract ever seen at that time in the NHL: U.S.$80,000 over two years, including a U.S.$25,000 signing bonus. Money was never better spent.

8.2 C. Jean Béliveau

Salary disclosure was almost unheard of during the six-team era, but when Jean Béliveau signed with Montreal in October 1953 the deal was so huge that it was impossible to keep the details from the media. Béliveau received $110,000 with a five-year guarantee and a slew of bonuses. He immediately became the league's highest-paid athlete, making more money than the league's best players, Maurice Richard and Gordie Howe. Many believe that Béliveau also made more money than Howe and Richard when he was playing minor pro hockey with the Quebec Aces of the Quebec Senior Hockey League. If so, Béliveau is the only minor pro star able to make such a claim.

8.3 B. $1.75 million over 10 years

Hull's 10-year contract worked this way: for the first five years the Golden Jet received $250,000 annually as player-coach, then in the final five years he got a stipend of $100,000 per annum. His signing bonus was an unprecedented $1 million. For the upstart league it was a bargain, considering Hull's value at the box office. Meanwhile, the Blackhawks were only offering their multiple 50-goal scorer $100,000 per season.

Frustrated by the impasse in negotiations with the Hawks, Hull tried to use the WHA as a bargaining ploy. As he recalled in *Sports Illustrated,* "I thought it (the WHA offer) was a joke. I pretended to go along with it, just to scare Chicago. Then my agent, Harvey Weinberg, said, 'Bobby, these guys are serious.'" Hull's signing gave the WHA instant credibility, and as Winnipeg general manager Annis Stukus said, "Bobby made us major league."

8.4 A. Less than $1 million

In 1978, after just eight games and six points with the Indianapolis Racers, 17-year-old rookie Wayne Gretzky (as well as Peter Driscoll and Eddie Mio) was sold for $850,000 by the team's owner, Nelson Skalbania, to Peter Pocklington of the WHA Edmonton Oilers. Skalbania had originally signed Gretzky to a personal-services contract ($825,000 for four years), but after losing $40,000 per game in Indianapolis, he severed his ties with Gretzky. Obviously that was a big mistake. Skalbania had a handshake deal with the Winnipeg Jets, but owner Michael Gobuty unwisely listened to his scouts, who said the kid was too small and wasn't worth the money. Another big mistake. Shortly after, Gretzky inked a new contract with Pocklington at centre ice before an Edmonton crowd at Northlands Coliseum. The contract expiry date was 1999, the year Gretzky eventually retired. "I remember when he got off that little jet I sent to get him," Pocklington recalled. "Here's this skinny little kid with peach fuzz. I thought, 'My God, I paid $850,000 for that.' Just kidding."

8.5 B. He bet on a racehorse

Acquiring Clancy was considered the biggest player deal of the 1930s, and Smythe did it with the help of a filly named Rare Jewel—a horse that rarely paid off. Smythe placed a huge sum on the long shot, and in the home stretch, Rare Jewel upset the field and stole the race. Smythe pocketed about $15,000, enough to make up the difference needed to buy King Clancy for $35,000 from the Senators. It was an astronomical amount at the time but Smythe needed a marquee name for his next big project, Maple Leaf Gardens. Clancy remained a hockey icon in Toronto for the next half-century.

8.6 C. Bellegarde, Saskatchewan

Rather than see their aging rink close because of debts of Cdn$5,000, Bellegarde's 41 residents held a local contest to raise money to keep the lights on. Participants had to guess which day in spring a 1968 Chevrolet Bel Air would break through just over three feet of ice on a man-made pond. Tickets were sold and the town raised Cdn$2,000, just enough to keep the rink open through the winter. But then the *National Post* ran a front-page story and started its own version of the contest. Soon Molson Inc. was on board, and through its Local Heroes fund, the brewery donated Cdn$10,000 to save the rink. The newspaper contest included a grand prize of a free trip to Bellegarde. The rusted old Chevy finally sank on April 14, 2002. There were 14 contestants who predicted that date. In a run-off draw, Jacques Dion of Asbestos, Quebec, won the prize.

8.7 C. No. 9

On the back of the Canadian $5 bill is an image of kids tobogganing, learning to skate and playing hockey. Four children are playing pick-up hockey and one girl is wearing a No. 9 jersey, in memory of Montreal Canadiens legend Maurice Richard. Next to the illustration is Quebecois writer Roch Carrier's words from his story *The Hockey Sweater:* "The winters of my childhood were long, long seasons. We lived in three places—the school, the church and the skating-rink—but our real life was on the skating-rink." Keeping the kids company on the reverse side of the $5 note is one-time Canadian prime minister Sir Wilfrid Laurier. When it was introduced in March 2002, the new $5 bill was worth only about U.S.$3.10.

8.8 B. Bobby Orr

Orr became hockey's first millionaire after signing a five-year U.S.$200,000-a-year contract with the Bruins in 1971. Shortly thereafter, a handful of players received seven-figure salaries, including Derek Sanderson and Bobby Hull, each of whom inked multi-year WHA deals in June 1972.

8.9 A. Pittsburgh's Mario Lemieux

Since team payrolls fluctuate slightly throughout the year because of trades, this answer depends on when you do the math. At the start of 2002–03, Paul Kariya's U.S.$10-million salary took a whopping 25.6 per cent of Anaheim's player payout of U.S.$39 million. After the March 2003 trade deadline, which our answer is based on, the Mighty Ducks bumped their payroll to U.S.$46 million, while Pittsburgh dumped players and dropped its payroll to U.S.$22.8 million, making Lemieux the highest-paid wage earner as a percentage of total team payroll. Lemieux earned U.S.$5.25 million, or 23 per cent of the Penguins' payroll. Jagr made 22.1 per cent (U.S.$11.5 million of $52 million), Kariya 21.7 per cent (U.S.$10 million of $46 million) and Alexei Yashin 20 per cent (U.S.$7.4 million of $37 million).

8.10 D. U.S.$10 million

In 1997, Philadelphia general manager Bobby Clarke really liked what he saw in Tampa Bay's six-foot-four, 218-pound centre Chris Gratton. Could he be another John LeClair? He signed Gratton to a five-year offer worth U.S.$16.5 million (which Tampa didn't match), U.S.$10 million of which was front-loaded in the first year. But after one season, Gratton failed to impress Clarke, who sent him back to the Lightning for the same player he gave up originally, Mikael Renberg. Clarke's self-admitted mistake was huge. By trading away Renberg, he broke up the Flyers' most productive scoring unit, the Legion of Doom, and, ultimately, cost the Flyers

U.S.$10 million (which Gratton received in his only season as a Flyer). The big centre scored 62 points in Philly in 1997–98, or U.S.$161,290.32 per point.

8.11 C. U.S.$115 million

In a wild spending spree just after the 2001 NHL Entry Draft, the Stanley Cup champion Colorado Avalanche doled out an unprecedented U.S.$115 million to re-sign three of its big stars: centre Joe Sakic, goalie Patrick Roy and defenseman Rob Blake. Altogether, Sakic (U.S.$9.8 million), Roy (U.S.$8.5 million) and Blake (U.S.$9.3 million) earned almost U.S.$28 million in 2001–02, a sum higher than the cost of an entire roster of seven NHL teams that year.

8.12 D. Philadelphia's John LeClair

John LeClair, who had scored the most total goals (235) over the preceding five years of any NHLer, had been underpaid for years by the Philadelphia Flyers. In August 2000, LeClair won a record-setting one-year arbitration award of U.S.$7 million, beating the previous high set by Pierre Turgeon of U.S.$4.6 million. Even so, LeClair didn't get what he wanted. He asked for U.S.$9 million, and the Flyers countered with U.S.$4.6 million. Still, his pay hike from U.S.$3.7 million in 1999–2000 to U.S.$7 million was a 90 per cent salary raise.

8.13 C. A 153 per cent increase

He was the goalie nobody wanted. Playing for the Canadian national team program, Fred Brathwaite caught fire in Calgary after a rash of injuries left the Flames with few options in 1999–2000. Brathwaite stayed for a team-high 61 games that season, earning a 25–25–7 record and a salary of U.S.$375,000 as one of the league's lowest-paid goalies. At the six-hour arbitration hearing, Brathwaite was looking to triple his annual salary to more than U.S.$1 million, while Calgary's qualifying offer included a standard 10 per cent raise. The decision: the

Flames were ordered to pay Brathwaite U.S.$950,000 in 2000–01 and U.S.$1.05 million in 2001–02, a 153 and 180 per cent increase in the first and second years.

8.14 C. The Boston Bruins

The first NHLer to become a free agent through arbitration was Dmitri Khristich, who signed with the Toronto Maple Leafs for U.S.$2.8 million after Boston walked away from an arbitrator's salary award in 1999. Khristich, who had two straight 29-goal seasons with Boston, slumped badly in a Maple Leaf uniform, scoring only 15 goals before being shipped to Washington, where he retired in 2002. The second player to become a free agent via arbitration was Bryan Berard, another Bruin cast-off. Boston refused the U.S.$2.51 million salary given to Berard after an arbitration hearing in 2003.

8.15 B. U.S.$3.6 million

Trying to get a new contract by refusing to play in 1999–2000 might have worked in any American city, but not in small-market Ottawa and not with Senators owner Rod Bryden, whose steadfast refusal to renegotiate cost Alexei Yashin and his agent Mark Gandler U.S.$3.6 million. Yashin, on the advice of Gandler, who completely misjudged Bryden's resolve, spent the season working out with Switzerland's Kloten Flyers in the hopes that his Ottawa contract would expire. But an independent arbitrator ruled in favour of the Senators and Yashin's loss seemed even greater. Had he played in 1999–2000, the U.S.$3.6 million would have been in the bank and he could have negotiated his "dream" contract in 2000–01, at a potential of U.S.$6 to $8 million a year. Instead Yashin was forced to play for U.S.$3.6 million in 2000–01. As a further insult, when Yashin took the arbitrator's decision to court to have the ruling overturned, he lost the NHLPA's backing and ultimately his right to restricted free agency. He was also ordered to pay the NHL's one-day legal fees of $27,649.39. Still, Yashin had the last laugh on NHL owners. In what is one of the most flagrant misuses of player money that could only hurt future league pay structures, Yashin signed a 10-year deal with the New York Islanders worth U.S.$87.5 million.

8.16 A. Sergei Fedorov

Fedorov's nickname dates back to 1996–97, when the Detroit star complained about the different standards for Russian players and those from North America, declaring things would be different "if my name were Sam Jones." During his lengthy contract impasse in 1997–98, some Detroit players were less than complimentary about Sam Jones. "Sam Jones is in Moscow now... losing a lot of money," said Slava Kozlov. Based on his $5-million salary, Fedorov forfeited $25,000 a day during his holdout. As it turned out, that sum was pocket change to Fedorov, whose patience paid off when he signed one of hockey's most substantial contracts, a $38-million deal with Detroit that included a $14-million signing bonus, $2 million in salary and another $12-million payment if the Wings reached the Western Conference finals. In the new NHL (post-lockout 2004–05), those kinds of dollars are ancient history.

8.17 C. U.S.$17.2 million

Tkachuk vaulted into the penthouse of NHL wage earners when he signed a five-year U.S.$17.2-million contract with the Winnipeg Jets in October 1995. An unrestricted free agent at the start of the 1995–96 season, Tkachuk was free to entertain offers from other teams when he and the Jets failed to ink a new deal. Chicago tried to steal him away by offering an enormous sum (a frontloaded contract worth U.S.$6 million in the first year alone), but the cash-strapped Jets bit the bullet and matched the offer.

8.18 A. Less than U.S.$100,000

Brodeur, NHL rookie of the year in 1994 and the centrepiece of the New Jersey Devils' 1995 Stanley Cup championship team, was the lowest-paid full-time NHLer in 1994–95. His paltry U.S.$140,000 salary, which was pro-rated to the 48-game schedule, worked out to about U.S.$80,000. After arbitration his income was considerably higher. According to the terms of the NHL Collective Bargaining Agreement, the maximum Brodeur could receive was U.S.$850,000.

8.19 D. U.S.$5 million

Instead of basking in the NHL spotlight in 1998–99, Carey, once Washington's Vezina-winning superstar goalie, was riding buses in the AHL, all the while collecting a U.S.$5-million salary. After his Vezina year in 1996, Carey slumped so badly that his freefall from greatness landed him with the Bruins' AHL farm team in Providence. With a guaranteed salary of U.S.$2.3 million on a one-way contract, Boston management was obligated to pay him U.S.$5 million for 1998–99 and 1999–2000. Carey lobbied for a buyout in the summer of 1998, but the Bruins resisted. In late 1998–99 the club sent him to St. Louis, where he played just four games. Carey is the highest-paid player in American League history.

8.20 D. U.S.$2.5 million

It's an astronomical sum of money to pay someone for playing in the minors, but when 36-year-old John MacLean cleared waivers around the league in November 2000, New York general manager Glen Sather was forced to send the unhappy MacLean to the Rangers' IHL farm club, the Manitoba Moose. Sather had already offered to pay 80 per cent (U.S.$2 million) in trade talks, leaving other NHL teams to cough up just U.S.$500,000. Then, Sather tried to buy out MacLean at U.S.$2 million, but over two years. MacLean refused. His punishment was full salary (U.S.$2.5 million) in the minors.

8.21 B. Kevin Lowe of the Edmonton Oilers

In an NHL first, Lowe called for Mike Comrie to ante up U.S.$2.5 million to complete a trade deal with Anaheim after the disgruntled centre turned down Edmonton's qualifying offer of U.S.$1.13 million. Comrie, who had cashed in on a front-loaded U.S.$12-million contract for 2½ seasons of work with the Oilers, cited "philosophical differences" as his justification for not wanting to join the club. Lowe didn't get the money and Comrie was later dealt to Philadelphia for prospect Jeff Woywitka and a draft pick.

8.22 D. Dominik Hasek of the Detroit Red Wings

Hasek's unconventional style between the pipes stopped a lot of rubber during his career, but the Gumby-like goalie may have saved his most unusual move for 2003–04, when he forfeited almost U.S.$3 million of his U.S.$6-million salary after a bad groin limited him to 14 games.

8.23 A. The Nashville Predators

After a disappointing finish in 2001–02, Predators owner Craig Leipold told fans that 2002–03's season-ticket price increase would be refunded if the team didn't make postseason. Without the offer, a club survey of season-ticket subscribers predicted only 70 per cent would renew. With the offer in place, the Predators managed to attract 83 per cent of their fans back, even though there was almost no upgrade in player personnel from the previous year. As it turned out, Nashville finished 24th overall, missed the playoffs by nine points and Leipold paid back the ticket-price increase to his customers. In a related story, an auditor determined the team is costing Nashville taxpayers about U.S.$7 million per year.

8.24 B. The New York Islanders

After insulting fans with the worst ticket-price gouge in recent memory, a 38 per cent hike on ducats for 2003–04, Islanders owner Charles Wang did a Savardian spinarama and offered free tickets for the first two playoff rounds of 2004 to anyone who purchased a season ticket package for the 2004–05 campaign. While the deal netted almost 1,500 loyal fans by the March 21 deadline, it cost the Islanders about U.S.$650,000 per playoff game. Wang said at the time he didn't need approval from the NHL, joking "They let me lose as much [money] as I want, any way I want."

8.25 D. U.S.$800,000

On April 18, 1999, in the Blues' last regular-season match, Pavol Demitra needed one point to hit the 90-point plateau and activate a U.S.$500,000 incentive clause in his contract. With time running out and St. Louis ahead 3–2, Demitra passed up an open net opportunity and fed the puck to Scott Young, who was one goal short of the 25 he needed to collect on his own U.S.$300,000 bonus. Unfortunately, neither man benefited from Demitra's generosity. Young's shot was blocked by Los Angeles defenseman Jaroslav Modry. Asked how he could pass up a certain half-million, Demitra said, "Scott needed a goal." Worse still, earlier in the game, Demitra almost had his 90th point when he assisted on a goal by Lubos Bartecko. The goal was called back after video replay determined Bartecko was in the crease.

8.26 C. U.S.$225,000

While some players get paid extra to score, the injury-prone Clark got bonus money in 1992–93 just for showing up. After all, in five previous years he averaged only 37 games per season. Clark's contract called for bonuses of U.S.$100,000 for playing 45 games, an additional U.S.$75,000 if he played 55 and U.S.$50,000 more if he appeared in 65 matches. The Maple Leafs captain managed a career-high 66-game season and earned his U.S.$225,000 bonus (but missed an additional U.S.$100,000 when he failed to achieve 40 goals or 80 points). Clark scored 17 goals and 39 points for his base salary of U.S.$600,000.

8.27 D. U.S.$4 million

After the 1994–95 Collective Bargaining Agreement, the NHL supposedly had controls on salaries, especially for players in the entry level system. But player agents soon found a way to circumvent the limits of the cap by establishing a player bonus structure that required the Atlanta Thrashers to pay rookie sensations Kovalchuk and Heatley U.S.$4.37 million and U.S.$4.19 million respectively. Heatley and Kovalchuk were 1–2 in the rookie scoring race and in Calder Trophy votes for rookie of the year.

8.28 C. Between U.S.$3 million and U.S.$4 million

Spezza triggered a U.S.$3.85-million bonus by achieving three of six clauses in his contract, the final component being a 20-goal season. The 20-year-old centre scored 22 goals and earned U.S.$1.2 million in base salary in 2003–04.

8.29 B. U.S.$502,000

Did the sentence fit the crime? In what was hockey's most sensational story of 2003–04, Todd Bertuzzi sucker punched Steve Moore from behind and then, coming down on top of him, drove his face into the ice, giving Moore a concussion and facial lacerations and breaking three of his cervical vertebrae. Bert's roundhouse right to Moore's head was in retaliation for the Avalanche forward's borderline hit on Markus Naslund in a February 16 game that left the Canuck captain with a concussion. Bertuzzi paid a steep price for following hockey's so-called "code" of retaliation. The Vancouver star put another player's career in doubt and he was suspended the rest of the regular season and the entire playoffs, worth U.S.$502,000.

8.30 C. Between U.S.$250,000 and U.S.$400,000

The $386,178 was deducted from Fedorov's $14-million paycheque thanks to his five-game suspension for a slashing incident in February 1999. Fedorov had swung his stick with his right hand and struck the Islanders' Zdeno Chara on the neck. Chara collapsed and remained on the ice for several minutes. Fedorov was also assessed a match penalty for deliberately injuring a player.

8.31 A. A water bottle

Jeremy Roenick, like Brett Hull, is no "pussy-footer" when venting his anger and frustration on national television. After a January 13, 2004, 6–2 loss to the Buffalo Sabres, Roenick, who had been high-sticked in the face without a penalty call to the offender, Rory Fitzpatrick, said in a post-game televised rant: "Look at me... I'm bleeding like a stuck pig... how does he [referee Blaine Angus] not see blood dripping all over my face, all over my jersey. Terrible. Absolutely, absolutely terrible." But Roenick's words were cheap compared to the cost of firing a water bottle at Angus after the referee's non-call on the play. Launched from the Flyer bench, it skipped across the ice and clipped the official just above the skates—a pretty good throw considering the distance, though the indiscretion earned Roenick a gross misconduct and an unsportsmanlike conduct penalty worth a one-game suspension and U.S.$91,463.41 to the NHL Players Emergency Assistance Fund. NHL commissioner Gary Bettman admitted that the ref blew the call, but said Roenick could have received three games for the bottle toss. That touched off another tirade by Roenick, who later apologized for criticizing the league. Perhaps the best quote at that time came from Roenick's wife, Tracy, who said: "I have to look at you across the dinner table. Will you stop messing up your face?"

8.32 B. Ted Leonsis of the Washington Capitals

In a bizarre incident following a 4–1 loss to Philadelphia in January 2004, Leonsis attacked Jason Hammer after the 20-year-old fan led a derisive chant and held up a sign that read "Caps Hockey; AOL Stock—See a Pattern?" at the MCI Center. According to witnesses, the Capitals owner and vice-chairman of America Online began choking Hammer, and security guards had to intervene. Leonsis later apologized but was suspended for a week and fined U.S.$100,000—a little more salt in the wound for the Capitals, who had a U.S.$30-million deficit in 2003–04.

8.33 C. U.S.$1,000

A number of players were outed for diving during the NHL's first-ever crackdown in 2002–03, including McCabe, Kasparaitis and DiPietro, who were among a slew of players fined U.S.$1,000. More embarrassing, however, was having their names listed in dressing rooms throughout the league. McCabe was most vocal after an incident with Vancouver's Todd Bertuzzi in March 2003. "They don't call half the [crap] that goes on," he told the *Toronto Star.* "I get speared in the [groin] the play before, then I get punched in the head and I go down and it's a dive?" Equally incensed were Edmonton's Marty Reasoner and Calgary's Oleg Saprykin, who figured they were owed penalty shots after being hauled down on breakaways during separate games in mid-March. Instead, both were called for diving and took penalties for their tumbles. Which begs the question: Who would ever dive on a breakaway? Mario Lemieux also weighed in on the NHL's new diving policy. "I don't think it's the place of the NHL to try to embarrass players. If they would just call the obstruction, nobody would have to dive," said Lemieux.

8.34 B. U.S.$100,000 to $150,000

Phoenix's Brad May lost U.S.$117,647 in salary after receiving the fourth-longest suspension in NHL history in November 2000. May's suspension for bashing Steve Heinze with a baseball-style swing across the face came shortly after Marty McSorley's year-long suspension for clubbing Donald Brashear in February 2000. May, then Brashear's Vancouver teammate, had responded to McSorley's slash by saying: "I have no respect for that guy ever again." Heinze was McSorley's teammate in Boston at the time of the Brashear attack. Was it a settling of accounts between tough guys? "I hope the McSorley incident had nothing to do with this," said Phoenix general manager Bobby Smith. May, known for his rugged play, had never been suspended before. He later apologized to Heinze, who needed nine stitches to close the gash.

8.35 D. The NHL uses it as an emergency fund for retired players and their families

Figures are rarely made public, but as an example, in 1992–93, the NHL collected supplementary discipline fines totalling U.S.$157,631, all of which was set aside to discreetly provide charitable assistance to retired players and their families.

8.36 C. U.S.$9,999

Following in the footsteps of football's Joe Montana and basketball's Michael Jordan, Wayne Gretzky held his first-ever fantasy camp for hockey's well-heeled fans. The U.S.$9,999 price tag, a neat tie-in to the game's most famous number, included airfare, luxury accommodations, meals and playing with and against Gretzky and other former pros such as Paul Coffey and Russ Courtnall. The four-day camp with a guest list of 72 participants was held in Scottsdale, Arizona.

8.37 D. More than U.S.$12,000

There may be larger inventories of hockey memorabilia outside the Hockey Hall of Fame, but few would compare in historical value to Mark Friedland's collection of hockey sticks, pucks and sweaters. The Aspen, Colorado, businessman owns more than 350 NHL game-worn jerseys, including a 1950 All-Star sweater worn by Maurice Richard that cost him U.S.$40,000. Among Friedland's most famous pucks is U.S. captain Mike Eruzione's game-winner from Team U.S.A.'s 4–3 victory against the Soviets at Lake Placid during the 1980 Olympics. That piece of vulcanized rubber sent the Americans to the gold-medal game, which they won against Finland. The puck cost Friedland U.S.$13,200.

8.38 B. The Maple Leafs' 1967 Stanley Cup banner

In the November 19, 2000, auction that stripped Maple Leaf Gardens down to bricks and mortar, everything that could be moved was sold off, including player banners, scoreboards, team benches, goal lights, penalty boxes, restroom signs and even the Zamboni. The priciest item was Toronto's 1967 Stanley Cup banner, which went to a telephone bidder for $60,000. The Zamboni sold for $26,000, a Leaf net sold for $10,500, the home penalty box brought $7,000 and George Armstrong's retired No. 10 banner earned $3,400. The most symbolic gesture of the day's proceedings was the sale of Conn Smythe's blue-and-white dressing room sign, "Defeat does not rest lightly on their shoulders." It fetched $7,600.

8.39 B. The Canadiens' 1993 Stanley Cup banner

Pierre Daoust, the owner of a suburban Montreal bar, spent $32,000 plus $4,000 in taxes for the Canadiens' most recent Stanley Cup banner. It was the highest price paid for any of the 145 items up for auction. The charity fundraiser drew 2,500 people who spent $726,750 on a wide array of memorabilia, including shot clocks, stick racks, autographed sweaters and even a latrine from the Forum washroom. One item that didn't go on the block was an original seat from Section 111. An ingenious thief, equipped with a pair of bolt cutters, had spirited it out of the Forum during a game a month earlier against the Ottawa Senators.

8.40 C. U.S.$6,500

At a Panthers' charity auction in February 2000, the bidding reached U.S.$6,500 for dinner with the Russian Rocket. But when Bure's then-girlfriend, tennis star Anna Kournikova, hopped onto the stage alongside the Florida sniper, the price nearly doubled to U.S.$12,500. The highest bidder won a dinner for eight, including the two celebrity athletes, at Bure's favourite restaurant in Miami's South Beach district.

8.41 C. U.S.$26,000

Every fan who attended Edmonton's Heritage Classic in November 2003 took home at least one piece of memorabilia: their ticket stub to the NHL's first outdoor game. Then the auctioning of the big-ticket items began. Gretzky's autographed jersey, one of three worn by the Great One during the geezer freezer, received the highest bid on eBay: U.S.$26,000. The sweater was purchased by an unidentified Edmonton man who also spent U.S.$9,600 on a Mark Messier jersey. "I thought it would be nice to keep them together," he said.

8.42 A. Steve Yzerman

Sales of 38-year-old Steve Yzerman's Detroit Red Wings sweater topped those of all NHL players' during 2003–04's regular season. In second place was Colorado's Peter Forsberg and in third was New Jersey's Martin Brodeur. The average age of the players with the NHL's top-10-selling sweaters was 34.8 years, far higher than other major sports and not a good sign for the league. All told, the NHL reaped U.S.$1.5 billion in sales of its licensed merchandise, which ranked fifth behind the NFL (U.S.$3.2 billion), NBA (U.S.$3 billion), MLB (U.S.$3 billion) and NASCAR (U.S.$2 billion).

8.43 D. 96 sweaters

You know the merchandising game has gotten out of hand when teams that have existed less than five years, such as the Minnesota Wild and Atlanta Thrashers, decide it's time to debut a third jersey. All told, there were 96 different uniforms worn by NHL teams, including two new All-Star team sweaters, in 2003–04. The Canucks, Oilers, Kings, Rangers and Bruins set a new record by wearing five each. The surge was sparked by the launch of the NHL's Vintage Hockey Program, which introduced home and away retro jerseys to the apparel sweepstakes.

GAME 8

Puck Crossword

IN THIS GAME EACH WORD is connected in the same way as a regular crossword. Starting at square number one, work clockwise around the four concentric rings or towards the centre along the spokes, filling in the correct answer from the clues below. Each answer begins with the letter of the previous word. Determine word length by using the clue numbers (e.g., the answer to "Around, number one" is eight letters long, since the next clue is number three).

Solutions are on page 563

AROUND

1. 1960s Montreal enforcer, John ________
3. Digit on back of jersey
5. 1970 Red Wing, Mickey ________
7. Enhancing drug
9. ________ Lindros
10. Wendel ________
12. 1970s Buffalo/LA D-man, Jerry ________
14. 1970s Flyers sniper, Bill ________
16. Buffalo coach, Lindy ________
17. Club; NHL ________
18. Too many ________ on the ice
19 ________ Broten
20. 1970s Detroit winger, Nick ________
21. 1970s Ranger, Walt ________
22. 1980s Toronto–New Jersey winger, Jim ________
23. ID on back of sweater
24. 1990s Montreal-Anaheim tough guy, Todd ________
25. 1970s Flyer winger, Simon _____
26. Drive or ________ into the boards
27. 1980s journeyman winger with the Sabres, Pens, Devils, Gary ________
28. 2000 Dallas veteran, Kirk ________
29. 1990s Boston-Dallas winger, David ________
30. Scoring champ Marcel ________
31. Old-timer Hab, ________ Lach
32. 1970s Boston's Derek ________
33. Hockey ________ in Canada
34. The Dallas Stars' state

TOWARDS CENTRE

1. ________ "the Fog" Shero
2. The Blues' hometown
4. The goalie is ________ the pipes
6. ________ it up in the corners
8. Eight-time Hab Cup-winner, Claude ________
11. Mario ________
13. New York team
15. NHL commissioner Gary________

9

The Rookies

EVEN THOUGH MIKE BOSSY averaged 77 goals per year playing junior for the Laval Nationals from 1972 to 1977, the knock against him at the NHL draft tables in 1977 was his defense and a belief by team scouts that he was too soft for the bang-bang play at the big league level. Incredibly, 14 teams passed on the CHL's all-time leading goal-scorer before the New York Islanders selected him 15th overall. Safe to say, the other 14 clubs suffered a little sniper envy during Bossy's rookie campaign. He shattered the old freshman mark of 44 with 53 goals in 1977–78, winning the Calder Trophy as top rookie, and reminded a lot of hockey managers that scoring goals is often the best defense against losing games. In this chapter, we wise up to some of hockey's best first-year wonders.

Answers are on page 214

9.1 At what age did the oldest player make his debut in an NHL game?

A. 35 years old
B. 37 years old
C. 39 years old
D. 41 years old

9.2 What is the fastest goal by a rookie in his first NHL game?

A. Less than 30 seconds
B. Between the one- and two-minute mark
C. Between the two- and five-minute mark
D. More than five minutes

9.3 What did rookie defenseman Thomas Pock accomplish in his first game with the New York Rangers in 2003–04?

A. He scored a goal
B. He scored a goal into his own net
C. He scored a goal that was called back
D. He scored a goal that was awarded to another player

9.4 Considering the NHL record for the fastest goal by a rookie is 15 seconds, what is the freshman record for the fastest assist?

A. 12 seconds
B. The same time, 15 seconds
C. 30 seconds
D. One minute

9.5 What is the record for most goals by a player in his first NHL game?

A. One goal
B. Two goals
C. Three goals
D. Four goals

9.6 What is the record for most points accumulated by a player in his first NHL game?

A. Three points
B. Four points
C. Five points
D. Six points

9.7 Which NHL rookie made an immediate impact in 1995–96, scoring four goals with his first four shots on net?

A. The Sharks' Jan Caloun
B. The Oilers' Miroslav Satan
C. The Canadiens' Brian Savage
D. The Islanders' Todd Bertuzzi

9.8 Which All-Star defenseman did Mario Lemieux beat to score his first NHL goal?

A. Boston's Ray Bourque
B. Montreal's Larry Robinson
C. Edmonton's Paul Coffey
D. Chicago's Chris Chelios

9.9 Which rookie scored two goals in four seconds in 1995–96 to tie the record for the fastest pair of goals in NHL annals?

A. The Hawks' Eric Daze
B. The Jets' Deron Quint
C. The Panthers' Radek Dvorak
D. The Senators' Daniel Alfredsson

9.10 Who was the first rookie in NHL history to score two penalty-shot goals in one season? It happened in 2000–01.

A. Brad Richards of the Tampa Bay Lightning
B. David Vyborny of the Columbus Blue Jackets
C. Marian Gaborik of the Minnesota Wild
D. Martin Havlat of the Ottawa Senators

9.11 When was the last time a rookie scored five goals in one game?

A. 1936–37
B. 1956–57
C. 1976–77
D. 1996–97

9.12 What is the most game-winning goals scored by an NHL rookie in a season?

A. Seven game-winners
B. Eight game-winners
C. Nine game-winners
D. 10 game-winners

9.13 Which NHLer holds the league record for the most power-play goals in a rookie season?

A. The Islanders' Mike Bossy
B. Calgary's Joe Nieuwendyk
C. Pittsburgh's Mario Lemieux
D. Edmonton's Wayne Gretzky

9.14 How long did Bernie Geoffrion's 1951–52 rookie record of 30 goals last?

A. One year
B. Five to 10 years
C. 10 to 15 years
D. More than 15 years

9.15 Who was the first NHL rookie to post a 50-goal season?

A. Rick Martin
B. Mike Bossy
C. Mario Lemieux
D. Joe Nieuwendyk

9.16 Who was the first NHL rookie to score 100 points?

A. Guy Lafleur
B. Peter Stastny
C. Bobby Clarke
D. Denis Savard

9.17 Whose NHL rookie scoring record did Gilbert Perreault break when he tallied 72 points for the Buffalo Sabres in 1970–71?

A. Toronto's Howie Meeker
B. Montreal's Bernie Geoffrion
C. Chicago's Bill Mosienko
D. Toronto's Frank Mahovlich

9.18 How many points did Teemu Selanne score in 1992–93 to pass Peter Stastny's NHL rookie record of 109 points, set in 1980–81?

A. 112 points
B. 122 points
C. 132 points
D. 142 points

9.19 Which rookie has recorded the most points in a season since Teemu Selanne in 1992–93?

A. Joé Juneau
B. Mikael Renberg
C. Eric Lindros
D. Jason Allison

9.20 Who is the only NHL rookie to score 100 points and not win the Calder Trophy as top freshman?

A. Joé Juneau
B. Neal Broten
C. Larry Murphy
D. Steve Yzerman

9.21 How many rookies have won an NHL goal-scoring race?

A. None
B. One rookie
C. Three rookies
D. Five rookies

9.22 With the exception of the NHL's first season, when all players could be considered an NHL rookie, what is the highest percentage of team goals recorded by a freshman in league history?

A. 17 per cent
B. 27 per cent
C. 37 per cent
D. 47 per cent

9.23 Which rookie of the year posted the biggest increase in points in his second season?

A. Pavel Bure
B. Mike Bossy
C. Mario Lemieux
D. Peter Stastny

9.24 Who holds the NHL record for most games played by a rookie goalie?

A. Martin Brodeur
B. Jim Carey
C. Ed Belfour
D. Arturs Irbe

9.25 Who holds the NHL mark for most wins by a rookie goaltender?

A. Terry Sawchuk
B. Tony Esposito
C. Ed Belfour
D. Martin Brodeur

9.26 Which NHL goalie collected the most shutouts in his rookie season?

A. Terry Sawchuk
B. Glenn Hall
C. Tony Esposito
D. Ken Dryden

9.27 If the NHL record for the longest undefeated streak by a goalie in one season is 32 games, what is the record for a rookie netminder?

A. 19 games
B. 23 games
C. 27 games
D. 31 games

9.28 Rookie netminder Patrick Lalime of the Pittsburgh Penguins set an NHL record for most consecutive undefeated games at the start of a career by going undefeated in how many games in 1996–97?

A. 10 straight games
B. 13 straight games
C. 16 straight games
D. 19 straight games

9.29 What is the age of the youngest goalie in NHL history?

A. 16 years old
B. 17 years old
C. 18 years old
D. 19 years old

9.30 What is the record for regular-season goals by a rookie defenseman?

A. 23 goals
B. 25 goals
C. 27 goals
D. 29 goals

9.31 Which defenseman scored the most points in his rookie season?

A. New York's Brian Leetch in 1987–88
B. Calgary's Gary Suter in 1985–86
C. Boston's Ray Bourque in 1979–80
D. Los Angeles' Larry Murphy in 1980–81

9.32 In what year did a rookie defenseman first record 50 assists in one season?

A. 1957–58
B. 1967–68
C. 1977–78
D. 1987–88

9.33 Who beat Bobby Hull as rookie of the year in 1957–58?

A. Stan Mikita
B. Ralph Backstrom
C. Tim Horton
D. Frank Mahovlich

9.34 Which goalie won the Calder Trophy as rookie of the year over Steve Yzerman in 1983–84?

A. Tom Barrasso
B. John Vanbiesbrouck
C. Pelle Lindbergh
D. Ed Belfour

9.35 In Wayne Gretzky's first NHL season, 1979–80, who won the Calder Trophy as NHL rookie of the year?

A. Ray Bourque
B. Mike Foligno
C. Peter Stastny
D. Wayne Gretzky

9.36 Who was the last rookie to be traded midway through the year he won the Calder Trophy?

A. Ed Litzenberger, in 1955
B. Roger Crozier, in 1965
C. Eric Vail, in 1975
D. It has never happened

9.37 Which goalie from the six-team era is the only Calder Trophy winner in NHL history to miss an entire season after copping rookie honours?

A. Toronto's Frank McCool in 1945
B. New York's Gump Worsley in 1953
C. Detroit's Glenn Hall in 1956
D. Detroit's Roger Crozier in 1965

9.38 Who was the first skater in NHL history to win the Calder Trophy as top rookie and a First All-Star berth in the same season?

A. Denis Potvin
B. Bobby Orr
C. Ray Bourque
D. Jacques Laperriere

9.39 Of all the players to win the Calder Trophy, which rookie amassed the most penalty minutes?

A. Bobby Orr in 1966–67
B. Denis Potvin in 1973–74
C. Gary Suter in 1985–86
D. Barret Jackman in 2002–03

9.40 Prior to Atlanta players Dany Heatley and Ilya Kovalchuk's 1–2 finish in Calder Trophy voting in 2001–02, when was the last time a club iced rookies who ranked top two in the balloting?

A. 1955–56
B. 1965–66
C. 1975–76
D. 1985–86

The Rookies

Answers

9.1 D. 41 years old

St. Louis defenseman Connie Madigan was a ripe 38 years old and had been bouncing from team to team, playing in three amateur and four semi-pro leagues (WHL, CHL, IHL and AHL), when the big call came from the Blues organization on February 6, 1973. Madigan stayed for just 20 games but earned three assists, 25 penalty minutes and the distinction by many in hockey as the league's oldest rookie—though Hugh Lehman might take issue, if he were alive today. On November 17, 1926, Lehman played his first NHL game at 41 years old. A long-time pro goalie on the old western teams, Lehman joined the NHL after the PCHA and WHL folded in 1926. His rookie status was by definition only, considering he was a Stanley Cup winner. Before the NHL played its first season in 1917–18, Lehman backstopped the Vancouver Millionaires to the Cup in 1915, which was 11 years prior to his first NHL game. He won it, a 4–1 Chicago victory against Toronto.

9.2 A. Less than 30 seconds

Gus Bodnar, the same man who assisted on the NHL's fastest hat trick, also holds another "fastest" league record—the quickest goal by a rookie. Bodnar, in his first NHL game, scored 15 seconds after the first puck was dropped on October 30, 1943. His victim was the Rangers' rookie netminder, Ken McAuley, also appearing in his first NHL game. Among modern-day players, Buffalo's Danny Gare has the fastest time. Just 18 seconds after the puck was dropped on October 10, 1974, Gare, a 20-year-old winger up from the Calgary Centennials, scored his first NHL goal on his first shift against the NHL's top scoring line, the Bruins' Phil Esposito, Wayne Cashman and Ken Hodge. Gare and the Sabres pounded the Bruins 9–5. More recently, Alexander Mogilny did it in 20 seconds in 1989.

9.3 A. He scored a goal

Every season has a few heartwarming stories of college players who suddenly become NHLers overnight after a regular goes down with an injury, and fate turns their dreams into reality—at least for one game. Consider University of Massachusetts defenseman Thomas Pock, who got to play in a Rangers game on March 23, 2004. Pock's invite came while he was hanging out with classmates at his off-campus apartment in Amherst, N.Y. That night, on a 50-foot wrist shot against Pittsburgh's J.S. Aubin, Pock hit the rookie jackpot and scored a goal in his first game. "When I was driving down with my roommate," Pock told the *Hockey News*, "I was joking and I told him I was going to score a goal in the game. He was laughing," said Pock. "And I was laughing back, like 'Yeah, right.' It's overwhelming." Pock played five more games for the Rangers in 2003–04.

9.4 A. 12 seconds

The NHL *Official Guide and Record Book* lists Toronto's Gus Bodnar as the fastest goal scorer from the start of a career. But who nailed the fastest point on an assist in his NHL debut and how long did he take? Fresh out of high school hockey in Massachusetts, 18-year-old Bobby Carpenter of the Washington Capitals assisted on a Ryan Walter goal 12 seconds after the opening faceoff against Buffalo on October 7, 1981.

9.5 C. Three goals

Two rookies are tied for this goal-scoring record, and they couldn't be further apart in experience. Réal Cloutier, a two-time WHA scoring champion, wasted no time after landing in the NHL, recording a hat trick in his first NHL game on October 10, 1979. Thirty-five years earlier, on January 14, 1943, Alex Smart, an unknown forward from Brandon, Manitoba, stepped onto Montreal Forum ice for his first match and scored three times. But while Cloutier's NHL career lasted six seasons and 344 points, Smart's scoring touch quickly faded: seven games later he was on the train home. Of some consolation, Smart's hat trick did earn Montreal a 5–1 win over Chicago, versus Cloutier's goals, which were in vain; Quebec lost to Atlanta 5–3.

9.6 C. Five points

Al Hill will never be anyone famous in hockey, but he is remembered for accomplishing something very big when he broke into the league on February 14, 1977. The blush of first love on that Valentine's Day must have brought a wide grin to the Philadelphia Flyers: Hill scored a league-record five points in his NHL debut. Called up earlier that day from the AHL Springfield Indians, Hill wasted no time getting on the scoreboard, blasting a 45-footer past St. Louis Blues goalie Yves Belanger only 36 seconds into the first period. Hill scored again on his second shot just 11 minutes later, and went on to add three assists in the Flyers' 6–4 win. Oddly, Hill was never able to duplicate the magic of his first game. He bounced back and forth between the Flyers and the minors for eight seasons, collecting an NHL career total of 95 points.

9.7 A. The Sharks' Jan Caloun

San Jose's 1992 fourth-round pick was not supposed to be one of the Sharks' premier prospects, but Caloun's startling NHL debut may have caused the team to reassess its opinion. After being called up from the Kansas City Blades of the IHL on March 18, 1996, the Czech scored in his first game against Boston, then added two more in his second game versus Winnipeg and a fourth against Calgary in Game 3; all in only four shots on net. Caloun ended the season with eight goals on 20 shots, an accuracy rate of 40 per cent.

9.8 A. Boston's Ray Bourque

Just 78 seconds after stepping onto the ice in his first NHL game, Lemieux scored his first professional goal. With the Bruins on the attack, Mario went to the point as Ray Bourque was about to fire a shot. The blast hit Lemieux in the pads. He picked up the loose puck, shifted around the Boston All-Star and was gone for a clean breakaway on goalie Pete Peeters. Lemieux deked Peeters out of position with a brilliant move to pot his first NHL goal. It came in Mario's first game, on his first shift, on his first shot.

9.9 B. The Jets' Deron Quint

Quint scored only five goals in 1995–96, but the rookie defenseman put two of them behind Joaquin Gage of the Edmonton Oilers on December 15, 1995, in an amazing four seconds, equalling a Nels Stewart record that had stood since 1931. The goals came at 7:51 and 7:55 of the second period of a 9–4 Winnipeg win.

9.10 B. David Vyborny of the Columbus Blue Jackets

A few players have managed two penalty-shot goals in one season and Pavel Bure established the record at three in 1997–98, but until Vyborny came along no rookie had ever scored more than one goal mano-a-mano. The Blue Jackets freshman scored against Chicago's Robbie Tallas on October 15, 2000, and against Nashville's Tomas Vokoun on March 19, 2001.

9.11 C. 1976–77

It was a night few will forget and a record not since duplicated by a rookie. In just his fourth NHL game, New York Ranger rookie Don Murdoch scored five times against Minnesota on October 12, 1976. He immediately became the darling of the hockey world. Murdoch picks up the story of his fifth goal with just 10 seconds on the clock in Chris McDonell's *The Game I'll Never Forget:* "I jumped out onto the ice like a kid in a candy store and glided down to the Minnesota end of the ice. That's where Espo (Phil Esposito) pulled me aside. 'Listen kid,' said Espo, 'Stay here. Don't move from here. If I win the draw, you'll get it. If I lose the draw, don't move. I'll get it to you.' I just looked at him and nodded." Murdoch stood in the exact spot where he was told to and waited. A moment later he rippled the net for his fifth of the night. Murdoch is the only teenager in NHL history to record a five-goal game.

9.12 C. Nine game-winners

Since 1966–67, when the NHL began tabulating such stats, no rookie has scored more game-winners than Steve Larmer. In 1982–83, Larmer notched an unprecedented nine game-winning goals in his 43-goal first season with Chicago. Sometimes teamed with scoring ace Denis Savard, Larmer established his credentials as a hard worker who could score crucial goals. He had great acceleration, a big slap shot and exceptional hand-eye coordination that produced consistently throughout his career. Larmer was also one of the league's best "wrong-shooting" wings, a natural right-winger who shot left. Joe Nieuwendyk's eight game-winners in 1987–88 ranks second; Tim Kerr, Barry Pederson and Teemu Selanne are third with seven game-winners in their respective rookie years. A number of other players notched six game-winning goals in their NHL debuts, including Wayne Gretzky in 1979–80.

9.13 B. Calgary's Joe Nieuwendyk

No rookie since 1967 has scored more on the power play than Joe Nieuwendyk. In his first NHL season, 1987–88, Nieuwendyk was used in almost every critical situation involving special teams, but especially when Calgary had the man-advantage. Of his 51 goals that season, Nieuwendyk amassed an awesome 31 power-play goals, far and away the most among rookies in NHL history, easily topping freshman Mike Bossy's 25 man-advantage goals in 1977–78 and just three short of the league-record 34 scored by six-year veteran Tim Kerr in 1985–86. Few NHLers have ever been given so much responsibility so early in their careers. Nieuwendyk was rejected by every NHL team before being selected 27th overall in 1985.

NHL Rookies with Most Power-Play Goals*

PLAYER	TEAM	SEASON	GP	G	PP
Joe Nieuwendyk	Calgary	1987–88	75	51	31
Mike Bossy	NYI	1977–78	73	53	25
Teemu Selanne	Winnipeg	1992–93	84	76	24
Rick Martin	Buffalo	1971–72	73	44	19

**Current to 2004–05*

9.14 D. More than 15 years

Among the many French Canadian superstars to come out of the fabled Montreal Canadiens dressing room during the dynasty years of the 1950s, few, with the exception of Jean Béliveau and Maurice and Henri Richard, could compare in spirit or shooting skill to Geoffrion. Yet, forever in Béliveau and Richard's shadow, Geoffrion had to be content with being the number-three star forward (almost as Ron Francis was to Mario Lemieux and Jaromir Jagr in Pittsburgh). With any other team, Geoffrion would have been a franchise player. But on the talent-rich Canadiens, he was expected to be great but was not honoured for his greatness. Indeed, when he won the NHL scoring race in 1954–55, Montreal fans booed him long and loud for "stealing" the scoring title from the suspended Maurice Richard. And among the Habs' historic jersey numbers, Geoffrion's No. 5 is still not retired by the club. Yet he won two scoring titles, five Stanley Cups and was the second NHLer to score 50 goals in a season. Perhaps his greatest scoring feat came in his rookie year when he scored an eye-popping 30 goals, a record that stood for 17 seasons until Danny Grant and Norm Ferguson ripped 34 goals in 1968–69.

9.15 B. Mike Bossy

You've heard of the scorer's touch? Mike Bossy had it in spades. His feel for a hockey stick was so precise that he'd send the sticks he ordered back to the manufacturer if they were an ounce too heavy. Bossy exhibited the same precision with his shots: not only did he get them away quickly, they were incredibly accurate. In his rookie season with the New York Islanders in 1977–78, for example, Bossy fired 53 goals behind opposition netminders. No other NHL rookie had ever scored so many goals. The dreaded sophomore jinx also held no terror for Bossy. The next year, he rifled in 69 goals to establish a new single-season record for right-wingers.

9.16 B. Peter Stastny

Still considered a rookie at 24, and after several seasons with Slovan in his native Czechoslovakia, Stastny turned the NHL inside out in his debut season, recording a 39–70–109 start. He potted his 100th point on a Michel Goulet goal on March 29, 1981. It was an NHL first for a rookie. (Wayne Gretzky, who scored 137 points in his freshman year, 1979–80, was not considered an NHL rookie because of his WHA service.)

9.17 C. Chicago's Bill Mosienko

Mosienko, who is best known for the fastest hat trick in NHL history (three goals in 21 seconds), established a new NHL record for points by a rookie when he collected 70 points with the Chicago Blackhawks in 1943–44. Mosienko's mark would stand for 27 years until Gilbert Perreault broke it in 1970–71. However, Perreault played 78 games that season while Mosienko set his standard in a 50-game schedule.

9.18 C. 132 points

In NHL history, no rookie has ever matched Selanne for sheer impact on the record books. In his freshman campaign he was christened the Finnish Flash after scoring an unprecedented 132 points, 23 more than Peter Stastny's old record of 109. Selanne's 76 goals shared the league lead in 1992–93 and he topped Mike Bossy's rookie mark of 53 by an extraordinary 23 goals. Moreover, Selanne's goal count was the fifth-highest total in history. His scoring streaks that year awed the hockey world; in one 17-game stretch he netted 20 goals and 14 assists. So how did an NHL rookie produce such a dramatic start? At 22, he was almost three years older than the average rookie; also, combined with his training in the Finnish elite league and his Canada Cup and Olympic experiences, Selanne was far more mature and prepared. Under the grind of an 84-game schedule, he proved his readiness and maturity, to say nothing of his hockey skills.

9.19 B. Mikael Renberg

Mikael Renberg was one of the first Flyers to benefit offensively from the play of Eric Lindros. In his rookie season in Philadelphia, the Swedish winger scored 82 points, the highest point total by an NHL freshman since Teemu Selanne netted 132 in 1992–93. Renberg finished first among rookies in goals (38), points (82) and shots (195) in 1993–94. He also broke Jorgen Pettersson's NHL record of 37 goals by a Swedish rookie (1980–81).

9.20 A. Joé Juneau

While Winnipeg's Teemu Selanne was tearing up the league establishing freshman records of 76 goals and 132 points, Juneau was quietly turning a few heads with his 102-point rookie effort. It's the highest total ever scored by a first-year player who didn't win Calder honours; and that includes Neal Broten's 98 points in 1981–82, Larry Murphy's 76 points in 1984–85 and Steve Yzerman's 87 points in 1983–84. Only five freshmen have ever topped the 100-point plateau. All, except Juneau, won rookie-of-the-year status.

The NHL's All-Time Top-Point-Scoring Rookies*

PLAYER	TEAM	SEASON	GP	G	A	PTS
Teemu Selanne	Wpg	1992–93	84	76	56	132
Peter Stastny	Que	1980–81	77	39	70	109
Dale Hawerchuk	Wpg	1981–82	80	45	58	103
Joé Juneau	Bos	1992–93	84	32	70	102
Mario Lemieux	Pit	1984–85	73	43	57	100

**Current to 2004–05*

9.21 C. Three rookies

A number of old-time players (Babe Dye, Charlie Conacher, Gord Drillon and Cooney Weiland) won goal-scoring titles in their second seasons, but only three players in NHL history have done it as rookies. The Montreal Maroons' Nels Stewart established his scoring might in 1925–26, firing a league-high 34 goals to become the first NHL freshman to win the goal-scoring race. In 1938–39, Boston Bruins rookie Roy Conacher scored 26 goals to top the goal-scorers' list. In 1992–93, the Winnipeg Jets' Teemu Selanne became the third rookie to lead the NHL in goals, tying Alexander Mogilny with 76.

9.22 C. 37 per cent

As rookie starts go, Nels Stewart's was nothing short of incredible. Although Stewart, at six foot one, 195 pounds, had the average height and weight of today's players, he towered above the rest of the league in his era. He may not have been as nimble as other forwards, but he used his size to shoot fast and play tough, assets that were evident from his first season. The Montreal Maroons freshman won the 1925–26 scoring title with 42 points, took home the Hart Trophy as MVP and scored six of Montreal's 10 playoff goals to lead the second-year Maroons to the Stanley Cup. At the same time he amassed 119 minutes in box time, an extraordinary penalty total for a forward. And few could stop him in goal scoring. Of the 91 goals scored by Montreal in Stewart's rookie season, he owned 34 of them, a 37.4 per cent share. Among modern-day freshmen, Teemu Selanne was responsible for 24 per cent of the Winnipeg Jets' total offensive output, scoring 76 of Winnipeg's 322 goals in 1992–93.

9.23 A. Pavel Bure

The sophomore jinx is no myth. Many star rookies have trouble improving in their second year, partly because other teams are more aware of them, but also because the expectations placed on them are so much greater. Calder Trophy winners who defy the odds and improve in year two are rare commodities. The largest leap in points by a Calder winner belongs to Pavel Bure. After posting 60 points with the Vancouver Canucks in 1991–92, he upped his output to 110 in his sophomore year, a jump of 50 points. The Russian Rocket's goal count alone zoomed from 34 to 60. Bure's totals in his rookie campaign would have undoubtedly been higher had he played a full season, but a contract wrangle with Russian hockey officials delayed his debut with the Canucks until November 1991.

Biggest Improvements in Points by Calder Trophy Winners*

PLAYER	TEAM	SEASONS	POINTS	INCREASE
Pavel Bure	Vancouver	1991–92	60	
		1992–93	110	50
Mario Lemieux	Pittsburgh	1984–85	100	
		1985–86	141	41
Mike Bossy	N.Y. Islanders	1977–78	91	
		1978–79	126	35
Peter Stastny	Quebec	1980–81	109	
		1981–82	139	30
Luc Robitaille	Los Angeles	1986–87	84	
		1987–88	111	27

**Current to 2004–05 (Peter Forsberg's 66-point leap in points in his second year is discounted because his rookie season was the lockout-shortened 1994–95 campaign)*

9.24 C. Ed Belfour

No rookie recorded more games played in his freshman year than Ed Belfour, who laced up for 74 games in 1990–91. Belfour won almost everything that year, including the Vezina Trophy as top goaltender, the Calder Trophy as top rookie, the Jennings Trophy for the best goals-against average and status as a member of the NHL All-Rookie and First All-Star teams. Old-timers

Johnny Bower, Terry Sawchuk, Glenn Hall and Roger Crozier split second place in this category; each played the maximum 70-game schedule during their rookie seasons.

9.25 A. Terry Sawchuk

Terry Sawchuk wasted no time establishing himself as an NHL star. The freshman goalie took the league by storm, recording 44 wins, 11 shutouts and a 1.99 goals-against average as he led the Detroit Red Wings to a first-place finish in 1950–51. Sawchuk's 44 victories set an NHL record for wins by a goalie that has since been surpassed by only one other netminder: Bernie Parent, who posted 47 for the Philadelphia Flyers during his eighth NHL campaign in 1973–74. Ed Belfour narrowly missed equalling Sawchuk's rookie standard when he notched 43 wins for Chicago in 1990–91.

9.26 C. Tony Esposito

After just 13 games and a Stanley Cup with Montreal in 1968–69, Tony Esposito moved to Chicago the following season and proved his number one status by establishing the NHL benchmark for shutouts. Esposito bagged a modern-day record 15 zeroes in 1969–70, his rookie NHL season. He was named to the First All-Star team, and won the Calder Trophy as top rookie and the Vezina Trophy as best goalie.

Rookie Shutout Kings*

PLAYER	TEAM	YEAR	GP	SO
Tony Esposito	Chicago	1969–70	63	15
George Hainsworth	Montreal	1926–27	44	14
Tiny Thompson	Boston	1928–29	44	12
Glenn Hall	Detroit	1955–56	70	12
Terry Sawchuk	Detroit	1950–51	70	11

**Current to 2004–05*

9.27 C. 27 games

Boston's Gerry Cheevers owns the league record with a 32-game undefeated streak of 24 wins and eight ties in 1971–72, but among rookie netminders, Philadelphia's Pete Peeters has the longest stretch without a loss. Peeters went undefeated in 27 games in 1979–80 as the Flyers set their own NHL record: a 35-game unbeaten streak. While the *NHL Official Guide and Record Book* refers to Grant Fuhr's 23-game streak in 1981–82 as the longest span by a goalie in his year, Peeters does edge Fuhr in this category. At issue is the fact that Peeters played five games in 1978–79, his first year, but not in his rookie season.

9.28 C. 16 straight games

Patrick Lalime's emergence as the main man in the Penguins net was as unexpected as it was sudden. The last goalie selected in the 1993 draft and the 156th player taken overall, Lalime had spent two very ordinary seasons in the minors before being promoted to the big club early in 1996–97 as a backup to Ken Wregget. When Wregget went down with a pulled hamstring, 22-year-old Lalime stepped into the breach and immediately went on a spectacular roll, going unbeaten in 16 straight games (14–0–2). His streak broke the NHL record of 14 games, shared by Montreal's Ken Dryden (12–0–2 in 1970–71) and Boston's Ross Brooks (11–0–3 in 1972–73). Colorado finally snapped the string by defeating Lalime and the Penguins 4–3 in overtime. Ironically, Lalime's goaltending opponent that night was none other than his idol, Patrick Roy.

9.29 B. 17 years old

Harry "Apple Cheeks" Lumley was signed by Detroit when he was only 16, and started his first NHL game at age 17.1 years on December 22, 1943, losing to Chicago 7–1. Lumley played two more games that season, including one the following night against his Detroit teammates when New York "borrowed" him after its goalie, Ken McAuley, went down. Lumley lost again, 5–3. It would be the only occasion the future All-Star netminder played for the Rangers in an outstanding 16-year career that took him to every one of the Original Six teams except Montreal. In 2001–02, Olivier Michaud made hockey headlines when he backstopped Montreal and became the NHL's next-youngest netminder at 18.1 years.

9.30 A. 23 goals

By the end of 1988–89, the Rangers knew that their first-round draft pick of 1986 had not been wasted on just another overrated star college player. Brian Leetch quickly demonstrated that his electrifying raw talent had impact at the NHL level. His hard, accurate shot and superior defensive skills made him a game-breaking defenseman of the calibre of Bobby Orr and Ray Bourque. His creativity as a playmaker and scorer was almost scary. In 1988–89, Leetch won the Calder Trophy, potting an NHL record of 23 goals by a rookie rearguard.

9.31 D. Los Angeles' Larry Murphy in 1980–81

Among the NHL's top point-earning blueliners, Murphy quietly went about his job, working hard on defense, leading attacks and directing power plays. Although he was one of the many offensive-minded D-men to come along and make their scoring presence known after Bobby Orr, Murphy was never as conspicuous as Ray Bourque, Brian Leetch or Chris Chelios. The exception might be Murphy's rookie year, 1980–81, when he grabbed the spotlight with his startling 76-point season to break the freshman mark of 65 points held by Bourque. Why was the first-year defenseman afforded all the ice time in Los Angeles? Coach Bob Berry believed that Murphy could easily make the transition from junior hockey to the NHL. In fact, Murphy's rookie record of 16–60–76 powered the Kings to a second-place finish in the Norris Division and the Triple Crown Line of Marcel Dionne, Dave Taylor and Charlie Simmer to its best season ever. Murphy finished fourth in team scoring, behind only Dionne, Taylor and Simmer, each of whom finished in the NHL's top 10. Murphy was runner-up to Quebec's Peter Stastny in Calder Trophy voting as top rookie.

The NHL's Top-Point-Scoring Rookie Defensemen*

PLAYER	TEAM	SEASON	G	A	PTS
Larry Murphy	Los Angeles	1980–81	16	60	76
Brian Leetch	NYR	1988–89	23	48	71
Gary Suter	Calgary	1985–86	18	50	68
Phil Housley	Buffalo	1982–83	19	47	66
Ray Bourque	Boston	1979–80	17	48	65
Chris Chelios	Montreal	1984–85	9	55	64

**Current to 2004–05*

9.32 C. 1977–78

The New York Islanders' Stefan Persson was a solid yet unspectacular defenseman who happened to find a place on a team of great destiny. In Sweden he had very low point totals, but with the Islanders he racked up an unprecedented 50 assists in his first season. Only rookies Chris Chelios and Larry Murphy have topped Persson in this category.

9.33 D. Frank Mahovlich

Although Bobby Hull's rookie regular-season record of 13–34–47 topped Mahovlich's 20–16–36, the Big M scored more points in Calder Trophy balloting than runner-up Hull. Mahovlich was teamed with Leaf linemates Ron Stewart and Dick Duff, two youngsters who complemented the St. Michael's College junior's long, powerful strides on the attack. And from his first NHL season, Mahovlich demonstrated an uncanny scoring ability, with masterful stickhandling and dead-accurate shots. Mahovlich played in three decades with three NHL teams, repeatedly delivering what had been predicted from the beginning: that he was a smooth-skating playmaker with the Midas touch around the net.

9.34 A. Tom Barrasso

In 1983–84, 18-year-old Steve Yzerman stepped into the NHL straight from junior hockey and had a rookie season most NHLers only dream about—scoring 39 goals and 48 assists to lead Detroit with 87 points. But Yzerman, chosen fourth overall in the 1983 draft, couldn't outscore the fifth pick, Barrasso, in Calder balloting. Barrasso, 18, also cracked the big leagues without playing one game on the farm, by compiling a strong 26–12–3 rookie record and the league's second-best average, 2.84. Besides winning top rookie honours, the Sabres freshman nabbed the Vezina Trophy and berths on both the NHL First All-Star team and the NHL All-Rookie team. Other rookie goalies who beat rookie snipers include: Ed Belfour over Sergei Fedorov (1991) and Ken Dryden over Rick Martin (1972).

9.35 A. Ray Bourque

Wayne Gretzky won almost every NHL award available to a forward but, like many of hockey's greatest, including Maurice Richard, Gordie Howe and Guy Lafleur, was denied the Calder Trophy. Because Gretzky played his first pro year of 1978–79 in the rival WHA (where he won the top rookie prize), the NHL disqualified him from the Calder race in 1979–80. That opened the door to Boston's Ray Bourque, who began his Hall of Fame career with a 17–48–65 record and top freshman honours. The rookie issue wasn't soon forgotten, however. Gretzky has long argued that if the NHL considers his WHA experience a pro year, shouldn't his WHA points count in his career totals?

9.36 A. Ed Litzenberger, in 1955

During the 1950s, Chicago was in a desperate situation. The floundering Blackhawks lived in the league basement, with nine last-place finishes in 11 seasons. Attendance had dropped to 4,500 per game. To beef up the Hawks' roster, the NHL asked teams to release almost a dozen players. In midseason, the Canadiens dealt Litzenberger to Chicago for a waiver fee. Chicago finished last again, but Litzenberger's hard shot and smooth skating earned him the Calder as top rookie. His

51 points on 23 goals and 28 assists ranked 12th best among all NHLers. Montreal's loss of Litzenberger had little bearing on its success. Montreal won five Stanley Cups between 1956 and 1960. Litzenberger, who played in a record 73 games during 1954–55's 70-game schedule (29 games in Montreal and 44 in Chicago), eventually won championships in Chicago in 1961 and Toronto in 1962, 1963 and 1964.

9.37 B. New York's Gump Worsley in 1953

Worsley got what he thought was his big break after the Rangers' Charlie Rayner suffered a career-ending knee injury in 1952. The raw rookie, fresh from the Saskatoon farm team, backstopped the weak New York team for the last 50 games of 1952–53, winning the Calder Trophy as top rookie with a 13–29–8 record. But when he asked for a $500 raise the next season, Worsley found himself in the WHL with Vancouver. "Everybody thinks Johnny Bower beat me out of a job but it had to be the money," says Worsley in Dick Irvin's book, *In the Crease.* "The next year, Camille Henry won the rookie award with the Rangers and he asked for a $500 raise. I got news for you: he ended up in Providence for most of the year." The celebrated Ranger centre, though healthy, didn't play a full NHL season until 1957–58. Such was the NHL during the six-team era.

9.38 C. Ray Bourque

Although a few goalies have been named both top rookie and a First All-Star (including Tony Esposito in 1970 and Glenn Hall in 1956), no skater, until Ray Bourque, had ever won both honours in the same year. No one. Not even Bobby Orr, Gordie Howe or Mike Bossy ever achieved the double honour. Bourque's first season, 1979–80, was a measure of his superb hockey instincts and a glimpse into the future. He won the Calder and his First All-Star team selection while setting an NHL record for rookie defensemen (65 points). His offensive production, like his work ethic, has been tireless through 22 seasons, making him the all-time leader in career goals (410), career assists (1,169) and career points (1,579). Like Doug

Harvey and Bobby Orr before him, Bourque's awesome talent lay in his skating and shooting skills, his deep passion for hockey and his timing and anticipation, which, as with Orr and Harvey, allowed him to orchestrate the pace of a game.

9.39 D. Barret Jackman in 2002–03

Denis Potvin owned this record among Calder winners for almost 30 years after amassing 175 minutes in 1973–74. Then, Jackman won with 190 bruising minutes in box time during 2002–03. Some griped about Detroit's flashy wing Henrik Zetterberg not copping the honour, but Jackman played a key role in helping the Blues post 99 points, eighth-best overall, during a season with team leader Chris Pronger sidelined. Jackman played well beyond his years and filled some very big skates, leading all Blues in plus-minus (plus 23) and games played (82) while averaging 20 minutes per game.

Rookie-of-the-Year Penalty Leaders*

PLAYER	TEAM	SEASON	SCORING	PIM
Barret Jackman	St. Louis	2002–03	3–16–19	190
Denis Potvin	NYI	1973–74	17–37–54	175
Gary Suter	Calgary	1985–86	18–50–68	141
Willi Plett	Atlanta	1976–77	33–23–56	123
Kent Douglas	Toronto	1962–63	7–15–22	105

**Current to 2004–05*

9.40 C. 1975–76

Only eight teammates have finished 1–2 in Calder voting since the trophy was first awarded in 1933. Prior to Heatley and Kovalchuk's first- and second-place finishes in 2001–02, the last club with the NHL's top two rookies was the New York Islanders in 1975–76, when Bryan Trottier won the Calder and Chico Resch finished runner-up.

GAME 9

The First Time

IN A POSITION THAT DEMANDS fending off attackers, few defensemen have ever been honoured as the league's most gentlemanly player. In fact, based on the number of blueliners to cop the Lady Byng Trophy, it's really become a forward's award, which may also have been Nicklas Lidstrom's conclusion after four runner-up finishes in Lady Byng balloting. The first winner among defensemen was Detroit's Bill Quackenbush, in 1949; the last, Red Kelly, won it with the Red Wings in 1951, 1953 and 1954. Match the other historic NHL firsts below with the blueliners responsible for them.

Solutions are on page 564

Mark Howe	Paul Coffey	Babe Pratt
Denis Potvin	Red Kelly	Ian Turnbull
Paul Reinhart	Bill Gadsby	Bobby Orr

1. ________ was the first defenseman to score 100 points for two NHL teams.
2. ________ was the first Norris Trophy winner as top D-man in the NHL.
3. ________ was the first blueliner in NHL history to get six assists in one game.
4. ________ was the first defenseman in history to collect 500 career points.
5. ________ was the first rearguard to score two playoff hat tricks.
6. ________ was the first blueliner to score two shorthanded goals in one game.
7. ________ was the first D-man to score five goals in an NHL game.
8. ________ was the first NHL defenseman to reach 1,000 career points.
9. ________ was the first modern-day NHL rearguard to score a hat trick in the playoffs.

10

United We Stand

GLORY OFTEN GOES TO THE INDIVIDUAL record holder, seldom to the club that helped land a player the hardware. For example, in 1976–77, while Guy Lafleur was turning goalies into pretzels and winning another scoring championship, Montreal was setting what all-time league record? During Lafleur's blitz the Canadiens gave no quarter to visiting teams on Montreal Forum ice for a record five-month stretch. They went undefeated in 34 home games (28–0–6) between November 1, 1976, to April 2, 1977. In this chapter we check out various team highs, from record-winning streaks to home sellouts.

Answers are on page 242

10.1 According to Chicago's original charter, what is the club's real name?

A. The Hawks
B. The Blackhawks
C. The Black Hawks
D. The Black-Eyed Hawks

10.2 Which NHL team has the oldest name in hockey?

A. Toronto—The Maple Leafs
B. Ottawa—The Senators
C. Boston—The Bruins
D. Montreal—The Canadiens

10.3 What is the longest streak by a team scoring the first goal in a game?

A. 10 games
B. 14 games
C. 18 games
D. 22 games

10.4 What is the fastest time in which one team has scored two goals?

A. Three seconds
B. Four seconds
C. Five seconds
D. Six seconds

10.5 What is the greatest number of goals scored by a team in the biggest third-period comeback in NHL history?

A. Three goals
B. Four goals
C. Five goals
D. Six goals

10.6 In 1992–93, the Pittsburgh Penguins set the NHL record for consecutive wins. How many games in a row did the club win?

A. 14 games
B. 17 games
C. 20 games
D. 23 games

10.7 Which team owns the NHL record for the longest winning streak from the start of a season?

A. The Buffalo Sabres in 1975–76
B. The Toronto Maple Leafs in 1993–94
C. The Edmonton Oilers in 1983–84
D. The Quebec Nordiques in 1985–86

10.8 What is the longest stretch of one-goal victories by one team?

A. Six wins
B. 10 wins
C. 16 wins
D. 22 wins

10.9 What is the NHL team record for most consecutive games without a goal?

A. Five games in a row
B. Six games in a row
C. Seven games in a row
D. Eight games in a row

10.10 In 1999–2000, a new record was set for most consecutive successful penalty kills by an NHL team. How many were recorded?

A. 23 straight penalty kills
B. 33 straight penalty kills
C. 43 straight penalty kills
D. 53 straight penalty kills

10.11 What is the most number of regular-season games one NHL team played before registering its first penalty shot in franchise history?

A. Fewer than 400 games
B. Between 400 and 600 games
C. Between 600 and 800 games
D. More than 800 games

10.12 Which team owns the record for scoring the most power-play goals in a season?

A. The Boston Bruins of 1971–72
B. The Edmonton Oilers of 1983–84
C. The Pittsburgh Penguins of 1988–89
D. The Detroit Red Wings of 1995–96

10.13 What is the most number of shorthanded goals scored by one team in a season?

A. 16 shorthanded goals
B. 26 shorthanded goals
C. 36 shorthanded goals
D. 46 shorthanded goals

10.14 What is the highest number of empty-net goals scored by one team in one NHL game?

A. Two empty-net goals
B. Three empty-net goals
C. Four empty-net goals
D. Five empty-net goals

10.15 Since the advent of the 44-game schedule in 1926–27, which is the only NHL team to go unbeaten on home ice for an entire season?

A. The Montreal Canadiens of 1943–44
B. The Montreal Canadiens of 1976–77
C. The New York Islanders of 1981–82
D. The Detroit Red Wings of 1995–96

10.16 Which NHL team holds the longest undefeated streak?

A. The Montreal Canadiens
B. The Detroit Red Wings
C. The Edmonton Oilers
D. The Philadelphia Flyers

10.17 From the time it entered the NHL, what is the record for the longest non-winning streak on the road by a team against another team?

A. 25 games
B. 35 games
C. 45 games
D. 55 games

10.18 From the time it entered the NHL, what is the record for the longest non-winning streak by a team against another team?

A. 14 games
B. 24 games
C. 34 games
D. 44 games

10.19 Which expansion team scored the most goals in its first NHL season?

A. The Edmonton Oilers in 1979–80
B. The Hartford Whalers in 1979–80
C. The Tampa Bay Lightning in 1992–93
D. The Florida Panthers in 1993–94

10.20 Which expansion team holds the NHL record for most points in its first year?

A. The Florida Panthers
B. The Philadelphia Flyers
C. The St. Louis Blues
D. The Anaheim Mighty Ducks

10.21 Which club holds the NHL record for road victories by a first-year team?

A. The San Jose Sharks
B. The Anaheim Mighty Ducks
C. The Tampa Bay Lightning
D. The Florida Panthers

10.22 What is the most number of consecutive wins posted by an expansion team in its first year?

A. Two straight wins
B. Three straight wins
C. Four straight wins
D. Five straight wins

10.23 Which expansion team set an NHL attendance record in its first season?

A. The Tampa Bay Lightning in 1992–93
B. The Mighty Ducks of Anaheim in 1993–94
C. The Atlanta Thrashers of 1999–2000
D. The Minnesota Wild of 2000–01

10.24 How many former Minnesota North Stars were still playing for the Dallas Stars when the Stars returned for the first time to play the Wild in Minnesota in 2000–01?

A. Only one, Mike Modano
B. Three players
C. Five players
D. Seven players

10.25 Which team first recorded 400 consecutive home sellouts?

A. The Toronto Maple Leafs
B. The New York Rangers
C. The Colorado Avalanche
D. The Boston Bruins

10.26 Which team averaged the highest attendance per game in one NHL season?

A. The Vancouver Canucks
B. The Montreal Canadiens
C. The Detroit Red Wings
D. The Chicago Blackhawks

10.27 What is the greatest number of regular-season and playoff games by a team in one season?

A. 106 games
B. 108 games
C. 110 games
D. 112 games

10.28 Which NHL team scored the most goals in one season?

A. The Boston Bruins in 1971–72
B. The Montreal Canadiens in 1976–77
C. The Edmonton Oilers in 1983–84
D. The Pittsburgh Penguins in 1990–91

10.29 What is the fewest goals allowed by a team in a minimum 80-game NHL schedule?

A. 154 goals
B. 164 goals
C. 174 goals
D. 184 goals

10.30 Which NHL team produced the first lineup with five 30-goal scorers in one season?

A. The Chicago Blackhawks
B. The Boston Bruins
C. The Edmonton Oilers
D. The Montreal Canadiens

10.31 Which NHL team in 1997–98 made hockey history by icing three teammates who each reached the 1,000-point plateau during the season?

A. The Washington Capitals
B. The New York Islanders
C. The Detroit Red Wings
D. The Edmonton Oilers

10.32 What is the most number of goalies one team has iced in one season?

A. Five goalies
B. Six goalies
C. Seven goalies
D. Eight goalies

10.33 What is the NHL record for most consecutive shutouts by a team to start a season?

A. Two games
B. Three games
C. Five games
D. Seven games

10.34 What is the greatest number of consecutive overtime games played in regular-season play by an NHL team?

A. Four overtime games
B. Five overtime games
C. Six overtime games
D. Seven overtime games

10.35 What is the NHL record for most overtime appearances by a team in one season?

A. 25 overtimes
B. 30 overtimes
C. 35 overtimes
D. 40 overtimes

10.36 Which team first recorded double digits in overtime wins in a year?

A. The Calgary Flames in 1999–2000
B. The Detroit Red Wings in 2000–01
C. The Vancouver Canucks in 2003–04
D. The St. Louis Blues in 2003–04

10.37 Name the only NHL team in history to place its players first, second, third and fourth in the scoring race in the same season.

A. The Pittsburgh Penguins
B. The Montreal Canadiens
C. The Edmonton Oilers
D. The Boston Bruins

10.38 Which NHL team has gone the longest without icing an NHL scoring champion?

A. The Toronto Maple Leafs
B. The Detroit Red Wings
C. The New York Rangers
D. The Chicago Blackhawks

10.39 Which is the only team in NHL history to score 100 more goals than any other team in the league?

A. The Boston Bruins of 1970–71
B. The Montreal Canadiens of 1976–77
C. The Edmonton Oilers of 1983–84
D. The Pittsburgh Penguins of 1992–93

10.40 Which is the only NHL team to score 200 more goals than it allowed in a season?

A. The Boston Bruins of 1970–71
B. The Montreal Canadiens of 1976–77
C. The Edmonton Oilers of 1984–85
D. The Detroit Red Wings of 1995–96

10.41 Of all defunct teams, which one recorded the greatest number of NHL wins?

A. The Montreal Maroons
B. The old Ottawa Senators
C. The California/Oakland Seals
D. The New York/Brooklyn Americans

10.42 Which team recorded the NHL's greatest point increase in a single-season turnaround?

A. The San Jose Sharks in 1993–94
B. The New York Islanders in 1974–75
C. The Boston Bruins in 1967–68
D. The Quebec Nordiques in 1992–93

Answers

10.1 B. The Blackhawks

Until 1986, the team's name was always written as two words: Black Hawks. But that year, someone in Chicago's front office discovered that the name had been written as one word, Blackhawks, in the team's original NHL charter of 1926, so club owner Bill Wirtz officially changed the spelling to conform to those documents. The name had been incorrectly written on everything from league scoresheets to club publicity for 60 years.

10.2 B. Ottawa—The Senators

The Senators' origins are rooted in the Ottawa City Hockey Club, which began playing the game around 1884 and later produced the famed multi-Stanley Cup-winning Silver Seven, a team named for its championship heroics during the era of the seven-man game prior to 1912. By the time the team won its fifth Stanley Cup in 1909, the team was called the Senators. The following season, 1909–10, when Montreal joined the National Hockey Association, the predecessor to the NHL, it was called the Canadiens. In North American professional sports, only Major League Baseball's Phillies (1883) and the National Football League's Cardinals (1899) have older names.

10.3 C. 18 games

During their dynasty years of the 1950s, the Montreal Canadiens were the greatest thing since, well, artificial ice was invented. Hockey's most-storied franchise produced some near-unbeatable team records, including this jewel: most consecutive games scoring the first goal. Between October 18 and November 29, 1959, the Canadiens scored the first goal in a record 18 straight games, of which they won 15 and tied three. The record for a club from the start of a season belongs to the 1985–86 Philadelphia Flyers and the 2003–04 Vancouver Canucks, who both notched the first goal in 12 consecutive matches.

Most Consecutive Games Scoring First Goal*

GAMES	TEAM	RECORD	STREAK
18	Montreal	15–0–3	Oct. 18–Nov. 29, 1959
15	Chicago	10–1–4	Dec. 10, 1967–Jan. 13, 1968
15	Montreal	13–1–1	Feb. 19–Mar. 18, 1972

**Current to 2004–05*

Most Consecutive Games Scoring First Goal from Start of Season*

GAMES	TEAM	RECORD	STREAK
12	Philadelphia	10–2–0	Oct. 10–Nov. 6, 1985
12	Vancouver	8–2–2	Oct. 9–Nov. 3, 2003

**Current to 2004–05*

10.4 A. Three seconds

Vegas oddsmakers wouldn't have given the Minnesota Wild better than million-to-one odds to crack this 73-year-old scoring record, an achievement that has held since the days of the Montreal Maroons in the 10-team NHL. Since then, four other clubs have equalled the Maroons' mark of four seconds for two goals. But the unlikely Wild managed goals just three seconds apart after getting third-period markers from Jim Dowd at 19:44 and then, with an empty Chicago net, from Richard Park at 19:47 to lift Minnesota to the 4–2 win over the Blackhawks on January 21, 2004.

10.5 C. Five goals

Toronto's Maple Leaf Gardens was the site of two fatal cave-ins, 13 years apart. In 1987, the Calgary Flames erased a 5–0 deficit with five third-period goals, then won the game on a goal by Colin Patterson at 1:30 of overtime. Toronto's Alan Bester gave up six goals in an elapsed time of 15:28. The St. Louis Blues' 2000 comeback at the Gardens began after coach Joel Quennville pulled goalie Roman Turek early in the third and put in backup Brent Johnson. The Blues roared back with six straight goals against Curtis Joseph in 15 minutes and seven seconds, the winning marker coming off the stick of Jochim Hecht, just 18 seconds into overtime. Besides the Maple Leafs as victims, the other constant in the two games was defenseman Al MacInnis, who played for the comeback team in both cases.

10.6 B. 17 games

The amazing surge of the 1992–93 Pittsburgh Penguins was sparked by the inspirational return of Mario Lemieux to the lineup after his seven weeks of treatment for Hodgkin's disease, a form of cancer. With Lemieux leading the charge, Pittsburgh put together a 17-game winning streak from March 9 to April 10, 1993. The streak ended on the last night of the season, when Pittsburgh was held to a 6–6 tie by the New Jersey Devils. Ironically, when the Devils made a run at the Penguins' record in 2000–01, it was Pittsburgh who stopped their streak at 13 straight wins. The next-best record belongs to the New York Islanders, who had 15 wins in 1981–82.

10.7 B. The Toronto Maple Leafs in 1993–94

In 1993–94, the Toronto Maple Leafs compiled the longest winning stretch from the start of a season in NHL history. Between October 7 and October 28 the Leafs won a record 10 consecutive games, outscoring their opponents 45–20. The streak fizzled in Montreal in a 5–2 loss against the Canadiens on October 30.

10.8 B. 10 wins

The Anaheim Mighty Ducks broke one of hockey's longest-standing records on February 12, 2003, when they defeated Calgary in a 4–3 win, their 10th straight one-goal victory. The streak began on January 12, a 2–1 win against St. Louis. In the 14-game stretch the Ducks lost four times (twice by one-goal margins of 2–1) but beat Columbus 4–3, Minnesota 1–0, Los Angeles 6–5, Ottawa 3–2, San Jose 4–3, Calgary 3–2, Phoenix 3–2, Carolina 2–1 and, finally, the Flames 4–3. The previous record of nine was held by the 1926–27 Ottawa Senators.

10.9 D. Eight games in a row

The Chicago Blackhawks went scoreless for an unprecedented eight straight games in 1928–29, losing or tying 1–0, 1–0, 1–0, 3–0, 3–0, 0–0, 3–0 and 0–0 in almost a month of action. The shutout streak began February 7 in New York against the Americans and ended mercifully March 2 with a 2–1 win over the Montreal Maroons. Chicago, in just its third NHL season and easily the league's worst team, was goose-egged another 12 times. The Hawks won only seven matches in the 44-game schedule.

10.10 D. 53 straight penalty kills

The Washington Capitals set an NHL record in 1999–2000 with 53 consecutive successful penalty kills, and tied another record by going 12 straight games without allowing a power-play goal. The Capitals established the new league mark between October 26 and November 24 with a 5–5–2 win-loss record. Despite the record, Washington still finished the season seventh overall in team penalty killing with 47 power-play goals allowed on 341 attempts by the opposition for an 86.2 per cent success rate.

10.11 D. More than 800 games

The New Jersey franchise played in 829 regular-season games (as the Devils, Kansas City Scouts and Colorado Rockies) before recording its first penalty shot, the longest wait in NHL history.

The historic shot came on December 17, 1984, as Rocky Trottier scored one-on-one against Edmonton's Andy Moog at the Meadowlands. The Devils' first penalty shot goal was also the first goal ever allowed in a penalty shot situation in Oilers history. Among expansion teams since 1990, Anaheim waited the longest to record a penalty shot—315 games before Joe Sacco's goal on November 12, 1997.

10.12 C. The Pittsburgh Penguins of 1988–89

The Penguins already had a dangerous power play thanks to the presence of Mario Lemieux, but when the club acquired defenseman Paul Coffey in a trade with Edmonton midway through the 1987–88 season, the unit moved up another notch. Powered by Lemieux's 31 power-play goals and Coffey's 11 in the following season, 1988–89, Pittsburgh amassed a league-record 119 man-advantage goals, setting a record that has never been surpassed. Remarkably, none of the NHL's highest-scoring teams (such as the 1980s Edmonton Oilers or the 1970s Montreal Canadiens) rank among the premier power-play clubs in the NHL record book. After the Pens, the 1992–93 Detroit Red Wings scored 113 times on the advantage and the 1987–88 New York Rangers 111 times.

10.13 C. 36 shorthanded goals

No team in NHL history has matched the offensive numbers of the Edmonton Oilers during the 1980s. In fact, during Edmonton's most productive season, 1983–84, losing a man to the penalty box actually helped on occasion. The Oilers scored a record 36 with a man short. Wayne Gretzky was the biggest benefactor of more ice space (even if it was at the expense of a fellow Oiler), notching 12 shorthanders or 33 per cent of Edmonton's record output. The Oilers also hold down the next three best league marks in this category with 28 shorthanded goals in 1986–87 and 27 in 1985–86 and 1988–89. Surprisingly, on the power play, Edmonton doesn't even rank among the top four goal-scoring teams in NHL history.

10.14 D. Five empty-net goals

You're the coach. It's the last game of the regular season. Your team, the Canadiens, is fighting for the final playoff berth. You need either a tie or at least five goals to avoid elimination. With Montreal down 3–2 in the third period, Chicago's Pit Martin connects twice in less than four minutes. The score: 5–2. The clock reads 10:44. Henri Richard looks over his shoulder at you and says: "It's like a bad dream." What would you do? Desperate times call for desperate measures. That's what Habs coach Claude Ruel figured on April 5, 1970. Win, lose or draw, three more goals would get the Canadiens into the playoffs. It was a slapstick finish to Montreal's season, with Ruel pulling Rogie Vachon on every faceoff and the Hawks capitalizing each time to score five empty-net goals in eight minutes. It's the only time in 45 years that the Canadiens missed the playoffs. And you wanted to be the coach?

10.15 A. The Montreal Canadiens of 1943–44

The Canadiens went unbeaten through 25 home dates in 1943–44's 50-game schedule. In all, they won 22 games and tied three at the Montreal Forum. Although they were not as dominant on the road, they only lost an NHL-record five games in a league ravaged by World War II recruiting, which claimed players from every position and team. Montreal, the least affected club, capitalized and finished first with 38 wins and 83 points, producing the greatest point spread (25 points) between first- and second-place teams during the six-team era. The Canadiens suffered their first defeat on home ice in 1943–44 during the first round of the playoffs, losing 3–1 to the Toronto Maple Leafs. In Game 2, Maurice Richard led the charge, scoring all five goals in a 5–1 victory; the Habs never looked back. They took the series in five games, then swept the Chicago Blackhawks four straight in the finals. The only other club to go unbeaten at home through an NHL season was the 1922–23 Ottawa Senators. But they only played a 24-game schedule that year, with a 11–0–1 home record.

10.16 D. The Philadelphia Flyers

From October 14, 1979, through January 6, 1980, the Flyers amassed an undefeated streak that is unrivalled in pro hockey, winning 25 games and tying 10 in 35 matches. The string ended with a 7–1 loss to Minnesota, before the Flyers tore off on another 13-game undefeated streak. One measly loss in 49 games. Wow!

10.17 B. 35 games

The record for the longest road drought in one city is owned by the Minnesota North Stars, who recorded their first victory in Boston on November 8, 1981, 14 years after joining the NHL as an expansion team in 1967. It was Minnesota's first road win after posting a 0–28–7 record against the Bruins. During that 14-year stretch the North Stars fared better at home versus Boston, with 10–17–8. Two other teams needed seven seasons to beat their rivals on the road: the Kansas City/Colorado/New Jersey franchise went through three different cities and 26 games (0–24–2) before scoring a victory against the Islanders at Long Island on December 11, 1984; and Washington played 23 winless games (0–22–1) against the Montreal Canadiens at the Forum before the team's first triumph on November 26, 1983.

10.18 C. 34 games

In what is considered the longest non-winning streak between teams, the Washington Capitals failed to record a victory against the Montreal Canadiens in almost six years—from 1974–75, their first NHL season, until February 19, 1980. The Caps played in 31 losses and three ties before notching their first victory against Montreal, a 3–1 win at the Capital Center. Not mincing words, Caps captain Ryan Walter said, "We had a barrier about beating Montreal." The winless streak ended after Bengt Gustaffson scored the go-ahead goal and Mike Gardiner potted an empty netter. Goalie Wayne Stephenson earned the Washington win. Overall, the Capitals own the top three of four spots in this category, falling short 26 consecutive times against Boston and 19 times against the Islanders.

10.19 B. The Hartford Whalers in 1979–80

It shouldn't be too surprising that the Whalers lead all NHL expansion teams in the goals-scored column. Playing alongside veterans like Gordie and Mark Howe, Dave Keon and Bobby Hull, Hartford had two 100-point players in Mike Rogers and Blaine Stoughton. In the 80-game schedule, the Whalers averaged 3.79 goals per game, or 303 goals, edging the Gretzky-led Oilers (301 goals). The Panthers had 233 goals and the Lightning 245 goals in 84 games. Among low-scoring expansion teams in a minimum 70-game schedule, the Oakland Seals potted the fewest goals: 153 in 1967–68.

10.20 A. The Florida Panthers

In 1993–94 the Panthers set an NHL expansion record, racking up 83 points in their inaugural season during the 84-game schedule and recording the longest unbeaten streak of nine games by a first-year team. But best remembered may be their tenacious season-long struggle for playoff contention, only to fall short by one point after folding in the last two games. The Panthers had the league's third-lowest goals-against with 233, but they finished 22nd in scoring with 233 goals.

10.21 B. The Anaheim Mighty Ducks

Their half-million-dollar Disney-produced home-opening extravaganza aside, the Ducks saved their best show for the road with a 19–20–3 record, a respectable 13th among the NHL's 26 teams. It was the best away record ever for a first-year expansion team and just ahead of the Panthers who posted 18–16–8 the same season, 1993–94. At home the Ducks were 14–26–2 in their first year or 25th overall in the home-wins column.

10.22 C. Four straight wins

Nine expansion teams have tied the NHL record for consecutive wins in their first season. The Columbus Blue Jackets became the ninth first-year club to win four straight after defeating San Jose (5–2) on November 9, Phoenix (2–1) on November 11, Dallas (3–2) on November 14 and Nashville (5–1) on November 16. Columbus' bubble burst in the fifth game after a 3–0 loss against Florida on November 17. Prior to the Blue Jackets, the last expansion club to win four-in-a-row was the 1993–94 Panthers.

10.23 D. The Minnesota Wild of 2000–01

Atlanta set an NHL expansion team record for attendance in 1999–2000, averaging 17,205 fans per game, including 14 sellouts. But audience loyalty brought few victories as the Thrashers challenged league standards in the win column, registering an embarrassing 14–61–7 record or fourth-worst by an expansion team since 1970. There was little doubt that when the Wild entered the league the following season it would top those numbers, both in attendance and wins, particularly considering Minnesota's long love of hockey and its defense-oriented coach, Jacques Lemaire. The Wild drew 751,472 fans in its first year for an average of 18,328 in 41 consecutive sellouts and registered a respectable 25–39–13–5. The official capacity of the Xcel Energy Center is 18,064. In its first two seasons it recorded 50 overflow crowds, including its biggest home game when 19,042 fans attended a game against the Dallas Stars on November 25, 2001.

10.24 B. Three players

When the Stars returned to Minnesota on December 17, 2000, for the first time since their move to Dallas (except for one neutral site game) in 1993, only three players from the original Minnesota team had survived: Mike Modano, Derian Hatcher and Richard Matvichuk. The Wild waxed the Stars 6–0 before a record crowd of 18,834. Three of the Wild's six goals were scored by Minnesota natives: Jeff Neilsen had one and Darby Hendrickson two.

10.25 C. The Colorado Avalanche

The turnstiles never stop turning in Denver. The Avalanche recorded its 400th consecutive sellout against the Phoenix Coyotes on November 6, 2000. Colorado won 2–1 as goalie Philip Sauve picked up his first NHL victory. Colorado's sellout streak is the longest in NHL history and the longest active streak of all major professional sports. To reach number 400, there were 199 sellouts at McNichols Sports Arena and 201 sellouts at the Pepsi Center. The run dates back to November 1995.

10.26 D. The Chicago Blackhawks

It was the hype surrounding the opening of Chicago's new United Center that caused the Blackhawks to set this record, rather than any great excitement about the team's on-ice performance or the truncated NHL season, which did not begin until January because of a labour dispute. The Hawks averaged 20,818 fans per game, just 46 more fans per game than the runner-up Montreal Canadiens, who attracted 20,772 at the Molson Centre in 1997–98.

10.27 B. 108 games

Both the Los Angeles Kings of 1992–93 and the Vancouver Canucks of 1993–94 shared a similar fate during the NHL's only 84-game schedules. Each team was eventually defeated in the Cup finals after playing 24 playoff games.

10.28 C. The Edmonton Oilers in 1983–84

Using coach Glen Sather's fire-wagon style of offense, the 1983–84 Edmonton Oilers pumped an NHL-record 446 goals past opposing netminders during an 80-game schedule. Wayne Gretzky led the offensive barrage, ringing up 87 goals, followed by Glenn Anderson's 54 red lights and Jari Kurri's 52. Defenseman Paul Coffey scored 40 times and Mark Messier had 37. So prolific were the Oilers in 1983–84 that even netminder Grant Fuhr had a great offensive year, compiling an NHL goalie record of 14 assists.

10.29 B. 164 goals

They've been criticized for being mind-numbingly dull and a negative influence on the game, but the New Jersey Devils are also one of hockey's best defensive clubs ever. In 2003–04, even without injured captain Scott Stevens, the Devils allowed just 164 goals, beating the previous minimum 80-game record of 165 goals set by the St. Louis Blues in 1999–2000. At the 50-game mark New Jersey had allowed only 94 goals, the lowest goals-against count through 50 games since the 1955–56 Montreal Canadiens gave up 91 goals, and just back of the 1953–54 Toronto Maple Leafs and their record low 84 goals. The best modern-day record for a full season belongs to those two teams: both the 1953–54 Maple Leafs and 1955–56 Canadiens allowed just 131 goals in a 70-game schedule.

10.30 A. The Chicago Blackhawks

In 1968–69 Chicago's offensive powerhouse scored 280 goals, second only to Bobby Orr's Boston Bruins with 303 goals. The scoring machine was sparked by Stan Mikita, Eric Nesterenko, Dennis Hull and Kenny Wharram, who each scored exactly 30 goals; Bobby Hull established an NHL record 58 goals. The Blackhawks, however, were less successful at winning. Although Chicago iced the first five 30-goal scorers in one season, the club finished last in the tough East Division.

10.31 A. The Washington Capitals

When Washington wants veterans, it goes all out. In 23 NHL seasons, no NHLer had scored his 1,000th career point as a member of the Capitals. Then, in 1997–98, Phil Housley, Adam Oates and Dale Hunter each hit the 1,000-point milestone with Washington, the first 1,000-point trio from one team in league annals. Oates knocked home number 1,000 on October 8, 1997; a month later, on November 8, Housley scored his 1,000th; Hunter made it a Washington hat trick on January 9, 1998. Washington's affinity for picking up veterans on the verge of their millennium point continued in 1998–99, when Brian Bellows scored career number 1,000 with the Caps.

10.32 C. Seven goalies

If any goalie has been through the revolving door it's Fred Brathwaite. Not once but twice he has suited up for teams in a goalie-crunch crisis no NHL general manager has ever faced before. He found his way out of minor-league obscurity during 1998–99 when Calgary signed a record eight netminders to contract. Brathwaite, the eighth goalie signed and sixth and final Flames goaltender to start that season, proved to be Calgary's silver lining with an 11–9–7 record in 28 games. Then, in 2002–03, Brathwaite was one of a record seven goalies to start with St. Louis, playing 30 games for a 12–9–4 mark. Besides Brathwaite, the Blues also iced Brent Johnson, Chris Osgood, Tom Barrasso, Curtis Sanford, Reinhard Divis and Cody Rudkowsky.

10.33 C. Five games

The Toronto Maple Leafs began the 1930–31 season by blanking their opponents in five straight games. After opening with a 0–0 draw on home ice against the New York Americans, Toronto stifled the Philadelphia Quakers 4–0. Then they headed out on the road and defeated the Montreal Canadiens 3–0, tied the Americans 0–0 and downed the Ottawa Senators 2–0. The Leafs' shutout streak ended in their next game when they were edged 2–1 by the Philadelphia Quakers. Philadelphia was an unlikely club to snap the streak: it won just four games all season and scored a league-low 76 goals in 44 games. After its fast start, Toronto posted only three more goose eggs the rest of the way, finishing second in the Canadian Division.

10.34 D. Seven overtime games

The 2003–04 Edmonton Oilers squandered leads, suffered through goal-scoring slumps and had trouble stealing a win, but what kept them in their frantic race for a playoff berth (which they missed by three points) was a record-setting seven-game overtime streak in late February and March. The Oilers went 2–0–2–3 during the streak, which began February 29 in a 5–4 loss to Dallas. From there, they beat Phoenix 5–4

(March 2), tied St. Louis 1–1 (March 4), edged Chicago 4–3 (March 7), equalled Calgary 1–1 (March 9) and ended the run with OT losses to Colorado 3–2 (March 10) and Vancouver 4–3 (March 12). "It's frustrating," said Shawn Horcoff after the Oilers' seventh overtime game. "We needed two points and these one-point games aren't doing it for us. Time is running out and we've got to start winning hockey games." The previous NHL record for consecutive overtime games was five, accomplished eight times by seven teams.

10.35 B. 30 overtimes

What started out as an overtime rule to decrease ties in 1983–84 has grown into a kind of game strategy to increase point production, especially after the rule changes of 1999–2000, which brought four-on-four hockey and a point for an OT loss. In 1983–84, only 16.6 per cent of games had an extra period. That number steadily increased to 25.6 per cent by 2003–04 as 315 games ended in overtime. The Boston Bruins set a new record that year with 30 overtimes, followed by Phoenix with 29 and Colorado with 28. The previous high was 28 overtimes by the Avalanche in 2002–03.

10.36 A. The Calgary Flames in 1999–2000

Since 1983–84 and the start of five-minute overtimes in regular-season play, few teams have been as successful as the Calgary Flames of 1999–2000. The Flames played 26 games with extra periods and won a league-high 11 overtimes, the first time any team had reached double digits in regular-season play. The Flames' success has been astounding, considering they were one of the league's lowest-scoring clubs and their 11 OT wins represented one of every three victories in their 31-win record of 1999–2000. Calgary's biggest single weapon was Phil Housley, an offensive defenseman with great puck control who suited open ice, four-on-four play perfectly. His confidence and composure sparked the entire team in tight games. Housley recorded a team- and league-high six overtime points. Four other teams have produced double digits in OT wins. In back-to-back years, 2000–01 and 2001–02, Detroit registered 10 extra-period wins and Vancouver and St. Louis tied Calgary's record of 11 in 2003–04.

10.37 D. The Boston Bruins

The Bruins of the 1970s made the NHL scoring totals their own personal race for six seasons from 1969 to 1975, with Phil Esposito and Bobby Orr alternating first and second positions each year—except 1972–73; and twice, four Boston players hogged the top four spots (1970–71 and 1973–74).

10.38 A. The Toronto Maple Leafs

It has been more than half a century (and counting) since Toronto produced an NHL scoring leader. The last Leaf scoring champion was Gord Drillon, who led the league with 52 points in 1937–38. New York fans have been watching and waiting almost as long. New York hasn't seen a Ranger win the crown since 1941–42, when Bryan Hextall Sr. led with 56 points.

10.39 A. The Boston Bruins of 1970–71

The transformation of the Bruins from league doormat to league powerhouse was triggered by the arrival of Bobby Orr in 1966–67 and the acquisition of Phil Esposito, Ken Hodge and Fred Stanfield in a one-sided deal with Chicago prior to the 1967–68 season. The Big Bad Bruins put the fear into everyone, especially at Boston Garden where they stomped opponents with malicious zeal. The most explosive Boston team of the era was the 1970–71 edition, which scored 399 goals, 108 more than any other team in the league that season, including the Montreal Canadiens with the next-highest goal count of 291. As our stat box on the next page indicates, not even the high-flying Edmonton Oilers teams of the 1980s could match that margin of domination.

Largest Margin in Goals Scored*

POINT-YEAR	MOST-GOALS TEAM	GOALS	SECOND-MOST-GOALS TEAM	GOALS	SPREAD
1970–71	Boston	399	Montreal	291	108
1983–84	Edmonton	446	NYI	357	89
1982–83	Edmonton	424	Montreal	350	74
1985–86	Edmonton	426	Calgary	354	72

**Current to 2004–05*

10.40 B. The Montreal Canadiens of 1976–77

Many believe that the Montreal teams of the late 1970s formed the most awesome dynasty of all time. The chart below supports that claim. The 1976–77 Canadiens squad was a juggernaut. Guy Lafleur, Larry Robinson, Ken Dryden and company posted a 60–8–12 mark and amassed an NHL-record 132 points. The team's dominance is reflected in its goals-for and goals-against numbers. The Habs scored 387 times while allowing opponents only 171, a difference of 216. That's 24 goals better than the closest team, the 1970–71 Boston Bruins.

Largest Goal-Differentials in a Season*

TEAM	SEASON	GF	GA	MARGIN
Montreal	1976–77	387	171	216
Boston	1970–71	399	207	192
Montreal	1977–78	359	183	176
Montreal	1975–76	337	174	163
Montreal	1974–75	374	225	149
Montreal	1972–73	329	184	145

**Current to 2004–05*

10.41 A. The Montreal Maroons

It's ironic that the first tenants of the old Montreal Forum, the Maroons, are still waiting to hang their championship banners for two Stanley Cups. The all-but-forgotten Maroons won 271 games between 1924–25 and 1937–38; the Senators earned 258 victories from 1917–18 to 1933–34.

10.42 A. The San Jose Sharks in 1993–94

The three-year-old Sharks went from being the second-worst NHL team in 1992–93 (with 24 points, losing 71 games) to playoff contenders the next year, 1993–94 (finishing eighth with 82 points in the Western Conference). It was a 58-point turnaround and a league record. Their playoff drive, which included upsetting the heavily favoured Red Wings and pushing Toronto to the brink in Game 7, proved the potency of the new Shark attack. Was it the new stadium, the new coach, Kevin Constantine, or the new system—to say nothing of the spectacular play of Arturs Irbe and Soviet veterans Igor Larionov and Sergei Makarov, who found their wheels while helping the Sharks achieve respectability? The previous record turnaround was 52 points, held by the 1992–93 Nordiques.

GAME 10

The Player's Choice

THE LESTER B. PEARSON AWARD, which goes to the NHL's outstanding player as selected by the players, is usually bestowed upon big scorers. Since its inception in 1971, only two goalies have copped the award. Mike Liut was the first goalie to win it (in 1981), after he led the upstart Blues to a second-place overall finish with a 107-point season. There are 17 family names of Pearson winners listed below. Their names, such as Joe **SAKIC**, appear in the puzzle horizontally, vertically, diagonally or backwards. After you've circled all 17 names and the word *award*, read the remaining 19 letters in descending order to spell our unknown Pearson-winning goalie and his team.

Solutions are on page 564

Bobby **ORR**

Sergei **FEDOROV**

Phil **ESPOSITO**

Bobby **CLARKE**

Jaromir **JAGR**

Wayne **GRETZKY**

Mark **MESSIER**

Eric **LINDROS**

Joe **SAKIC**

Jean **RATELLE**

Marcel **DIONNE**

Guy **LAFLEUR**

Jarome **IGINLA**

Steve **YZERMAN**

Mario **LEMIEUX**

Brett **HULL**

Mike **LIUT**

AWARD

O	R	R	E	L	L	E	T	A	R
L	T	D	V	O	R	O	D	E	F
E	A	I	O	D	I	O	N	N	E
I	K	F	S	M	I	N	N	I	G
X	G	R	L	O	R	G	A	J	R
U	R	I	A	E	P	K	M	H	E
E	E	A	N	L	U	S	R	S	T
I	I	E	L	L	C	R	E	K	Z
M	S	C	I	K	A	S	Z	B	K
E	S	H	U	L	L	U	Y	F	Y
L	E	F	T	D	R	A	W	A	A
L	M	O	S	O	R	D	N	I	L

11

Hockey's Who's Who and Fred Saskamoose

IT'S A NAME THAT COULD ONLY belong to a hockey player. Fred Saskamoose, a Cree from the Sandy Lake Reserve, Saskatchewan, played only 11 games with the Chicago Blackhawks in 1953–54 but will forever be remembered, if not for his name then for being the first of Canada's aboriginal players in the NHL. Saskamoose recorded no points and six penalty minutes in his brief big league stint. In 1962, when he was a playing coach with the Kamloops Chiefs, the Shuswap and Chilcotin Indians of the B.C. Interior proclaimed him "Chief Thunder Stick," an honorary title he later used when he served as chief of the Sandy Lake Reserve. In this chapter, we pick our best Who's Who from hockey's most famous players roster, but also from that group of NHLers we couldn't help but admire for their small place in history.

Answers are on page 268

11.1 Who was known as the Babe Ruth of Hockey?

A. Gordie Howe
B. Howie Morenz
C. Eddie Shore
D. Aurèl Joliat

11.2 Who is the youngest team captain in NHL history?

A. Vancouver's Trevor Linden
B. Detroit's Steve Yzerman

C. The Minnesota North Stars' Brian Bellows
D. Tampa Bay's Vincent Lecavalier

11.3 Teddy Saunders was featured on the cover of the Ottawa Senators' media guide in 1999–2000? Who is Teddy Saunders?

A. The first owner of the Ottawa Senators
B. The last Ottawa-born goalie to win a Stanley Cup
C. The first Ottawa Senator to score a goal
D. The last surviving member of the original Ottawa Senators

11.4 Who was "Lefty" Wilson?

A. A pro baseball pitcher turned NHL star in the 1940s
B. A famous Boston team doctor
C. A New York mobster who ran Madison Square Garden
D. A long-time practice goalie for Detroit

11.5 Which NHL 500-goal scorer was known as "The Little Ball of Hate"?

A. Dino Ciccarelli
B. Pat Verbeek
C. Stan Mikita
D. Theo Fleury

11.6 Who was Fast Eddie?

A. Ed Mio
B. Ed Belfour
C. Ed Giacomin
D. Gary Edwards

11.7 Who was the first player to break one of Wayne Gretzky's 61 NHL records?

A. Brett Hull
B. Ray Bourque
C. Joe Sakic
D. Ron Francis

11.8 Who was Hobey Baker?

A. Hockey's most traded American player

B. Hockey's first American superstar

C. The first American-born player to play in the Soviet Elite League

D. The first American to win the NHL's scoring race

11.9 Which old-time NHL penalty leader was nicknamed "Box-Car" because he spent so much time in the penalty box?

A. Pat Egan

B. Gus Mortson

C. Lou Fontinato

D. John Ferguson

11.10 Who was the NHL's last player-coach?

A. The New York Rangers' Doug Harvey

B. The Minnesota North Stars' Charlie Burns

C. Boston's Dit Clapper

D. Montreal's Toe Blake

11.11 Who was the NHL's first Hispanic player?

A. Philadelphia's Dave Hoyda

B. Chicago's Moose Vasko

C. New Jersey's Scott Gomez

D. Buffalo's Jim Lorentz

11.12 Which nickname did Boston fans give to Frank Brimsek when he posted 10 shutouts in his rookie season of 1938–39?

A. Mr. Zero

B. Brimsek the Blanker

C. Zilch Man

D. Dr. Goose Egg

11.13 Who is "Mad Mike"?

A. Mike Modano
B. Mike Keenan
C. Mike Milbury
D. Mike Richter

11.14 Who was the only player from the six-team era between 1942 and 1967 to play with all six clubs?

A. Bronco Horvath
B. Pat Egan
C. Ed Litzenberger
D. Vic Lynn

11.15 Who was the only NHLer to play for all five of the NHL's first chartered teams in 1917–18?

A. Joe Malone
B. Dave Ritchie
C. Newsy Lalonde
D. Georges Vezina

11.16 Who was shortest player?

A. Cecil "Tiny" Thompson
B. Roy "Shrimp" Worters
C. Harry "Pee-Wee" Oliver
D. Wilfred "Shorty" Green

11.17 In 1943, Conn Smythe, the powerful owner of the Toronto Maple Leafs, said: "I will give $10,000 to anyone who can turn Herb Carnegie white." Who was Herb Carnegie?

A. A lacrosse player
B. A singer
C. A boxer
D. A hockey player

11.18 Who was Joe Turner?

A. A little-known goalie with a championship trophy named after him
B. A journeyman defenseman with an NHL goal-scoring record
C. A little-league referee who became an NHL president
D. A fourth-line centre who played backup goalie in more NHL games than any other forward

11.19 Which brothers played as teammates with the most teams?

A. Bobby and Dennis Hull
B. Des and Earl Roche
C. Frank and Pete Mahovlich
D. Mark and Marty Howe

11.20 Who was Lady Byng?

A. The wife of NHL president Frank Calder
B. The wife of Canada's governor general
C. The NHL's first female executive
D. England's Duchess of York

11.21 Which family is considered hockey's royal family?

A. The Howes
B. The Patricks
C. The Sutters
D. The Richards

11.22 Who is Peter Demers?

A. A French Canadian play-by-play announcer
B. The inventor of the net-cam
C. The NHL's first goal judge
D. A long-time team trainer

11.23 Who scored the first NHL goal?

A. Toronto's Jack Adams
B. Montreal's Joe Malone
C. The Montreal Wanderers' Dave Ritchie
D. Ottawa's Frank Nighbor

11.24 Who first earned the nickname "Terrible Ted"?

A. Ted Lindsay
B. Ted Harris
C. Ted Green
D. Ted Kennedy

11.25 Who is known as Mr. Goalie?

A. Montreal's Ken Dryden
B. Chicago's Glenn Hall
C. Detroit's Terry Sawchuk
D. Buffalo's Dominik Hasek

11.26 Who outscored Wayne Gretzky to set an Ontario Junior A scoring record of 192 points in 1977–78?

A. Al Secord
B. Ken Linseman
C. Bobby Smith
D. Keith Acton

11.27 Who is Freddy Charles?

A. The only goalie ever awarded the Lady Byng Trophy
B. The L.A. Kings' national-anthem singer
C. Eric Lindros's ex-agent
D. Hockey's most-traded player

11.28 Who is the last NHLer to play without a helmet?

A. Mark Messier
B. Craig MacTavish
C. Al Secord
D. Dale Hunter

11.29 Who is Stanislav Gvoth?

A. The artist who designed Curtis Joseph's goalie mask
B. The inventor of the Zamboni
C. The president of the International Ice Hockey Federation
D. The Chicago Blackhawks' all-time scoring leader

11.30 Who are Mr. and Mrs. Lou Reese?

A. The married couple who founded the Hockey Hall of Fame
B. The parents of Jeff Reese, the only NHL goalie with three assists in one game
C. The only married couple who have their names on the Stanley Cup
D. The married couple who got hit by separate pucks during an NHL game

11.31 Which goaltender from 2000–01 went by the nickname "Moose"?

A. Dan Cloutier of the Vancouver Canucks
B. Johan Hedberg of the Pittsburgh Penguins
C. Brent Johnson of the St. Louis Blues
D. Roberto Luongo of the Florida Panthers

11.32 Who is Lloyd Percival?

A. The logo designer of the NHL crest
B. The silversmith who cast the Stanley Cup
C. The author of the book that taught the Russians hockey
D. Broadcaster Don Cherry's tailor

11.33 Who performed a celebratory dance that became popularly known as "The Goldy Shuffle"?

A. Bill Goldsworthy
B. Bob Goldham
C. Bobby Hull
D. Glenn Goldup

11.34 Who is Jay North?

A. The first high-school player drafted by an NHL team

B. The first full-blooded Native Canadian NHL player

C. The first NHLer assessed a fighting major

D. The first goal-scoring leader not elected an All-Star

11.35 Called "Old Poison" because of his lethal touch around the net, he became the only rookie to win an NHL scoring crown. He was:

A. Toe Blake

B. Nels Stewart

C. Howie Morenz

D. Gordie Howe

11.36 Who is Ryan Malone?

A. The first hometown player for the Pittsburgh Penguins

B. The first hometown player for the Los Angeles Kings

C. The first hometown player for the Philadelphia Flyers

D. The first hometown player for the Buffalo Sabres

11.37 Who was dubbed "the Rodney Dangerfield of the NHL" when he was left off the roster for the 1996 NHL All-Star game?

A. Ron Francis

B. Alexei Zhamnov

C. John LeClair

D. Trevor Linden

11.38 Which goalie was known as "Jimmy Buffer" to his team-mates in 2003–04?

A. Ed Belfour of the Toronto Maple Leafs

B. Manny Legace of the Detroit Red Wings

C. Nikolai Khabibulin of the Tampa Bay Lightning

D. Martin Brodeur of the New Jersey Devils

11.39 Who did the Montreal hockey press call "The 12 Apostles"?

A. The 12 Stanley Cup-winning Canadiens coaches
B. The first 12 Canadiens in the Hall of Fame
C. The only 12 five-time members of the NHL's First All-Star team
D. The 12 players from the 1956 to 1960 Stanley Cup dynasty

11.40 Who is Joe Hockey?

A. An NHL publicity director
B. A hockey trivia expert
C. A man who knows nothing about hockey
D. A party animal in a TV beer commercial

Hockey's Who's Who and Fred Saskamoose

Answers

11.1 B. Howie Morenz

American sportswriters nicknamed Morenz the Babe Ruth of Hockey. He was the NHL's first real superstar, a player of unparalleled speed who drew audiences to arenas and brought fans to their feet during his headlong rushes. In the 1920s he racked up totals of 40 goals in 44 games in one season and 28-in-30 in another. But statistics do little to describe the thrill of watching Morenz, the box-office attraction who truly was hockey's Babe Ruth.

11.2 C. The Minnesota North Stars' Brian Bellows

Okay, Bellows gets this honour but not without an asterisk. He was just 19.2 years old when he was named the North Stars' co-captain after Craig Hartsburg went down with a serious knee injury two games into 1983–84. Lecavalier earned full captaincy when he was 19.5 years old, after Chris Gratton was traded in late 1999–2000. Both are the only two teenage captains in NHL annals. Linden was tri-captain at 20.6 years and Yzerman at 21.5 years.

11.3 D. The last surviving member of the original Ottawa Senators

Saunders played only 18 games for the old Ottawa Senators franchise, far fewer than the big names who won the club numerous Stanley Cups during its heyday. But the current Senators club featured him on their 1999–2000 media guide because he was the last player link between the current Senators and the first Senators franchise, which folded after the 1933–34 campaign. Saunders was best known for his wrist shot. He scored one goal and three assists during his 18-game stint in Ottawa. He died on May 21, 2002, at age 90.

11.4 D. A long-time practice goalie for Detroit

Before the two-goalie system, teams found spare goalies wherever they could; in Detroit they relied on "Lefty" Wilson, a trainer and practice goaltender who actually played three NHL games. Wilson first tended nets on October 10, 1953, replacing an injured Terry Sawchuk in period three of a 4–1 loss to Montreal. He played twice more in league action. Oddly, both times he faced his own team, the Red Wings. Wilson was loaned to Toronto to replace an injured Harry Lumley on January 22, 1956, and to Boston to sub for an injured Don Simmons on December 29, 1957. Lefty's career consisted of three games for three different teams—twice against his own team.

11.5 B. Pat Verbeek

It might just be the way he played, full of emotion and dirty tricks, but, somewhere along the way, Verbeek picked up the nickname the Little Ball of Hate. Actually, the dubbing of the five-foot-nine, 190-pound Verbeek came courtesy of goalie Glenn Healy in the mid-1990s, when the two men were with the New York Rangers. Verbeek was all fire and brimstone. He scored his 500th on March 22, 2000, while sparking Detroit's number one line of Steve Yzerman and Brendan Shanahan. The Little Ball of Hate, a third-liner on the 1999 Dallas Cup winners, couldn't contain himself as he jumped up and down and pumped his fist into the air.

11.6 C. Ed Giacomin

During New York's 54-year drought between Stanley Cups, the Rangers had a few inspirational puck stoppers who nearly altered the fortunes of the Cup-starved club. Both Chuck Rayner (1950) and John Davidson (1979) reached Cup finals in their eras, but neither garnered the kind of intense loyalty that Ranger fans lavished on Ed Giacomin. Fast Eddie played 10 seasons in New York, led the league in victories three times and helped the team reach the postseason on nine occasions. His peak came in 1972 when the Rangers lost a tough six-game Cup final against Bobby Orr and the Boston Bruins. In late October 1975, New Yorkers were stunned to learn that Giacomin, 36 years old, had been sent to Detroit. His first return to Madison Square Garden just days later sparked one of that rink's most emotional nights. In a salute to their faithful goalie, fans started chanting his name during the national anthem and erupted in deafening ovations several more times throughout the game. One of his former teammates even apologized for scoring. Giacomin faced 46 shots in a 6–4 Detroit win. "I've never been an emotional man, but I couldn't hold back the tears tonight," he said after the November 2, 1975, game. "When the people started cheering me at the beginning, the tears came down my face. A couple of times, I thought I would collapse from the emotion." Today, Fast Eddie is one of only three Rangers whose sweater number has been retired by the club.

11.7 B. Ray Bourque

Few would have figured a defenseman to be the first to break one of Wayne Gretzky's 61 NHL scoring records. But that record breaker was Ray Bourque, hockey's all-time leading point earner among rearguards. Bourque broke Gretzky's mark of 12 All-Star game assists on February 6, 2000, when he assisted on a goal by Tony Amonte at 12:14 of the second period at the 2000 All-Star game. Five minutes later Mark

Messier also notched his 13th career All-Star assist on a Ray Whitney goal. The first player to break a Gretzky regular-season record was Adam Oates. Oates toppled the Great One's career record of 15 overtime assists in 2001–02 when he collected his 14th, 15th and 16th overtime helpers with the Capitals and Flyers.

11.8 B. Hockey's first American superstar

Hobart "Hobey" Baker was the perfect All-American collegiate sports hero. The award named after him, which goes to the U.S. college hockey player of the year, honours that individual who exhibits hockey skills on and off the ice and excels in scholastic achievement and sportsmanship, much like Hobey himself did in his Princeton days. An exceptional skater and stickhandler, it was once reported that Baker, after being checked over the boards, dashed along the bench, leapt back into the action, got the loose puck and scored. Baker captained his team to two intercollegiate titles in the 1910s, but he never made the NHL. He died flying with the famous Escadrille Lafayette in World War I. He is the only individual inducted into both the Hockey Hall of Fame and the Collegiate Hall of Fame in the United States. Winners of the Hobey Baker Award include Neal Broten (1981), Paul Kariya (1993) and Chris Drury (1998).

11.9 A. Pat Egan

Scrappy defender Pat Egan played with four NHL clubs in 11 years during the 1940s and early 1950s. He earned his tough-guy reputation and the nickname Box-Car in 1941–42, when he accumulated a league-high 124 minutes in box time. In subsequent years he was usually among the top penalty leaders to lay on the lumber, including 1944–45, when he won the penalty crown again by accumulating 86 minutes. Box-Car quit the NHL with 776 penalty minutes in 554 games.

11.10 B. The Minnesota North Stars' Charlie Burns

Centre Charlie Burns of the Minnesota North Stars was the last player-coach in the NHL. Better known as one of only four players to wear a helmet full-time in 1969–70, Burns was appointed Minnesota's bench boss in December when ill health forced Wren Blair to quit his coaching duties. Burns's double role may have split his effectiveness in both positions. He scored a career-low 16 points and coached his North Stars to third place with a 19–35–22 record in the weak West Division.

11.11 C. New Jersey's Scott Gomez

Gomez is believed to be the first Mexican-American to play in the NHL. Born in Alaska, Gomez turned in the hottest performance by a rookie in 1999–2000 with a league-leading 70 points on 19 goals and 51 assists. Commenting on his Latino status, Gomez said, "It's not like I'm breaking any barriers, not like Jackie Robinson."

11.12 A. Mr. Zero

Frank Brimsek's toughest assignment came in his rookie year when he replaced 10-year Bruin veteran Tiny Thompson, whom Boston fans adored. In his first game, Brimsek, playing at home, was blanked 2–0 by Montreal—a difficult start in the wake of the past heroics of Thompson. But the next three games changed everything. The rookie came back and notched back-to-back-to-back shutouts and totalled six goose eggs in his first eight games. By the end of the season Boston fans had almost forgotten Thompson. Their new zero hero was Brimsek, who won not only their hearts but the Vezina and Calder Trophies and, finally, the Stanley Cup. Yet among all the awards and accolades bestowed on him that first season, few are remembered more today than the title given him by his fans: Mr. Zero.

11.13 C. Mike Milbury

Calling himself "Mad Mike," Milbury sliced and diced his Islanders roster into an almost unrecognizable team in just a few short years after taking office in December 1995. Some league general managers publicly questioned his deals, and as one hockey writer said, "Milbury... makes George Steinbrenner look like the picture of restraint." He was working under some financial pressures, but still, the Isles lost 40-goal man Ziggy Palffy; Roberto Luongo, the promising Quebec goaltender; and his entire defensive corps of Bryan Berard, Wade Redden, Darius Kasparaitis, Bryan McCabe and Eric Brewer. Then, to completely prove his madness and ineptitude as the league's worst GM, Milbury convinced free-spending Isles owner Charles B. Wang to sign sourpuss star Alexei Yashin with U.S.$87.5 million to a 10-year deal that skyrocketed player salaries around the league. Sooner or later, something had to click for Mad Mike, though: After signing Yashin, Michael Peca, Roman Hamrlik, Adrian Aucoin and Mark Parrish, Milbury turned his perennial losers into playoff contenders by engineering a 44-point turnaround in 2001–02. But Mad Mike's report card, after almost a decade of shuffling bodies, shows his performance was a near-disaster, one that ruined the confidence of many young players, chased away several rising stars and pushed league salaries beyond small-market limits. And really, what's he got on Wang?

11.14 D. Vic Lynn

Lynn is the only NHLer to suit up for all teams of the Original Six. He played with the New York Rangers (one game), Montreal (two games), Detroit (three games), Chicago (40 games), Boston (68 games) and Toronto (213 games). Bronco Horvath was signed by all six teams but never played with Detroit when he first came up from the minors in 1955.

11.15 B. Dave Ritchie

Ritchie was the only player to don sweaters with all five original NHL clubs. When the league began in 1917–18, Ritchie's rights were owned by the Quebec Bulldogs. Since Quebec did not ice a team that year, he joined the Montreal Wanderers for four games before they withdrew from the league. The Ottawa Senators picked up Ritchie for the remaining 14 games of 1917–18. During the next several years the defenseman played with the Toronto Arenas, Quebec and the Montreal Canadiens, where he ended his career in 1925–26.

11.16 B. Roy "Shrimp" Worters

The Shrimp was only five foot three, but height is no indication of stature. Worters was the first NHL goalie to win the Hart Trophy as League MVP and is one of only four netminders so honoured; "Pee-Wee" Oliver came up big in the Bruins' first Stanley Cup, 1928–29; and "Shorty" Green, as captain of the Hamilton Tigers, staged the NHL's first strike in 1925. As for "Tiny" Thompson, he was actually five foot 10. In 12 seasons, he won four Vezinas and zeroed the opposition 81 times, ranking fourth-best in all-time shutouts. Tiny, Shrimp, Pee-Wee and Shorty were anything but small fry; all are Hockey Hall of Fame members.

11.17 D. A hockey player

Although Boston's Willie O'Ree became the first black NHLer in 1958, he wasn't the first to try and break the league's one-time colour barrier. In *Too Colourful for the League,* a TV documentary examining the obstacles preventing the acceptance of black players in the NHL, Herb Carnegie said of Smythe's "$10,000" declaration: "I was conscious of carrying Conn Smythe's remark with me all the way through my hockey career. I always played the game as if to say there's somebody bigger than Conn Smythe who will say, 'Come and play for us.' Never did I at any time play a losing game because

I said, 'Aw, what's the use?' I never had that mindset. But I was denied the opportunity to even try out, that's what really bothers me the most..." Carnegie starred in the Quebec Provincial Hockey League in the 1940s, winning three MVP titles as a centre on a high-scoring, all-black line with his brother Ossie and Manny McIntyre. He later played alongside Montreal Canadiens great Jean Béliveau in the Quebec Senior League. "He had the ability to play in the NHL," said Béliveau in the film. "But I suppose the different owners or different managers maybe were afraid to be the first one to hire a coloured person."

11.18 A. A little-known goalie with a championship trophy named after him

Joe Turner may be the goaltending fraternity's most famous one-game wonder. Although more than 70 goalies have NHL careers of a single game, Turner stands out, not because of his 3–3 tie against Toronto after replacing an injured Johnny Mowers in the Detroit net on February 5, 1942, but because his story champions the heroics of all minor-league goalies who had little chance of making it to the big time. After his NHL debut, the Canadian-born Turner joined the U.S. Marine Corps to fight overseas. Unfortunately he was killed in action in January 1945. As a tribute, the new IHL named its championship trophy after him. The Turner Cup was presented annually to the playoff winners until the league folded in 2001.

11.19 B. Des and Earl Roche

In their four NHL seasons together, Des and Earl seemed to be joined at the hip, moving together from team to team with more consistency than any other two players in league history. The brothers played together for four different clubs from 1930–31 to 1934–35: Montreal Maroons, Ottawa, St. Louis Eagles and Detroit.

11.20 B. The wife of Canada's governor general

A true upper-crust Brit, Lady Evelyn, wife of Canada's 12th governor general, Baron Byng of Vimy, loved the "Canadian game" but not Canadian fans, whom she regarded as "childish" for showering the rink with garbage and coins to show their displeasure with referees and players. Perhaps that's why she donated a trophy in 1925 to reward the most gentlemanly player in the game.

11.21 B. The Patricks

No single family has contributed more to the improvement and quality of hockey than the Patricks. As the game grew up, one generation of Patricks succeeded another, both on the ice and behind the scenes, changing the rules, the style of play and the organization, taking a fledgling game out of dank, poorly lit arenas and turning it into one of North America's four major professional team sports. Brothers Lester and Frank built Canada's first artificial rinks, painted the first blue lines for offside calls and introduced the penalty shot and playoff format. Lester's sons Lynn and Muzz coached and served as general managers in the NHL, as did Lester's grandson, Craig, who today continues his family's name and its rich hockey heritage as GM of the Pittsburgh Penguins. More than hockey directors or innovators, all the Patricks were players first; some were great, others ordinary, but each developed a view of the game from the faceoff circle out. All five Patricks have won the Stanley Cup.

11.22 D. A long-time team trainer

Peter Demers is one of the longest-serving trainers in NHL hockey. In 2003–04, Demers, at 60 years old, was in his 32nd year treating the walking wounded of the Los Angeles Kings. He has massaged, iced, stitched up and stroked the egos of everyone from Marcel Dionne to Wayne Gretzky to Ziggy Palffy, working more than 2,500 games. Although to get a dressing-room story from him about a player would be breaking the trainer's code of silence, he reveals a lighter moment on the very serious subject of concussions, during the era of helmetless players: "The joke going around was, you'd hold up three fingers and ask the guy, 'How many fingers?' If he said 'two' or 'four,' you'd say: 'Close enough,'" said Demers.

11.23 B. Montreal's Joe Malone
C. The Montreal Wanderers' Dave Ritchie

The first goal in NHL history was scored on December 19, 1917. Two players share in the credit since two games were played that night: The Montreal Canadiens beat the Ottawa Senators 7–4 at the Arena on Laurier Avenue in Ottawa; and the Montreal Wanderers defeated Toronto at Westmount Arena in Montreal. As reported in the December 20th *Ottawa Citizen,* the "Canadiens started off with a blinding blast of speed and soon had Eddie Gerard and his Senators on the defensive." Montreal's Joe Malone "took a pass and dodged in for the first goal in 6 minutes and 30 seconds..." In the 10–9 game between the Wanderers and Toronto that same night, defenseman Dave Ritchie of the Wanderers scored first at the one-minute mark. The *Montreal Gazette* even credited the game's officials: "To Riley Hern, once a wonder-goalkeeper, fell the honor as umpire of lighting the first goal light, but the score was pretty evenly divided between himself and Jack Lowe." Interestingly, the *Gazette* also reported that goal lights at the Westmount Arena were "perched upon the top right hand corner of the nets and are protected by miniature barbed-wire entanglements."

11.24 A. Ted Lindsay

More than one Ted was nicknamed Terrible Ted, but Lindsay owned it first. So just how terrible was he? By the time his 17-year NHL career ended in 1964–65, Lindsay had served nearly 2,000 penalty minutes, the most box time of any Original Six player, and had battled through many epic fights and earned numerous fines for his stickwork. It is said he stopped counting the number of stitches in his face after he reached 400. But his aggressive, fearless approach to the game doesn't begin to describe the superior quality of Lindsay's hockey skills nor the immeasurable difference he made as Detroit's physical and emotional leader. His contribution to the Wings' Production Line brought Detroit four Stanley Cups between 1950 and 1955 and netted Lindsay the Art Ross Trophy as 1949–50's scoring leader. He was named to the First All-Star team as best left-winger eight times. Lindsay was one of hockey's most ferocious competitors, as his numbers indicate: 379 goals, 851 points and 1,808 penalty minutes in 1,068 games.

11.25 B. Chicago's Glenn Hall

No puck stopper in NHL history deserves the moniker Mr. Goalie more than Glenn Hall; few have had such an impact on their profession. In fact, today's netminders all have a little of Hall in their style. Hall revolutionized the position with his butterfly stance and honed the fundamentals of skating, puckhandling and positioning as one of the elite goalies of the 1950s and 1960s.

11.26 C. Bobby Smith

In 1977–78, 20-year-old Bobby Smith of the Ottawa 67s waged a year-long battle with 17-year-old rookie Wayne Gretzky of the Sault Ste. Marie Greyhounds for the Ontario Hockey Association scoring title. When the smoke finally cleared, Smith had bested Gretzky by 10 points, 192 to 182. Smith would enjoy a distinguished 16-year NHL career with the Minnesota North Stars and Montreal Canadiens, but he never outpointed the Great One again.

11.27 D. Hockey's most-traded player

You won't find stats on Freddy Charles in any hockey guide—he's fictional! The name, coined by NHL players, is hockey slang for the trade term "future considerations," as in: "He was traded for Freddy Charles."

11.28 B. Craig MacTavish

Craig MacTavish, who signed a player's contract prior to the 1979 cutoff date for exemption from the NHL's helmet rule, is the last helmetless NHLer. Although the league reversed this rule in 1992, permitting players to go bareheaded (Greg Smyth did it for a while with Calgary), none have done so on a permanent basis.

11.29 D. The Chicago Blackhawks' all-time scoring leader

Stanislav Gvoth was born on May 20, 1940, in Sokolce, Czechoslovakia. When the Communists seized control of the country in 1948, Mr. and Mrs. Gvoth made the difficult decision to send their son to Canada to live with his Uncle Joe and Aunt Anna in St. Catharines, Ontario. Little Stan took his aunt and uncle's last name, Mikita, as his own. He would later make it one of the most famous names in NHL annals. The 1,467 career points that Mikita compiled during his 22-year career are the most by a player in a Blackhawks uniform.

11.30 D. The married couple who got hit by separate pucks during an NHL game

March 28, 1943, was a busy night in the Red Wings' infirmary, not for injured players but for the fans—and one married couple in particular. First, Mrs. Reese took four stitches after being struck in the face by a puck. Then, moments after she returned to her seat, another stray puck cut her husband for two stitches. The Wings won 4–2 over Toronto.

11.31 B. Johan Hedberg of the Pittsburgh Penguins

How does a five-foot-eleven, 185-pound Swedish goalie come to be called "Moose"? Because he used to be one, that's how. Hedberg spent most of the 2000–01 season tending goal for the Manitoba Moose of the International Hockey League. The goalie mask he wore for Manitoba was a sky-blue colour with a moose painted on it. On March 12, 2001, the Penguins acquired Hedberg in a trade with San Jose, and brought him up for a tryout. The 27-year-old with the distinctive headgear was sensational, losing only one of nine games to close out the season. Pittsburgh fans began chanting "Mooooose!" every time he made a save. The Winnipeg team's Web site was swamped by fans searching for souvenir moose antlers and Hedberg's game-worn jerseys. The rookie continued his roll in the postseason, leading Pittsburgh to victories over Washington and Buffalo, before New Jersey ended the Moose's Cinderella run.

11.32 C. The author of the book that taught the Russians hockey
Even though the first edition of Percival's *Hockey Handbook* was published in the 1950s, the Handbook is still considered the definitive technical book on the game. You have to read only the first few lines to see why: "Skating is to hockey what throwing is to baseball, what tackling is to football, or what footwork is to tennis. It is the most important fundamental. Our research has shown that in the average full-length game players skate from two to three miles. When poor line changes are used, players skate as far as four miles per game. Skating is what the player does most. It is the foundation on which everything else is built." When the coaches who introduced the game to the Soviet Union read this, the *Hockey Handbook* became their bible. Percival's ideas on conditioning programs, precision-passing drills and coaching techniques inspired the Soviets to implement a brand-new approach to hockey—an approach virtually ignored by the NHL until our eyes were opened at the Summit Series in 1972. Percival, who was tutored by the legendary Knute Rockne of Notre Dame, applied scientific principals to coaching, training and performing in an effort to make the game faster and better. Wayne Gretzky, who never met Percival, unwittingly paid the coach his greatest compliment when he said: "We've learned more from the Soviets than they from us." Yes, Percival was the hockey genius we overlooked.

11.33 A. Bill Goldsworthy

While in Minnesota, Bill Goldsworthy developed his own post-goal choreography called "The Goldy Shuffle." Never construed as deft footwork, the on-ice jig became a fan favourite, with everyone expecting the simple shuffle and pump motion after a Goldsworthy goal.

11.34 A. The first high-school player drafted by an NHL team

A number of famous high schoolers have gone directly from their school books to the NHL record books. Before Bobby Carpenter made history as the first player drafted directly from high school into the NHL in 1981, Jay North and seven other high-schoolers were chosen in 1980. North, from Bloomington-Jefferson High School in Minnesota, was selected by Buffalo 62nd overall. But his league first made little impact: he never made it to the big time.

11.35 B. Nels Stewart

As the triggerman on the Montreal Maroons' "S" Line with Hooley Smith and Babe Siebert in the late 1920s and early 1930s, Nels Stewart displayed a deadly touch around the net. "Old Poison" lost his NHL goal-scoring record of 324 goals to Maurice Richard in 1952–53, but no one has equalled another of Stewart's scoring benchmarks: leading the league in scoring as a rookie. In his freshman season, in 1925–26, Stewart tallied 34 goals and 42 points, six points better than runner-up Cy Denneny of the Ottawa Senators. Only one other first-year player has topped the NHL's point parade, Joe Malone, in 1917–18. But no one in the league was classified as a rookie that season since it was the NHL's first year of operation.

11.36 A. The first hometown player for the Pittsburgh Penguins

Ryan Malone, a fourth-round pick in 1999, became the first Pittsburgh-born-and-trained player to suit up for the Penguins in 2003–04. He is also the first native Pittsburgher to reach the NHL, 36 years after the team joined the league, in 1967–68.

Malone was fourth among rookies with 22 goals and 43 points, the best freshman goal count by a Penguin since Shawn McEachern in 1992–93. Malone wore the same No. 12 his father, Greg, wore with the Penguins. Greg Malone is the team's head scout.

11.37 A. Ron Francis

Even though Francis was off to the best season of his career, he was not named to the roster of the Eastern Conference All-Stars by a selection committee of general managers. The slight prompted Pittsburgh's public relations office to compare Francis to Rodney Dangerfield, the comedian who "gets no respect." The Pens' centre did play in the game, however, but only after NHL commissioner Gary Bettman intervened on his behalf.

11.38 B. Manny Legace of the Detroit Red Wings

Detroit's backup since 2000–01, Legace kept finding himself in the spotlight during 2003–04. With a U.S.$15-million stable of goalies to contend with, the Red Wings still had trouble handing their number one job to, well, their number one goalies, after an injury epidemic felled both Dominik Hasek and Curtis Joseph. The Wings' number three man, Legace drew the most assignments in the goaltending soap opera. He became the man in the middle, literally. Because Legace's locker was located in no-man's land between the stalls of Hasek and Joseph, teammates figured he would be a buffer for the two feuding goalies and called him Jimmy Buffer, presumably a reference to singer Jimmy Buffet.

11.39 D. The 12 players from the 1956 to 1960 Stanley Cup dynasty

The "12 Apostles" helped turn winning the Stanley Cup into a Montreal spring rite in a record five consecutive seasons. In predominantly Catholic Quebec, the glory and soul of the

Canadiens dynasty were the 12 holy men from the five championship teams: Maurice Richard, Jean Béliveau, Jacques Plante, Dickie Moore, Claude Provost, Doug Harvey, Jean-Guy Talbot, Donnie Marshall, Bernie Geoffrion, Tom Johnson, Bob Turner and Henri Richard. The only Apostle to play every minute of every playoff game during the five straight Cups was Jacques Plante.

11.40 C. A man who knows nothing about hockey

Gordie Howe may have officially trademarked his nickname Mr. Hockey, but there is nothing he can do about Joe Hockey. In fact, Mr. Hockey, Joe that is, doesn't even know who Howe is. And he understands little about the made-in-Canada game. That's because Joe Hockey is Australian, and there isn't much stick-and-puck culture in the land of kangaroos and crocodiles. Born to parents of Palestinian and Irish descent, the family name Hockedunian was anglicized Down Under. Ever since, he's been Joe Hockey. As a member for North Sydney in the Australian parliament and that country's Minister of Tourism and Small Business, he's been to Canada but has no real sense of his name's power. "I've had Canadians try and buy my Web site," he said in a *National Post* story. "They always ring me up. When I registered joehockey.com, a Canadian offered me U.S.$100,000 for [it]. I turned it down." That decision proved unwise, considering a hockey league has since used www.joe-hockey.com.

GAME 11

Big Trades

CERTAINLY THE BIGGEST TRADE in hockey history has to be the Wayne Gretzky deal of 1988. It not only changed the fortunes of both the players and teams involved but the game itself. Gretzky's move put hockey on the front page in Los Angeles and thousands more Kings fans in the Great Western Forum. Moreover, it sparked new franchises in San Jose, Anaheim and Phoenix. Match the major players in trades between the right and left columns.

Solutions are on page 565

1. Patrick Roy, Mike Keane
   Montreal
2. Ray Bourque, Dave Andreychuk
   Boston
3. Todd Bertuzzi, Bryan McCabe
   New York Islanders
4. Mats Sundin, Garth Butcher
   Quebec
5. Brett Hull
   Calgary
6. John LeClair, Eric Desjardins
   Montreal
7. Wayne Gretzky, Mike Krushelnyski, Marty McSorley
   Edmonton

A. Wendel Clark, Todd Warriner, Sylvain Lefebvre
   Toronto

B. Mark Recchi
   Philadelphia

C. Rob Ramage, Rick Green
   St. Louis

D. Brian Rolston, Martin Grenier
   Colorado

E. Trevor Linden
   Vancouver

F. Jimmy Carson, Martin Gelinas, with draft picks/cash
   Los Angeles

G. Andrei Kovalenko, Martin Rucinsky, Jocelyn Thibault
   Colorado

12

This Side of Ken McAuley

WHEN THE NEW YORK RANGERS called up minor pro goalie Ken McAuley in 1943–44, they expected the worst. Ranger GM Lester Patrick had already asked the NHL to allow his team to withdraw from the league during the war years because his best players were serving overseas. When the league said play on, McAuley stepped into the breach and played all 50 games of the schedule. He won just six contests. Lester Patrick was right. The Rangers were a train wreck as McAuley gave up an all-time-high 310 goals. Almost 40 years later, Hartford's Greg Millen suffered the worst embarrassment this side of Ken McAuley when he allowed 282 goals in 60 games during 1982–83.

Answers are on page 294

12.1 Who was the first butterfly-style goalie?

A. Glenn Hall
B. Tony Esposito
C. Terry Sawchuk
D. Georges Vezina

12.2 Who was the last maskless NHL goaltender?

A. Cesare Maniago
B. Ed Giacomin
C. Andy Brown
D. Gump Worsley

12.3 What famous hockey first was little-known New York Rangers backup Joe Schaefer involved in?

A. The NHL's first masked goalie, Jacques Plante
B. The NHL's first goal by a goalie, accredited to Billy Smith
C. The NHL's first female goalie, Manon Rheaume
D. The NHL's first scoreless tie, by Clint Benedict and Jake Forbes

12.4 What is the highest number of wins in a season by a goalie? Name the netminder.

A. 45 wins—Martin Brodeur
B. 47 wins—Bernie Parent
C. 49 wins—Tom Barrasso
D. 51 wins—Grant Fuhr

12.5 Since Terry Sawchuk's magical 44-win season in his rookie year, 1950–51, what modern-day goalie has the next-best record for most rookie wins?

A. Chicago's Tony Esposito in 1969–70
B. Montreal's Ken Dryden in 1971–72
C. Philadelphia's Ron Hextall in 1986–87
D. Chicago's Ed Belfour in 1990–91

12.6 What is the most number of wins recorded by a goalie on an NHL expansion team?

A. 12 wins
B. 22 wins
C. 32 wins
D. 42 wins

12.7 How many wins did goalie Michel Belhumeur post in the 35 games he backstopped Washington for in 1974–75, the year the Capitals set so many NHL losing and winless team records?

A. No wins
B. One win

C. Five wins
D. Nine wins

12.8 According to New Jersey's Martin Brodeur, how many games does a great goaltender steal for his team during the course of a season?

A. Three games
B. Five games
C. Seven games
D. Nine games

12.9 What is the NHL record for most wins in a row by a netminder?

A. 13 wins
B. 17 wins
C. 21 wins
D. 25 wins

12.10 Which goalie recorded the most NHL wins after his 39th birthday?

A. Johnny Bower
B. Jacques Plante
C. George Hainsworth
D. Gerry Cheevers

12.11 Which goalie holds the NHL career record for all-time wins?

A. Terry Sawchuk
B. Jacques Plante
C. Patrick Roy
D. Martin Brodeur

12.12 Which coach was behind the Montreal Canadiens bench when Patrick Roy posted his first NHL win?

A. Pat Burns
B. Jacques Lemaire
C. Bob Berry
D. Jean Perron

12.13 Which goalie earned the last wins at both the Montreal Forum and Maple Leaf Gardens?

A. Curtis Joseph
B. Jocelyn Thibault
C. Felix Potvin
D. Patrick Roy

12.14 Who was the last goalie from a first-place team to get credit for all of his club's victories during a season?

A. Philadelphia's Bernie Parent in 1973–74
B. Chicago's Tony Esposito in 1969–70
C. Detroit's Roger Crozier in 1964–65
D. Montreal's Jacques Plante in 1961–62

12.15 What is the most goals allowed in an NHL game?

A. 15 goals
B. 17 goals
C. 19 goals
D. 21 goals

12.16 What is the highest number of goals allowed by one netminder in a career?

A. 1,700 to 2,000 goals
B. 2,000 to 2,300 goals
C. 2,300 to 2,600 goals
D. More than 2,600 goals

12.17 Which Original Six goalie is famous for attempting to score goals?

A. Johnny Bower
B. Sugar Jim Henry
C. Bill Durnan
D. Charlie Rayner

12.18 Who was the first NHL goalie to score a game-winning goal?

A. Billy Smith
B. Ron Hextall
C. Chris Osgood
D. Martin Brodeur

12.19 Who was the first goalie scored upon by his brother in NHL action?

A. Tiny Thompson in the 1930s
B. Tony Esposito in the 1960s
C. Gary Smith in the 1970s
D. It has never happened

12.20 Which team chased Patrick Roy from the net by scoring nine goals on him in his last game for the Montreal Canadiens, December 2, 1995?

A. The Pittsburgh Penguins
B. The New York Rangers
C. The Detroit Red Wings
D. The Philadelphia Flyers

12.21 What is the most number of consecutive games in which one NHL team has allowed two goals or less? Name the goalie.

A. Eight straight games
B. 18 straight games
C. 28 straight games
D. 38 straight games

12.22 What is the highest number of goals allowed by a goalie whose NHL career lasted just one game?

A. Eight goals
B. 10 goals
C. 12 goals
D. 14 goals

12.23 What is the fewest number of career games played by a goalie who shut out the opposition in his first NHL game?

A. Three games
B. Six games
C. Nine games
D. 12 games

12.24 What is the fewest number of career games played by a goalie who recorded only one shutout?

A. One game
B. Two games
C. Four games
D. Eight games

12.25 Which goalie set a modern-day NHL record for the longest shutout sequence during the 2003–04 season?

A. Marty Turco of the Dallas Stars
B. Brian Boucher of the Phoenix Coyotes
C. Martin Brodeur of the New Jersey Devils
D. José Théodore of the Montreal Canadiens

12.26 When Brian Boucher set a modern-day mark for longest consecutive scoreless minutes of 332:01 in 2003–04, how close did the Phoenix Coyote goalie come to breaking the all-time record?

A. Under 10 minutes
B. Between 10 and 60 minutes
C. Between 60 and 120 minutes
D. More than 120 minutes

12.27 What is the highest number of shutouts recorded by a goalie in his first season?

A. Nine shutouts
B. 11 shutouts
C. 13 shutouts
D. 15 shutouts

12.28 What is the greatest number of different teams one goalie has shut out in one season?

A. Five teams

B. Seven teams

C. Nine teams

D. 11 teams

12.29 Who was the last goalie to shut out all opposing teams in one season?

A. Tony Esposito of the Chicago Blackhawks

B. Ed Giacomin of the New York Rangers

C. Charlie Hodge of the Montreal Canadiens

D. Roger Crozier of the Detroit Red Wings

12.30 What is the record for the longest shutout sequence by a goalie from the start of a career?

A. 60 minutes

B. 80 minutes

C. 100 minutes

D. 120 minutes

12.31 What did opposing netminders Zac Bierk of Phoenix and Michael Leighton of Chicago accomplish in a Coyotes–Blackhawks game on January 8, 2003?

A. An NHL shutout first

B. An NHL shots-against record

C. An NHL minutes-played record

D. An NHL empty net first

12.32 What is the highest number of shutouts recorded by a goalie in his last NHL season?

A. Six shutouts

B. Nine shutouts

C. 12 shutouts

D. 15 shutouts

12.33 Who is the only modern-day goalie to post shutouts with six different NHL teams?

A. Sean Burke
B. Bob Essensa
C. Grant Fuhr
D. Gary Smith

12.34 Who holds the NHL record for most games played in one season?

A. Ed Belfour in 1990–91
B. Grant Fuhr in 1995–96
C. Martin Brodeur in 1995–96
D. Felix Potvin in 1996–97

12.35 Which NHL goalkeeper went unbeaten in a record 32 straight games?

A. Ken Dryden
B. Bernie Parent
C. Gerry Cheevers
D. Pete Peeters

12.36 What is the most regular-season games played by an NHL goalie who never appeared in a playoff game?

A. Between 150 and 200 games
B. Between 200 and 250 games
C. Between 250 and 300 games
D. More than 300 games

12.37 Who was Chicago's backup goalie during Glenn Hall's record 502 consecutive-games streak?

A. Al Rollins
B. Denis DeJordy
C. Henry Bassen
D. Harry Lumley

12.38 What is the most losses amassed by a goalie in a single NHL season?

A. 38 losses
B. 48 losses
C. 58 losses
D. 68 losses

12.39 Which goalie suffered the most losses in his career?

A. Gump Worsley
B. Terry Sawchuk
C. Gilles Meloche
D. Glenn Hall

12.40 Which celebrated NHL goalie made a surprise visit to the USSR dressing room just before Game 1 of the 1972 Canada–Russia Summit Series?

A. Jacques Plante
B. Glenn Hall
C. Ken Dryden
D. Tony Esposito

12.41 Which NHL goalie set a modern-day record for the best goals-against average in 2003–04?

A. Montreal's José Théodore
B. Dallas' Marty Turco
C. New Jersey's Martin Brodeur
D. Calgary's Miikka Kiprusoff

Answers

12.1 A. Glenn Hall

Goalies are remembered in many ways: some for their game-winning saves, others for their Stanley Cup victories or unique personalities. In Hall's case, he will be forever linked to one of hockey's most important innovations, the inverted-V style, or butterfly stance, which he pioneered long before its modern-day practitioners such as Ed Belfour and Patrick Roy. Hall, a lanky six-footer, "got into the butterfly kind of by accident" when the game changed offensively with the slap shot and defensively with more screened shots. Not comfortable with the traditional stance of stand-up goalies, who stayed on their feet and kept their legs together, Hall spaced his feet wide apart and hugged his knees. When he dropped to the ice his knees were together and his legs splayed to either side, forming a wall of pads 10 inches high across the goalmouth. It was a goalie first that few purists endorsed at the time, yet Hall's new crouch-and-drop technique made him faster and more agile post-to-post and gave him a better view on screen shots. He could also get back on his feet more quickly than a stand-up netminder down on the ice. It wasn't until the next generation of goalies came along, including Tony Esposito, that Hall's butterfly was copied. As it turned out, the inverted-V became goaltending's most enduring style.

12.2 C. Andy Brown

A journeyman goalie, Brown staked his claim to fame in his last game as a Pittsburgh Penguin on April 7, 1974. Although Brown continued to play barefaced with the WHA Indianapolis Racers the following season, no other NHL goalie would again enter the nets without face protection. Gump Worsley's contempt for the mask is well known. He was the last goalie of his generation to go barefaced, yielding only in his final season, 1973–74—14 years after Jacques Plante first wore a mask in 1959.

12.3 **A. The NHL's first masked goalie, Jacques Plante**

One of hockey's least-known details about that fateful night in 1959, when Plante first wore his famous mask, concerns Joe Schaefer, the Rangers' assistant trainer and practice goalie. Plante's Montreal Canadiens were playing in New York when, as long-time Rangers general manager Emile Francis tells it: "After Andy Bathgate's backhand forced Plante into the Garden's medic room for stitching, Jacques gave coach Toe Blake two options: 'Play me with my mask or get yourself a backup.' In those days the home team supplied both teams with the spare goalie, and in New York, it was Joe Schaefer. Earlier, Joe had played for Chicago and he let in five goals in two periods of play. After the game, the press boys say, 'Was it a thrill to play tonight?' And Joe says, 'Oh yeah.' They ask, 'What's your weakness?' Joe says, 'Shots!' Well, Blake knew Schaefer's reputation for soft goals. So when Plante refused to play without his mask, Blake's choice was obvious. Plante wore his mask. When he skated out, I couldn't believe it."

12.4 **B. 47 wins—Bernie Parent**

No goalie in NHL history recorded as many wins in a single season as Philadelphia's Bernie Parent in 1973–74, when the Flyers racked up a 50–16–12 season. After seven average seasons, including one year in the WHA, Parent caught fire and won an astonishing 47 games to smash the 22-year record set by Terry Sawchuk with 44 wins in 1951–52. Parent's 47-victory campaign included 12 shutouts, a miserly 1.89 goals-against average and Vezina Trophy honours as top netminder, an award he shared with Tony Esposito of Chicago.

12.5 **D. Chicago's Ed Belfour in 1990–91**

A number of freshmen have challenged Sawchuk's 44-win rookie season of 1950–51. Tony Esposito recorded 38 rookie wins in 1969–70, Ken Dryden topped that with 39 in 1971–72 and Hextall had 37 in 1986–87. But in 1990–91 Ed Belfour struck the closest, recording 43 rookie wins with Chicago—just one short of Sawchuk's awesome mark.

12.6 B. 22 wins

Until 2000–01, the Minnesota North Stars' Cesare Maniago and Florida's John Vanbiesbrouck were the winningest expansion team goalies in modern-day NHL play. Each had notched 21 victories (Maniago in 1967–68 and Vanbiesbrouck in 1993–94) and come within a win of the all-time NHL record set by Lorne Chabot in the New York Rangers' first season, 1926–27. But then came Ron Tugnutt to defy the hockey experts and their predictions that he couldn't win more than 20 games with the expansion Columbus Blue Jackets. (The projection wasn't unrealistic, considering the unknowns of an inaugural season.) It was the kind of criticism the smallish netminder faced for most of his 13-year NHL career; he would then battle back and surprise his detractors. In fact, Tugnutt's 22–25–5 performance with the Blue Jackets in 2000–01 tied his previous best mark of 22 wins and four shutouts, but also equalled one of hockey's longest-standing marks: Chabot's 74-year record for most wins by an expansion team goalie. Tugnutt's 22nd victory came in a 4–3 overtime win against Chicago on April 8, 2001.

12.7 A. No wins

The 1974–75 Capitals established a number of spectacular NHL lows (some later broken by the hapless Ottawa Senators in the early 1990s). In fact, no team in history has set more losing or winless streaks than Washington in its first year of play. It wasn't just bad, it was ugly. The Caps went 17 games in a row without a win, 11 straight without a victory at home, incurred 37 consecutive road losses and allowed an all-time record-high 446 goals. Their worst loss was 12–1, which they suffered twice, to Boston and Pittsburgh, and they incurred five more defeats in the double digits. The year was costly on the coaches, too.

Three bench bosses were wasted and 39 players made the rounds before the smoke cleared. Through it all, goalie Michel Belhumeur allowed 162 goals in 35 games for a goals-against average of more than five goals per game. He failed to record a single win. Belhumeur (which in French means good humour) must have had a great sense of humour to survive with his confidence intact. He played another seven games for Washington the following season and, again, failed to record a win. Belhumeur never played in the NHL again.

12.8 B. Five games

On being asked how many games a great goaltender steals in a season, Martin Brodeur humbly responded, "By myself, I probably steal up to five games that we have no business winning." Long-time Devils defenseman Ken Daneyko, asked the same question about Brodeur, thought his backstopper was a little conservative. "I think probably eight," said Daneyko.

12.9 B. 17 wins

Boston Bruins goalies have carved out a few NHL marks, including the longest winning streak in one season. Boston's Tiny Thompson in 1929–30 and Ross Brooks in 1973–74 set the standard at 14 straight wins. Then, two years after Ross, fellow Bruin Gilles Gilbert recorded an amazing 17-game streak between December 26, 1975, and February 29, 1976. During that two-month stretch the Bruins played 28 games split among three netminders: Gilbert, Dave Reece (whose last NHL game was an 11–4 wipeout by Toronto on February 7) and Gerry Cheevers (back from oblivion and the WHA). To keep his string intact, Gilbert had some luck. In a 7–5 loss at St. Louis on January 17, he and Reece split the nets but Reece registered the loss. In those 17 wins, Gilbert recorded one shutout and allowed just 34 goals on almost 500 shots. The Bruins scored 79 times on the opposition. The streak earned Gilbert a 33–8–10 record and the fewest losses by a starter in 1975–76.

12.10 C. George Hainsworth

Despite a lengthy and successful pro career before the NHL came calling, Hainsworth still figured he had something to prove after joining the league in 1926–27. He was old enough to retire at 31 years old, but the future Hall of Famer played ironman for the next 10 seasons, uninterrupted except for two games in 1929–30, when Montreal won its first of two back-to-back Cups. In 1934–35's 48-game schedule, Hainsworth won 30 games for Toronto—tops in NHL history among goalies aged 39 or older. But that number could be bettered by another Maple Leaf goalie, Ed Belfour, who turned in a 34-win season at age 38 in 2003–04. One more solid season for Belfour and he will have rewritten this record and broken Hainsworth's 70-year hold.

Most Wins by Goalies Aged 39 or Older*

PLAYER	SEASON	TEAM	WINS	AGE
George Hainsworth	1934–35	Toronto	30	39 yrs., 266 days
Gerry Cheevers	1979–80	Boston	24	39 yrs., 121 days
Jacques Plante	1970–71	Toronto	24	42 yrs., 77 days
Johnny Bower	1963–64	Toronto	24	39 yrs., 135 days
George Hainsworth	1935–36	Toronto	23	40 yrs., 269 days
Tony Esposito	1982–83	Chicago	23	39 yrs., 346 days

**Current to 2004–05; courtesy of the* Hockey News

12.11 C. Patrick Roy

Roy has established so many important records that his dominance in the goaltending section of the NHL record book is Gretzky-like. And like the Great One, few of Roy's records will soon be beaten. As long as the great Terry Sawchuk played and as much as he won during his career, Roy has still recorded more minutes and more games than Sawchuk or any other netminder, topping Sawchuk's 447 victories with a regular-season total of 551. As well, Roy leads all goalies with the most 30-or-more-win seasons (13). St. Patrick also owns some prime real estate in the playoff record book. He is the leader in victories, games played and shutouts.

12.12 B. Jacques Lemaire

The date was February 23, 1985. The Canadiens were hosting the Winnipeg Jets. Because of a rash of injuries, Roy had been called up from the Granby Bisons of the Quebec Junior Hockey League to back up starter Doug Soetaert. The 19-year-old didn't expect to play, but just before the start of the third period, with the score knotted 4–4, Montreal coach Jacques Lemaire decided to stir the pot. "Lemaire walked into the dressing room and said, in English, 'Roy, get in the net!' My English wasn't very good. Well, it's still not very good, but there have been a lot improvements since then," Roy recalled in an ESPN interview. "I turned around and said to Guy Carbonneau, 'Did he just mention my name here?' Carbo said, 'Yeah, you're going in.' I said, 'Whoa.' It was a big thrill for me to get in net for those 20 minutes." Roy faced only two shots in the period, but got credit for his first NHL victory as Montreal scored twice to win 6–4. Soon afterwards, Roy was sent back to Granby. Lemaire, who was replaced after the season, should have kept him around. The next fall, Roy rejoined the Habs and led them to the Stanley Cup.

12.13 B. Jocelyn Thibault

More than 130 years of hockey were played at Maple Leaf Gardens and the Montreal Forum, but the last games in both old barns were won by the same netminder: Jocelyn Thibault. Backstopping the Canadiens, Thibault defeated Dallas 4–1 March 11, 1996, in the Forum's finale. Then, almost three years later, as a Blackhawk, T-Bo humbled Toronto 6–2 on February 13, 1999, in the last match at MLG. "I'm a pretty historic goalie," laughed Thibault after realizing he was 2–0 in arena closings. Also that night at the Gardens, Thibault, 24, joined an elite group of goaltenders for another reason. He notched his 100th career NHL victory. (Only four other active goalies had won 100 games so early in their careers: Martin Brodeur, Patrick Roy, Grant Fuhr and Tom Barrasso.)

12.14 C. Detroit's Roger Crozier in 1964–65

Prior to the advent of the two-goalie system in the late 1960s, it wasn't unusual for a netminder to play all of his team's games in a season, thereby getting credit for all games in the win column. However, performing this ironman stunt for a first-place team over a 70-game schedule is still a rare feat. Since the adoption of the 70-game schedule in 1949–50, only four goalies have done it: Terry Sawchuk with Detroit in 1950–51 and 1951–52, Glenn Hall with Detroit in 1956–57, Jacques Plante with Montreal in 1960–61 and 1961–62 and Roger Crozier with Detroit in 1964–65. Crozier's record for the first-place Red Wings was 40–22–7.

12.15 D. 21 goals

On December 11, 1985, Edmonton's Grant Fuhr and Chicago's Murray Bannerman and Bob Sauve made hockey history by allowing a record number of goals, to equal one of the NHL's longest-standing offensive team records: a 14–7 goal-fest in 1919–20 between Toronto and Montreal. That infamous mark stood unchallenged for more than six decades, until 1985 when Bannerman, Sauve and Fuhr gave up a mind-numbing 21 goals in the Oilers' 12–9 decision over the Blackhawks. In all, 62 points were tallied between the clubs, another team record.

12.16 D. More than 2,600 goals

The leading candidates for the distinction of hockey's "most scored upon" are some of the sport's best puck stoppers. Typically, they either played a consistently good game with bad or mediocre teams or, through longevity, acquired a higher goals-against count. The winner (or loser, depending on your viewpoint) is Gilles Meloche. His 2,756 goals in 18 NHL seasons outdistances all other netminders, but the statistic is deceiving. Meloche was better than most of the teams he backstopped, including the California Seals and Cleveland Barons. When the Barons merged with Minnesota, Meloche had his finest hour tending the nets in the 1981 Stanley Cup finals against the New York Islanders.

12.17 D. Charlie Rayner

Rayner's ambition was to score a goal in the NHL. His penchant for playing the point on a delayed penalty or late in the game as an extra attacker put him in good position on numerous occasions. On December 28, 1946, with his Rangers down 2–1 and 35 seconds left on the clock, coach Frank Boucher stationed Rayner just inside Detroit's blue line instead of pulling him for an extra attacker during a faceoff in the Red Wings end. Rayner didn't score, but teammate Hal Laycoe did, potting the winner against Harry Lumley with just seven seconds remaining. Five days later against Toronto, the Rangers goalie raced up the ice to Toronto's blue line with less than a minute remaining to try and help notch the tying goal in a 5–4 game. This time New York failed to score. Then, on January 25, while defending a 1–0 shutout (with the Maple Leafs' Turk Broda on the bench for the extra attacker), Rayner dashed 30 feet for a loose puck in the dying seconds and fired the puck up-ice, barely missing the empty net. Rayner made several more attempts for a goal but never scored in NHL action. Still, his dream did come true while playing with his Rangers teammates on a barnstorming tour through the Canadian Maritimes in 1951. Facing the Maritime Senior League All-Stars, Rayner deked out the defense and tucked a pretty backhander into the net.

12.18 D. Martin Brodeur

Only a handful of netminders have scored in NHL action, but the first to score a game-winner was Brodeur, who was credited with the goal after Philadelphia misplayed the puck into its own vacated net on a delayed penalty on February 15, 2000. The Devils' goalie was the last player to touch the puck. "If I'm going to score, it might as well be a game-winner," said Brodeur after the 4–2 win. It was the second NHL goal of his career.

12.19 A. Tiny Thompson in the 1930s

Only a few brothers have become NHL skater-goalie combinations. Before Phil and Tony Esposito became household names in the 1970s, Brian and Gary Smith played against each other in 1967–68, when Brian was with Los Angeles and Gary was with Oakland. But the first brothers combo to face each other was Paul and Tiny Thompson. After playing against each other for the first time on December 4, 1928, brothers Tiny and Paul Thompson made history in their 14th NHL meeting, when Paul scored on Tiny during a clash between the Boston Bruins and the New York Rangers on March 18, 1930. The goal came at 14:48 of the second period. Boston won 9–2.

12.20 C. The Detroit Red Wings

Big-league pressures mean even the best have a bad night. But on December 2, 1995, when Detroit's scoring machine rolled into Montreal, Patrick Roy's bad night assumed profound importance—both for his career and the Canadiens. The Red Wings chased Roy from the net just 31:57 into the game, scoring nine goals on 26 shots. After the seventh goal, Sergei Fedorov took a long slapper, which Roy handled easily; disgruntled Forum fans responded with mock applause. Roy raised both arms high in a derisive salute to the sellout crowd. Two goals later he was finally yanked by rookie coach Mario Tremblay. Roy skated off the ice embarrassed and angry. Unbeknownst to anyone at the time, it was his last appearance for Montreal. As Roy walked behind the player's bench to the backup goalie's stool, he stopped in midstride beyond Tremblay, wheeled around and took several steps back behind the bench to the box seat of Canadiens president Ronald Corey. Roy pressed up against Corey and snorted, "This is my last game for Montreal." Roy then pushed past a glaring Tremblay, sat on the stool, cocked his head back and said, "Did you understand?" Roy, an icon of the game and the Habs' most popular player, was through in Montreal. Four days later, he was traded to Colorado, where he would help the Avalanche win the 1996 Stanley Cup. Ironically, the Avalanche defeated the Red Wings—the team whose shelling had prompted Roy's trade from Montreal—in the Western Conference finals.

12.21 B. 18 straight games

Fronted by perhaps the era's best defensive duo in the NHL—Norris Trophy-winners Doug Harvey and Tom Johnson—Montreal's Jacques Plante allowed two goals or less for a record 18 games in 1959–60. Interestingly, the streak, which began on October 22 and ended in Game 19 after a 7–4 loss to the Rangers December 3, also set a little-known league record for most consecutive games by a team scoring the first goal. The Canadiens, man for man, may have had added incentive to win for their star netminder. It was during this period that Plante faced his stiffest criticism by becoming hockey's first masked goalie. Plante's record during the streak was 14–1–3.

12.22 B. 10 goals

What number of games have more goalies played in their career than any other number? One game. Discounting the position players, trainers, coaches and practice goalies who replaced injured or penalized netminders in hockey's early days, some 65 goalies to date have had one-game careers in the NHL. They either filled in as temporary replacements for a night or for a period or were called up as legitimate tryouts. Among those one-game wonders, Winnipeg's Ron Loustel allowed an unprecedented 10 goals in a 10–2 whipping against Vancouver on March 27, 1981. But the worst goals-against average belongs to Jim Stewart, who made his debut with the Boston Bruins on January 10, 1980. Stewart allowed three goals in the first four minutes and two before the period ended. He was yanked after 20 minutes and five goals with a humbling 15 goals-against average. Neither Stewart nor Loustel ever backstopped another NHL team.

12.23 A. Three games

Dave Gatherum, Gord Henry and Claude Pronovost are among more than 20 goalies who recorded shutouts in their NHL debuts. Unfortunately, the big league wasn't so kind in subsequent games. Each had the NHL lifespan of a fruit fly, backstopping two more games before being swatted back to the minors.

12.24 B. Two games

NHL history is rich in hero-to-zero stories, such as the saga of the two-game career of Joe Ironstone. After allowing three goals in two periods for the New York Americans in a 1925–26 game, Ironstone was sent back to minor pro until March 28, 1928, when he was called up by Toronto GM Conn Smythe to replace an injured John Ross Roach in a Toronto–Boston match. In what proved to be his downfall, Ironstone agreed to play at Smythe's request but not at his price. Because the invite was last-minute on game day, Smythe met Ironstone's demands for a top-dollar wage. The replacement goalie proved worthy of every penny, playing 70 minutes of shutout hockey in the scoreless overtime tie. But Smythe didn't like Ironstone's cheekiness. The goalie never saw NHL action again.

12.25 B. Brian Boucher of the Phoenix Coyotes

Boucher is not the first nobody to put his name in the NHL record book, but even among the unlikeliest candidates to break Bill Durnan's 1949 modern-day shutout record of 309:21, his candidacy would be a stretch. Boucher, a backup for most of his five-year career, was riding the pines in Phoenix as the number three man after getting beat out by Zac Bierk as Sean Burke's caddy at camp in 2003–04. It only got worse when the

Coyotes put him on waivers and there were no takers. Then, in late December, fate came calling. Injuries opened up a spot and Boucher seized the day. His streak began in Nashville on December 22 in a 3–3 tie against the Predators. After giving up a goal at 19:15 of the second period to Scott Walker, Boucher barred the door with a 4–0 win against Los Angeles on December 31, followed by road victories over Dallas 6–0, Carolina 3–0, Washington 3–0 and Minnesota 2–0. Boucher's run ended with a goal he had no way of stopping. A wrist shot fired by Atlanta's Randy Robitaille glanced off the chest of Phoenix defenseman David Tanabe and into the net at 6:16 of the first period in a 1–1 tie against the Thrashers on January 11. The native of Woonsocket, Rhode Island, broke two 55-year-old records by reeling off five straight shutouts and not allowing a goal for 332 minutes and one second. In that span he made 146 saves. But, according to Tanabe, Boucher's real test may have come when he wasn't even practising with the team in November. "A lot of us sat back and watched the professional way he reacted to that... those things earn a lot of respect from teammates, and it makes you proud to stand in front of the guy and do everything you can," said Tanabe. Boucher, holder of more than five hours of shutout hockey, was humbled by the accomplishment. "There's a lot of history in this game and to be a small part of it is something I'm very proud of," he said.

12.26 D. More than 120 minutes

Brian Boucher's five straight shutouts from December 31 to January 9, 2003, broke Bill Durnan's modern-day record of four zeroes in 1948–49 but fell far short of the all-time mark set by Alex Connell of the old Ottawa Senators. Playing in an era before forward passing was allowed, Connell stoned opponents in six games for 461 minutes and 29 seconds, besting Boucher's shutout sequence of 332 minutes and one second by more than two complete games, 129:28.

12.27 D. 15 shutouts

Only a handful of rookies have reached the double-digit shutout mark. Legendary netminders such as George Hainsworth (14 zeroes), Glenn Hall (12), Terry Sawchuk (11) and Ken Dryden (8) broke into the league and earned quick recognition for their singular performance in the nets. But despite the fact that Hall, Sawchuk and Dryden all won the Calder Trophy as top freshman, not one of them could touch Tony Esposito's Calder accomplishment of 15 rookie shutouts in 1969–70. Esposito also led the league in wins (38) and goals-against average (2.17), earning him not only the Calder but the Vezina Trophy as top netminder, a feat only achieved once before, by Frank Brimsek in 1939, and not duplicated for another 14 years, until Tom Barrasso in 1984.

12.28 D. 11 teams

In 1997–98 Dominik Hasek stormed the 26-team NHL, goosing 11 different teams in his 13-shutout season. Hasek blanked Boston, Anaheim, Tampa Bay, Montreal, Ottawa, Washington, Pittsburgh, Calgary, Edmonton and Los Angeles once, and the New York Rangers three times.

12.29 B. Ed Giacomin of the New York Rangers

Goalies today have a snowball's chance in hell of duplicating Giacomin's shutout feat of zeroing all teams in one season. In what turned into a slow year for shutouts, just 29 in 1966–67, Giacomin ruled the league with nine, blanking Toronto three times, Chicago and Detroit twice and Montreal and Boston once in the six-team NHL. During Tony Esposito's record-setting 15-shutout run in 1969–70, he notched shutouts against nine of the NHL's other 11 teams. The only clubs Esposito failed to shut out were Minnesota and Giacomin's Rangers.

12.30 C. 100 minutes

The longest shutout sequence by a first-time goalie belongs to Detroit rookie Dave Gatherum. A fill-in for an injured Terry Sawchuk, Gatherum played three games in October 1953, goosing Toronto 4–0 in his NHL debut on October 11 and then blanking Chicago until 00:21 of the third period five nights later. Gatherum earned a 2–2 tie against the Hawks and set the shutout mark at 100 minutes and 21 seconds from the start of a career. In his third game, the rookie recorded another win, but his 2–0–1 rookie record meant little when Sawchuk returned. Gatherum never backstopped another game in the six-team NHL.

12.31 A. An NHL shutout first

Zac Bierk and Michael Leighton are the first opposing goalies to record their first career shutouts in the same game. They did it backstopping Phoenix and Chicago in the scoreless tie. Bierk stopped 40 shots and Leighton 31. The NHL has had more than 150 scoreless games since its first season in 1917–18.

12.32 D. 15 shutouts

Before forward passing in all three zones was permitted in 1929–30, NHL goalies dominated hockey. The Brodeurs and Haseks of the 1920s routinely recorded double-digit shutout totals in 44-game seasons, almost half the length of today's schedule. Remarkably, in 1927–28, six starting goalies in the 10-team NHL all notched 10 shutouts or more. Boston's Hal Winkler, a 36-year-old veteran, collected a league-high 15 zeroes that season. It was his swan song in the NHL. The Bruins replaced Winkler with rookie sensation Tiny Thompson in 1928–29. No goalie has gone out with such huge numbers in the shutout column. As a tribute, when Boston won the Cup with Thompson between the pipes in 1928–29, Winkler was listed on the Cup as the team's "sub-goaltender," an NHL first in the days when teams played without backups or spares.

12.33 A. Sean Burke

In 1999–2000, Burke joined old-timer Lorne Chabot as one of only two netminders to register shutouts with six NHL teams. Chabot logged zeroes with each of the six teams he played for: the New York Rangers, Toronto Maple Leafs, Chicago Blackhawks, Montreal Canadiens, Montreal Maroons and New York Americans. Burke has posted goose eggs with six of the seven teams he has played for: the New Jersey Devils, Hartford Whalers, Carolina Hurricanes, Philadelphia Flyers, Florida Panthers and Phoenix Coyotes. Burke did not earn a shutout with the Vancouver Canucks in the 16 games he played for the club in 1997–98.

12.34 B. Grant Fuhr in 1995–96

Fuhr backstopped Mike Keenan's St. Louis Blues in a league-record 79 games in 1995–96, his first season with the Blues after signing as a free agent in July 1995. Keenan rescued Fuhr's career as a backup in Los Angeles, Buffalo and Toronto by making the 14-year veteran his number one starter. During 1995–96 Fuhr battled with the Devils' Martin Brodeur in the games-played statistical category. In the test of endurance each survived the gruelling schedule, but after 82 games Fuhr had a two-game edge: 79 matches to Brodeur's 77. Yet despite having played two more games, Fuhr logged 4,365 minutes—68 minutes fewer than Brodeur's season count of 4,433, a new league record which has since been topped by the Devils goalie himself (4,555 minutes in 2003–04).

12.35 C. Gerry Cheevers

The Boston Bruins of the early 1970s were famed for their blitzkrieg offense and smash-mouth physical play, but an overlooked ingredient of the Bruins' success was their goaltending. Cheevers may not have put up flashy shutout or goals-against numbers, but no one was better at making clutch saves with the game on the line. As he once admitted: "I don't care much about my average. My philosophy has always been that the other team can fill the net on me as long as we get one more goal." In 1971–72, Cheevers went unbeaten in 32 straight games with 24 wins and eight ties, and helped lead Boston to the league title and its second Stanley Cup in three years. The next year he jumped ship to play in the WHA, and the Bruins crashed and burned in the quarterfinals.

Longest Undefeated Streak by a Goalie*

GOALIE	TEAM	SEASON	STREAK
Gerry Cheevers	Boston	1971–72	32 games
Pete Peeters	Boston	1982–83	31 games
Pete Peeters	Philadelphia	1979–80	27 games
Frank Brimsek	Boston	1940–41	23 games
Chico Resch	N.Y. Islanders	1978–79	23 games
Grant Fuhr	Edmonton	1981–82	23 games

**Current to 2004–05*

12.36 C. Between 250 and 300 games

Dunc Wilson logged 287 games with five NHL teams between 1969–70 and 1978–79, and never once appeared in a playoff match. Each of his five clubs—Philadelphia, Vancouver, Toronto, New York and Pittsburgh—were among the worst in the NHL during Wilson's time with each club. When his teams did make the playoffs, such as Toronto in 1974 and Pittsburgh in 1977, Wilson sat on the bench, watching in frustration as his clubs were eliminated.

12.37 B. Denis DeJordy

Like Bobby Hull, Pierre Pilote and other young, talented juniors, DeJordy came from Chicago's farm team, the St. Catherines Teepees of the Ontario Hockey League. DeJordy joined the Teepees in Glenn Hall's first year as a Blackhawk, 1957–58, but unlike Hall, who made the NHL club immediately, DeJordy waited out Hall's streak over five seasons before playing his first NHL game. Like Pilote before him, DeJordy honed his skills with the Hawks' affiliate in the American Hockey League, the Buffalo Bisons, and with the EPHL's Sault Ste. Marie Thunderbirds. During that time he led his respective leagues in wins four times and in shutouts twice. But as long as Hall was healthy in Chicago, DeJordy was little more than long-distance injury insurance in the one-goalie system of the six-team NHL. The long wait for DeJordy finally ended in November 1962, when a back problem forced Hall out of a game against Boston. DeJordy replaced him in a 3–3 tie against the Bruins and played two nights later in Montreal for a 3–1 win over the Canadiens, ending Hall's amazing iron-man record. Over the next two seasons DeJordy played just 11 games and didn't get any consistent NHL action until 1964–65, when he managed 30 games as Hall's regular backup. By that time DeJordy had spent seven seasons in wait. He was already in his prime at age 26.

12.38 B. 48 losses

The most disastrous season for a goalie in recent times may be Marc Denis's 41-loss campaign with Columbus in 2002–03, but even his numbers pale in comparison to the record defeats accumulated by Gary "Suitcase" Smith. Smith may best be remembered as the journeyman goalie who played on a record eight teams, but his 15-year career featured another sorry feat: 48 losses. Smith's undressing happened in 1970–71 when he was playing for the California Seals, an awful team (20–53–5) with the league's most porous defense and lifeless offense. Smith grew so frustrated with his club's performance during one game that he tried to score a goal himself on opposition goalie Ed Giacomin of the Rangers. Smith took off for the New York end and crossed centre ice before being stopped by Rod Seiling, the last Ranger back. Had Smith been able to deke Seiling, he would have had a remarkable breakaway, a one-on-one goalie versus goalie shootout.

The NHL's Top Single-Season Losing Goalies*

PLAYER	TEAM	SEASON	GP	LOSSES
Gary Smith	California	1970–71	71	48
Al Rollins	Chicago	1953–54	66	47
Peter Sidorkiewicz	Ottawa	1992–93	64	46
Harry Lumley	Chicago	1951–52	70	44

**Current to 2004–05*

12.39 A. Gump Worsley

Although the Gumper won four Stanley Cups late in his career with the powerhouse Montreal Canadiens of the 1960s, he paid his dues during the 1950s with some terrible New York Rangers teams. His rise from "duck in a shooting gallery" to Cup champion produced two completely opposite NHL records. No goalie in league history has been defeated more often (352 losses) than Worsley, yet he holds the game's lowest career goals-against average among modern-day netminders in Stanley Cup finals action: 1.82 in 16 games. Gilles Meloche, who never won a Cup, has 351 losses, just one less than Worsley. John Vanbiesbrouck also retired in time to avoid this record, with five fewer losses or 346 defeats between 1981–82 and 2001–02.

12.40 A. Jacques Plante

Before the opening game of the 1972 Summit Series, Vladislav Tretiak received an unusual visit from NHL veteran Jacques Plante, who, through a translator and with blackboard diagrams, instructed the young Soviet goalie on how to stop Canada's top snipers. Whatever possessed Plante, perhaps hockey's most learned goalie, to reveal such hockey secrets is not clear; perhaps he felt sorry for Tretiak, a fellow gatekeeper up against overwhelming odds. But the game is now hockey lore. The Soviets humiliated Canada 7–3, exposing Canada's biggest weakness—its lack of game preparation, particularly in properly assessing Soviet strengths, such as Tretiak. After the loss, Pete Mahovlich unwittingly remarked that Tretiak had played him like he'd known him throughout his career, which leads us to wonder how Plante reacted to Canada's defeat that night. Was he smiling at his tutorial success, or regretful?

12.41 D. Calgary's Miikka Kiprusoff

He played in less than half of Calgary's games in 2003–04, but Kiprusoff attracted honourable mentions for league MVP after posting a modern-era-low 1.69 goals-against average and a striking 24–10–4 record. Along with Jarome Iginla's 41-goal blitz, Kiprusoff's spiffy play led the Flames to their first playoff spot since 1996, a nice career boost considering he was San Jose's odd man out before being plucked in mid-November from the depths of the Sharks system by Calgary coach and general manager Darryl Sutter. Kiprusoff topped Marty Turco's goals-against record of 1.72 in 2002–03 and produced the lowest average by a regular since 1939–40, when Ranger Davey Kerr's 48-game performance netted a 1.54.

GAME 12

Backup to the Greats

SCOTT CLEMMENSEN DOESN'T get much attention. There are no fat contracts, shiny trophies, catchy nicknames or sweet endorsement deals in the job as backup to Martin Brodeur. Heck, a little more playing time would be nice, but for the Devils rookie, 2003–04 was still good: three wins, two shutouts and a warm seat at the end of New Jersey's bench. In this game, match these famous Stanley Cup-winning goalies and their backups.

Solutions are on page 565

PART 1

1.________	Dominik Hasek/Detroit 2002	A. David Aebischer
2.________	Gump Worsley/Montreal 1966	B. Rick Wamsley
3.________	Mike Vernon/Calgary 1989	C. Roman Turek
4.________	Bernie Parent/Philadelphia 1975	D. Manny Legace
5.________	Ed Belfour/Dallas 1999	E. Charlie Hodge
6.________	Gerry Cheevers/Boston 1970	F. Wayne Stephenson
7.________	Patrick Roy/Colorado 2001	G. Eddie Johnston

PART 2

1.________	Martin Brodeur/New Jersey 2003	A. Ken Wregget
2.________	Bill Ranford/Edmonton 1990	B. Roland Melanson
3.________	Ken Dryden/Montreal 1978	C. Don Simmons
4.________	Mike Richter/NY Rangers 1994	D. Glenn Healy
5.________	Johnny Bower/Toronto 1964	E. Corey Schwab
6.________	Tom Barrasso/Pittsburgh 1992	F. Michel Larocque
7.________	Billy Smith/NY Islanders 1983	G. Grant Fuhr

13

The Big Lines

AT ONE TIME, IT SEEMED as though every team had its big line—a trio of forwards who combined breathtaking speed with gritty play and awesome scoring power. This three-way chemistry transformed otherwise ordinary teams into championship-winners. These lethal combos were game-winners and dynasty builders. Whatever happened to hockey's great scoring lines? In this chapter, we look at the lines that could hurt you on every shift.

Answers are on page 320

13.1 How many goals did the New York Rangers' GAG (Goal-A-Game) Line score during its peak season, the 78-game schedule of 1971–72?

A. Exactly 78 goals
B. Between 79 and 99 goals
C. Between 100 and 129 goals
D. More than 129 goals

13.2 Which team iced the Mattress Line in 2003–04?

A. The Tampa Bay Lightning
B. The Vancouver Canucks
C. The Dallas Stars
D. The Ottawa Senators

13.3 Which left-winger played the longest on the Edmonton Oilers' Wayne Gretzky–Jari Kurri line?

A. Dave Semenko
B. Esa Tikkanen

C. Mike Krushelnyski
D. Craig Simpson

13.4 What 1970s team had a famous line named after an Academy Award-winning movie?
A. The New York Rangers
B. The Buffalo Sabres
C. The Los Angeles Kings
D. The Minnesota North Stars

13.5 Why were Penguins Syl Apps Jr., Lowell MacDonald and Jean Pronovost dubbed the Century Line in the 1970s?
A. Their line scored more than 100 goals in 1973–74
B. Their ages totalled 100 years
C. Each player scored his 100th NHL goal in 1974–75
D. Their jersey numbers added up to 100

13.6 Which Flyer helped nickname the Eric Lindros–John Leclair–Mikael Renberg line the Legion of Doom?
A. Jim Montgomery
B. Rod Brind'Amour
C. Craig MacTavish
D. Ron Hextall

13.7 The players on which line finished the 1949–50 season ranked first, second and third in the NHL scoring race?
A. Detroit's Production Line
B. Montreal's Punch Line
C. Boston's Kraut Line
D. Chicago's Pony Line

13.8 Who centred Gordie Howe and Ted Lindsay on Detroit's Production Line after Sid Abel retired in 1952?
A. Earl Reibel
B. Norm Ullman
C. Glen Skov
D. Alex Delvecchio

13.9 Which NHL team iced the so-called 700-Pound Line in 2003–04?

A. The Dallas Stars
B. The Boston Bruins
C. The St. Louis Blues
D. The Philadelphia Flyers

13.10 In what year did the U.S. Olympic hockey team feature The Diaper Line?

A. 1980
B. 1984
C. 1992
D. 1994

13.11 What line was the first to finish 1–2–3 in the NHL scoring race?

A. Montreal's Punch Line of Blake–Lach–Richard
B. Toronto's Kid Line of Jackson–Primeau–Conacher
C. Boston's Kraut Line of Dumart–Schmidt–Bauer
D. Detroit's Production Line of Lindsay–Abel–Howe

13.12 Which NHL team iced the GAS Line in 2000–01?

A. The New Jersey Devils
B. The Calgary Flames
C. The Boston Bruins
D. The Detroit Red Wings

13.13 Which forward line was considered the first power trio in the NHL?

A. The Montreal Maroons' S Line
B. Toronto's Kid Line
C. New York's A Line
D. Detroit's Production Line

13.14 Which 1970s team featured the Mafia Line?

A. The Detroit Red Wings
B. The Chicago Blackhawks
C. The New York Rangers
D. The Philadelphia Flyers

13.15 What was the name of Stan Mikita's famous line in Chicago?

A. The Scooter Line
B. The Pony Line
C. The Reject Line
D. The Million-Dollar Line

13.16 Which was the first line to feature three 100-point scorers?

A. New York's GAG Line of Ratelle–Gilbert–Hadfield
B. Boston's Nitro Line of Esposito–Hodge–Cashman
C. Buffalo's French Connection Line of Perreault–Martin–Robert
D. Los Angeles' Triple Crown Line of Dionne–Simmer–Taylor

13.17 What NHL team iced the Crash Line during the mid-1990s?

A. The Toronto Maple Leafs
B. The Tampa Bay Lightning
C. The Dallas Stars
D. The New Jersey Devils

13.18 Why was Toronto's Flying Forts Line given that name?

A. The entire line came from Fort William, Ontario
B. All three linemates played over the age of 40
C. Each linemate played junior hockey in Fort Francis, Ontario
D. The linemates lived as rookies in a Toronto hotel known as Fort Knox

13.19 Who formed Toronto's most celebrated scoring trio, the Kid Line?

A. Frank Selke
B. Charlie Conacher
C. Conn Smythe
D. King Clancy

13.20 What 1997–98 team produced the Grind Line?

A. The New York Rangers
B. The Detroit Red Wings
C. The Phoenix Coyotes
D. The Vancouver Canucks

13.21 Which country did the KLM Line play for in international hockey competition?

A. U.S.A.
B. Sweden
C. The Soviet Union
D. Holland

13.22 Which old-time duo was called the Gold Dust Twins?

A. Chicago's Bobby Hull and Stan Mikita
B. Montreal's Odie and Sprague Cleghorn
C. The Rangers' Bill and Bun Cook
D. Ottawa's Cy Denneny and Punch Broadbent

13.23 Who formed the famous S Line?

A. The Maroons' Nels Stewart, Babe Siebert and Hooley Smith
B. The Bruins' Derek Sanderson, Al Sims and Fred Stanfield
C. The Hawks' Glen Skov, Tod Sloan and George Sullivan
D. The Rangers' Alex Shibicky, Clint Smith and Earl Seibert

13.24 Over its lifetime, how many Canadian forwards played regularly on Montreal's Doughnut Line?

A. One forward: John Ferguson, the team's policeman
B. Two forwards: Guy Lafleur and Steve Shutt

C. Two forwards: Jean Béliveau and Henri Richard
D. Three forwards: Maurice Richard, Elmer Lach and Toe Blake

13.25 Which two wingers did Bryan Trottier centre on the New York Islanders' Long Island Lighting Co.?
A. Clark Gillies and Mike Bossy
B. John Tonelli and Bob Nystrom
C. Duane Sutter and Brent Sutter
D. Butch Goring and Bill Harris

13.26 As brothers, we formed a complete offensive line. Our stay together was brief, but it was a feat not repeated until Quebec made linemates of Peter, Marion and Anton Stastny in 1981. Who were we?
A. Larry, Wayne and Floyd Hillman
B. Lionel, Charlie and Roy Conacher
C. Max, Doug and Reg Bentley
D. Marcel, Jean and Claude Pronovost

13.27 What name was given to Philadelphia's line of centre Daniel Lacroix and wingers Dan Kordic and Brantt Myhres in 1997–98?
A. The Sin Bin Line
B. The Bus Line
C. The KLM Line
D. The Left Hook Line

13.28 What was the name of the Winnipeg Jets line that Bobby Hull, Anders Hedberg and Ulf Nilsson played on in the WHA?
A. The Golden Jet Line
B. The Hot Line
C. The International Line
D. The Swedish Express

13.29 Which team iced the FLY Line in 2001–02?
A. The Washington Capitals
B. The New York Rangers
C. The Vancouver Canucks
D. The St. Louis Blues

13.30 The LCB Line played for which Stanley Cup-winning team during the 1970s?
A. The Boston Bruins
B. The Philadelphia Flyers
C. The Montreal Canadiens
D. The New York Islanders

13.31 Which NHL team created the AMP Line in 2002–03?
A. The Toronto Maple Leafs
B. The Detroit Red Wings
C. The Tampa Bay Lightning
D. The Colorado Avalanche

13.32 Which scoring line was the first unit to have all of its three members inducted into the Hall of Fame?
A. Detroit's Production Line
B. Montreal's Punch Line
C. Toronto's Kid Line
D. The New York Islanders' Long Island Lighting Co.

The Big Lines

Answers

13.1 D. More than 129 goals
Vic Hadfield, Jean Ratelle and Rod Gilbert played together on the New York Rangers' GAG Line for more than a decade—from the early 1960s to the mid-1970s. Even though they never won

a Stanley Cup, at least longevity was on their side. It proved an important factor during their best season, 1971–72, when they produced 139 goals in the 78-game schedule. Only Phil Esposito and Bobby Orr's spectacular one-two finish topped the GAG Line's surprising third-, fourth- and fifth-place ranking in the NHL scoring derby—a race that included such snipers as Bobby Hull, Frank Mahovlich and Yvan Cournoyer. Bolstered by the GAG Line's scoring production, the Rangers reached the Cup finals that year, only to lose in six games to the Bruins.

13.2 B. The Vancouver Canucks

After three years of trying to find someone who would make a second line out of Daniel and Henrik Sedin, the Canucks thought they had their sniper for the Swedish twins' puck-control game in right wing Jason King, a Newfoundland native and draft-day gamble picked 212th overall in 2001. In early 2003–04, King led all Canucks with 10 goals and all NHL rookies with 14 points. Things soon cooled off for the rookie (and his line fit for a king), but not before every hockey fan in the Lower Mainland of British Columbia was telling this Newfie joke: "How many Newfies does it take to get the Sedin twins to live up to their potential?" The answer? "One... Jason King." The trio was dubbed the Mattress Line—two twins and a King.

13.3 B. Esa Tikkanen

With the exception of Philadelphia's Legion of Doom Line, few teams in the 1980s and 1990s found the right player combination to form a potent threesome. Two-man units with the third forward in rotation became the norm. It's not because of any particular hockey philosophy, but today there are more clubs, less talent on each team and fewer coaches willing to let lines develop as pressure mounts for instant success. When Wayne Gretzky and Jari Kurri teamed up in the early 1980s, their mobility and natural offensive skills became the vanguard for the Oilers' flying assault. Kurri could switch lanes in mid-attack to feed Gretzky. In turn, Gretzky, from any angle but especially from behind his opponents' net, would set up Kurri for a one-timer or score himself on the wraparound. They knew each other's positions on the ice almost without looking. Playing together became second nature. Although many left-wingers guested on their line, the most frequent one was Esa Tikkanen, who played with the duo for almost three full seasons, winning two Stanley Cups and racking up his best numbers. In 1986–87, the trio combined for 369 points.

13.4 B. The Buffalo Sabres

The hit movie *The French Connection* was the inspiration for Buffalo's greatest scoring unit of Rick Martin, Gilbert Perreault and Rene Robert. All native Quebeckers, the trio played together for eight years and in its most productive season, 1974–75, combined for 131 goals. During the playoffs, the French Connection Line was the driving force behind the Sabres' run to the Stanley Cup finals. The name was the inspiration of Buffalo reporter Lee Coppola, who thought it up one night while operating Memorial Auditorium's scoreboard.

13.5 A. Their line scored more than 100 goals in 1973–74

Often forgotten and never as flashy as Buffalo's French Connection or the Flyers' LCB line, Pittsburgh's Century Line of Apps, Pronovost and MacDonald was one of the best offensive trios of the mid-1970s, notching 107 goals in 1973–74, second only to Phil Esposito's line in Boston.

13.6 A. Jim Montgomery

The "Legion of Doom" nickname developed out of a comment Montgomery made to Les Bowen of the *Philadelphia Daily News* at a Flyers practice, just a few days after the big trade. In his observations about the line's size, Montgomery, a huge wrestling fan, remarked that the new Philly forward unit resembled the Legion of Doom, a pro wrestling tag team.

Many other nicknames were suggested (Bob's Big Boys, among them), but nothing rivalled Montgomery's characterization of the biggest line of 1994–95.

13.7 A. Detroit's Production Line

Perhaps hockey's greatest trio, the fabled Production Line of Gordie Howe, Sid Abel and Ted Lindsay, finished first-second-third in 1949–50's scoring race with Lindsay's record of 23–55–78, Abel's 34–35–69 and Howe's 35–33–68. It was not the first time three linemates had led the NHL in scoring, but it gave notice of Detroit's future as an NHL powerhouse. The Red Wings won seven straight regular-season championships and four Stanley Cups in five years with the Production Line motoring their offense. Like other formidable scoring lines, the Production Line had great chemistry. Abel was the unit's veteran, the savvy leader who centred the younger Lindsay and Howe. The pair blended superb skills and bone-jarring toughness—a lethal combination. Both men won NHL goal-scoring titles and often ranked among the league leaders in penalty minutes. Howe, on right wing, could do everything. His enormous strength and coordination made him a scoring champion for four straight years while playing with Lindsay and Abel. The Production Line played together for almost six years before Abel moved to Chicago as a player-coach.

13.8 D. Alex Delvecchio

One minute you're a 20-year-old slogging it through America's industrial belt on the junior circuit, the next you're centring one of hockey's biggest power lines, partnered with Gordie Howe and Ted Lindsay during Detroit's reign of championships. That was the heady reality Alex Delvecchio woke up to in 1952 after Sid Abel retired and left the Wings without a centre for the Production Line. Manager Jack Adams figured Delvecchio's pinpoint passing and lightning-fast skating skills would prove the perfect complement for the famed Detroit wingers. Adams nailed it right. The following season, 1952–53,

Delvecchio finished fifth in league scoring and was named centre on the Second All-Star team. He dominated offensively during the 1954 and 1955 Stanley Cups and played faithfully for the Wings until 1974. (Worth noting: before Delvecchio became a permanent pivot, other players centred the line, including rookie Earl Reibel, who recorded a 15–33–48 in 1953–54.

13.9 B. The Boston Bruins

One of the NHL's most dominant lines of 2003–04, the Bruins' 700-Pound Line of Mike Knuble (six foot three and 225 pounds), Joe Thornton (six foot four and 220 pounds) and Glen Murray (six foot three and 225 pounds) weighed 670 pounds. In full gear, Knuble, Thornton and Murray tipped the scales at more than 750 pounds, about half the weight of a compact car.

13.10 B. 1984

The U.S. Olympic hockey team of 1984 had none of the gold-medal success of their predecessors four years earlier, but they did have some impressive moments, particularly from a forward unit dubbed The Diaper Line. The mighty trio of teenagers included Pat LaFontaine, David A. Jensen and Ed Olczyk. The American team finished seventh in the standings.

13.11 C. Boston's Kraut Line of Dumart–Schmidt–Bauer

The Bruins' potent scoring line of Milt Schmidt, Woody Dumart and Bobby Bauer was formed in 1937–38, and almost immediately became known as the Kraut Line, a reference to the trio's Germanic hometown—Kitchener, in southern Ontario. In their first season, the wide-eyed kids from Kitchener combined for 46 goals and 88 points, not enough for a top-10 finish among them, but it was obvious that Schmidt, Dumart and Bauer read one another very well. The following season Boston won the Stanley Cup and the year after that the Kraut Line paced the league one-two-three in scoring. Boston took another Cup in 1941 before the entire

Kraut Line joined the Royal Canadian Air Force to play for the Allan Cup-winning Ottawa Hurricanes during World War II. Their NHL return three years later showed that the trio had lost none of its playmaking chemistry. The three players never won another Cup together but each maintained his scoring drive. Bauer retired in 1946–47 after a career-high 30-goal season. Dumart and Schmidt played on until the mid-1950s. Dumart recorded five 20-goal years and three All-Star berths. Schmidt won the Hart Trophy as league MVP in 1951. The Kraut Line's final game was on March 18, 1952. Bauer came out of retirement to play with his hometown teammates one more time at a game honouring Schmidt and Dumart. That night, Boston fans saw again what three boys from a small Canadian town could do together on ice, as Schmidt scored his 200th career goal.

13.12 C. The Boston Bruins

They had the pedal to the metal for a stretch during 2000–01, but by the All-Star break Boston coach Mike Keenan's so-called GAS Line of Bill Guerin, Jason Allison and Sergei Samsonov was running on empty with some uninspired play. Keenan periodically broke up the unit, moving Samsonov to play with centre Joe Thornton and right-winger Andrei Kovalenko.

13.13 C. New York's A Line

The first hockey triumvirate to earn a nickname that stuck was the New York Rangers' A Line of Frank Boucher and brothers Bill and Bun Cook, three players from the disbanded Western Hockey League who joined the expansion Rangers in 1926–27. In their first NHL season with New York, the team finished atop the American Division and Bill Cook won the scoring title with a 33–4–37 record. The next season, the Rangers claimed the Stanley Cup, turning New Yorkers into lifelong hockey fans. As Frank Boucher explained in Stan Fischler's *20th Century Hockey Chronicle,* he and the Cook brothers clicked as a line from the start. "We never put diagrams on paper.

Somehow, just in describing our ideas, we'd all grasp it. Bill would do most of the talking. He'd say, 'Now look, when I want that puck I'll yell for it, and you get that damn puck to me when I yell. Don't look up to see where I am; just put it there and I'll be there.'" One of their most innovative plays was the drop pass, a ploy they worked to perfection. The trio was named after the Eighth Avenue subway line, the A Train, which was built along Eighth Avenue beneath the old Madison Square Garden. The A Line played together from 1926–27 to 1935–36.

13.14 C. The New York Rangers

During the 1978–79 season, the Rangers were led by the Mafia Line of "Godfather" Phil Esposito on left wing and his two dons—Don Murdoch at centre and rookie Don Maloney on right wing. Murdoch might never have played on the infamous New York line if his year-long suspension for cocaine possession had not been commuted to 40 games. Maloney scored 20 points in the playoffs that year, setting an NHL record by a rookie.

13.15 A. The Scooter Line

The Blackhawks have a rich history of monikers for their scoring lines, from Bill Mosienko and brothers Doug and Max Bentley's Pony Line in the 1940s to the early 1990's Reject Line, which teamed fourth-liners Greg Gilbert, Christian Ruuttu and Dirk Graham. The Scooter Line was Bobby Hull, Bill Hay and Murray Balfour before they later became the Million-Dollar Line. Chicago's real Scooter Line was powered by Doug Mohns, Stan Mikita and Kenny Wharram, a trio of speedsters who in 1964–65 accounted for almost half of Chicago's goals.

13.16 D. Los Angeles' Triple Crown Line of Dionne–Simmer–Taylor

The Kings' Triple Crown Line possessed everything required of an elite scoring unit. In Marcel Dionne, the line had the consummate goal scorer and puck-carrying centre. Dave Taylor was the hulking cornerman and an excellent puck handler.

Charlie Simmer, the finisher, was immovable in the crease while waiting for rebounds and tip-ins. More than individual speed, skill or strength, the trio meshed because all three players shared good communication—the ability to read off each other. In six seasons together, they averaged 284 points per year. Their best year was 1980–81, when each recorded more than 100 points: Dionne scored 58 goals and 135 points; Taylor, 47 goals and 112 points; and Simmer, 56 goals and 105 points.

13.17 D. The New Jersey Devils

The Devils' Jacques Lemaire is one of the few NHL coaches to consistently play four lines each game, even in the playoffs. And after forming the Crash Line of Bobby Holik, Randy McKay and Mike Peluso in 1993–94, he made good on his four-line system, using the fourth unit through the entire 1995 Stanley Cup playoffs. The Crash Line combined to score 23 individual points in the postseason.

13.18 A. The entire line came from Fort William, Ontario

The Flying Forts Line was formed in 1943–44 when rookie Gus Bodnar joined two other Fort William natives, Gaye Stewart and Bud Poile, to became part of Toronto's rebuilding scheme. Despite a Stanley Cup in 1947, manager Conn Smythe dealt the entire line in the "trade of the century" to get Chicago scoring champ Max Bentley.

13.19 C. Conn Smythe

Conn Smythe's rebuilding job of the Leafs in the late 1920s began in earnest with the signing of youngster Joe Primeau in 1927. Primeau spent two years in the minors for seasoning. Then, in 1929, Smythe brought up a couple of kids, Busher Jackson and Charlie Conacher, from Frank Selke's old junior team, the Toronto Marlboros. On December 29, 1929, Smythe sent Jackson and Conacher out on a line with the struggling Primeau. It was pure magic. Chemistry on ice. They became the Kid Line and quickly developed into a trio of fearless young bloods characterized by their on-ice flair, bravado and scoring skill. In 1931–32, the threesome finished first, second and fourth in the scoring race and helped Toronto win its first Stanley Cup under the Maple Leaf banner. Smythe had built his Cup-winner and, in the process, one of hockey's most enduring skating and scoring legacies, the Kid Line.

13.20 B. The Detroit Red Wings

Detroit coach Scotty Bowman put together some great scoring lines in his time, but few have been as successful at not scoring as his combination of Kris Draper, Kirk Maltby and Joe Kocur. Better known as the Grind Line, the trio specialized in grinding down first-line opponents along the boards.

13.21 C. The Soviet Union

The famed unit of Vladimir Krutov, Igor Larionov and Sergei Makarov dominated Russian and international hockey for eight years during the 1980s, winning four world championships (1982, 1983, 1986, 1989) and two Olympic gold medals (in 1984 in Sarajevo and in 1988 in Calgary). The Krutov–Larionov–Makarov troika powered the Central Red Army Team to eight straight Soviet League titles. Makarov was named Soviet player of the year three times, Larionov once, and Krutov won the Gold Stick in 1986–87 as the outstanding player in Europe. When Soviet emigration restrictions eased, a number of players joined the NHL ranks in 1989, including Larionov and Krutov (who went to Vancouver) and Makarov (who went to Calgary). Krutov, considered the best pro prospect, was a bust after one season. Makarov, at 31, won the Calder Trophy as rookie of the year in 1990 and played six NHL seasons with Calgary and San Jose. Larionov, after stints in Vancouver and San Jose, centred Scotty Bowman's five-man Russian unit in Detroit.

13.22 D. Ottawa's Cy Denneny and Punch Broadbent

During the 1920s, the old Ottawa Senators were the team to be reckoned with in the NHL. They finished in first place six times and won four Stanley Cups. Three of those championships came on the backbone of linemate wingers Denneny and Broadbent, who were called the Gold Dust Twins for their sparkling and gritty playing style. Acting as both policemen and triggermen, they kept the opposition honest while providing a potent offensive combination. In 1921–22's 24-game schedule, the Twins finished one-two in the NHL scoring race, Broadbent leading with a 32–14–46 record to Denneny's 27–12–39. In the 1923 best-of-three final series against Edmonton, Denneny and Broadbent each scored game-winners to claim the Stanley Cup. The pair was split up in 1924 when Broadbent moved to the Montreal Maroons.

13.23 A. The Maroons' Nels Stewart, Babe Siebert and Hooley Smith

The S Line of Stewart, Siebert and Smith was formed in the late 1920s and played together for five seasons with the Montreal Maroons. Stewart centred the line and was its leading point earner, but the unit's real strength was its combination of scoring power and tough play. Running roughshod over opponents, the S Line usually topped 200 minutes in box time, a high penalty count for a scoring line in that era. They became hockey's most feared threesome: Stewart, the gifted goal scorer; Siebert, the fierce competitor with great athletic strength; and Smith, with his sweeping hook-check, one of the game's best two-way players. But as powerful and punishing as they were together, the line was broken up by two sudden trades in 1932. Stewart went to the Bruins and Siebert to the Rangers. Unlike most other scoring trios, however, their best years were not behind them after they were split up. Stewart would win the NHL scoring crown again in 1937, Smith captained the Maroons to a Stanley Cup in 1935 and Siebert developed into an MVP-winning defenseman and Cup-winner with the Rangers and Canadiens. All three S Line members are in the Hockey Hall of Fame.

13.24 B. Two forwards: Guy Lafleur and Steve Shutt

Lafleur and Shutt's 1970s scoring line was known as the Doughnut Line because the two wingers played with "a hole in the centre" filled by a few pivots, including Pete Mahovlich and, finally, Jacques Lemaire. None of the centres lasted more than two years with the Lafleur-Shutt duo, but over seven seasons they were instrumental in five Montreal Stanley Cups. Except for Mahovlich, no Doughnut Line members were very big, but they were all great puck handlers and skaters. "Lafleur had to control the puck, I could dart to the holes and Lemaire could read the play from behind," Shutt once said.

13.25 A. Clark Gillies and Mike Bossy

Some great lines just happen; others are designed by general managers and coaches for success. For the Long Island Lighting Co. (a.k.a. the Grande Trio), it was "intuition" according to ex-Islanders general manager Bill Torrey, who drafted Trottier and Gillies in 1974 and Bossy in 1977. Bossy, the gifted junior from Quebec, had trouble finding his place on the roster until he was teamed with rising stars Gillies and Trottier. They clicked halfway through their first game together, on an unforgettable play. "It was like tic-tac-toe," Torrey recalls, "and then the puck was in the net." As the unit gelled they went on to score 134 goals in 1977–78, including Bossy's league rookie-record of 53. The Long Island Lighting Co. was together nine seasons and helped the Islanders win four Stanley Cups between 1980 and 1983.

13.26 C. Max, Doug and Reg Bentley

On January 1, 1943, Chicago coach Paul Thompson introduced the all-Bentley line, playing brothers Max, Doug and Reg Bentley together as a unit against the Rangers. It was the first time three brothers were linemates in an NHL game. The Hawks defeated New York 6–5, but the novel experiment failed to click and the trio was soon broken up.

13.27 D. The Left Hook Line

Lines are usually named for their scoring prowess. In Philadelphia, where hockey is a serious passion, even a checking line of tough guys gets christened. Lacroix, Kordic and Myhres combined for only two goals and seven points in 1997–98, but their penalty totals of 135, 210 and 169 minutes reflect their gritty moniker, the Left Hook Line.

13.28 B. The Hot Line

What the name lacked in originality (several teams have iced a Hot Line), the unit made up in on-ice performance, becoming the most explosive scoring force in the WHA. Regardless of their position on the ice, each linemate somehow knew where the other was going to be. According to Anders Hedberg in *WHA—Same Game, Different Name*, "We never really had plays or planned where to move. We could interchange positions. It was a style Bobby always wanted to play." In its first season, 1974–75, the Hot Line combined for an amazing 362 points, with Hull scoring 50 goals in 50 games to tie Maurice Richard's historic 50-in-50 record and then, later that year, eclipsing the 76-goal mark of Phil Esposito. Hull amassed 142 points, Nilsson counted 120 points (including 94 assists) and Hedberg earned 53 goals and 100 points. Nilsson once said: "I may have had the toughest role on that line because Bobby and Anders both wanted to score goals. Bobby yelled at me if I passed the puck to Anders. I heard the same, only in Swedish, from Anders, if I gave the puck to Hull. When I took a shot on goal, I got an earful from both of them."

13.29 B. The New York Rangers

Until Eric Lindros ran into injury problems midway through 2001–02, he and his two wingers, Theo Fleury and Mike York, formed the league's highest-scoring trio. The FLY Line, as the New York media dubbed it, was an unconventional unit, with the hulking Lindros flanked by two speedy but undersized wingers. Joked Fleury: "I don't understand all this talk about Lindros needing a big winger. If you put me and Yorkie together, we're 11 foot one."

13.30 B. The Philadelphia Flyers

Not all of those brawling Flyers from the 1970s were Broad Street Bullies. Philadelphia's two consecutive Stanley Cups in 1974 and 1975 were won not only by intimidation through thuggery but also by great goaltending from Bernie Parent, the offense of 50-goal scorer Rick MacLeish and the LCB Line of Reggie Leach, Bobby Clarke and Bill Barber. From day one the threesome connected. Clarke, the gritty centre, was the line's workhorse and spark plug; Barber and Leach its tenacious scoring wingers. They came together by design, the handiwork of Flyers general manager Keith Allen, who in 1974 picked up Leach from California and then, three days later, sent Bill Flett (the line's original right wing) to Toronto. The move was a natural considering Leach and Clarke's junior days in Flin Flon, Manitoba. "I knew of their great success together, so I wanted to see if they could do it again here," Allen recalls. The combo clicked, and in 1975–76 they scored 141 goals. No Flyer line, including the Legion of Doom, has topped that incredible season. The LCB Line played together for nine years.

13.31 D. The Colorado Avalanche

The AMP line of Alex Tanguay, Milan Hejduk and Peter Forsberg was arguably the best line of 2002–03. Hejduk scored 50 goals to become the first player in Colorado history to lead the league in goals. Meanwhile, Forsberg led the league in scoring (106 points) and assists (77). Tanguay came back from a poor season in 2001–02 to collect 26 goals and 41 assists. During the final 37 games of 2002–03 the trio combined for 59 goals and 90 assists. The line's name is an anagram of the players' first names.

13.32 B. Montreal's Punch Line

Only a small number of scoring units have been inducted into the Hall of Fame. In 2002, the Islanders line of Mike Bossy, Bryan Trottier and Clark Gillies earned that distinction when Gillies was finally elected to the Hall. The first trio with full Hall of Fame membership was the Punch Line of Toe Blake, Elmer Lach and Maurice Richard, who were all inducted by 1966, just six years after Richard retired in 1960 and 18 years after the line broke up in 1948. Despite its fame, the Punch Line played together less than five seasons, but in that short time revitalized the sagging Canadiens franchise with Stanley Cups in 1944 and 1946. The line's most revered contribution to hockey is the NHL's first 50-goal season by Richard.

GAME 13

Rearguard Records

THE NHL RECORD BOOKS are home to the league's most famous defensemen. Listed below are the first names of 22 record-setting goal scorers, point producers, plus-minus leaders and award winners who have plied the blue line. Once you figure out their family names, find them in the puzzle by reading across, down or diagonally. Following our example of Larry **ROBINSON**, connect the family names using letters no more than once. Start with the letters printed in heavy type.

Solutions are on page 566

Nicklas	__________	Paul	__________
Ray	__________	Al	__________
Doug	__________	Chris	__________
Rob	__________	Bobby	__________
Phil	__________	Denis	__________
Larry	__________	Larry	__________
Gary	__________	Ian	__________
Brian	__________	Chris	__________
Steve	__________	Tom	__________
Serge	__________	Doug	__________
Rod	__________	Eddie	__________

L	I	W	U	M		O	E	N	S	P
S	P	R	C	L	I	R	B	H	E	R
H	O	N	H	E	R	O	S	O	C	O
Y	T	L	A	D	O	N	U	Y	U	N
R	U	B	I	U	Q	R	E	D	G	L
R	O	B	E	N	R	V	R	E	S	E
N	S	L	S	A	Y	O	M	H	O	E
I	B	Y	I	O	H	E	R	R	E	T
R	N	U	A	D	N	T	L	S	C	H
E	N	L	W	G	S	D	R	A	U	S
T	I	S	L	A	N	Y	H	O	V	A
C	U	N	L	O	P	E	F	F	O	E
A	M	I	V	T		B	L	A	K	C

14

Box Time

IT'S NOT OFTEN THAT HOCKEY-PLAYING brothers rumble, so when the brothers Primeau duked it out during a 1997 Buffalo–Hartford game, it got noticed. Brother Wayne, 20, ran Hartford goalie Sean Burke, so brother Keith, 25, entered the fracas to defend his netminder. The brothers dropped their gloves and Keith won the decision after Wayne hit the ice first. "There was some hesitation," Keith said. "I knew who he was. That's blood, man." The elder Primeau was so upset, he called his parents between periods to apologize. Hartford coach Paul Maurice concluded: "It must have been pretty tough at the Primeau dinner table when there was only one pork chop left." Blood sport or not, in this round we go toe-to-toe with hockey's heavyweight legends. Put 'em up.

Answers are on page 344

14.1 Who holds the record for most penalties in one game?

A. Dave Schultz
B. Jim Dorey
C. Chris Nilan
D. Terry O'Reilly

14.2 Which team iced the "Bruise Brothers"?

A. The Detroit Red Wings
B. The Philadelphia Flyers
C. The Boston Bruins
D. The Calgary Flames

14.3 What is the most penalty minutes recorded by two teams in one NHL game?

A. 319 penalty minutes
B. 359 penalty minutes
C. 419 penalty minutes
D. 459 penalty minutes

14.4 Toronto coach and former defenseman Pat Quinn played nine NHL seasons, but he is best remembered for delivering a crushing bodycheck that knocked out which superstar?

A. Bobby Orr
B. Guy Lafleur
C. Bobby Clarke
D. Phil Esposito

14.5 What rivalry produced the so-called "Good Friday Massacre"?

A. The Battle of New York—Islanders vs. Rangers
B. The Battle of Alberta—Oilers vs. Flames
C. The Battle of Quebec—Canadiens vs. Nordiques
D. The Battle of Pennsylvania—Flyers vs. Penguins

14.6 In 1986, which mayor threatened police action if brawls continued to take place at his city's rink?

A. Calgary's mayor Ralph Klein
B. New York's mayor Ed Koch
C. Boston's mayor Ray Flynn
D. Montreal's mayor Jean Drapeau

14.7 When was the NHL's last bench-clearing brawl?

A. The 1960s
B. The 1970s
C. The 1980s
D. The 1990s

14.8 Which goalie is best known for playing a key role in starting a fight that led to a team brawl before the start of a 1987 playoff game?

A. Philadelphia's Chico Resch
B. The Islanders' Billy Smith
C. Edmonton's Grant Fuhr
D. Philadelphia's Ron Hextall

14.9 What is the longest suspension handed out to goalie Ron Hextall?

A. Three games
B. Six games
C. Nine games
D. 12 games

14.10 Which NHLer holds the record for most penalty minutes in one game?

A. Dave "Tiger" Williams
B. Tie Domi
C. Randy Holt
D. Basil McRae

14.11 What is the most penalty minutes assessed to one player during a single NHL season?

A. 300 to 350 minutes
B. 350 to 400 minutes
C. 400 to 450 minutes
D. 450 to 500 minutes

14.12 Which old-time hockey hooligan boasted that he had been involved in "50 stretcher-case fights" during his career?

A. Red Horner
B. Eddie Shore
C. Sprague Cleghorn
D. Black Jack Stewart

14.13 Which Detroit player beat up Colorado's Claude Lemieux in 1997, to avenge a vicious blindside hit that Lemieux had laid on Red Wing Kris Draper during the 1996 playoffs?

A. Brendan Shanahan
B. Darren McCarty
C. Martin Lapointe
D. Jamie Pushor

14.14 How many seconds in the Avalanche–Red Wings game on November 11, 1997, did it take Colorado's Claude Lemieux and Detroit's Darren McCarty to start fighting another round in their ongoing feud?

A. Three seconds
B. 33 seconds
C. 66 seconds
D. 99 seconds

14.15 What is the highest number of penalty minutes amassed by one NHL team in one regular season?

A. Between 1,000 and 2,000 penalty minutes
B. Between 2,000 and 3,000 penalty minutes
C. Between 3,000 and 4,000 penalty minutes
D. More than 4,000 penalty minutes

14.16 What is the "Piestany Punch-up"?

A. A 1972 Summit Series fracas
B. A 1980 fight between police and Czech hockey fans
C. A World Junior Championship brawl
D. A Soviet enforcer tactic

14.17 Which future NHLer punched his own goalie at the 1992 World Junior Championships?

A. Jason Arnott
B. Saku Koivu
C. Radek Bonk
D. Darius Kasparaitis

14.18 Despite being best friends, which two opposing goalies duked it out in a 1998 brawl that saw all 12 players on the ice ejected from the game?

A. Detroit's Chris Osgood and Colorado's Patrick Roy
B. Washington's Olaf Kolzig and Boston's Byron Dafoe
C. Dallas' Ed Belfour and Philadelphia's Ron Hextall
D. Tampa Bay's Daren Puppa and Pittsburgh's Tom Barrasso

14.19 In what decade did two goalies fight for the first time in NHL playoff action?

A. The 1920s
B. The 1930s
C. The 1940s
D. The 1950s

14.20 Which goalie earned his team's first ever fighting major?

A. Ron Low of the Washington Capitals
B. Billy Smith of the New York Islanders
C. Jeff Hackett of the San Jose Sharks
D. Mike Dunham of the Nashville Predators

14.21 Which tough guy owns the NHL record for most fights in a season?

A. Dave Williams of the Toronto Maple Leafs
B. Mike Peluso of the Chicago Blackhawks
C. Tie Domi of the Winnipeg Jets
D. Paul Laus of the Florida Panthers

14.22 How many fighting majors did Philadelphia's Dave Schultz collect when he set the single-season NHL record with 472 penalty minutes in 1974–75?

A. 26 fighting majors
B. 36 fighting majors
C. 46 fighting majors
D. 56 fighting majors

14.23 Who holds the record for most fighting majors by a rookie?

A. Bob Probert of the Detroit Red Wings
B. Chris Nilan of the Montreal Canadiens
C. Joe Kocur of the Detroit Red Wings
D. Reed Low of the St. Louis Blues

14.24 Which legendary enforcer scored two goals and won a fight against the league's meanest player in his first NHL game?

A. Ted Lindsay
B. John Ferguson
C. Dave Schultz
D. Chris Nilan

14.25 In his rookie WHA season, which future NHL All-Star was speared by Gordie Howe after beating up Marty Howe?

A. Mark Howe
B. Wayne Gretzky
C. Mike Gartner
D. Michel Goulet

14.26 Who recorded the most goals in the same season that he led the league in penalty minutes?

A. Maurice Richard
B. Ted Lindsay
C. Bob Probert
D. Dave Williams

14.27 Who is the only NHLer to score 40 or more goals in a season while collecting more than 300 minutes in penalties?

A. Al Secord
B. Rick Tocchet
C. Clark Gillies
D. Keith Tkachuk

14.28 Who holds the NHL record for compiling the most penalty minutes in a season in which he scored 50 goals?

A. Keith Tkachuk
B. Brendan Shanahan
C. Kevin Stevens
D. Gary Roberts

14.29 What is the record for most points in a season by an NHL penalty leader?

A. 42 points
B. 52 points
C. 62 points
D. 72 points

14.30 What is the fewest points scored by an NHL penalty leader?

A. Zero points
B. One point
C. Four points
D. Nine points

14.31 What is the shortest NHL career for an NHL penalty leader?

A. 18 games
B. 38 games
C. 68 games
D. 98 games

14.32 How long did the infamous Bob Probert–Marty McSorley fight-fest last on February 4, 1994?

A. 40 seconds
B. One minute
C. One minute and 40 seconds
D. Two minutes

14.33 Which NHL scrapper was told by the league to drop his hand-wiping act after winning a fight in 2000–01?

A. Donald Brashear
B. Tie Domi
C. Matthew Barnaby
D. Chris Simon

14.34 What kind of penalty did Toronto's Glenn Anderson serve after scoring his 1,000th career point on February 22, 1993?

A. Fighting major
B. Delay of game
C. Misconduct for an obscene gesture
D. Unsportsmanlike conduct

14.35 Who was the first NHLer to rack up 1,000 career penalty minutes?

A. Eddie Shore
B. Red Horner
C. Ted Lindsay
D. Lou Fontinato

14.36 In a story that made national headlines in Canada, what did Edmonton coach Craig MacTavish do to Calgary's mascot, Harvey the Hound, during a game in January 2003?

A. Tore out its tongue
B. Boxed its ears
C. Sprayed it with a water bottle
D. Pulled off its head

14.37 During a playoff game in the 1950s, which top scorer raised his stick towards the crowd and pretended to shoot it like a gun?

A. Detroit's Ted Lindsay
B. Boston's Fleming Mackell
C. Montreal's Henri Richard
D. New York's Andy Bathgate

14.38 What unusual NHL first did Syd Howe face after mistakenly serving a teammate's penalty in 1935?

A. He became the first player assessed a $500 fine
B. He became the first player stripped of his captaincy
C. He became the first player assessed a game misconduct
D. He became the first player penalized for such an action

14.39 What criminal sentence did Marty McSorley receive in an October 2000 court ruling after clubbing Donald Brashear during a Vancouver–Boston game on February 21, 2000?

A. McSorley was found not guilty
B. McSorley was fined $50,000
C. McSorley received an 18-month conditional discharge
D. McSorley was sentenced to 18 months in jail

14.40 What was Tie Domi's punishment for decking Ulf Samuelsson with a sucker punch in October 14, 1995?

A. A five-game suspension and a $500 fine
B. An eight-game suspension and a $1,000 fine
C. A 10-game suspension and a $5,000 fine
D. A 15-game suspension and a $2,000 fine

Answers

14.1 C. Chris Nilan

It wasn't a good night for hockey on March 31, 1991, when Hartford met Boston in a 3½-hour free-for-all that saw 10 misconducts handed out. Nilan's pugilistic skills made him the busiest man on the ice that night. He collected 42 penalty minutes in a record 10 penalties, including six minors, two majors, one 10-minute misconduct and one game misconduct.

14.2 A. The Detroit Red Wings

In Jake and Elwood Blues's hometown, Red Wing fans readily embraced the team's two toughest hit men—Bob Probert and Joe Kocur—and nicknamed them the Bruise Brothers. Together, Probert and Kocur forged a reputation as the NHL's best one-two punch on the same team. Probert, despite his struggle with substance abuse, became the league's undisputed heavyweight champion. Kocur was the strongest and meanest fighter on the ice, a goon with fists that packed the force of a runaway freight train. The Bruise Brothers' reign of terror in Detroit ended when Kocur was traded in 1991 and Probert in 1994.

14.3 C. 419 penalty minutes

It must have brought tears to Dave Schultz's eyes, the way the Philadelphia Flyers pounded it out with the Ottawa Senators on March 5, 2004. His former team's 5–3 win featured five brawls in the final two minutes and 16 player ejections, and set a new NHL record with 419 penalty minutes (breaking the mark of 406 minutes set in a Boston–Minnesota game on February 26, 1981). The born-again Broad Street Bullies also established the highest box time total ever for a team in one game (213 minutes; surpassing Minnesota's 211) and smashed the league's penalty-minute count in one period (209 minutes). Meanwhile their adversaries gave as good as they got (200 minutes all told for Ottawa), breaking Calgary's December 2001 record of 190 penalty minutes in one period and Philadelphia's 23-year NHL mark of 188 minutes set in March 1979. Even Schultz's old teammate, Flyer GM Bobby Clarke, couldn't resist trying for a little revenge. He had to be restrained by arena personnel in his search for Senators coach Jacques Martin, who Clarke called "that gutless puke" because of an earlier February 26 match that included some nasty stick-work by Ottawa forward Martin Havlat on Mark Recchi. In all, 20 players got fighting penalties and only five players were left on the bench at the final buzzer. Officials needed 90 minutes after the game to figure everything out. Yes, Schultzie would have been proud.

14.4 A. Bobby Orr

Pat Quinn played 617 NHL games, including playoffs. He scored 132 points and recorded 971 penalty minutes. As a brute defenseman with few skills, almost all of his nine-year career has been forgotten except for one incident during his rookie playoff season—a bone-crushing bodycheck on the great Bobby Orr. It happened at Boston Garden on April 2, 1969, as Orr was fighting off Toronto's Brit Selby for the puck. The Bruins defenseman lost control of the puck between his legs. Quinn motored in at full speed and pounded the preoccupied Orr with such force that the two were thrown in opposite directions. Orr collapsed, knocked out cold near the boards. Quinn got a five-minute elbowing major and a rough time from Bruin fans, who tried to exact their own revenge on him. Quinn swung his stick to defend himself and broke a pane of protective glass, which showered down on a policeman. The fans were screaming "We want Quinn" as the besieged rookie escaped to the Toronto dressing room. Shaken, Orr stumbled off the ice to the Boston room. The Bruins annihilated Toronto 10–0 and swept the quarterfinals.

14.5 C. The Battle of Quebec—Canadiens vs. Nordiques

Perhaps no two NHL teams have vented more mutual spite than Montreal and Quebec; certainly no game better demonstrated that once-bitter rivalry than the mêlée on Good Friday in 1984. As one report noted, it was "a vendetta... that became frightening in its bitterness and duration." For 35 minutes the fighting raged, clearing the benches twice: at the end of the second period and the beginning of the third. Bodies and equipment littered the Forum ice. Officials scurried from skirmish to skirmish, hopelessly tugging at sweaters to separate the combatants. On the card: every dressed player. The main event featured Louis Sleigher, who sucker punched Jean

Hamel and put him out of the game; Chris Nilan, who ambushed a defenseless Randy Moller and pummelled his face with several blows, and Peter Stastny, who suffered a broken nose at the hands of Mario Tremblay. It was referee Bruce Hood's nightmare come true, made worse by the fact that the players who were serving game misconducts returned to the ice for the third period only to wage another free-for-all that even pitted brothers Dale and Mark Hunter against each other. When it was all over, 10 players had been ejected and 252 penalty minutes called, only 46 minutes short of the playoff record set by the Red Wings and Blues in 1991.

14.6 C. Boston's mayor Ray Flynn

Prompted by a bench-clearing 1986 Bruins–Canadiens brawl that spread to fighting among fans in the stands, Ray Flynn sent letters warning Boston team owners they had to "take effective action to strongly discourage incidents of violence." Otherwise, the mayor said, he would send the police onto the ice if necessary to stop the fighting. Boston fans were skeptical; team owners used doublespeak, saying something about a "disadvantage competitively"; and John Ziegler offered the weirdest response. "The subject is too trite to comment on," said the ex-NHL boss. The Garden brawl was started by Canadiens goon Chris Nilan, a Boston native.

14.7 C. The 1980s

Until anti-brawling legislation was introduced during the late 1970s and beefed up in the early 1980s, bench-clearing battles were relatively common in hockey, with sometimes five or six incidents per year. But the third-man-in rule, game misconducts and heavy fines (levied against anyone intervening in an altercation or anyone who didn't go to the bench area during a fight) soon eliminated them. The last full-scale mêlée was on February 26, 1987, when the Quebec Nordiques and the Boston Bruins emptied both benches in a battle that led to nine ejections and 167 penalty minutes. Ironically, the fight came one night after Boston city council rejected a proposed ordinance allowing city police to arrest athletes in the middle of a game for assault. (Later, on May 14, 1987, another all-out brawl occurred between Montreal and Philadelphia, but that was a pre-game situation that erupted over players' rituals during the warm-up skate.)

14.8 A. Philadelphia's Chico Resch

During the 1987 Wales Conference finals between Montreal and Philadelphia, a bizarre pre-game brawl erupted after the warm-up in Game 6. Chico Resch and Ed Hospodar tried to prevent two Canadien players from performing their pre-game ritual of shooting the puck into the Flyers' empty net. (In previous games, Claude Lemieux and Shayne Corson would stay on the ice to pot a goal after both teams had left the ice for their dressing rooms.) The Flyers didn't like the routine, so mild-mannered Resch and hit man Hospodar were elected as on-ice watchmen. Resch picks up the story in Dick Irvin's *In the Crease:* "I threw my stick to try and knock the puck away from him [Lemieux]. I was still in the mood that this was just fooling around. Hospodar took a different approach and he charged at Lemieux and jumped him.... I skated over and yelled at him, 'Ed, what are you doing?' And Lemieux looked up and he says, 'Yeah Ed, what are you doing?' Within seconds both teams had poured out onto the ice, some players half-dressed and with bare feet. A full-scale brawl ensued for 11 minutes before officials were notified and able to restore order. The league handed out $24,000 in fines.

14.9 D. 12 games

Ron Hextall has defended his crease and teammates more vigorously and with more menace than any other goalie in recent memory. His competitive aggressiveness became one of his trademarks as he laid out victims and piled up penalties; his rap sheet includes three suspensions of six, eight and 12 games. Hextall's bad-boy reputation was established during his rookie season, 1986–87, when he logged a record 104 penalty minutes. Then, in the Stanley Cup final that season, he felled

Edmonton's Kent Nilsson with a wicked slash to the back of his legs that earned Hextall an eight-game suspension in his sophomore year. In 1989–90, he missed Philadelphia's first 12 games for attacking Chris Chelios of the Montreal Canadiens with his blocker in 1989's Wales Conference finals. His third-longest suspension was a six-gamer in 1991–92 for slashing Detroit's Jim Cummins in a preseason game.

14.10 C. Randy Holt

It was during a Flyers–Kings brawl on March 11, 1979, that nine NHL penalty records were set, three of them by Holt, who was assessed a record 67 minutes for nine penalties—all during a wild first period that ended with a 12-minute mêlée that carried across the ice to the Los Angeles bench. Referee Wally Harris ejected 10 players, five from each team, and handed out 352 penalty minutes, including one minor, three majors, two 10-minute misconducts and a triple game misconduct to Holt.

14.11 D. 450 to 500 minutes

Few players, including even the toughest goons, have ever exceeded the 400 penalty-minute mark—and that includes heavyweights such as Marty McSorley, Bob Probert and Chris Nilan. But Dave "The Hammer" Schultz epitomized thuggery. His Broad Street Bullies style of playing equated ice-fighting to goal scoring. In 1974–75, Schultz hammered enough opponents to establish an NHL record of 472 penalty minutes—the equivalent of almost eight complete games in the box.

14.12 C. Sprague Cleghorn

Many old-timers insist that Cleghorn was the nastiest customer to ever lace on a pair of skates. During his 18-year career, he carved out a notorious reputation. Jack Adams, who played against Cleghorn, called him "an unwashed surgeon." In one game alone in 1921, Cleghorn disabled three Ottawa Senator players. After the game, the Ottawa police offered to arrest him for assault. During the 1923 playoffs, Cleghorn stick-whipped Lionel Hitchman of the Ottawa Senators so severely that Cleghorn's own manager, Leo Dandurand of the Canadiens, fined him $200 and suspended him. Before he died in 1953, Cleghorn boasted, "All told, I figure I was in 50 stretcher-case fights. I didn't lose any."

14.13 B. Darren McCarty

The March 26, 1997, match was the first time Claude Lemieux had played in Detroit since the 1996 playoff incident, and by Darren McCarty's accounting it was a great game—"like old-time hockey." The press dubbed the bloodletting the "Brawl in Hockeytown" and continued replaying its highlights for days afterwards. The fight began in retaliation for Lemieux's nasty backside cross-check on Draper during Game 6 of 1996's Western Conference finals. Lemieux got a two-game suspension, but Draper sustained multiple fractures and required major facial and oral surgery. Fast forward to Lemieux's next meeting with Detroit, 10 months later. With two minutes left in the first period, Igor Larionov and Peter Forsberg collided along the boards. No big deal. But in the ensuing scuffle, McCarty took revenge and sucker punched Lemieux to the ice. Lemieux turtled while McCarty continued pummelling away. Patrick Roy stormed out of his crease to help Lemieux, but Brendan Shanahan intercepted Roy with a heavy check at centre ice. That caused Wing backstopper Mike Vernon to enter the fray, and the two goalies slugged it out toe-to-toe, with Vernon winning the bout. After 60 minutes of bloody hockey, 18 fighting majors and 148 penalty minutes, the game went into overtime tied 5–5. Who scored the winner? On a nice offensive move, Shanahan pulled Roy to the right side of the goal and passed to McCarty, who fired home the tie breaker. McCarty settled a couple of scores that night. Draper said he felt "a sense of closure" after the fight-filled game. Detroit's 6–5 win was its first after three consecutive losses to Colorado, along with the series loss in the 1996 Western Conference finals.

14.14 A. Three seconds

The Claude Lemieux–Darren McCarty feud was sparked by an incident in the 1996 playoffs when Lemieux's nasty blindside cross-check sent the Wings' Kris Draper to the hospital for reconstructive facial surgery. In retaliation for his teammate's injuries, McCarty bloodied Lemieux with a sucker punch in a brawl-filled game in Detroit in March 1997. Lemieux hardly defended himself, meekly turtling under McCarty's blows. In their next regular-season meeting, November 11, 1997, Lemieux switched his wing at the opening faceoff so he could get closer to McCarty. Lemieux jawed with McCarty and the two squared off again, dropping their gloves just three seconds into the game. They fought toe-to-toe, Lemieux landing several rights and lefts to McCarty's face before the pair tumbled to the ice. "If you're going to do it, do it right off the bat," Lemieux said of the old score that needed settling. "Last year, the guys fought their hearts out for me. This was my payback for them." McCarty concluded: "He wanted to prove something to himself and his teammates. It was more or less his move. In my mind, he's still an idiot because he hasn't apologized to Drapes."

14.15 B. Between 2,000 and 3,000 penalty minutes

No NHL team has amassed more box time in one season than the 1991–92 Buffalo Sabres—a record 2,713 penalty minutes. Leading the assault were Rob Ray with 354 minutes, Gord Donnelly with 316 and Brad May with 309. The three Sabre tough guys accumulated almost 1,000 minutes.

14.16 C. A World Junior Championship brawl

It was the most violent battle in the history of international hockey. The Soviets, out of medal contention, had nothing to lose. Team Canada was applying the pressure, trying to increase a 4–2 lead and go for the gold medal. Then it happened. Canadian and Soviet players, fed up with stickwork and running at each other, dropped their gloves and engaged in a 20-minute brawl that cleared the benches. With the fight out of control, the officials left the ice and the arena lights dimmed. The game never resumed. Both teams were disqualified and their records erased.

14.17 D. Darius Kasparaitis

Kasparaitis is known as the mad Lithuanian, with good reason. The rugged rearguard earned a spot in hockey lore by punching his own goalie in the nose at the 1992 World Junior Championships. Kasparaitis's team, the former Soviet Union, known that year as the Commonwealth of Independent States (CIS), was filing off the bench to console goalie Ildar Muhametov after a 5–1 loss to the Czech Republic when Kasparaitis struck. "I was mad because the Czech team was bad that year and they had still beat us. So, I snapped," confessed Kasparaitis in an interview with the *National Post*. "I got fined for it but it was worth it. That goalie didn't play anymore after that and Nikolai Khabibulin was the backup, and he played unbelievable the rest of the tournament." Improbably, the CIS rebounded to win the gold medal; Kasparaitis was named the tourney's outstanding defenseman.

14.18 B. Washington's Olaf Kolzig and Boston's Byron Dafoe

Sitting pretty with three first-period goals, Bruins coach Pat Burns sensed the fight coming. "You could feel it when we got the big lead in the first period. It's something that goes back to last year's playoffs," Burns said. At the 12-minute mark, Burns's "feeling" turned ugly, erupting into a 12-player free-for-all that pinned best friends Kolzig and Dafoe in a toe-to-toe dance amidst the debris of hockey equipment, blood and bodies strewn over the ice. Referee Mark Faucette tossed all 12 players and assessed 264 minutes in penalties in that first period. "It's tough fighting your best friend. You can joke about it all you want, but when you're out there it's tough to throw a punch," Kolzig said. Boston prevailed over Washington 5–4 in the game, November 22, 1998.

14.19 C. The 1940s

Probably the first clash between two netminders in playoff action came on April 10, 1948, when Toronto's Turk Broda and Harry Lumley of Detroit squared off after a brawl erupted during a fight between Gordie Howe and Howie Meeker. Lumley (six foot, 195 pounds), three inches taller and 15 pounds heavier than Broda (five foot nine, 180 pounds), had the clear advantage in size but no winner was declared. Toronto won 4–2.

14.20 B. Billy Smith of the New York Islanders

It's not hard to fathom this from Battlin' Billy Smith, a guy who often refused to shake hands with winning playoff opponents. Smith once said: "I just try to give myself a little extra working room." On this occasion, October 21, 1972, Smith dropped the gloves with New York Rangers winger Rod Gilbert and became the first player on the expansion Islanders to receive a fighting major.

14.21 D. Paul Laus of the Florida Panthers

NHL players have been fighting since the league's inaugural season in 1917–18. Unfortunately, figures are not available prior to 1953–54, when the NHL began to keep statistics, but since then the league's leading pugilists have gone from four or five fights in a 70-game schedule to six times that amount during the 1990s. For example, NHL hardrock John Ferguson shared the lead (with Reggie Fleming) with eight fighting majors in 1966–67. Today, heavyweight battlers such as Paul Laus customarily rack up 30 or more fights in a season. Laus leads all punchers with 39 majors for Florida in 1996–97.

14.22 A. 26 fighting majors

Considering the record for most fighting majors in a single season is Paul Laus's 39, Schultz's rap sheet looks almost modest. The Flyers' lead goon supplemented his 130 fighting minutes with 122 minutes on 61 minors and a whopping 220 minutes on misconducts.

14.23 C. Joe Kocur of the Detroit Red Wings

Rookie Reed Low had a few hockey people scratching their heads when he finished 2000–01 with a team-high 159 penalty minutes and second in the NHL with 23 fighting majors. Not that those bruising numbers weren't anticipated from the six-foot-four, 225-pound right-winger, but did Low's 23 majors set the rookie standard? Hello, Joey. Kocur traded punches with anyone who was willing in his first full season, 1985–86, amassing a league-high 377 PIM in just 59 games. He answered the bell 37 times, which set a new rookie record that fell just two majors short of Paul Laus's mark of 39. Until broken bones in his hands forced him to cut back on hostilities, Kocur was the most feared knockout artist.

14.24 B. John Ferguson

Montreal Canadiens coach Toe Blake gave Ferguson specific instructions prior to his first NHL game against the Boston Bruins on October 8, 1963. "You'll be playing on a line with Béliveau and Geoffrion tonight. Don't let those Boston buggers bother my big scorers or push them around." Blake undoubtedly had Bruin defenseman "Terrible" Teddy Green in mind. Ferguson didn't wait long to introduce himself to the Bruins' resident psycho. Just 12 seconds into the game the two collided and the gloves flew off. Ferguson sent a message by thumping out a resounding decision. But the hard-nosed rookie wasn't done. He later scored two goals and then set up the game-tying marker by Bernie Geoffrion in a 4–4 deadlock. With Ferguson handling policing duties, Montreal would capture five Cups in the next eight years.

14.25 D. Michel Goulet

Gordie Howe and his sons Mark and Marty played together seven seasons: six in the WHA after signing in unison with Houston in 1973–74, and one as NHL Whalers in 1979–80. A favourite story involves rookie Michel Goulet, who took on Marty Howe in a fight one night. Goulet won against the younger Howe, but after the penalties were served, Goulet faced Gordie in the faceoff circle. "What I remember next was clutching my stomach. Gordie had speared me and yelled into my ear, 'Never touch my son.'" Blood is thicker than water, even on ice. The Howes' first pro goal together came on November 18, 1973, when Mark scored on assists by Gordie and Marty in an 8–3 Houston loss to the Quebec Nordiques.

14.26 D. Dave Williams

Williams did more than just rack up box time pummelling players; he scored with relative consistency, topping every other NHL penalty leader in most goals in a PIM-leading season, including the great Maurice Richard, one the league's toughest players of all time. In 1980–81 with Vancouver, Williams scored 35 goals and 62 points and logged a league-high 343 penalty minutes. Bob Probert scored 29 goals but tied Williams's 62 points in 1987–88, and Richard had 28 goals for 61 points in 1952–53. But while Richard, Probert and Williams all played in 70 or more games to accumulate their goal- and league-leading penalty totals, little-known Joe Lamb made his mark in the 44-game schedule of 1929–30.

Most Goals Scored in a Season by a Penalty Leader*

PLAYER	TEAM	SEASON	GP	GOALS	PIM
Dave Williams	Vancouver	1980–81	77	35	343
Joe Lamb	Ottawa	1929–30	44	29	119
Bob Probert	Detroit	1987–88	74	29	398
Maurice Richard	Montreal	1952–53	70	28	112

**Current to 2004–05*

14.27 A. Al Secord

It's doubtful that the Boston Bruins would have traded Secord if coach Don Cherry had not been fired prior to the 1980–81 season. Secord fit Cherry's definition of an ideal Bruin: big, tough, with a deft touch around the net. But on December 18, 1980, general manager Harry Sinden sent the burly left-winger to Chicago in exchange for defenseman Mike O'Connell. Playing on Chicago's top line with Denis Savard and Steve Larmer, Secord developed into one of the league's premier power forwards. In 1981–82, he scored 44 goals and racked up 303 penalty minutes. No other 300-PIM man has ever scored as many goals.

14.28 C. Kevin Stevens

Putting the "pow!" in power forward, Stevens accumulated a team-leading 254 penalty minutes in 1991–92 while notching 54 goals for the Pittsburgh Penguins. The six-foot-three, 230-pound left-winger ranked second in league scoring that season with 123 points, only eight behind teammate Mario Lemieux.

Most Penalty Minutes by 50-Goal Scorers*

PLAYER	TEAM	SEASON	G	PIM
Kevin Stevens	Pittsburgh	1991–92	54	254
Keith Tkachuk	Phoenix	1996–97	52	228
Brendan Shanahan	St. Louis	1993–94	52	211
Gary Roberts	Calgary	1991–92	53	207
Al Secord	Chicago	1982–83	54	180

**Current to 2004–05*

14.29 C. 62 points

Players who spend a lot of time in the penalty box don't usually bag many points, but Bob Probert and Dave Williams both managed to compile a respectable 62 points during a season in which they also led the NHL in penalty minutes. In 1987–88, Probert notched 29 goals and 33 assists for the Detroit Red Wings while racking up 398 penalty minutes. Both marks were career highs. In 1980–81, Williams posted 35 goals and 27 assists for the Vancouver Canucks to go with 343 penalty minutes.

14.30 B. One point

No NHL penalty leader has ever gone pointless during the year he led the league in penalties, but Detroit defenseman Harvey "Hard Rock" Rockburn came within a single assist after a 0–1–1 season in 1930–31. Hard Rock, one of only three NHL regulars to score one point that year, sat in the box for a league-best 118 penalty minutes. Among today's penalty leaders no one can top Buffalo bad boy Rob Ray. Despite no appreciable hockey skills at the NHL level, Ray carved out an NHL career as arguably the league's number one fighter while scoring only 41 goals during a 16-year career. As penalty leader in 1998–99, Ray sat in the box for a league-high 261 minutes and established a modern-day low of just four points (all assists) in 76 games. Jody Shelley collected five points and 249 minutes in 2002–03.

14.31 B. 38 games

The shortest NHL career for a penalty leader belongs to Montreal Canadiens old-timer Joe Hall, the two-time penalty king from the league's first two seasons in 1917–18 and 1918–19. Hall played only 38 games over the two 24-game schedules before he died from influenza during the 1919 Stanley Cup finals. In modern play, Montreal's Mike McMahon had the next-shortest NHL career among penalty leaders. A defenseman with the Quebec Aces in the Quebec Senior Hockey League, McMahon joined the Canadiens in 1943–44, amassed a league-leading 98 minutes (and 24 points) in the 50-game schedule and helped Montreal win its first Stanley Cup in 13 years. In the playoffs he matched his defensive partners in points with three in eight games while collecting the second-most penalty minutes (16) in the postseason. Parachuted into the NHL's top team, things couldn't have been better for the five-foot-eight, 215-pound McMahon. He even stood next to Maurice Richard in the team photo for the Stanley Cup. But the following season he was demoted to the Montreal Royals of the QSHL. McMahon survived only another 15 NHL games, split between Montreal and Boston in 1945–46, before spending his remaining years in the minors. McMahon's 57-game career is the briefest among modern-day NHL penalty leaders.

14.32 C. One minute and 40 seconds

As hockey fights go, boxing aficionados say it ranked with the "Thrilla in Manila" and the "Rumble in the Jungle." It was a heavyweight classic: McSorley, six foot one, 235 pounds, barefisted it with Probert, six foot three, 225 pounds, the two going toe-to-toe, launching rapid-fire blows for 1:40 until the pummelling bloodied their knuckles and complete exhaustion set in. Only after a gash opened over McSorley's right eye did the linesmen step in. Each got five minutes, and they weren't worth skate laces for the rest of the game.

14.33 A. Donald Brashear

No fines or disciplinary action were levied, but Vancouver's Donald Brashear received notice from the league to stop his hand-wiping taunts after officials saw videos of the tough guy wiping his hands following an October 12, 2000, dust-up with Greg de Vries of Colorado. Buffalo Sabres tough guy Rob Ray admitted "We've all done it, we're all guilty of it," but said Brashear's timing couldn't have been worse. "Right now Brash is the last guy who should be doing that," said Ray, referring to recent testimony from Marty McSorley that taunting contributed to his stick-swinging assault on Brashear in February 2000. When league officials called Canucks general manager Brian Burke with a request that Brashear stop it, Burke said: "I told them until there's a rule prohibiting it, don't bug my guy."

14.34 B. Delay of game

Neither Vancouver's electronic scoreboard nor the public address system recognized his historic achievement, but Glenn Anderson's Toronto teammates certainly let everyone know, storming over the boards en masse to congratulate him on the third-period breakaway goal that marked his 1,000th career point. Referee Denis Morel promptly whistled a two-minute delay-of-game penalty at the Leafs bench. Anderson served the penalty, but nothing could wipe the grin off his face after he became the 36th NHLer with 1,000 points.

14.35 B. Red Horner

The Toronto Maple Leafs' hardrock player led the league in penalty minutes a record eight straight seasons from 1932–33 to 1939–40. Horner became the first NHLer to reach 1,000 penalty minutes in 1936–37. Two years later, Eddie Shore became the second player to crack the milestone.

14.36 A. Tore out its tongue

It was not the first time a coach had attacked a team mascot during a game. To our knowledge, the first coach to take down a mascot was the usually even-tempered Don Jackson, bench boss of the IHL Cincinnati Cyclones, on February 4, 1995. Jackson completely lost it after the Atlanta Knights' mascot Sir Slap Shot banged on the glass partition separating the fans from the bench and knocked the Cyclones coach into his players. Seconds later, Jackson climbed over the glass divider and began pummelling Sir Slap Shot, to the consternation of many fans. In January 2003, after being taunted by Harvey the

Hound from behind the partition, MacTavish grabbed Harvey's 12-inch red tongue, tore it out and threw it into the crowd. When the Flames' mascot continued to goad the coach, MacTavish threatened and chased Harvey away with a stick.

14.37 A. Detroit's Ted Lindsay

During the 1956 Red Wings–Maple Leafs semifinals, an anonymous caller, probably unhappy with Detroit's 2–0 series lead, telephoned Toronto newspapers threatening: "Don't worry about Howe and Lindsay tonight. I'm going to shoot them." Plainclothes policemen were assigned to watch the Wings and their two targeted players, who by game time were extremely anxious, given all the publicity. Into the third period the threat seemed to be working. Detroit was down 4–2. But, as time ticked away, the mounting pressure fortified the Wings, and Howe and Lindsay each scored big goals to push the game into overtime. Then, at 4:22 of OT, Lindsay took a Bob Goldham pass at the Toronto goalmouth and whacked it beyond Leaf netminder Harry Lumley. After the game-winning goal, in defiance of the Toronto crowd, Lindsay raised the butt of his stick towards the stands and pretended to fire it like a gun. Lindsay's Hall of Fame career was defined by many such well-publicized events. He was one of old-time hockey's toughest and most feared players, yet he had league-wide respect as a goal scorer. He never backed down from anything or anyone: not his on-ice opponents, his team's management, league owners, and certainly not from disgruntled fans.

14.38 D. He became the first player penalized for such an action

During a November 24, 1935, game against Toronto, Red Wings rearguard Ralph Bowman was given a minor penalty, but teammate Syd Howe mistakenly went to the box instead. After the penalty expired, the Leafs complained that the wrong Detroit player had served it. The referee agreed and assessed Howe a minor, the first time another player was penalized for serving a teammate's penalty. Detroit's Wally Kilrea protested the call and was assessed a misconduct for his trouble. Despite the gaffe, Detroit won 2–1.

14.39 C. McSorley received an 18-month conditional discharge

Was it just tough guys playing hockey or assault with a weapon? That was the issue at Marty McSorley's trial in October 2000 when B.C. judge William Kitchen rendered a guilty verdict to the veteran enforcer. Judge Kitchen found McSorley guilty of assault with a weapon and handed him an 18-month conditional discharge, which spared him from serving jail time or having a criminal record.

14.40 B. An eight-game suspension and a $1,000 fine

Sure Tie Domi forfeited eight games and $1,000 for dinging Ulf Samuelsson, but his sucker punch was worth every bruised knuckle on his mangled left hand—to say nothing of his stock. His popularity rose immeasurably among players and fans around the league, who considered the sneak attack fair comeuppance for the Swede's career of cheap shots and dirty hits. Domi and Samuelsson initially bumped behind the Rangers' net and continued to jostle as they made their way to the front of the crease. Domi then slyly dropped his left glove and delivered a blow with his fist, striking the unsuspecting Samuelsson squarely on the chin. In an instant Samuelsson fell and struck his head on the ice. Four stitches closed the wound, but he suffered a concussion. The next day, reports from the Vancouver dressing room said Canuck players let out a collective cheer upon hearing of Domi's sucker punch.

GAME 14

The Ultimate 30–Goal Man

WHO IS THE ONLY NHLER to score 30 goals with five different teams? Unscramble the names of the other well-known 30-goal scorers below by placing each letter in the correct order in the boxes. Each name starts with a bolded letter. Then unscramble the letters in the circled boxes to spell out our ultimate five-team 30-goal man. To help you out, the two blackened circles are his initials.

Solutions are on page 566

K Y Z T R E **G**

S T R I L E T

U R **K** I R

S T O O P I **E** S

A R M E N Z **Y**

W **H** E O

I N N **D** O E

15

The Blue Line Corps

DURING THE SIX-TEAM ERA, the defenseman's primary role was to take care of his own end. Traditional rearguards, such as Allan Stanley, Leo Boivin and Butch Bouchard, plied their trade with heavy hits and solid defensive positioning and produced some of the most competitive low-scoring games in hockey history. But there was another approach, taken by a small group of intrepid blueliners whose skills surpassed the standard defensive positional play of their contemporaries. These men could control the tempo and flow of the game, lead a headlong rush through traffic or deliver pinpoint passing right on the tape. If Bobby Orr changed hockey by revolutionizing his position, he did it in the tradition of such maverick D-men as Doug Harvey, Pierre Pilote and Tim Horton.

Answers are on page 372

15.1 Which defenseman posted the NHL's all-time-highest plus-minus rating for one season?

A. Brian Leetch
B. Bobby Orr
C. Larry Robinson
D. Mark Howe

15.2 As of 2004–05, how many times has Scott Stevens been a minus in plus-minus ratings during his 22-year career?

A. Never
B. Only once
C. Three times
D. Five times

15.3 Which defenseman took six seasons to score his first goal? It was the first goal in the Buffalo Sabres' history.

A. Al Hamilton
B. Jean-Guy Talbot
C. Doug Barrie
D. Jim Watson

15.4 How many games did Larry Murphy miss during his 21-year career?

A. Less than 30 games
B. Between 30 and 60 games
C. Between 60 and 90 games
D. More than 90 games

15.5 Which team's defense corps boasted the "Big Three"?

A. The Edmonton Oilers
B. The Washington Capitals
C. The Montreal Canadiens
D. The Boston Bruins

15.6 Which NHL defenseman blocked the most shots in 1998–99, the first year the league tracked the statistic?

A. Ray Bourque
B. Rob Blake
C. Brian Leetch
D. Ken Daneyko

15.7 Who was the first NHL defenseman to play a full season without registering a penalty?

A. Doug Harvey
B. Jacques Laperriere
C. Red Kelly
D. Bill Quackenbush

15.8 In which year did a defenseman first record a 20-goal season?

A. 1917–18, when the NHL was formed

B. 1929–30, when forward passing was permitted in all three zones

C. 1944–45, when Maurice Richard recorded his 50-goals-in-50-games milestone

D. 1968–69, when Bobby Orr scored 21 goals

15.9 What was the greatest number of goals Doug Harvey ever scored in one season?

A. Under five goals

B. Between five and 10 goals

C. Between 11 and 15 goals

D. Between 16 and 20 goals

15.10 Which old-time rearguard was the first skater to replace an injured goalie for an entire NHL game?

A. Harry Mummery

B. Eddie Shore

C. Sprague Cleghorn

D. Eddie Gerard

15.11 Who was the last defenseman to win the Lady Byng Trophy as the league's most gentlemanly player?

A. Pat Stapleton

B. Doug Harvey

C. J.C. Tremblay

D. Red Kelly

15.12 Which Hall of Fame defenseman is famous for wearing a cape onto the ice before the opening faceoff?

A. Emile "Butch" Bouchard

B. Eddie Shore

C. Bill "Flash" Hollett

D. John "Black Jack" Stewart

15.13 Who is the only blueliner in NHL history to record a five-goal game?

A. Edmonton's Paul Coffey
B. Calgary's Gary Suter
C. Philadelphia's Tom Bladon
D. Toronto's Ian Turnbull

15.14 If the NHL record for the most shorthanded goals in one season is 13 by a forward, what is the record by a defenseman?

A. Seven shorthanded goals
B. Nine shorthanded goals
C. 11 shorthanded goals
D. 13 shorthanded goals

15.15 What is the record for most goals scored by two defensemen (as teammates or opponents) in one game?

A. Four goals
B. Six goals
C. Eight goals
D. 10 goals

15.16 Between Butch and Pierre Bouchard, how many goals did father and son score in their combined 23 years with the Montreal Canadiens?

A. Less than 50 goals
B. 50 to 100 goals
C. 100 to 200 goals
D. More than 200 goals

15.17 Which two defensemen have produced the most 20-goal seasons?

A. Bobby Orr and Paul Coffey
B. Paul Coffey and Denis Potvin
C. Denis Potvin and Ray Bourque
D. Ray Bourque and Bobby Orr

15.18 Who was the youngest blueliner in NHL history to score 20 goals in a season?

A. Bobby Orr
B. Paul Coffey
C. Phil Housley
D. Denis Potvin

15.19 After Bobby Orr, who was the next rearguard to score 30 goals in a season?

A. Larry Robinson
B. Paul Coffey
C. Denis Potvin
D. Doug Wilson

15.20 Which trio of defensemen became the first to each score 20 goals for one team in a single season?

A. The Oilers' Paul Coffey, Charlie Huddy and Kevin Lowe
B. The Capitals' Kevin Hatcher, Sylvain Côté and Al Iafrate
C. The Bruins' Bobby Orr, Carol Vadnais and Dallas Smith
D. The Canadiens' Serge Savard, Larry Robinson and Guy Lapointe

15.21 Who is the only defenseman to score more goals than any other member of his team in one season?

A. Bobby Orr of the Boston Bruins
B. Doug Wilson of the Chicago Blackhawks
C. Carol Vadnais of the Oakland Seals
D. Kevin Hatcher of the Washington Capitals

15.22 Who was the first NHL defenseman in history to lead a first-place team (overall) in scoring?

A. The Bruins' Ray Bourque
B. The Rangers' Sergei Zubov
C. The Islanders' Denis Potvin
D. The Bruins' Bobby Orr

15.23 Who was called the Bobby Orr of the WHA after he became only the second defenseman in pro hockey to lead his team in scoring?

A. Chicago's Pat Stapleton
B. Winnipeg's Lars-Erik Sjoberg
C. Quebec's J.C. Tremblay
D. New England's Rick Ley

15.24 Who was the first defenseman to compile six assists in a game?

A. Babe Pratt
B. Tom Johnson
C. Lionel Conacher
D. Babe Siebert

15.25 What is the longest consecutive point-scoring streak by a defenseman?

A. 16 games
B. 20 games
C. 24 games
D. 28 games

15.26 Which defenseman's record for most points in a season did Bobby Orr break in 1968–69?

A. Chicago's Pierre Pilote's
B. Detroit's Red Kelly's
C. Montreal's Doug Harvey's
D. Toronto's Tim Horton's

15.27 Who was the first rearguard to break one of Bobby Orr's NHL scoring records?

A. Tom Bladon
B. Ian Turnbull
C. Paul Coffey
D. Ron Stackhouse

15.28 Which defenseman's record for most goals in a rookie season did Brian Leetch break in 1988–89?

A. Buffalo's Phil Housley
B. Detroit's Reed Larson
C. Colorado's Barry Beck
D. Calgary's Gary Suter

15.29 How many goals did Bobby Orr score in his best offensive season?

A. 38 goals
B. 42 goals
C. 46 goals
D. 50 goals

15.30 How long did Bobby Orr's single-season goal-scoring record for blueliners last?

A. One year
B. 11 years
C. 22 years
D. It has never been broken

15.31 In his last great season, 1974–75, Bobby Orr scored a league-leading 135 points to win the NHL scoring race. If runner-up Phil Esposito was eight points back with 127, how far back was the next-best defenseman? Who was he?

A. Less than 30 points back
B. Between 30 and 40 points back
C. Between 40 and 50 points back
D. More than 50 points back

15.32 Bobby Orr led all NHL defensemen in scoring seven times. What was his largest single-season lead over the runner-up in points?

A. 29 points
B. 42 points
C. 60 points
D. 76 points

15.33 Who was the first rearguard in NHL history to score 300 career goals?

A. Ray Bourque
B. Denis Potvin
C. Bobby Orr
D. Paul Coffey

15.34 After Paul Coffey, Ray Bourque and Denis Potvin, who was the fourth blueliner to score 300 career goals?

A. Phil Housley
B. Al MacInnis
C. Chris Chelios
D. Larry Murphy

15.35 In NHL annals, how many defensemen have had 100-point seasons?

A. Two defensemen
B. Three defensemen
C. Four defensemen
D. Five defensemen

15.36 Who was the first NHL rearguard to score 500 points in a career?

A. Doug Harvey
B. Red Kelly
C. Bobby Orr
D. Bill Gadsby

15.37 Who was the first blueliner to amass 1,000 career points?

A. Brad Park
B. Paul Coffey
C. Denis Potvin
D. Larry Robinson

15.38 Which Washington Capitals player was known as the Secretary of Defense?

A. Larry Murphy
B. Rod Langway
C. Kevin Hatcher
D. Scott Stevens

15.39 Defensive great Serge Savard scored just 106 goals in 1,040 career games, or one goal about every 10 games. What is the worst games-per-goal total among players with 1,000 NHL games?

A. About 12 games per goal
B. About 24 games per goal
C. About 36 games per goal
D. About 48 games per goal

15.40 How many defensemen rank among the top-10 all-time American-born NHL point leaders?

A. Two defensemen
B. Three defensemen
C. Four defensemen
D. Five defensemen

15.41 Which defenseman scored the most regular-season goals in NHL history?

A. Denis Potvin
B. Ray Bourque
C. Paul Coffey
D. Bobby Orr

Answers

15.1 B. Bobby Orr

Larry Robinson gave it a valiant try in 1976–77 when the Canadiens lost just eight games all season. But even his awesome plus 120 rating couldn't equal Bobby Orr's 1970–71 mark of plus 124. Orr's rating is almost unbeatable, considering the best rating by a forward is Wayne Gretzky's plus 98 in 1984–85. Orr is, and probably always will be, the standard against which all good defensemen measure their hockey skills.

15.2 A. Never

During his 22-year career Scott Stevens has never been a minus—not once. The New Jersey defenseman had a flat zero in 1985–86 and a few plus-ones in 1988–89 and 1989–90 during his years in Washington, but with the Devils he has fared better, including a career-high and league-leading plus 53 in 1993–94.

15.3 D. Jim Watson

The expansion Buffalo Sabres had a soft spot for milestone goals by veteran defensemen held goal-less in their careers. The first Sabre goal in franchise history wasn't scored by future star forwards such as Gilbert Perreault or Gerry Meehan, but by Jim Watson, a veteran blueliner without a goal in six seasons with Detroit, where he played just 77 games. Al Hamilton, another veteran rearguard, waited four long years to score his first NHL goal, which he also earned in the Sabres' first year, 1970–71. Watson's goal, the first in the Sabres' history, was scored at 5:01 of the second period in a 2–1 win over Pittsburgh on October 10, 1970.

15.4 B. Between 30 and 60 games

When 20-year man Larry Murphy slipped into runner-up position on the NHL's all-time games-played list (second only to Gordie Howe) in 1999–2000, he was asked if could ever catch the indomitable Howe. "Gordie's a few years away. If I'm still playing at that point, I'm sure he will come back and play again. I think it'll be impossible to catch him," Murphy told the *Detroit Free Press.* Murphy played one more season and capped his career with 1,615, only 152 games shy of Howe's 1,767. He has since been passed by Mark Messier, Ron Francis and Scott Stevens in the Catch-Howe sweepstakes, but the veteran blueliner is still unsurpassed in games missed. In more than two full decades of hockey, Murphy missed only 53 games, almost half of them (25 matches) in his final season, 2000–01.

15.5 C. The Montreal Canadiens

The old sports saying "Offense wins games; defense wins championships" was proven true time and again by the "Big Three" on the Canadiens dynasty teams of the 1970s. Very big both in size and playmaking abilities, the defensive trio of Serge Savard, Larry Robinson and Guy Lapointe gave Montreal the balance, speed and muscle to completely control the game in any zone on the ice. No team before or since has ever boasted three All-Star rushing defensemen. Ken Dryden knew that better than anyone. Stuck in his familiar goalie pose of "The Thinker," he often watched the action from the far end of the rink.

15.6 C. Brian Leetch

In 1998–99, three of the top shot-blockers played for the New York Rangers, but no player blocked more than Leetch, with 212. Other top-flight defenders—including Ray Bourque (113 shots blocked), Rob Blake (139) and Al MacInnis (128)—didn't even approach the numbers of the Rangers captain. It's both a science and an art. Timing is essential. "There are certain ways to go down," noted Craig Ludwig, another savvy shot-blocker, in a *National Post* story. "If you are seven or eight feet from the guy, you do not go down on both knees and have your head in the way. You have to be smart enough to go down when your head is facing the corner and not the net, because they are trying to score a goal and you have to keep your head away from the play. But half the time you do not think about it. It just becomes part of your game."

The NHL's Top Shot-Blockers of 1998–99

PLAYER	TEAM	GP	SB	AVG
Brian Leetch	NYR	82	212	2.58
Ulf Samuelsson	NYR/Detroit	71	179	2.52
Peter Popovic	NYR	68	178	2.61
Igor Ulanov	Montreal	76	163	2.14
Ken Daneyko	New Jersey	82	159	1.93

15.7 D. Bill Quackenbush

It's not surprising that, in 1948–49, Quackenbush earned the honour of being hockey's first rearguard to play a penalty-free season. The position demands the sublime discipline of stealing the puck from an attacker, something Quackenbush did more effectively than anyone else in the six-team era, checking players without holding or tripping and stopping a rush cold without boarding. His low penalty totals are indicative of his clean style of play, which never betrayed the Hall of Famer in 14 NHL seasons. In that time, Quackenbush accumulated just 95 career penalty minutes and became the NHL's first Lady Byng winner from the defense corps. But his longevity had as much to do with his airtight defense as with his offensive skills, which often equalled those of the great Doug Harvey for puck control and Red Kelly's talent for playmaking.

15.8 C. 1944–45, when Maurice Richard recorded his 50-goals-in-50-games milestone

A few old-time guards scored 18 goals, but no D-man cracked the 20-goal barrier until 1944–45, when Detroit's Bill "Flash" Hollett scored 20 times in the 50-game schedule. Hollett played first in Toronto and later in Boston, where he developed superb rushing and stickhandling skills under the guidance of Eddie Shore and Dit Clapper. In the stay-at-home era of blueliners, Hollett excelled in both setting up plays and goal production. He twice registered 19-goal seasons before his record-setting 20-goal performance in 1944–45, the same season as Maurice Richard's benchmark of 50-in-50. No other NHL blueliner topped Hollett's total until Boston's Bobby Orr scored 21 times in 1968–69. As of 2005, Hollett has not been named to the Hockey Hall of Fame.

15.9 B. Between five and 10 goals

Doug Harvey was one of hockey's greatest D-men, though in a career that included 19 NHL seasons, seven Norris Trophies as outstanding defenseman, 13 All-Star appearances and six Stanley Cups, he never scored more than nine goals in a season. But when it came to controlling a game, Harvey was peerless. Rarely did he direct an errant pass or rush a play without his winger in position. He used to say, sarcastically, that he didn't score because there were no bonuses in his contract for goals. Still, Harvey wasn't the stay-at-home low-scoring rearguard typical of his era; his offensive style was the forerunner to Bobby Orr's. Harvey could kill time on a penalty or lead a rush up-ice with equal deftness, manoeuvring in and out almost effortlessly among forecheckers to deliver a soft pass to Canadiens forwards before returning to defend the blue line. Harvey scored only 88 goals but assisted on 452 in 1,113 games.

15.10 A. Harry Mummery

In old-time hockey, when a goalie was too badly injured to continue, another player from the team donned his equipment and replaced him in the net. The first skater to stand in for an injured netminder during an NHL game was Quebec Bulldog defenseman Harry Mummery, who subbed for goalie Frank Brophy three times—February 4, March 8 and March 10, 1920—during the 1919–20 season. But Mummery played a better defensive game manning the blue line than between the pipes. In his three "goalie" games he won one but allowed 18 goals for an awful 7.61 goals-against average. High numbers in any era but not as bad as some of the nights when number one goalie Frank Brophy backstopped the Bulldogs. On March 3, 1920, Brophy, playing with an injured leg, allowed a record 16 goals in a 16–3 shellacking by the Montreal Canadiens. It is still the NHL record for most goals scored by one team in one game. Mummery went between the pipes again on January 21, 1922, when he replaced Hamilton Tiger goalie Howie Lockhart in a 7–6 win against Ottawa. All four games Mummery worked as a substitute goalkeeper were against the old Ottawa Senators.

15.11 D. Red Kelly

The last time a D-man nailed gentlemanly play honours was in 1954, when Kelly won his third Lady Byng with Detroit. Defense is a tough position to play while avoiding penalties, and Kelly was among the few NHL rearguards who combined playmaking excellence with clean hockey, finishing sixth with 49 points and only 18 minutes in penalties in 1953–54. Kelly won one more Lady Byng in 1961, when he was playing forward with Toronto.

15.12 B. Eddie Shore

Shore played in the Roaring Twenties and Dirty Thirties hockey era, which witnessed great changes not only to the rules but in the marketing of the game. When the native of

Fort Qu'Appelle, Saskatchewan, blew into Boston in 1926, the Bruins knew they had themselves a gate attraction who could play skilled hockey and check, punch and scrap with the best of them. The Bruins indulged press and public alike—and their fast-rising star's flair for the unusual. After the warm-up skate, with all the players on the ice, the Garden's house lights would be dimmed, a spotlight would appear and out would skate Shore, outfitted in a black-and-gold cape, blowing kisses to the tune of "Hail to the Chief" playing over the loudspeakers. Boston fans would go wild while the opposition cringed at the antics of the NHL's first major marketing phenomenon.

15.13 D. Toronto's Ian Turnbull

Turnbull's hard shot, speed and natural ability made him one of the league's top defensemen in the 1970s. But his scoring touch could never compensate for his lackadaisical attitude and lapses in defense. His play was often uneven, though when he wanted to he could turn it on. His best offensive night occurred after being shut out for 30 straight games. He exploded for five goals on five shots against Detroit at Maple Leaf Gardens on February 2, 1977. It remains the NHL's only five-goal game by a blueliner.

15.14 B. Nine shorthanded goals

Paul Coffey's career year for goals was 1985–86, when the former Edmonton rearguard scored an amazing 48 times, nine of them shorthanded, to set the NHL standard for defensemen. The shorthanded record among forwards is held by Mario Lemieux (13 goals in 1988–89).

15.15 C. Eight goals

One of the most unusual scoring marks established in one game is the record for most goals by two defensemen. Interestingly, the record wasn't set during the careers of hockey's highest-scoring defensemen, Bobby Orr and Paul Coffey, but more than 40 years earlier on November 19, 1929.

Between Toronto's Hap Day and Pittsburgh's Johnny McKinnon, the two defensemen scored eight times, four goals apiece, in the Pirates' 10–5 bombing of the Maple Leafs. The goal surge was likely due to the new offside and forward passing rules introduced at the start of 1929–30. Forward passing was legal in all three zones (there was no red line until 1943) and there were no illegal offsides except for passes from one zone to another. This caused a league-wide goal explosion that forced the NHL to rethink its new rules. Less than a month after that game, one of the offside rules was amended on December 21, 1929, restricting attacking players from preceding the play when entering the opposing defensive zone.

15.16 B. 50 to 100 goals

The Canadiens knew what they were getting in 1970 when they assigned Butch Bouchard's son, Pierre, to their defense unit. Like father, like son. Both were big as redwoods. And both played in the same manner: low in goal production, tops in defensive skills. Bouchard the elder bluelined 15 seasons for Montreal, manhandling the opposition and steering away potential goals for backstoppers Bill Durnan and Gerry McNeil. The younger Bouchard duplicated his father's role for eight years with Ken Dryden, as a hard-nosed defensive defenseman. Their stay-at-home gamesmanship wasn't measured in goals but in quality of years of service. The Bouchards played 1,274 regular-season games for a combined 65 goals in 23 seasons with the Canadiens.

15.17 C. Denis Potvin and Ray Bourque

Bobby Orr could have won this race had his surgery-ravaged knees not given out after nine seasons. Orr recorded seven consecutive 20-or-more-goal years during his brief career, two less than the league-leading nine seasons set by both Ray Bourque and Denis Potvin. Bourque might have been the runaway leader in this category had he scored just one goal more in each of four 19-goal seasons during his career. Coffey produced eight 20-goal years and Al MacInnis, seven.

15.18 A. Bobby Orr

When Orr scored 33 goals in 1969–70, it was difficult to choose the more impressive feat: recording the NHL's first 30-goal season by a rearguard or his age—just 22. After three respectable 41-, 31- and 64-point seasons between 1966 and 1969, Orr unleashed the offensive force that would dominate individual point scoring for five NHL seasons and, ultimately, change the defensive position forever. No one had ever controlled an up-ice rush like Orr. In that 1969–70 season, his 120 points led all players, another NHL first for a defenseman.

15.19 C. Denis Potvin

Six years after Bobby Orr registered the NHL's first 30-goal season by a defenseman with 33 goals in 1969–70, Potvin potted 31 goals in 1975–76. Although often compared to the great Boston defenseman, Potvin was no Orr, but his longevity and scoring touch earned him the 1,000-point mark, something Orr never achieved.

15.20 B. The Capitals' Kevin Hatcher, Sylvain Côté and Al Iafrate

The first time an NHL team ever produced three 20-goal scorers among defensemen was in 1992–93, when Hatcher (34 goals), Iafrate (25 goals) and Côté (21 goals) teamed up to provide Washington with extra firepower up front after a series of trades and injuries hurt the forward lines. The Capitals' defense corps all chipped in to become the highest-scoring defense in NHL history, tallying 95 goals—29 per cent of Washington's 325 goals.

15.21 C. Carol Vadnais of the Oakland Seals

Similar to the fate of many snipers who played in the long shadow of Wayne Gretzky, Vadnais came into the NHL at the same time as Bobby Orr. While Orr was producing the greatest regular season by a defenseman, with league records for assists and points, a Stanley Cup-winning goal and four major individual trophies, Carol Vadnais was also having a pretty good year with the anemic Seals in Oakland in 1969–70. True, it was nothing compared to what Orr was accomplishing with the high-powered Bruins, but Vadnais, one of his era's most gifted offensive defensemen, led Oakland with 24 goals—the first and only time a blueliner topped his teammates in goals in regular-season play. Seals centre Earl Ingarfield recorded 21 goals that year. The only other rearguard to challenge Vadnais in this category is Washington's Kevin Hatcher, who shared the team lead with teammate Kelly Miller (24 goals in 1990–91).

15.22 B. The Rangers' Sergei Zubov

Although many blueliners, including Brian Leetch, Denis Potvin and Ray Bourque, have all led their teams in season point totals, no defenseman had ever achieved it on a club finishing first overall. Not until 1993–94, when the Rangers were number one and Sergei Zubov, who missed six games shuffling between Mike Keenan's doghouse and New York's Binghamton farm team, racked up 89 points to lead all Blueshirt point-getters (and all NHL defensemen, with 77 assists). Bobby Orr's first scoring championship in 1969–70 almost qualified him as the answer here, but Orr's Bruins only tied Chicago for most points (99) in the standings that season. The Blackhawks were awarded first because they won five more games than Boston.

15.23 C. Quebec's J.C. Tremblay

Similar to Bobby Orr in 1969–70, when he led the Boston Bruins in point totals with 33–87–120, Tremblay established himself as Quebec's defensive mainstay in the WHA during 1972–73, notching a team-high 89 points to become only the second rearguard in history to capture his team's scoring title. Tremblay also led the WHA that season with 75 assists.

15.24 A. Babe Pratt

Pratt was one of old-time hockey's best rushing rearguards. He could play the blue line, but it was his offensive numbers that stood out, especially during his record-setting 57-point season with Toronto in 1943–44. Pratt's best performance came on January 8, 1944, when he recorded the NHL's first six-assist game by a defenseman in a 12–3 Toronto romp over Boston. His MVP-winning 57-point season stood for 21 years; his six-assist game wasn't equalled until Chicago's Pat Stapleton did it in March 1969. Since then only four other rearguards have recorded six assists in a game.

15.25 D. 28 games

When it comes to scoring streaks Paul Coffey is far ahead of the pack, an illustrious group that includes Ray Bourque, Brian Leetch and Bobby Orr. None have cracked 20 games, never mind the 25-game barrier. Coffey netted 55 points in a record 28 straight games with Edmonton during 1985–86.

15.26 A. Chicago's Pierre Pilote's

Before Bobby Orr scored 64 points in 1968–69 to establish the new NHL season point total for defensemen, Chicago captain Pierre Pilote held the record with 59 points in 1964–65. Pilote, one of the game's great rushers and thumpers and a three-time Norris Trophy winner, broke Babe Pratt's 21-year-old mark of 57 points, set in 1943–44. Doug Mohns, a sometimes-blueliner, wasn't playing rearguard in 1967–68, the season he scored 60 points on a line with Stan Mikita and Kenny Wharram. Red Kelly's highest season total as a defenseman was 54 points in 1950–51.

15.27 A. Tom Bladon

Except for a few records, such as most assists or points in one season by a defenseman, many of Bobby Orr's 14 rearguard marks have been broken. The first one fell to Philadelphia's Tom Bladon, who, on December 11, 1977, scored eight points on four goals and four assists against Cleveland to best Orr's single-game mark of seven points, established in November 1973.

15.28 C. Colorado's Barry Beck

Selected second overall by Colorado in 1977, Beck tore out of the starting blocks and fired 22 tallies to establish a new NHL rookie goal-scoring mark for defensemen—a record that went unequalled until Leetch's 23-goal surge in 1988–89. The six-foot-three, 216-pound Beck took runner-up honours in Calder Trophy voting and compiled 60 points for the Rockies. Interestingly, besides Beck, two other defensemen during 1977–78 broke the old rookie goal-scoring record of 17 goals: Minnesota's Brad Maxwell with 18 and Detroit's Reed Larson with 19.

15.29 C. 46 goals

The NHL has always had a few great rushing defensemen. For blueliners such as Eddie Shore, Bill Hollett and Doug Harvey, the position meant more than blocking shots, skating off attackers and staying back to defend their netminders. Unlike the majority of rearguards, they could take over on offense, move the puck and set up plays. Then came Bobby Orr and his electrifying, game-breaking brand of hockey. His puck carrying and shooting skills were unlike those of any defenseman before him and have since influenced a generation of Bourques, Leetches and Lidstroms. Still, no defenseman but Orr has won a league scoring title. He twice accomplished the feat, including his 135-point season in 1974–75, the year of his highest goal output (46).

15.30 B. 11 years

At the time, no one in hockey could imagine another defenseman smashing Bobby Orr's 46-goal effort of 1974–75—or at least not in just 11 years. But in 1985–86, Paul Coffey pulled off what looked impossible and lit 48 red lights to break Orr's mark by two goals. It was an epic season for Coffey, who established a number of other offensive standards for blueliners, including beating Ray Bourque's 17-game point streak and tying Tom Bladon's mark of eight points in a game. Coffey played the last game of the season just two goals short of the coveted 50-goal mark, and one point to tie Orr's record point total of 139. But the Norris Trophy winner went pointless, finishing with a head-turning 138 points.

15.31 D. More than 50 points back

Bobby Orr's second scoring title in 1974–75 was his last great hurrah in NHL action. He led the league in points and assists and scored 46 goals, 18 more than Canadiens defenseman Guy Lapointe's runner-up total of 28. More impressive, Orr finished a staggering 59 points ahead of second-place Denis Potvin of the New York Islanders. Potvin had 76 points to Orr's 135.

15.32 D. 76 points

You can get a sense of Bobby Orr's impact on hockey by this astounding number. In 1969–70, the Bruins rearguard posted a league-high 120 points, shattering his own record for a blueliner by 56 points. The next-highest point total by a defenseman that season was 44, shared by Oakland's Carol Vadnais and Toronto's Jim McKenny. The next season, Orr turned it up another notch, amassing 139 points, which again was precisely 76 points better than runner-up J.C. Tremblay of Montreal, who had 63.

15.33 B. Denis Potvin

Potvin became the NHL's first 300-goal defenseman in his final season on January 14, 1987. The milestone goal came against Quebec rookie Ron Tugnutt, who Potvin beat with a wrist shot from the slot in the 8–5 win. Potvin was the 65th player in NHL history to score 300 goals. He did it in his 1,023rd career game. The 15-year Islander capped his remarkable career with 310 goals, 40 more than Orr's total of 270. Coffey netted number 300 in 1990–91 with Pittsburgh; Bourque reached the mark with the Bruins in 1993–94.

15.34 A. Phil Housley

Calgary's Phil Housley became the fourth defenseman in league history to reach the 300-goal plateau in a 3–1 loss to Chicago, March 17, 1999. "It's a great feeling to be in that crowd, with those great players," said Housley, who had six goals in his last 15 games (after scoring only three in his first 52 of 1998–99) to reach the career milestone. Al MacInnis notched his 300th the following season, 1999–2000. (Worth noting: although Housley was a rearguard, early in his career he moved between centre and defense. In 1983–84, Housley picked up seven of his 31 goals as a forward.)

15.35 D. Five defensemen

Bobby Orr, Denis Potvin, Paul Coffey, Al MacInnis and Brian Leetch are the only blueliners to record 100-point seasons in the NHL, each accomplishing the feat once except for Orr and Coffey, who did it multiple times during their careers. Orr had six consecutive 100-point seasons in Boston, while Coffey recorded three in Edmonton and another two in Pittsburgh.

15.36 D. Bill Gadsby

A superb two-way defenseman, Gadsby narrowly beat Doug Harvey in the race to be the first rearguard to record 500 points. Gadsby scored the league's first 500th in his 17th season on November 4, 1962, just months ahead of Harvey's 500th on February 6, 1963. Red Kelly, who amassed 452 points while patrolling the blue line for Detroit, would have been the first to reach to the mark, but he was converted into a centre after his trade to Toronto in 1959–60. Bobby Orr did it the fastest, amassing 500 points in under six seasons, from 1966–67 to 1971–72. When Gadsby retired in 1965–66, he ranked 20th among NHL scorers.

15.37 C. Denis Potvin

The eventful 1,000th point occurred on April 4, 1987, when a Mikko Makela shot ricocheted off Potvin's arm and sailed past

Buffalo goalie Jacques Cloutier into the Buffalo net. Potvin recorded 290 goals and 710 assists to reach point number 1,000. Coffey recorded his 1,000th point on December 22, 1990, Bourque on February 29, 1992. Neither Park nor Robinson ever hit 1,000 points.

15.38 B. Rod Langway

Langway quarterbacked the Capitals in the same manner of all great defensemen who become team captains. Over his 11-year term wearing the "C" in Washington, he became a standard-bearer of the club, winning two Norris Trophies as the NHL's top blueliner in 1983 and 1984. In America's capital, where the world's most powerful men play with the world's most dangerous weapons, Langway's leadership on the Caps earned him the title of Secretary of Defense. Raised in Randolph, Massachusetts, Langway is the first American to win the Norris Trophy.

15.39 D. About 48 games per goal

In 17 seasons, defenseman Craig Ludwig scored just 38 goals in 1,256 games, or one goal every 33 games. Ken Daneyko has 36 goals in 1,283 games and Luke Richardson 32 in 1,247 games (as of 2004–05). Yet, in comparison to Brad Marsh, Ludwig, Daneyko and Richardson are almost snipers. Although Daneyko set the NHL record with a 256-game goal-scoring drought, Marsh is the least effective goal scorer among 1,000-game NHLers. The stone-handed rearguard scored just 23 times in 1,086 games, an average of 47.2 games for every goal.

15.40 C. Four defensemen

As of 2004–05, Phil Housley, Brian Leetch, Chris Chelios and Gary Suter all ranked among the top 10 U.S. scorers. Housley retired in 2002–03 as the most prolific U.S.-born scorer, with 1,232 points. Many of his best scoring years were as a Winnipeg Jet after his trade for Dale Hawerchuk in 1990. In successive seasons with the Jets, the fleet-footed rearguard scored

76, 86 and 97 points, the last as a contributor to 56 of Teemu Selanne's record 76-goal and 132-point rookie season.

Top 10 U.S.-Born Point Leaders*

PLAYER	YEARS	GOALS	ASSISTS	POINTS
Phil Housley	1982–2003	338	894	1,232
Jeremy Roenick	1988–2004	475	645	1,120
Mike Modano	1989–2004	458	648	1,096
Joe Mullen	1979–1997	501	561	1,063
Pat LaFontaine	1984–1998	468	545	1,013
Brian Leetch	1988–2004	242	745	996
Neal Broten	1980–1997	289	634	923
Chris Chelios	1983–2004	178	736	914
Gary Suter	1985–2002	203	641	844
Keith Tkachuk	1992–2004	431	401	832

**Current to 2004–05*

15.41 B. Ray Bourque

For much of their careers, Ray Bourque and Paul Coffey traded off first place as all-time goal-scoring leaders among defensemen. When the dust settled Bourque had 410 goals to Coffey's 396. Interestingly, with playoff goal totals of 41 for Bourque and 59 for Coffey, the positions reverse: Coffey leads Bourque, 454 to 451 career goals. Each had many significant markers, but Bourque's final NHL goal was an historic one. When the 40-year-old defenseman blasted a shot past New Jersey Devils goalie Martin Brodeur in Game 3 of the 2001 Stanley Cup finals, he became the oldest player to score in a final series. (This record was broken by Igor Larionov in the 2002 Cup finals.)

GAME 15

Goalie Gunners

ALTHOUGH BILLY SMITH is credited with the first NHL goal by a netminder, Michel Plasse, playing with Kansas City of the Central Hockey League, is the first pro goalie to score. Plasse potted one against Oklahoma—while the net was empty for an extra attacker—on February 21, 1971. His goal came eight years before Smith's famous marker in 1979. In this game, match the nine goalie snipers below and their NHL scoring firsts.

Solutions are on page 567

José Théodore	Billy Smith	Ron Hextall
Tiny Thompson	Grant Fuhr	Evgeni Nabokov
Damian Rhodes	Jeff Reese	Martin Brodeur

1. ________ First goalie to score an NHL goal
2. ________ First goalie to shoot and score a goal
3. ________ First goalie to score a game-winning goal
4. ________ First goalie to score a goal and record a shutout in the same game
5. ________ First goalie to shoot and score a goal and record a shutout in the same game
6. ________ First goalie to score a power-play goal
7. ________ First goalie to receive credit for an assist
8. ________ First goalie to score 10 points in one season
9. ________ First goalie to score three points in one game

16

Great Expectations

AFTER THE EARLY ROUNDS of most NHL drafts, general managers seldom expect to find players destined to make regular rotation on their club. Nevertheless, a surprising number of low picks have later become superstars, such as Pavel Bure (113th), Doug Gilmour (134th), Brett Hull (117th) and Luc Robitaille (171st). Others, drafted high after careful scrutiny, have been equally unpredictable, sometimes firing blanks instead of bullets. Trades are just as quirky, resulting in the erosion of a team after a bad deal or, on occasion, adding just the right chemistry to produce a winner. Hey, this wheeling and dealing is part intuition, timing and luck—but never a science. Judge for yourself.

Answers are on page 397

16.1 Who is the youngest first-overall pick in NHL draft history?

A. Pierre Turgeon in 1987
B. Mike Modano in 1988
C. Ed Jovanovski in 1994
D. Joe Thornton in 1997

16.2 Who was the original number one in the first NHL draft in 1963?

A. Peter Mahovlich
B. Walt McKechnie
C. Orest Romashyma
D. Garry Monahan

16.3 Who was the first defenseman drafted first overall since the NHL Amateur Draft began in 1969?

A. Rick Green
B. Greg Joly
C. Denis Potvin
D. Larry Robinson

16.4 Who was the first U.S. college player drafted number one overall?

A. Joé Juneau
B. Pat LaFontaine
C. Joe Murphy
D. Brian Lawton

16.5 Who was the first Russian to be selected in a first round of the NHL draft?

A. Alexei Kovalev
B. Pavel Bure
C. Ilya Kovalchuk
D. Alexei Yashin

16.6 Who was the first player to jump directly from high school to the NHL?

A. Brian Lawton
B. Bobby Carpenter
C. Tom Barrasso
D. Phil Housley

16.7 Which goalie from the 1970s was the first netminder to jump directly from junior into the NHL?

A. Ken Dryden
B. John Davidson
C. Billy Smith
D. Gilles Gilbert

16.8 Most future NHL greats are spotted early in their careers by scouts, but that's not always the case. Which star netminder was not drafted as a junior?

A. Patrick Roy
B. Ed Belfour
C. Olaf Kolzig
D. Martin Brodeur

16.9 Since the NHL Entry Draft began in 1969, what is the highest draft position awarded to a goalie?

A. First pick overall
B. Second pick overall
C. Third pick overall
D. Fourth pick overall

16.10 What was the age of the oldest player ever selected in the NHL Entry Draft?

A. 24 years old
B. 28 years old
C. 32 years old
D. 36 years old

16.11 Who was the lowest-drafted player to win the regular-season scoring championship?

A. Brett Hull
B. Bryan Trottier
C. Jaromir Jagr
D. Jarome Iginla

16.12 Besides New York's Steve Durbano, who was the only other NHL penalty leader picked in the NHL draft's first round?

A. Marty McSorley
B. Tie Domi
C. Jimmy Mann
D. Bob Probert

16.13 Which brothers are the NHL's highest combined draft picks?

A. Sylvain and Pierre Turgeon
B. Ron and Rich Sutter
C. Scott and Rob Niedermayer
D. Daniel and Henrik Sedin

16.14 What is the highest draft position of a player who waited the longest before playing his first game?

A. First overall
B. Fourth overall
C. Eighth overall
D. 16th overall

16.15 In the 1993 NHL draft, Paul Kariya was chosen fourth overall, Chris Gratton third (Tampa Bay) and Chris Pronger second (Hartford). Who was the first pick who, when asked how it felt being chosen, said, "Nobody remembers who was picked second"?

A. Roman Hamrlik of the Tampa Bay Lightning
B. Eric Lindros of the Philadelphia Flyers
C. Alexandre Daigle of the Ottawa Senators
D. Ed Jovanovski of the Florida Panthers

16.16 What is the most number of times one player has been through successive expansion drafts?

A. No player has been through more than one expansion draft
B. Two straight expansion drafts
C. Three straight expansion drafts
D. Four straight expansion drafts

16.17 When was the last time a first-place team selected first overall in the following year's NHL draft? Name the team.

A. It has never happened
B. 1971, the Montreal Canadiens
C. 1975, the Philadelphia Flyers
D. 1982, the Boston Bruins

16.18 What was the highest draft position of a player (who didn't sign with his original club) who later re-entered the draft?

A. First overall
B. Fifth overall
C. Ninth overall
D. 19th overall

16.19 What is the greatest number of career games played by an NHLer who was drafted and then traded in the same summer?

A. 64 games
B. 364 games
C. 664 games
D. 964 games

16.20 Which player, traded or acquired as a free agent, cost his new team the most first-round picks as a penalty?

A. Wayne Gretzky
B. Scott Stevens
C. Eric Lindros
D. Kevin Stevens

16.21 What NHL policy is a result of Eric Lindros not signing with the Quebec Nordiques?

A. No player can refuse to sign once drafted
B. Clubs can negotiate prior to the draft
C. Any drafted player refusing to sign loses NHL eligibility for two years
D. Drafted players have limited freedom of club choice

16.22 How many players on the 1996 Stanley Cup-winning Colorado Avalanche were connected to the 1993 Eric Lindros deal that sent Lindros from the Quebec Nordiques (later the Avalanche) to the Philadelphia Flyers?

A. Three players
B. Five players

C. Seven players
D. Nine players

16.23 How many players were involved in the 1988 Edmonton–Los Angeles trade of Wayne Gretzky?

A. Four players
B. Six players
C. Eight players
D. 10 players

16.24 At the 2003 trade deadline a new record was set for most deals. How many transactions took place to break the old record of 21 deals in 1999?

A. 22 deals
B. 24 deals
C. 28 deals
D. 32 deals

16.25 What is the highest finish in the scoring race by a player who was traded midseason?

A. Second overall
B. Fourth overall
C. Sixth overall
D. Eighth overall

16.26 Which NHLer traded midseason holds the distinction of scoring the most points during the season of his trade?

A. Jean Ratelle with Boston and the New York Rangers in 1975–76
B. Bernie Nicholls with Los Angeles and the New York Rangers in 1989–90
C. John LeClair with Montreal and Philadelphia in 1994–95
D. Teemu Selanne with Winnipeg and Anaheim in 1995–96

16.27 Although Jaromir Jagr was traded from Pittsburgh to Washington the season after he won the NHL scoring title, which scoring champion was the first to have this happen to him?

A. Max Bentley
B. Wayne Gretzky
C. Phil Esposito
D. Ted Lindsay

16.28 What is so unusual about the trade history between Randy Wood and Benoit Hogue?

A. Both were traded to three different teams in the same season
B. Both were traded to the same three teams in the same season
C. Both were traded to the same team three times
D. They were first traded for each other; and, later, with each other

16.29 Which Boston GM engineered "The Trade" that sent Pit Martin, Gilles Marotte and Jack Norris to Chicago in exchange for Phil Esposito, Ken Hodge and Fred Stanfield?

A. Lynn Patrick
B. Hap Emms
C. Milt Schmidt
D. Harry Sinden

16.30 Who did the Toronto Maple Leafs trade to Detroit to get Red Kelly in 1960?

A. Howie Young
B. Marc Réaume
C. Marcel Pronovost
D. Hank Bassen

16.31 How many players changed teams in the largest trade in NHL history?

A. Six players
B. Eight players
C. 10 players
D. 12 players

16.32 Which Hall of Fame goalie did the Montreal Canadiens receive in a seven-player trade that dealt away the famed Jacques Plante?

A. Charlie Hodge
B. Gump Worsley
C. Rogie Vachon
D. Tony Esposito

16.33 Who was the first major "free agent" signed in the NHL? It happened in 1975.

A. Marcel Dionne
B. Ken Hodge
C. Bobby Orr
D. Frank Mahovlich

16.34 Which compensation, if any, did the Bruins receive from Chicago when Bobby Orr became a Blackhawk in 1976?

A. Nothing
B. Players
C. Cash
D. Future draft picks

16.35 What did New York Rangers GM Phil Esposito give up to acquire coach Michel Bergeron in 1987?

A. Bergeron was hired without compensation to Quebec
B. Bergeron for future considerations
C. Bergeron for cash
D. Bergeron for cash and a New York first-round draft pick

16.36 Which NHL GM made a trade to acquire his son as a player on his team?

A. Bob Gainey of the Dallas Stars
B. Pierre Lacroix of the Colorado Avalanche
C. Bob Pulford of the Chicago Blackhawks
D. Doug Wilson of the San Jose Sharks

16.37 Who was the first underage European to sign a North American professional contract? He played in the International Hockey League at age 17, in 1993–94.

A. Radek Bonk
B. Dmitri Kvartalnov
C. Vladimir Tsyplakov
D. Ruslan Salei

16.38 Which Norris Trophy-winning defenseman was traded by his original team for an NHL penalty leader?

A. Paul Coffey
B. Rod Langway
C. Doug Harvey
D. Chris Chelios

16.39 Even though he was not eligible, which NHL team tried to draft 17-year-old Russian phenom Alexander Ovechkin at the 2003 NHL Entry Draft?

A. The Buffalo Sabres
B. The Florida Panthers
C. The Los Angeles Kings
D. The Calgary Flames

Answers

16.1 A. Pierre Turgeon in 1987

Pierre Turgeon, of the Granby Bisons, was 17 years and 10 months old when he was selected first overall by the Buffalo Sabres in 1997. Brian Bellows was the same age when he was picked at the 1982 Entry Draft, but Bellows was chosen second overall by Minnesota. Joe Thornton was only a month older than Turgeon on his draft day in 1997. As of 2004–05, four players are tied as the next-youngest at 18 years old: Mike Modano (1988), Ed Jovanovski (1994), Rick Nash (2002) and Marc-Andre Fleury (2003).

16.2 D. Garry Monahan

The predecessor of today's Entry Draft was the NHL Amateur Draft, which when first held on June 5, 1963, drafted players of qualifying age (17 years and older) who were not already signed to NHL-sponsored junior clubs. Monahan, an unsigned 17-year-old winger playing for St. Michael's High School in Toronto, was picked first overall by Sam Pollock and Scotty Bowman of the Montreal Canadiens. With the $8,000 signing bonus, Monahan was on his way. He bought himself a 1955 Chevy, and within a few years the original number one draft was playing in the big league, mostly with Toronto and Vancouver throughout the 1970s. He scored 285 points in 748 games and 12 NHL seasons. Mahovlich was picked second by Detroit, Romashyma, third by Boston and McKechnie, sixth by Toronto.

16.3 C. Denis Potvin

When Islanders general manager Bill Torrey drafted Potvin first overall in 1973, he was establishing the infrastructure for a team that would soon dominate the NHL. It didn't hurt that Torrey later drafted Clark Gillies, Bryan Trottier and Mike

Bossy, but in Potvin he found the player to build his dynasty around. Potvin won the Calder Trophy as top rookie in 1973–74, scoring 54 points while manning the blue line. He soon became one of the game's most complete players: a run-and-gun threat on the rush, a quarterback on the power play and a punishing checker who left opponents groggy. After scoring 101 points in 1978–79, Potvin captained New York to four straight championships, including a 25-point postseason in 1981's 18-game march to the Stanley Cup. When Potvin retired in 1988, he was the highest-scoring defenseman of all time, with 310 goals and 742 assists for 1,052 points.

16.4 C. Joe Murphy

Joe Murphy, a Canadian-born centre playing at Michigan State, was chosen first overall by Detroit in 1986, the same year he won the Central Collegiate Hockey Association's rookie of the year honour with 61 points in 35 games for the Spartans. Murphy played for seven teams in 15 NHL seasons, notching a career high 35–47–82 with Edmonton in 1991–92.

16.5 A. Alexei Kovalev

While Kovalchuk (2001) and Alexander Ovechkin (2004) are number one draft picks, Kovalev is the first player from the former Soviet Union picked in the first round, after being selected by New York Rangers GM Neil Smith 15th overall in 1991. Other notable Russians picked high: Evgeni Malkin, second overall in 2004; Alexei Yashin, second overall in 1992; and Oleg Tverdovsky, second overall in 1994.

16.6 B. Bobby Carpenter

One of the most highly touted American amateur players ever, Carpenter made the cover of *Sports Illustrated* while still in high school at St. John's Prep in Massachusetts. Carpenter proved Washington had drafted wisely (first pick, third overall) by notching his first point 12 seconds into his NHL debut and scoring his first goal before the night was out. Carpenter earned 32 goals and 67 points in his freshman year, 1981–82. It's still a Capitals rookie record. Housley (1982), Lawton (1983) and Barrasso (1983) also jumped from high school into the NHL.

16.7 B. John Davidson

Few netminders jump from junior to the ranks of the NHL, but Davidson's brilliant play with the Calgary Centennials in the Western Canadian Junior Hockey League earned him a fifth overall pick by St. Louis in 1973 and this NHL first among goalies. Davidson split the Blues' cage duties with Wayne Stephenson and played 39 games in 1973–74. He was just 20 years old.

16.8 B. Ed Belfour

A Stanley Cup winner with the Dallas Stars in 1999, Belfour is one of the best goalies to appear from nowhere. A native of Carman, Manitoba, he played his junior hockey for the Winkler Flyers in the low-profile Manitoba Junior Hockey League. Ignored by NHL scouts, Belfour was never drafted as a junior. He was later signed as a free agent by the Chicago Blackhawks, whose scouts obviously caught the Eagle's stand-out season with the NCAA's University of North Dakota Fighting Sioux in 1986–87.

16.9 A. First pick overall

Because goaltenders tend to mature at a different pace than skaters (it's often difficult to assess a junior league goalie's full potential), general managers rarely select them in early draft rounds. But some GMs have skated on thin ice, risking a high draft position on a gut feeling—with varying results. Tom Barrasso and John Davidson were selected in the first round, fifth overall, by Scotty Bowman and Sid Abel respectively. Then, at the 1997 Entry Draft, Val-d'Or goalie Roberto Luongo was selected fourth overall by New York Islanders GM Mike Milbury. Two years later, Milbury, with an eye on history, made an even bolder move by trading Luongo and picking up Boston

University netminder Rick DiPietro first overall in 2000. In 2003, Pittsburgh didn't chance losing Marc-Andre Fleury of the Cape Breton Screaming Eagles and selected him with their first overall pick. Prior to 1969, when team sponsorships still played a role in the availability of juniors, the highest-drafted goalie was Michel Plasse, who was chosen first overall by Montreal in 1968.

16.10 D. 36 years old

In the final round of the 1989 NHL Entry Draft, the Minnesota North Stars selected retired Soviet forward Helmut Balderis. The Latvian was only two weeks shy of his 37th birthday. The gamble failed as Balderis was clearly past his prime. He played just 26 games for the North Stars during the 1989–90 season, scoring nine points, before returning home.

16.11 B. Bryan Trottier

Because the NHL only began the draft in 1963 and much of the top talent during that era had already signed player contracts to NHL-sponsored junior teams, our answer is someone after Guy Lafleur, the first scoring champion ever drafted. Since Lafleur there have been no spectacularly late picks that fooled everyone and went on to win the NHL's scoring title. Although a few champions were never drafted, including Martin St. Louis, who was overlooked by every club during the 1990s, and Wayne Gretzky, who was never drafted because he had signed a long-term deal with the WHA Oilers before their merger into the NHL in 1979. While Jaromir Jagr went fifth overall in 1990 and Jarome Iginla was 11th overall in 1995, Bryan Trottier is the latest pick (chosen 22nd overall in 1974) to win a scoring title. Brett Hull managed runner-up status to Gretzky in the 1991 scoring race after his 117th selection in 1984's draft.

16.12 C. Jimmy Mann

Although many penalty leaders never get a chance to hear their name being called on draft day, some have been called as early as the first round. Jimmy Mann, a hard-hitting winger and First All-Star with the Sherbrooke Beavers in the Quebec juniors, was Winnipeg's first choice (19th overall at the 1979 draft). Mann had size, toughness and potential, but after leading the league with 287 penalty minutes during his rookie year, he never managed a full NHL season again. He was later traded to Quebec and Pittsburgh to become each team's designated fighter. Steve Durbano, chosen 13th overall by the New York Rangers in 1971, is the highest overall pick among NHL penalty leaders. He led the league in penalties with 370 in 1975–76, a season split between Pittsburgh (161) and the Kansas City Scouts (209).

16.13 A. Sylvain and Pierre Turgeon

Sylvain, who was taken second overall by Hartford in 1983, and Pierre, first overall by Buffalo in 1987, are the highest-drafted brothers in NHL history. Other sibling combos, such as the Sedins, were chosen second and third overall in 1999; the Niedermayers were selected third and fifth overall in 1991 and 1993; and the Sutters were picked fourth and 10th in 1982.

16.14 C. Eighth overall

Although first-rounders usually get plenty of opportunities to prove themselves with the big club, that wasn't the story for defenseman Jason Herter, the Canucks' first choice and eighth overall pick of 1989. Herter played in the WCHA, the IHL and the AHL for four years before being signed as a free agent by Dallas in 1993. But his signing by the Stars changed little. Herter's next stop was Kalamazoo, another team in the IHL. In 1995–96, six years after first being drafted, Herter was traded by the Stars to the News York Islanders, where he played his lone NHL game. He recorded an assist, rare for a one-game wonder, and hasn't set foot on NHL ice since.

16.15 C. Alexandre Daigle of the Ottawa Senators

After a stellar Canadian junior career with Victoriaville, where he was named 1992's rookie of the year and selected to the

QMJHL First All-Star team in 1993, Daigle seemed the perfect fit for Ottawa. The Senators, with only 11 wins in their first season, needed an offensive star to sell tickets and help fill their new $185-million arena. Daigle's junior numbers were impressive and he was camera savvy in Canada's two official languages—a star-in-waiting capable of bridging both cultures in Canada's bilingual capital. The Senators were so hot on Daigle (considered the best French Canadian junior since Mario Lemieux), some say they tanked a few games in 1992–93 to get the first pick. On the morning of the draft, Daigle was signed to an unprecedented five-year, $12.5-million deal. Unfortunately, the fairy tale went bust. The Senators got their new arena, but in 1998, after four more frustrating seasons, they traded their number one pick to Philadelphia. As one Ottawa headline declared: "He Was the Can't Miss Kid, Who Did." Just after the trade, Flyer Chris Gratton, who went third in Daigle's draft, was asked if he had reminded his new teammate of his 1993 comment, "Nobody remembers who was picked second." Gratton laughed: "Not yet, but I'm sure I'll bring it up once or twice, maybe when I get him in the corner during practice."

16.16 C. Three straight expansion drafts

Originally drafted 185th overall by the Washington Capitals in 1984, Jim Thomson was kicked around by three teams—Washington, Hartford and New Jersey—before arriving in Los Angeles where he was yo-yoed in league expansion drafts to Minnesota in 1991, Ottawa in 1992 and Anaheim in 1993. Clearly, Thomson was your borderline player. His best friend was league expansion.

16.17 C. 1975, the Philadelphia Flyers

Only two teams have ever had the first overall pick after finishing first: the 1969 Canadiens, who were awarded the top two French Canadian players for the last time; and the 1975 Flyers, who snagged Mel Bridgman after trading Don MacLean, Bill

Clement and their 1975 first-rounder for the Washington Capitals' first overall choice. In our two other choices, the Canadiens finished fourth in 1971, while taking Guy Lafleur first in that year's draft; Boston selected Gord Kluzak first in 1982, after its fourth-place finish.

16.18 C. Ninth overall

The most obvious example of a first-rounder who almost re-entered the draft was Eric Lindros, who never blinked after boycotting the Quebec Nordiques, his 1991 draft team. After more than a year of frustration with the future star, Quebec prudently dealt Eric to Philadelphia, preventing Lindros from re-entering the draft the next season. The highest position of a player who re-entered the draft belongs to Nick Boynton, Washington's ninth overall choice in 1997. The Capitals failed to sign Boynton, who returned to the OHL and won MVP status at the Memorial Cup in 1999. He was Boston's first choice, 21st overall at the 1999 draft.

16.19 D. 964 games

The most successful players drafted and traded in the same summer are Doug Jarvis and Bob Bourne. In one of hockey's most amazing coincidences, both Bourne and Jarvis played the exact same number of career games (964 matches), won the exact same number of Stanley Cups exactly the same way (four straight Cups for their respective traded-to teams) and retired in the same season (1987–88). Bourne was drafted 38th overall by Kansas City in 1974 before being traded in September to the New York Islanders. Jarvis, hockey's all-time ironman, was chosen 24th overall by Toronto and dealt to Montreal just weeks after the 1975 Entry Draft.

16.20 B. Scott Stevens

There was no spirit in St. Louis after the Blues forfeited an unprecedented five number-one picks to the Washington Capitals for signing free agent Scott Stevens in 1990. Worse, the

Blues not only gave up first-rounders in 1991, 1992, 1993, 1994 and 1995 for the All-Star defenseman, but Stevens played just 78 games in 1990–91 before being sent to New Jersey for compensation—when the Blues signed free agent Brendan Shanahan.

16.21 B. Clubs can negotiate prior to the draft

Any club drafting first overall is allowed to bargain and sign a player before the NHL draft. Once the first pick has been signed, the team choosing second can begin negotiations with the second pick overall.

16.22 D. Nine players

Eric Lindros has a bad habit of making his own decisions. First he snubbed Sault Ste. Marie and was traded to Ottawa of the OHA. Then he slighted the Quebec Nordiques for his first NHL home, Philadelphia. And when Bobby Clarke of the Flyers traded for Eric it cost his club (wait for it) six players, two first-round picks and U.S.$15 million. All Clarke got in return was one Stanley Cup appearance (a sweep by Detroit in 1998) and a lot of headaches from the Lindros family. Meanwhile, the Nordiques shifted their franchise to Colorado and won the Stanley Cup in 1996 with nine members in the lineup that can be traced to the Lindros deal: Peter Forsberg, Mike Ricci, Chris Simon, Adam Deadmarsh, Patrick Roy, Mike Keane, Uwe Krupp, Claude Lemieux and Sylvain Lefebvre.

16.23 C. Eight players

On August 9, 1988, Edmonton Oilers owner Peter Pocklington became the most hated man in Canada after trading Wayne Gretzky to Los Angeles with Marty McSorley and Mike Krushelnyski for the Kings' Jimmy Carson, Martin Gelinas, three first-round drafts and U.S.$15 million in cash. The picks were Jason Miller in 1989, Martin Rucinsky in 1991 and Nick Stajduhar in 1993. Including Gretzky, eight players exchanged jerseys. Some people blamed No. 99's new wife, Janet Jones, for his move to L.A. But it was mostly about money and Pocklington's failure at other business ventures. Pocklington later moved to Southern California, the same market where Gretzky once dazzled on ice and now lives.

16.24 B. 24 deals

A few new marks were set at the trade deadline on March 11, 2003. A record 46 players changed teams in a league-high 24 deals. Highlighting the day, Detroit picked up Mathieu Schneider from Los Angeles, Toronto got greybeards Phil Housley from Chicago and Doug Gilmour from Montreal and St. Louis shored up its crease with Chris Osgood from the Islanders.

16.25 A. Second overall

Between 1917–18, when the NHL began operations, and 2004–05, at least 20 players dealt midseason finished among the top 10 in league scoring. Two players, both traded from defunct NHL teams, finished second in the scoring race after their trades. Babe Dye went from Hamilton to Toronto in 1920–21 and Syd Howe moved from St. Louis to Detroit in 1934–35. In another oddity, Hall of Fame centre Duke Keats was traded in consecutive years, 1926 and 1927, and had top 10 finishes both seasons. The best placement involving a traded player since 1967–68 is John Cullen, who finished fifth overall after being dealt by Pittsburgh to Hartford in March 1991. Although Cullen amassed 110 points that year, the Penguins got Ron Francis and Ulf Samuelsson, two core players of their Stanley Cup wins in 1991 and 1992.

16.26 B. Bernie Nicholls with Los Angeles and the New York Rangers in 1989–90

One season after he posted his career year of 150 points in 1988–89 with Wayne Gretzky in Los Angeles, the Kings traded Nicholls midseason to New York for Tony Granato and Tomas

Sandstrom on January 20, 1990. It proved to be Nicholls's second-best season ever: he scored 112 points between the Kings and the Rangers, the highest point total for a player traded midseason.

The Highest Point Totals for Players Traded Midseason*

PLAYER	SEASON	TEAMS	GP	PTS	TP
Bernie Nicholls	1989–90	L.A.	47	75	
		NYR	32	37	112
John Cullen	1990–91	Pit	65	94	
		Htf	13	16	110
Teemu Selanne	1995–96	Wpg	51	72	
		Ana	28	36	108
Jean Ratelle	1975–76	NYR	13	15	
		Bos	67	90	105

**Current to 2004–05*

16.27 A. Max Bentley

Jaromir Jagr's trade to Washington was all about the money, or the lack of it in bankrupt Pittsburgh. The trade of Bentley, Chicago's two-time scoring champion in 1945–46 and 1946–47, was an on-ice manoeuvre, designed to add more depth to the Blackhawks, a club winless in all six starts of 1947–48. It produced the biggest deal at the time, as Bentley, along with Cy Thomas, was traded to Toronto for Gus Bodnar, Bud Poile, Gaye Stewart, Bob Goldham and Ernie Dickens. Bentley never claimed another scoring race, but he probably didn't mind, considering he won three Stanley Cups with the Maple Leafs.

16.28 D. They were first traded for each other; and, later, with each other

Eight players were swapped in the 1991 Pat LaFontaine–Pierre Turgeon trade between the Islanders and the Sabres, including Randy Wood to Buffalo and Benoit Hogue to New York. Then, in separate deals three months apart in 1995, Toronto traded with the Sabres to get Wood and with the Islanders to get Hogue. Halfway through the next season, in January 1996, the Maple Leafs dealt Wood and Hogue together for Dallas' Dave Gagner. It is one of the few times in NHL history that two players who were once traded for each other were later traded as teammates.

16.29 C. Milt Schmidt

A member of Boston's storied Kraut Line with Woody Dumart and Bob Bauer during the Bruins' Stanley Cup years of 1939 and 1941, Schmidt orchestrated another Cup-winning event on May 15, 1967. Robbing Chicago of Esposito, Hodge and Stanfield (coupled with Bobby Orr's arrival) turned the basement-dwelling Bruins into Stanley Cup champions three years later, while the Hawks dive-bombed from first to fourth before crashing into the NHL cellar.

16.30 B. Marc Réaume

One of the worst NHL one-for-one trades ever, today's equivalent of the Kelly-Réaume deal might be Markus Naslund for Alex Stojanov, between Pittsburgh and Vancouver in 1996. Penguins GM Craig Patrick's uncharacteristic blunder (he got two goals out of Stojanov and gave away Naslund) must have had Wings manager Jack Adams chuckling in his grave. Adams, believing Red Kelly was washed up in 1960, traded the veteran All-Star defenseman for Marc Réaume, a low-impact Toronto rearguard. In the next seven seasons, Kelly, who was moved from defense to forward, helped lead the Maple Leafs to four

Stanley Cups, the last in 1967. Réaume managed just five points in 77 NHL games; or almost the same numbers as Stojanov in Steeltown, six points in 45 games.

16.31 C. 10 players

There have been two NHL trades that involved 11 players each, but in both cases future draft picks dominated the deal. First, on July 3, 1981, Philadelphia and Hartford exchanged Rick MacLeish for Ray Allison in a deal that included six draft picks; then, on June 15, 1985, Montreal dealt Mark Hunter and others to St. Louis for five picks. But the biggest trade among players immediately exchanging teams sent 10 NHLers to two different clubs. Doug Gilmour was the prize catch when Calgary sent him, along with Ric Nattress, Jamie Macoun, Rick Wamsley and Kent Manderville, to Toronto, on January 2, 1992, in exchange for Gary Leeman, Craig Berube, Jeff Reese, Alexander Godynyuk and Michel Petit. The Maple Leafs got the nod in this deal, as Gilmour led Toronto to semifinal finishes in the next two seasons. It was the Leafs' best playoff performance in 25 years.

16.32 B. Gump Worsley

In a blockbuster trade with New York, Montreal dealt their multiple Vezina Trophy-winning goalie, the ever-temperamental Plante, to the Rangers (with Donny Marshall and Phil Goyette) for Gump Worsley (and Dave Balon, Leon Rochefort and Len Ronson). For Worsley, it was a new beginning after years of suffering on inept Ranger teams. For Plante, it was a big demotion. He played 98 games over the next two seasons before retiring. Meanwhile, in Montreal, Worsley and Charlie Hodge were winning Stanley Cups. After expansion in 1967, Plante was lured back between the pipes to play for St. Louis, Toronto and Boston before his second NHL retirement in 1973. Worsley hung up the pads a year later in 1974 as a Minnesota North Star. Both goalies began their NHL careers in 1952–53.

16.33 A. Marcel Dionne

On June 17, 1975, Dionne became the first big-name free agent in history after signing with Los Angeles. In accordance with a 1975 agreement between the NHL and the players' association (which states that any player whose contract expires can move to a new team, provided equal compensation is awarded to the player's former club), the NHL forced the Kings to give up Dan Maloney, Terry Harper and a second-round draft choice as compensation to Detroit for Dionne and Bart Crashley.

16.34 A. Nothing

On his last knees, Orr signed with Chicago after, unbeknownst to him, his agent Alan Eagleson turned down two Bruin contract offers (including the famous 18.5 per cent team ownership deal) that would have kept the All-Star defenseman in Boston. Instead, Orr unhappily left the Bruins and became a Blackhawk for a $3-million-dollar, five-year package, without compensation to Boston. The deal was struck just two months before the NHL's new Collective Bargaining Agreement, which included a provision for team compensation. The Bruins challenged the Blackhawks in federal court on compensation and tampering charges but the case was dismissed by a Chicago judge. The deal is the only one of its kind involving a player of Orr's stature that did not include some form of compensation.

16.35 D. Bergeron for cash and a New York first-round pick

On paper, the match was ingenious. Bring hockey's most colourful bench boss to the NHL's loudest and most vibrant city. Bring the scrappy, blood-boiling Michel Bergeron to cosmopolitan, sports-mad New York to coach the Rangers. Phil Esposito thought he had found the right man at the right time to spark his struggling team. So, in June 1987, Espo "traded" $100,000 and the Rangers' 1988 first-round draft pick to Quebec for the Nords' heart and soul, the feisty Bergeron, known as "le petit tigre," or "Little Tiger." The Esposito-

Bergeron tandem didn't last long, though. The men were too similar; Bergeron was gone from New York after less than two seasons, replaced by Espo himself.

16.36 B. Pierre Lacroix of the Colorado Avalanche

Ten days after winning the Stanley Cup in 1996, Colorado Avalanche general manager Pierre Lacroix dealt goalie Stephane Fiset and a first-round pick in 1998 to the Los Angeles Kings for his son, Eric Lacroix, and the Kings' first-round choice in 1998. Eric played two seasons and scored 67 points in 170 games with the Avalanche before he asked his father to trade him (to Los Angeles) in early 1998–99. There had long been suggestions that Eric's presence in the dressing room was causing some conflict within the team because he was suspected of being a spy for his father.

16.37 A. Radek Bonk

In 1993, when he signed with the IHL's Las Vegas Thunder, Bonk was 17, a fresh-faced centre from Krnov in the Czech Republic. Because of his age, many expected a difficult adjustment in a men's pro league, but Bonk, who earned $100,000, proved his big-league skills by scoring 42 goals and 87 points in 76 games with the Thunder. Bonk was Ottawa's first choice, third overall in the 1994 NHL Entry Draft.

16.38 C. Doug Harvey

In 1961, Montreal traded six-time Norris Trophy-winner Doug Harvey to the New York Rangers for tough guy Lou Fontinato. The Canadiens, looking to toughen up their lineup, chose well: Fontinato led the league with 167 penalty minutes in 1961–62. But Harvey, who became the Rangers' player-coach, won the Norris a record seventh time.

16.39 B. The Florida Panthers

In an effort to secure the surefire number one pick of 2004 a full year ahead of any other team, Florida chucked the Gregorian calendar and tried drafting Russian sensation Alexander Ovechkin at the 2003 Entry Draft. At the time, Ovechkin was 17 years old and ineligible until his 18th birthday on September 17, two days too late for the 2003 draft. But the Panthers chose him anyway, trying to fine-tune the space-time continuum with this theory: since there were four leap years since Ovechkin's birth in 1985, there would be four "extra" days, making him old enough to be drafted. In a *National Post* story, Professor Norman Murray of the Canadian Institute for Theoretical Astrophysics called Florida's argument "clever." "The usual definition [of age] is not how many days old you are, but how many birthdays you have. Yes, 365 days times 18, that's how many days old he would be on September 11—four days before the September 15 draft eligibility date, but that's not 18 years because years... are actually 365-and-a-quarter days long," said Murray. In reality, birthdays are celebrated by years, not by days, which was how the NHL saw it, rejecting Florida's innovative approach to aging. Instead the team picked Nanaimo Clippers forward Tanner Glass, 265th overall in the ninth round.

GAME 16

Stanley Cup Captains

IN PLAYOFF HISTORY ONLY one team has ever won the Stanley Cup while scoring fewer goals than any other club during the regular season. More impressive, our mysterious team has done it twice, including once with the only goalie to captain a Cup-winner. There are 29 names of Cup-winning captains listed below. Their names, such as Wayne **GRETZKY**, appear in the puzzle horizontally, vertically, diagonally or backwards. After you've circled all 29 names, read the remaining 12 letters in descending order to spell our unknown goalie captain.

Solutions are on page 567

Scott **STEVENS**
Ted **LINDSAY**
Guy **CARBONNEAU**
Wayne **GRETZKY**
Hap **DAY**
Sylvio **MANTHA**
Yvan **COURNOYER**
Joe **SAKIC**
Lionel **HITCHMAN**
Cooney **WEILAND**
Kevin **HATCHER**
Doug **YOUNG**
Dit **CLAPPER**
Bobby **CLARKE**
Toe **BLAKE**
Sid **ABEL**
Steve **YZERMAN**
Lanny **MCDONALD**
Syl **APPS**
George **ARMSTRONG**
Jean **BÉLIVEAU**
Denis **POTVIN**
Eddie **GERARD**
Mark **MESSIER**
Bob **GAINEY**
Maurice **RICHARD**
Ted **KENNEDY**
Sprague **CLEGHORN**
Mario **LEMIEUX**

S	H	U	P	U	A	E	V	I	L	E	B
C	T	A	O	H	Y	A	S	D	N	I	L
G	R	E	T	Z	K	Y	R	E	M	U	Y
E	E	N	V	C	L	A	R	K	E	C	O
R	P	N	I	E	H	K	L	A	S	D	U
A	P	O	N	C	N	E	G	L	S	A	N
R	A	B	I	A	B	S	R	B	I	Y	G
D	L	R	G	A	I	N	E	Y	E	Z	N
Y	C	A	H	T	N	A	M	R	R	E	R
D	L	C	O	U	R	N	O	Y	E	R	O
E	K	D	D	L	A	N	O	D	C	M	H
N	A	G	N	O	R	T	S	M	R	A	G
N	S	I	H	I	T	C	H	M	A	N	E
E	S	P	P	A	X	U	E	I	M	E	L
K	N	E	D	N	A	L	E	I	W	R	C

17

Getting Networked

When actor Paul Newman laced up the blades for the movie *Slap Shot,* he turned in a performance worthy of Bull Durham and revealed a hockey player's less-than-glorious life in the minors. Newman portrayed Reggie Dunlop, the player-coach of a fictitious team whose fortunes turn around after it acquires the Hansons, three brothers in horn-rimmed glasses who are better at cracking skulls than potting goals. In classic Hollywood fashion, Newman's team starts winning games and the hometown crowds return to cheer on their misguided heroes. In this chapter: our favourite show-biz trivia, bruises and all.

Answers are on page 423

17.1 Which famous hockey incident did the Canadian rock band the Tragically Hip write about in their song "Fifty-Mission Cap"?

A. The 1923 disappearance of the Stanley Cup
B. The 1951 death of Toronto's Bill Barilko
C. The 1955 Richard Riot in Montreal
D. The 1972 Summit Series between Canada and Russia

17.2 Which national team was featured on a Wheaties cereal box after the 1998 Olympics?

A. The 1998 U.S. Olympic men's hockey team
B. The 1998 Canadian Olympic women's hockey team
C. The 1998 Czech Republic Olympic men's hockey team
D. The 1998 U.S. Olympic women's hockey team

17.3 In the NHL version of Monopoly, the board game, what two franchises occupy Boardwalk and Park Place?

A. The New York Rangers and the Montreal Canadiens
B. The Montreal Canadiens and the Toronto Maple Leafs
C. The Toronto Maple Leafs and the Detroit Red Wings
D. The Detroit Red Wings and the Los Angeles Kings

17.4 The NHL refused to allow an advertisement for spark plugs on which goalie's mask during the 1970s?

A. Bernie Parent's
B. Ed Giacomin's
C. Tony Esposito's
D. Gary Smith's

17.5 What ever happened to Foster Hewitt's famous broadcast booth, the gondola?

A. It's stored in Maple Leaf Gardens
B. It was trashed
C. The Hewitt family has it
D. It's on display in the Hockey Hall of Fame

17.6 Which goalie appeared on NBC's *The Tonight Show* with Jay Leno during the 2003 playoffs?

A. Martin Brodeur of the New Jersey Devils
B. Patrick Lalime of the Ottawa Senators
C. Marty Turco of the Dallas Stars
D. Jean-Sébastien Giguère of the Anaheim Mighty Ducks

17.7 What children's song is unofficially banned by the NHL?

A. "Humpty Dumpty"
B. "Three Blind Mice"
C. "Here We Go Round the Mulberry Bush"
D. "Rock-a-Bye Baby"

17.8 What was the name of the fictional minor-league hockey team that the Hanson brothers played for in the 1977 film *Slap Shot*?

A. The Dayton Daggers
B. The Wheeling Wildcats
C. The Charlestown Chiefs
D. The Nashville Knights

17.9 Which sportswear manufacturer produced television commercials starring fictional down-on-their-luck goalies in 1997?

A. Easton
B. Nike
C. Starter
D. CCM

17.10 Who wrote the theme for the CBC's *Hockey Night in Canada*?

A. Canadian singer-songwriter Paul Anka
B. Jingle composer Dolores Claman
C. Canadian country singer Stompin' Tom Connors
D. Amateur songwriter Billy Cochrane, who won a contest

17.11 What two NHLers cameoed in the film *The Mighty Ducks*?

A. Basil McRae and Mike Modano
B. Basil McRae and Dave Gagner
C. Basil McRae and Mark Tinordi
D. Basil McRae and Russ Courtnall

17.12 What song did the organist play after a tear-gas bomb exploded at the Montreal Forum on the night of the famous Richard Riot in 1955?

A. The Platters' "Smoke Gets in Your Eyes"
B. Jackie Wilson's "Lonely Teardrops"

C. Percy Faith's "My Heart Cries for You"
D. Connie Francis's "Who's Sorry Now?"

17.13 Where and when was NHL hockey first broadcast on a pay-per-view basis?
A. In New York for the 1979 Challenge Cup
B. In Long Island for the 1983 All-Star game
C. In Minnesota for the 1991 Stanley Cup
D. In Chicago for the 1992 Stanley Cup

17.14 How many times did North Stars fans sing the "Na Na Hey Hey (Kiss Him Goodbye)" song during their team's drive to the Stanley Cup final in 1991?
A. About four times per playoff game
B. About six times per playoff game
C. About eight times per playoff game
D. About 12 times per playoff game

17.15 Which Olympic hockey team saw its country's leading opera company base a musical on its gold-medal performance?
A. U.S.A., 1980
B. Sweden, 1994
C. The Czech Republic, 1998
D. Canada, 2002

17.16 Which rock star was the inspiration for the naming of the Jacksonville Lizard Kings of the East Coast Hockey League?
A. Gene Simmons
B. Ozzy Osbourne
C. Jim Morrison
D. Alice Cooper

17.17 What did the Philadelphia Flyers do to try and psych out the Bruins during Game 6 of the 1974 finals?

A. They wore new playoff jerseys
B. They painted the Stanley Cup on the ice at the Spectrum
C. They hired a famous singer to belt out "God Bless America"
D. They handed out white pompoms to the spectators

17.18 In a 1995 episode of *Seinfeld,* the NBC TV sitcom featured a crazed New Jersey hockey fan wearing a Devils jersey. Which player's name and number made it to prime time?

A. Mike Peluso's No. 8
B. Martin Brodeur's No. 30
C. Claude Lemieux's No. 22
D. Scott Stevens's No. 4

17.19 In the TV sitcom *Cheers,* how does Carla's husband, goalie Eddie Lebec, die?

A. At the hands of Carla, who goes temporarily insane after finding out Eddie cheated on her
B. In a freak Zamboni accident at an ice show
C. In an on-ice brawl at Boston Garden
D. He's electrocuted at Sam's bar while installing a jukebox

17.20 Which NHL tough guy fronted a rock band called Grinder?

A. Derian Hatcher of the Detroit Red Wings
B. Georges Laraque of the Edmonton Oilers
C. Darren McCarty of the Detroit Red Wings
D. Matthew Barnaby of the New York Rangers

17.21 Which NHL goalie played Team U.S.A. goalie Jim Craig in the action scenes of *Miracle,* a feature-length film about the 1980 U.S. Olympic gold-medal-win in men's hockey?

A. Jim Craig
B. Tom Barrasso
C. Bill Ranford
D. Chris Osgood

17.22 Which company did Wayne Gretzky and the great Russian goalie Vladislav Tretiak endorse together on television?

A. Coca-Cola
B. American Express
C. Gillette
D. Pro-Set Table-Top Hockey

17.23 Who was the first hockey player to appear on the cover of *Time* magazine?

A. Chicago goalie Lorne Chabot
B. Montreal forward Jean Béliveau
C. Chicago sniper Bobby Hull
D. Detroit legend Gordie Howe

17.24 Which singer wrote the 1988 hit "Big League"?

A. k.d. lang
B. Stompin' Tom Connors
C. Tom Cochrane
D. Bryan Adams

17.25 Which Canadian goalie refused to allow his likeness to appear on a Swedish postage stamp?

A. Corey Hirsch
B. Trevor Kidd
C. Sean Burke
D. Craig Billington

17.26 On January 9, 1998, a naked fan streaked across the ice at Calgary's Saddledome during overtime in a Flames–Panthers game. Which song did the public-address system play to accompany the streaker?

A. The Village People's "Macho Man"
B. David Rose's "The Stripper"
C. Carly Simon's "You're So Vain"
D. Ray Stevens's "The Streak"

17.27 Which beer maker produced a 1998 television commercial in which a road-hockey game breaks out on a busy street?

A. Molson
B. Budweiser
C. Labatt
D. Coors

17.28 Which big-name country singer helped promote the Nashville Predators in a 1997–98 advertising campaign?

A. Garth Brooks
B. Tricia Yearwood
C. Shania Twain
D. Clint Black

17.29 Who was the first hockey player to have his image appear on a Campbell's soup can?

A. Gordie Howe
B. Maurice Richard
C. Bobby Orr
D. Wayne Gretzky

17.30 Which broadcaster broke the story of Wayne Gretzky's retirement?

A. Ron MacLean
B. John Davidson
C. Mike Lange
D. Don Cherry

17.31 The FOX network unveiled an electronic puck at the 1996 NHL All-Star game. What colour was the halo that surrounded the puck on TV screens?

A. Red
B. Blue
C. Green
D. Orange

17.32 Who was the first NHLer to make the cover of *Sports Illustrated*?

A. Bobby Hull
B. Gordie Howe
C. Maurice Richard
D. Jean Béliveau

17.33 How many times has Wayne Gretzky appeared on the cover of *Sports Illustrated*?

A. Eight times
B. 12 times
C. 16 times
D. 20 times

17.34 In the Kansas City Blades' regular-season IHL finale April 17, 1999, the club sponsored a promotion called Toothless Night in which fans with missing teeth got in for free. How many of the 9,325 fans in attendance qualified?

A. Less than 40 fans
B. Between 40 and 400 fans
C. Between 400 and 1,000 fans
D. More than 1,000 fans

17.35 In which city did the first North American telecast of an NHL game take place?

A. Toronto
B. Montreal
C. New York
D. Chicago

17.36 What was the Web site www.nogoal.com dedicated to?

A. NHLers who have never scored a goal
B. Goals disallowed by video replay
C. The Stanley Cup-winning goal of 1999
D. NHL shutout records

17.37 Who was the little boy Don Cherry famously picked up during one of the show openings of CBC's *Coach's Corner*?

A. A child actor
B. Patrick Roy's son
C. Don Cherry's nephew
D. An unidentified four-year-old Canadiens fan

17.38 What special feature was included in some trading card packs in the Be a Player 2000–2001 Memorabilia Series?

A. Official NHL bubble gum
B. Holographic player pictures
C. Genuine player autographs
D. Swatches of actual equipment fabric

17.39 What important Toronto Maple Leaf historical artifact did former Leafs broadcaster Brian McFarlane save from destruction in 1970?

A. The Leafs' Stanley Cup banners
B. Archival film footage of the Leafs' games
C. Foster Hewitt's broadcasting gondola
D. The Leafs' original team charter

17.40 Which Canadian rock band was featured on the NHL's official 2002 video game?

A. Blue Rodeo
B. Nickelback
C. The Tragically Hip
D. The Barenaked Ladies

17.41 After a number of high-profile stick-swinging incidents in 1999–2000, the NHL made it onto *The Late Show* with David Letterman in unceremonious fashion. In Letterman's list of top-10 new NHL slogans, what was his number one NHL slogan?

A. Dirtiest Game on Earth
B. Stick It to Me, Baby
C. We Will, We Will Sock You
D. He Shoots, He Scars

Answers

17.1 B. The 1951 death of Toronto's Bill Barilko

Shouts of "Barilko!" became the ritual whenever the Tragically Hip played Maple Leaf Gardens. It was a chant for "Fifty-Mission Cap," a rock hymn about rugged Leaf defenseman Bill Barilko, who, just months after scoring a spectacular goal to win the 1951 Stanley Cup, vanished with a friend while on a fishing trip in northern Ontario. Barilko's Cup-winner is considered MLG's most famous goal. To add to the tragedy and mystery of Barilko's disappearance, his downed plane wasn't found for another 11 years—when, on June 6, 1962, forest rangers found the wrecked aircraft and two skeletons in dense bush. The discovery came just weeks after the Leafs clinched their first Stanley Cup since the accident. Apparently, the plane had run short of fuel but was still on course—halfway between Rupert House and Timmins. Barilko's No. 5 has never been worn by another Toronto player.

17.2 D. The 1998 U.S. Olympic women's hockey team

Wheaties has featured many great athletes on its cereal boxes since the 1930s, when Johnny Weismuller first endorsed "The

Breakfast of Champions." Indeed, after the Americans beat Canada 3–1 to win the first-ever Olympic gold medal in women's hockey, 15 members of the team posed for the front of the Wheaties box. "Every Olympic athlete's dream. First a gold medal and then your own Wheaties box," quipped captain Cammi Granato after making one of the most prestigious covers in American sports culture.

17.3 B. The Montreal Canadiens and the Toronto Maple Leafs

In 1999, Parker Brothers, the makers of Monopoly, issued an NHL version of the popular board game. It was the first Monopoly game devoted to a professional league, in which players in the game become team owners who can buy and sell franchises, acquire broadcasting partners and hammer out deals in arena luxury boxes. The two most prestigious properties, Boardwalk and Park Place, are occupied by hockey's two oldest franchises, the Canadiens and the Maple Leafs.

17.4 B. Ed Giacomin's

After his trade to the Detroit Red Wings, Giacomin swung a deal with Champion Spark Plugs to carry a "Spark with Eddie" advertisement on his mask. The league torpedoed the arrangement but Eddie kept the motif he had designed and wore it on his final mask, as a Red Wing.

17.5 B. It was trashed

Two generations of Canadians grew up listening to Foster Hewitt call the play-by-play from the gondola in Maple Leaf Gardens. In 1979, the famous announcers booth was torn down to make room for private luxury boxes.

17.6 D. Jean-Sébastien Giguère of the Anaheim Mighty Ducks

Giguère, in the middle of a prolonged layoff before the start of the 2003 Cup finals and fast becoming a household name in southern California, guest-starred on NBC's *The Tonight Show* on

May 23, 2003. During the interview Leno quipped: "You don't look like a hockey guy, you have teeth and everything." Giguère smiled and shot back: "I'm a goalie. I've got a mask." Upon hearing about Giguère's appearance, Cup finals opponent Martin Brodeur of the Devils said: "I wish I could be." Giguère became the first goalie and only the second NHLer to appear on Leno's show. Detroit forward Brendan Shanahan appeared with Leno after the Red Wings won the Cup in 1997.

17.7 B. "Three Blind Mice"

In the 1950s this children's ditty was a favourite among arena organists, who would stir the crowd by piping out "Three Blind Mice" whenever the three on-ice officials, in the organist's opinion, made a bad call against the home team.

17.8 C. The Charlestown Chiefs

The 1977 comedy *Slap Shot* starred Paul Newman as playing coach of the Charlestown Chiefs, a hapless minor-league hockey team that achieves success thanks to the violent antics of a trio of bespectacled goons known as the Hanson brothers. Not only were the actors who portrayed the Hansons real hockey players, Newman's character, Reg Dunlop, was modelled on John Brophy, a playing coach with the Johnstown Jets of the old Eastern Hockey League. The silver-haired Brophy later coached the Toronto Maple Leafs in the 1980s. Some may be surprised to learn that *Slap Shot*'s raunchy script was penned by a woman, Nancy Dowd. She was aided in her realistic grasp of jock banter by her brother, Ned, a player with the Johnstown Jets, who sneaked a tape recorder onto the team bus.

17.9 B. Nike

The four hockey ads featuring fictitious down-and-out goalies were created by Nike, the planet's largest athletic apparel retailer. Nike got into hockey in 1994 by buying Canadian-owned Canstar, the makers of Bauer skates and Cooper pads.

Ever since, the Nike admen have pitched their hockey products just like their court gear: hype a superstar in artful over-the-top campaigns that sell "cool" and redefine "attitude" for every kid watching. Indeed, Nike's hockey ads focus on four former NHL goalies (in full gear) whose careers were ruined after their "weak glove-hand" or "weak stick-hand" was exposed by the likes of Mats Sundin, Sergei Fedorov or Jeremy Roenick, and "the effortless way he skates the puck through traffic... in his shiny Nike skates." Each unemployed goalie now works either as a janitor, a panhandler, a burger flipper or, in the most hilarious scenario, as a French Canadian cabbie who drives even more badly than he tends goal.

17.10 B. Jingle composer Dolores Claman

Da En Da En Da Da Naaa. So familiar is Claman's opening to *Hockey Night in Canada* that it has been called Canada's unofficial national anthem. Playing each Saturday night in hockey season since 1967, the theme has been indelibly etched into the Canadian consciousness. HNIC producers asked Claman to write a big, brassy opener like the popular themes from American action TV shows of the 1960s (e.g., *Mission Impossible*). Claman submitted two potential musical lead-ins. The CBC's pick has been HNIC's signature tune ever since.

17.11 A. Basil McRae and Mike Modano

Disney scored big bucks at the box office in 1992 with *The Mighty Ducks,* the story of a team of peewee misfits reluctantly coached by one Gordon Bombay (played by Emilio Estevez). Under Bombay, the Ducks gel into a winning team featuring two girls, a black-and-white threesome known as "the Oreo Line" and an on-ice manoeuvre called "the Flying V." On the road to victory, Bombay confronts his hockey past and introduces Basil McRae and Mike Modano to the team.

17.12 C. Percy Faith's "My Heart Cries for You"

The events leading up to the Richard Riot are well known. On the eve of the 1955 playoffs, during a Detroit–Montreal match, someone set off a tear-gas bomb in the Forum to protest the suspension of Maurice Richard. Richard, the pride of French Canada, had hit a linesman in a previous match. But to what music did the crowd exit? As putrid smoke filled the Forum, fans began their exodus and the organist, choking back his own tears, played "My Heart Cries for You."

17.13 C. In Minnesota for the 1991 Stanley Cup

Hockey's introduction to pay-per-view TV received rave reviews and generated huge revenues, spurred on by the North Stars' Cinderella performance in the 1991 playoffs. Viewers were charged U.S.$9.95 per game in the first two rounds and U.S.$12.95 per game for the Conference and Cup finals. Minnesota's 11 home games attracted 300,000 viewers and brought in U.S.$3.5 million.

17.14 D. About 12 times per playoff game

Commonly chanted at sporting events when the home team is about to win or an opposing player is removed from the ice, Steam's 1969 hit, "Na Na Hey Hey (Kiss Him Goodbye)" was sung 125 times during Minnesota's 11 home playoff games at the Met Sports Center in 1991. North Stars fans, delirious over their team's playoff run, were belting out the "Hey Hey" song almost every five minutes of playing time. But there was no song in their hearts on May 25, 1991, when the Penguins embarrassed the North Stars 8–0 to win the Cup.

17.15 C. The Czech Republic, 1998

Czech fans in Prague are as fanatical about their hockey as any rabid North American puckhead. They've even taken to the 2004 production of *Nagano,* the Czech opera company's musical based on that country's 1998 Olympic win in Japan. In this opera about the Czechs' passion for the game, performers act out the roles of stars such as Dominik Hasek, Robert Reichel and Jaromir Jagr—including a particularly memorable scene where fans run through the streets chanting "Hasek is god!"

17.16 C. Jim Morrison

As hockey has moved deeper into the American sunbelt, all kinds of odd creatures have turned up in team names, including Amarillo Rattlers, New Mexico Scorpions, South Carolina Stingrays, Orlando Solar Bears and Louisville Riverfrogs. Larry Lane, owner of Jacksonville's 1996–97 entry in the ECHL, called his team the Lizard Kings as a tribute to his favourite rock star. Jim Morrison, the charismatic singer-poet of The Doors, had a fascination with dreams, death and insanity and often used these themes in his lyrics, especially in his poem "Celebration of the Lizard" ("I am the Lizard King, I can do anything"). Clad in black leather and slithering on stage, Morrison became the Lizard King for generations of music fans.

17.17 C. They hired a famous singer to belt out "God Bless America"

Live or on tape, Kate Smith's version of "God Bless America" has a remarkable win-loss record for the Flyers at the Spectrum in Philadelphia. To gain the edge during Game 6 of the 1974 finals against Boston, the Flyers flew Smith in for the real thing. Smith, an avid Flyers supporter ("I really do love those Flyers!") belted out the patriotic anthem for U.S.$5,000 instead of her usual U.S.$25,000 fee. Philadelphia became the first expansion team to win the Cup.

17.18 B. Martin Brodeur's No. 30

During this memorable *Seinfeld* episode, Elaine dates a hockey fan who turns out to be a "face painter," someone who, in this case, paints his face green and red for Devils games. The fan also wears a New Jersey sweater with the No. 30 and the name

BRODEUR on the back. Interestingly, the program aired the evening prior to Martin Brodeur recording his third shutout against the Boston Bruins in the Eastern Conference quarter-finals. It marked only the fifth time a goalie posted three shutouts in a best-of-seven format since 1939.

17.19 B. In a freak Zamboni accident at an ice show

The producers of *Cheers* kill off the show's Eddie Lebec character—who has joined a travelling ice show as a skating penguin—by having Eddie make the ultimate sacrifice. He dies while saving a fellow penguin from a berserk Zamboni. Bonus question: What's Carla and Eddie's special song? "O Canada," of course.

17.20 C. Darren McCarty of the Detroit Red Wings

Long-time supporter of various charity causes, McCarty is also the founder and lead singer of a Michigan rock band called Grinder. The band, which cited the Clash and MC5 as its musical influences, recorded a CD to raise funds for the families of former Red Wing defenseman Vladimir Konstantinov and trainer Sergei Mnatsakanov, who both suffered serious injuries in a car crash in June 1997.

17.21 C. Bill Ranford

Ranked by *Sports Illustrated* as the greatest sports moment of the 20th century, Team U.S.A.'s gold-medal-win at the 1980 Olympics was nothing short of a miracle. Coach Herb Brooks sold a bunch of college kids on the notion that they could do the impossible and beat the unbeatable Soviets. Later, some called it the greatest coaching performance in the history of American sports and the most incredible sales job ever done on the minds of athletes who won "something that just never, ever should've been possible." Broadcaster Al Michaels's "Do you believe in miracles?" phrase best described the staggering upset by the Americans. In the Hollywood blockbuster *Miracle,* producers stocked the cast of the U.S. team with several first-time actors. American goalie Jim Craig was played by actor Eddie Cahill and by former NHLer Bill Ranford during the action sequences. "To add authenticity to the scenes, I tried duplicating some of Jim's signature moves," Ranford wrote in a story for the *Hockey News.* "I'd try to copy the way he played the puck with his glove hand near the bottom of his stick to help clear it out of the zone, or the way he'd hold his glove high on the crossbar so he could watch guys behind the net." Although it was a 4–2 victory over Finland that officially clinched the gold medal, the real miracle was the previous match, a 4–3 win over the Soviet Union.

17.22 C. Gillette

Even without his skates, Wayne Gretzky has scored some major accomplishments, particularly as a spokesperson in the big-league world of advertising. Over the years, he has done endorsements for McDonald's, Hudson's Bay, Campbell's Soup, Zurich Financial and Coca-Cola. Perhaps one of his most memorable pitches was the Gretzky–Tretiak commercial for Gillette—the first North American TV ad to use a Soviet athlete. It featured a nose-to-nose matchup between two of hockey's greatest—playing table-top hockey.

17.23 A. Chicago goalie Lorne Chabot

Sports figures have been the focus of a surprising number of cover stories in *Time* magazine, but only a half-dozen or so have been about hockey players. Wayne Gretzky graced *Time*'s cover in March 1985 (though the Great One had to share it with basketball superstar Larry Bird). Flyers goalie Bernie Parent also made *Time,* in February 1975, as did the Canada–Russia series in October 1974, Phil Esposito in October 1972, Bobby Hull in March 1968 and old-time goalies

Davey Kerr in March 1938 and Lorne Chabot in February 1935. (Chabot may have been considered a newsworthy figure because he replaced recently deceased Chuck Gardiner in the net of the defending champion Blackhawks. It must have been a slow news week.)

17.24 C. Tom Cochrane

Every parent hopes to see his or her children succeed. But when kids are in sports, the challenge to succeed begins sooner in life and fills a parent's head with what might be, as Cochrane so aptly wrote in his hit "Big League." Cochrane's inspiration came while on tour in western Canada. Before a concert he was approached by a man whose son was a big Cochrane fan and, also, a promising hockey player with an athletic scholarship. Unfortunately, before the boy could fulfill his lifelong dream of playing in the big leagues, he was killed in a car accident. Grief-stricken, the father made himself a promise to meet his son's musical hero. So moved was he by his fellow westerner's tragedy, Cochrane penned "Big League."

17.25 A. Corey Hirsch

For Swedish hockey fans, the 1994 Olympics symbolized the pinnacle of success. After several frustrating years of silver- and bronze-medal finishes, Sweden's moment came in dramatic fashion: a final-round shootout that pitted star forward Peter Forsberg against Team Canada goalie Corey Hirsch. It was over in a second, and Sweden had its first Olympic gold medal. Many commemorative items would honour that historic goal, including a Swedish postage stamp that would have depicted the likeness of Hirsch being deked out by Forsberg. But the Canadian netminder said "No way." So Sweden cast their national hero triumphantly scoring on an unidentifiable goalie.

17.26 A. The Village People's "Macho Man"

With 1:22 remaining in overtime, spectator Julian Vaudrey, 21, jumped the glass and ran around the rink wearing only a smile and a whistle for almost four minutes. He then stopped at centre ice to wave to 17,000 roaring fans. Calgary's public-address officials got into the act, playing the disco hit "Macho Man" before security escorted Vaudrey to a dressing room. Florida Panther Kirk Muller laughed till he cried and said, "I knew the guy had to be from up here [Calgary] because he didn't have a very good tan."

17.27 C. Labatt

The ad, part of Labatt's old "Out of the Blue" marketing campaign, starts with a young man flicking a crumpled can at the feet of a passerby on a busy street. Both men have hockey sticks and a road-hockey game ensues. Another businessman gets into it by playing goalie, using his umbrella and briefcase as a stick and blocker and a bicycle rack as his net. Other pedestrians join in, playing or cheering, until someone yells "Streetcar!"—ending the game. The spot was shot in mid-January in Toronto. The soundtrack was the hockey-arena anthem "Rock and Roll, Part II," by Gary Glitter.

17.28 A. Garth Brooks

To promote their premier NHL season, the Nashville Predators recruited Brooks and other celebrities, including Amy Grant and Vince Gill, to pose for print ads showing each of them with their front teeth blacked out. The ad slogan—"Got Tickets?"—was a takeoff on the familiar "Got Milk?" campaign that features famous people with milk mustaches.

17.29 D. Wayne Gretzky

The term superstar took on new meaning for Gretzky in 1996–97, when he became the first person to appear on a

Campbell's soup label. The image of Gretzky (clad in a generic uniform), along with his signature, appeared on 50 million labels of Campbell's Chunky.

17.30 B. John Davidson

Just weeks before the conclusion of the 1998–99 season, Davidson announced on the Madison Square Garden network and later on Fox's *Game of the Week* and CBC's *Hockey Night in Canada* that there was a better-than-80-per-cent chance that Wayne Gretzky would retire. What tipped Davidson off? Sticks and pucks. Davidson observed that No. 99 was stockpiling memorabilia. The all-time leading scorer in the game was using more sticks and saving more pucks than usual and storing them away. The deduction proved correct. Gretzky confirmed what Davidson had suspected: he was considering leaving the game. From there, a media frenzy of will-he-or-won't-he reports set the stage for the Great One's last two NHL contests, in Ottawa and New York.

17.31 B. Blue

American audiences have long complained that they have problems following the fast-moving puck on television. So the FOX network came up with a solution—a method of visually enhancing the puck with computer-generated graphics. The gimmick was introduced at the 1996 NHL All-Star game, when viewers saw a shimmery, blue aura surrounding the puck. Whenever the disk reached speeds of 70 mph or more, it turned red and sprouted a fiery comet tail. The network dubbed its glowing puck FoxTrax. Its clever name aside, most hockey fans hated the innovation. In a *Hockey News* poll, 91 per cent of respondents gave the thumbs down to FOX's psychedelic puck effects, claiming they were an annoying distraction.

17.32 D. Jean Béliveau

Despite the phenomenal popularity and widespread press coverage of the rivalry between the game's two best players, Howe and Richard, Béliveau got the big ink and landed the *Sports Illustrated* cover on January 23, 1956, two years after the magazine was first published in 1954.

17.33 C. 16 times

No hockey player was covered more by *Sports Illustrated* than Wayne Gretzky. From his early days in Edmonton when *SI* billed him as the Great Gretzky to his farewell skate in New York, No. 99 appeared on *SI*'s coveted front cover an unprecedented 16 times, including 12 exclusive covers and four covers on which his photo wasn't the primary image. In 1982, for his third cover, Gretzky was named *SI*'s sportsman of the year. Bobby Hull and Bobby Orr follow Gretzky with five *SI* covers each; Gordie Howe has notched four appearances. When the Great One retired, he was number eight on the list of all-time cover subjects, one behind Pete Rose and two ahead of Mike Tyson, Bill Walton and Arnold Palmer. By comparison, Gretzky's mug graced the cover of the *Hockey News* 70 times.

17.34 B. Between 40 and 400 fans

They called it a promotion with real bite. A total of 269 fans were admitted free as part of Toothless Night at the Blades' final home game of 1998–99. Another 48 fans with a chipped tooth qualified for a half-price deal. No one bothered to count the number of dentists in attendance.

17.35 C. New York

Contrary to what Canadians believe, televised coverage of NHL games actually began in the U.S. As Brian McFarlane notes in his book *The Rangers,* the first hockey telecast took place in New York City on February 15, 1940. The game, between the

Montreal Canadiens and the Rangers, was shown on an experimental station set up by NBC. It did not a have a large viewing audience, as there were only about 300 TV sets in the city. In fact, it was one of the rare times in history that the live audience at a sporting event outnumbered the number of fans watching on TV. The CBC can't even claim credit for being the first station to regularly broadcast NHL games. During the 1946–47 season, the Chicago Blackhawks began televising their home games to a local market on station WBKB. The CBC did not launch its TV coverage until the 1952–53 season.

17.36 C. The Stanley Cup-winning goal of 1999

After the Dallas Stars won the Stanley Cup on Brett Hull's so-called "tainted goal" (yes, Brett's foot was in the crease, but he had control of the puck), Buffalo fan Jeffrey Spring designed a Web site "so that people won't forget the only time they didn't finish the Stanley Cup finals," said Spring. The site—www.nogoal.com—offered surfers the famous overhead shot of Hull's goal, plus "No Goal" T-shirts, caps and bumper stickers.

17.37 B. Patrick Roy's son

CBC's opening to *Coach's Corner* once featured a barking dog (Cherry's bull terrier, Blue), Cherry himself standing on the Bruins bench with outstretched arms and Cherry hoisting Jonathan Roy, Patrick's son, the little boy wearing the Canadiens sweater.

17.38 D. Swatches of actual equipment fabric

They're similar to most other hockey trading cards, with cool artwork, career stats, a brief bio and an action shot of an NHL star, except that Be a Player cards periodically included a 1½-by-¾-inch patch of fabric affixed to the card back. Sometimes it was leather bits of Hall of Famer Gerry Cheevers or Bernie Parent's goalie pads or gloves; or, as in the 2000–01 edition, scraps of the ancient pads once worn by hockey's first great netminder, Georges Vezina, who played his last game in 1925. Cutting up Vezina's famous pads into swatches of leather and fabric for sale may seem a sacrilege to many hockey fans, who would rather see the pads—intact—in the Hockey Hall of Fame, but to card companies it was just part of the burgeoning trend in memorabilia collecting that gave everyone a chance to own a bit of hockey antiquity. In total, only 320 "Vezina pad cards" were issued, giving buyers about a 1:2,400 chance of finding an authentic swatch of the great netminder's pads. (Some of those cards contained the actual leather exterior, others had the fabric from inside the pad.) Today, Vezina's artifacts are so rare that the Hockey Hall of Fame owns only one pair of the Hall of Famer's skates.

17.39 B. Archival film footage of the Leafs' games

In 1970, Harold Ballard, then part-owner of the Toronto Maple Leafs, ordered a storage room at Maple Leaf Gardens cleaned out and hundreds of canisters of film tossed in the garbage. Brian McFarlane, a broadcaster and hockey historian, learned about the stockpile just as it was about to be destroyed and rescued a total of 796 cans. He then stored them at his own expense at a film distribution outlet in Toronto. The cache included all of the Leafs' game footage from 1962 to 1969, the era in which the club won four Stanley Cups. The film remained in storage until 2001, when the club prepared to launch Leafs TV. McFarlane then sold the film to Molson Inc., Leafs TV's major sponsor. The footage was still in pristine condition, and is considered one of Leafs TV's most valuable assets.

17.40 D. The Barenaked Ladies

It just might be the all-time best Canadian music gig. Not only did the Toronto band contribute three songs to the NHL 2002 video-game soundtrack, the game's designers even included the band members in the game alongside the NHL players.

"Seeing myself as a member of the Toronto Maple Leafs is a boyhood fantasy," said Ladies drummer Tyler Stewart. "For me it was very exciting to know that I could make it to the NHL—even if it is only on a digital level."

17.41 D. He Shoots, He Scars

If we could replay 1999–2000, we'd see a train wreck of concussions, suspensions and player violence that's almost unparalleled in NHL history. We'd zap from Mike Modano's near career-ending crash into the boards courtesy of Ruslan Salei's hit from behind, to Marty McSorley's two-hander across the temple of Donald Brashear, to Ed Belfour's assault on hotel security guards and his mace-in-the-face arrest, to Bryan Berard's sickening stick-in-the-eye injury, to Scott Niedermayer's clubbing of Peter Worrell and Worrell's subsequent throat-slashing gesture directed at the Devils' bench and, finally, to numerous hospital head-trauma units where Eric Lindros, Jaromir Jagr and Peter Forsberg all spent time with concussions. It would be a gruesome view of hockey. As a poignant close, the finale would go to David Letterman's top 10 list:

David Letterman's Top 10 NHL Slogans

10. It's Like an Episode of "Cops" on Ice
9. See for Yourself What Canadian Blood Looks Like
8. The "H" Is for "Hematoma"
7. It's Like Watching Really, Really Primitive Dentistry
6. A Sport That Combines Your Two Favourite Things: Ice Skating and Head Trauma
5. You Can't Spell "Unhealthy" Without "NHL"
4. Share the Excitement or We'll Beat Your Brains in with a Piece of Wood
3. We Injure More People by 9 p.m. Than Pro Football Does All Year
2. Don't Worry, Kids—They're Just Saying "Puck"
1. He Shoots, He Scars

GAME 17

Mario's Big Comeback

WHEN ASKED IF HE COULD visualize his first goal, the unretired Mario Lemieux answered immediately: "Breakaway. Top shelf." That's how Lemieux scored his very first NHL goal in 1984—on a clear breakaway with All-Star Ray Bourque hopelessly in pursuit. Lemieux's quote was among dozens that made headlines during his comeback in December 2000. In this game, match the hockey men below and their opinions on Mario's return.

Solutions are on page 568

Brett Hull	Martin Brodeur	Wayne Gretzky
Luc Robitaille	Jaromir Jagr	Mario Lemieux
Gary Bettman	Jeremy Roenick	Coach Ivan Hlinka
NHL spokesman Frank Brown		

1. ________ "It's not a big problem who's going to be captain.... Whatever he wants me to do, I'll do."
2. ________ "A fire hydrant could score 40 goals with him."
3. ________ "It's a little scary for us goaltenders."
4. ________ "There is no constitutional or bylaw provision that would prohibit an owner from playing."
5. ________ "This takes things up another notch."
6. ________ "I don't know how anybody could quit and want to come back. I'm dying to get out of this game."
7. ________ "He doesn't need a coach."
8. ________ "I have no intention of coming back."
9. ________ "None [no salary] deferred this time."
10. ________ "You know how much Keith Tkachuk gets pulled down, tackled, mugged in front of the net. It's ridiculous. Mario's in for a huge surprise."

18

Super Sweaters

IN A PROFESSION WHERE superstitious players obsessively perform detailed routines, former San Jose Shark Jamie Baker didn't ever worry, at least not about the No. 13 on his back. In 1993–94 the Ottawa-born native was the only North American regular in the NHL to sport No. 13, an unlucky number on this side of the Atlantic but popular overseas—just look at the European NHLers bearing No. 13s, including Mats Sundin and Teemu Selanne. Wearing the bad-luck number was the inspiration of an Ottawa Senator trainer who, at the 1992 training camp, suggested Baker take it because 13 was a baker's dozen.

Answers are on page 447

18.1 Bobby Orr is synonymous with No. 4, but the Bruins great actually wanted another number when he joined Boston in 1966–67. Which number?

A. No. 2
B. No. 6
C. No. 9
D. No. 13

18.2 When did Wayne Gretzky first start tucking part of his hockey sweater into his pants?

A. In the Brantford Atom league
B. With the Toronto Young Nations in Junior B
C. With the Sault Ste. Marie Greyhounds in Junior A
D. In the WHA

18.3 Which NHL team introduced a new third jersey in 1996–97, with a woman's image on the crest?

A. The St. Louis Blues
B. The New York Rangers
C. The Philadelphia Flyers
D. The Vancouver Canucks

18.4 In 1990, the Buffalo Sabres retired Gilbert Perreault's No. 11. Why did Perreault originally wear No. 11?

A. It was picked for him by a fortune teller
B. It was his number in junior hockey
C. It was the same number as his birthdate
D. It was Buffalo's winning lottery number in the 1970 Entry Draft

18.5 If "C" on sweaters means "Captain," what does "A" stand for?

A. Assistant captain
B. Associate captain
C. Alternate captain
D. Affiliate captain

18.6 Why did Maurice Richard choose No. 9 for his jersey?

A. He had no choice; No. 9 was assigned to him
B. As a tribute to Gordie Howe's No. 9
C. His newborn daughter weighed nine pounds
D. No. 9 was his first jersey number in city league

18.7 When Joé Juneau joined Boston, he asked for a certain uniform number but was turned down by the player who had previously worn it. Who was the player and what number did Juneau want?

A. Bobby Orr's No. 4
B. Phil Esposito's No. 7
C. Johnny Bucyk's No. 9
D. Milt Schmidt's No. 15

18.8 In which decade did player numbers first appear on hockey jerseys?

A. The 1910s
B. The 1920s
C. The 1930s
D. The 1940s

18.9 Which was the first NHL team to put players' names on the backs of their jerseys?

A. The Detroit Red Wings
B. The Montreal Canadiens
C. The Los Angeles Kings
D. The New York Americans

18.10 Toronto owner Harold Ballard made headlines by doing what in 1977?

A. Replacing the old Maple Leaf crest with a more stylized emblem
B. Camouflaging player names on sweaters
C. Changing the double stripe on the sleeve to a triple stripe to match the socks
D. Removing the small maple leaf on the shoulder

18.11 In which international hockey series did two teams first exchange jerseys on ice after the winning goal was scored?

A. The Summit Series in 1972
B. The Canada Cup of 1976
C. The Challenge Cup of 1979
D. The Canada Cup of 1981

18.12 Which NHL goalie wears a sweater number that pays tribute to Soviet netminder Vladislav Tretiak?

A. Ed Belfour
B. Nikolai Khabibulin
C. Arturs Irbe
D. Olaf Kolzig

18.13 Why does Pittsburgh's Jaromir Jagr wear No. 68?

A. He wanted a number close to Lemieux's No. 66
B. To commemorate the 1968 Soviet invasion of Czechoslovakia
C. He was born on February 15, 1968
D. He scored 68 points in his first season with Kladno, his junior Czech team

18.14 What was the sweater size of the Red Wings jersey that decorated the Spirit of Detroit statue during the Wings–Flyers Stanley Cup finals in 1997?

A. Size 60
B. Size 160
C. Size 260
D. Size 360

18.15 What role did little-known Sault Ste. Marie Greyhounds player Brian Gualazzi play in Wayne Gretzky's famous decision to wear No. 99 for the first time?

A. Gualazzi taped an extra nine on Gretzky's practice jersey
B. Gualazzi was already wearing the Greyhounds' No. 9 (Gretzky's favourite number)
C. Gualazzi threatened Gretzky if he asked for No. 9
D. Gualazzi was the first Greyhound to wear a number higher than 33

18.16 Who owns the No. 99 jersey that Wayne Gretzky wore when he scored his 801st goal to tie Gordie Howe's career goal-scoring record?

A. Wayne Gretzky's close friend and agent, Mike Barnett
B. Wayne Gretzky's father, Walter Gretzky
C. Wayne Gretzky himself
D. The Hockey Hall of Fame

18.17 What is the highest sweater number worn by an NHLer since Wayne Gretzky retired?

A. No. 95
B. No. 96
C. No. 97
D. No. 98

18.18 What is the highest sweater number worn by a goalie?

A. No. 60
B. No. 80
C. No. 93
D. No. 95

18.19 Which team banned the wearing of high sweater numbers in 1997–98?

A. The Calgary Flames
B. The Tampa Bay Lightning
C. The Ottawa Senators
D. The Anaheim Mighty Ducks

18.20 In 2000–01, sweater manufacturers moved their trademark logos on NHL jerseys. Where were they relocated on players' jerseys?

A. Above the player nameplate
B. On the right shoulder
C. Below the team crest
D. Below the player number

18.21 The New York Islanders wore whose name and number on their sweaters during the pre-game warm-up on October 20, 2001?

A. Clark Gillies's No. 9
B. Bryan Trottier's No. 19
C. Mike Bossy's No. 22
D. Bob Nystrom's No. 23

18.22 Prior to 1997–98 when Mark Messier wore No. 11, when was the last time that a Vancouver Canucks player wore No. 11? Name the player.

A. 1972–73
B. 1982–83
C. 1992–93
D. No Canuck had ever worn No. 11 before Mark Messier

18.23 Who was the first NHLer to have his jersey retired?

A. The Canadiens' Howie Morenz
B. The Bruins' Lionel Hitchman
C. The Maple Leafs' Ace Bailey
D. The Canadiens' Maurice Richard

18.24 Which goalie was the first to have his sweater number retired by an NHL team?

A. Toronto's No. 1, Turk Broda
B. New York's No. 1, Ed Giacomin
C. Montreal's No. 1, Jacques Plante
D. Philadelphia's No. 1, Bernie Parent

18.25 Name the only Chicago Blackhawk to wear No. 9 after Bobby Hull signed with the WHA in 1972?

A. Pit Martin
B. Dennis Hull
C. Dale Tallon
D. Ivan Boldirev

18.26 After Pavel Bure was traded to the New York Rangers in March 2002, he switched to No. 9 in honour of which former player?

A. Gordie Howe
B. Maurice Richard
C. Andy Bathgate
D. Valery Kharmalov

18.27 Canadian astronaut Robert Thirsk took whose hockey sweater and Stanley Cup ring into orbit on a 1996 NASA shuttle mission?

A. Joe Sakic's
B. Wayne Gretzky's
C. Bobby Orr's
D. Patrick Roy's

18.28 On what NHL team did Bernie Nicholls not wear No. 9 on his jersey?

A. The Los Angeles Kings
B. The Chicago Blackhawks
C. The New Jersey Devils
D. The New York Rangers

18.29 How did import player Tony Job make headlines in the Italian League in 1995–96?

A. He scored eight goals in one game
B. He married an Italian movie star
C. He tried to set fire to an opponent's sweater
D. He sang on stage with Luciano Pavarotti

18.30 Why did Brett Hull change his jersey number and wear No. 80 at the start of 2003–04?

A. To honour a scoring legend
B. To honour a coach
C. To honour his father, Bobby Hull
D. To honour a scoring record

18.31 Toronto's No. 6 jersey, worn by the great Ace Bailey, was retired in the 1930s, unretired in the 1960s and then retired again. Why?

A. To comply with an old Harold Ballard policy
B. Another Maple Leafs player wanted No. 6
C. The Maple Leafs ran short of sweater numbers
D. Bailey wanted another Maple Leaf to wear No. 6

18.32 Why did Darryl Sittler cut the captain's "C" off his sweater in 1979–80?

A. He wanted out of his no-trade contract
B. Because he was put on recallable waivers
C. Because of the Lanny McDonald trade
D. To protest the return of coach Punch Imlach

18.33 What jersey number was Gordie Howe wearing when he scored his first NHL goal in 1946?

A. No. 7
B. No. 17
C. No. 27
D. Howe always wore No. 9

18.34 Why does Alexander Mogilny wear No. 89?

A. He defected in 1989
B. He escaped on Flight 89 from Stockholm
C. He was drafted 89th overall by Buffalo
D. No. 89 is Mogilny's street address in Amherst, New York

18.35 Which Soviet player was the first to have his number retired in Russia?

A. Vladimir Krutov
B. Vladislav Tretiak
C. Anatoli Tarasov
D. Valery Kharlamov

18.36 Why did NHL teams begin wearing different sweaters for home and away games?

A. The away sweaters had names on the back
B. To make teams easier to distinguish on television
C. It was an NHL publicity move
D. Some teams had similar-coloured uniforms

18.37 When did Mario Lemieux first wear No. 66?

A. In 1978, in Pee Wee with the Ville Emard Hurricanes
B. In 1980, in Midget AAA with the Ville Emard Hurricanes
C. In 1981, in the QMJHL with the Laval Voisins
D. In 1984, in the NHL with the Pittsburgh Penguins

18.38 Which defunct NHL club first used a ferocious-looking animal on its team crest?

A. The Hamilton Tigers
B. The St. Louis Eagles
C. The Montreal Wanderers
D. The Quebec Bulldogs

18.39 What symbol was on the front of the Montreal Canadiens jersey during the club's founding years, between 1910 and 1914?

A. A "CH," like today
B. A hockey stick
C. A maple leaf
D. A flaming torch

Super Sweaters

Answers

18.1 A. No. 2

Bobby Orr wanted No. 2, which he had worn during his junior career with the Oshawa Generals of the Ontario Hockey Association. But that digit had been retired in honour of Boston Bruins defenseman Eddie Shore. Orr was assigned No. 27 when he joined the Bruins in 1966–67, but when Al Langlois, who had been wearing No. 4, was cut from the team before the start of the season, Orr took Langlois's number because it was the closest to No. 2 that he could get.

18.2 A. In the Brantford Atom league

Ever since he began playing organized hockey, Wayne Gretzky tucked in his sweater. When No. 99 was a small fry at age six on a team of 10-year-olds, his big sweater kept catching the butt end of his stick. Walter Gretzky tried the simplest solution. "My dad did it so [the sweater] wouldn't look so big on me," said Gretzky. Later, in the NHL, he used Velcro to make sure his sweater tuck stayed put. "I always cut off the fight strap—even for the All-Star game," he admitted.

18.3 B. The New York Rangers

The Rangers' new third jersey, introduced in 1996–97, received mostly positive reviews. Its crest featured the crowned visage of Lady Liberty emblazoned above the letters NYR. The idea of using the famous landmark originated with Ranger president and general manager Neil Smith. "We wanted a look that was identifiable with New York, and the Statue of Liberty was a better choice than, say, the Empire State Building," said Smith.

18.4 D. It was Buffalo's winning lottery number in the 1970 Entry Draft

When Buffalo and Vancouver entered the NHL in 1970, league officials decided which expansion team would get the first draft pick by spinning a roulette wheel. The Canucks chose the low numbers (1–8), while the Sabres had the high numbers (9–16). The wheel stopped at 11. Buffalo picked the premier junior player, Gilbert Perreault. Recognizing an auspicious omen when he saw one, Sabres general manager Punch Imlach gave Perreault uniform No. 11. Perreault wore it with great honour for 17 seasons before retiring in 1987 as Buffalo's all-time scoring leader.

18.5 C. Alternate captain

Teams have often played for years with alternate captains, choosing not to name a full captain for a variety of reasons.

From 1967 to 1973, the Bruins had no "C"s, relying on Esposito, Orr and Bucyk as alternates. This was coach Harry Sinden's way of making every player a leader on the ice.

18.6 C. His newborn daughter weighed nine pounds

Although many stars of the 1930s wore No. 9, it wasn't until the Rocket that 9 became hockey's most famous and requested number. Richard began his career in 1942 wearing No. 15, but after daughter Huguette was born, he switched to match her weight. She was truly the apple of her famous father's eye.

18.7 C. Johnny Bucyk's No. 9

Ever since he began playing organized hockey in his native Quebec, Juneau's favourite jersey number was No. 9. As a kid, he'd always arrive early to get the first sweater pick. But in Boston, No. 9 was hanging from the rafters, retired after the 21-year career of Bruin great Johnny Bucyk. So Juneau asked Bucyk if he would mind "unretiring" his No. 9. Bucyk happily agreed, but on the condition that Juneau hand over his six-figure signing bonus. Juneau, ever the creative hockey mind, laughed along with Bucyk at the proposal, then came up with No. 49, in honour of Bobby Orr's No. 4 and Bucyk's No. 9.

18.8 A. The 1910s

Based on what researchers now know, the first numbers on athletic uniforms appeared in 1908 on a few American college football teams. The practice of hockey numbers dates to 1911–12, when the Pacific Coast Hockey Association and the Montreal Wanderers of the National Hockey Association began using numbers one through 15 on team jerseys. In that era, much higher numbers were usually reserved for irregulars and backup goalies.

18.9 D. The New York Americans

The Americans' management adopted an aggressive and unconventional approach to marketing after the club joined the NHL in 1925. The between-periods entertainment at home games included barrel-jumping contests and dogsled races. In 1926, the Americans put player names on the backs of their flashy coloured jerseys, a first in pro sports and an innovation that the NHL didn't make mandatory until the 1970s.

18.10 B. Camouflaging player names on sweaters

Ballard refused to comply with an NHL rule requiring that all teams display players' names on the backs of their sweaters. Ballard figured sales of player programs would drop. In protest, he had blue letters sewn on the Leafs' blue uniforms, making it impossible to read the names. The stunt lasted one game.

18.11 B. The Canada Cup in 1976

It was an emotional moment few will forget. At the Montreal Forum, in sudden-death overtime, Canada defeated the defending world champion Czech team on a goal by Darryl Sittler. After the ceremonial handshakes, a group of Czechs corralled Bobby Orr, slapping him on his back and tugging at their own sweaters—and in a spontaneous act of sportsmanship, both teams exchanged jerseys. Bob Gainey slipped on Frantisek Pospisil's No. 7; Rogie Vachon exchanged No. 1s with Vladimir Dzurilla, and Sittler traded his No. 27 to get Bohuslav Ebermann's No. 25.

18.12 A. Ed Belfour

Belfour wears No. 20 in honour of his most influential goalie coach, Vladislav Tretiak, who began coaching in Chicago in Belfour's rookie season, 1990–91. That year, Belfour walked away with all of hockey's top awards for goaltenders. Tretiak never played in the NHL but his famous jersey number endures on the back of his star pupil. Belfour's No. 20 is the lowest double-digit number currently worn by an NHL goalie.

18.13 B. To commemorate the 1968 Soviet invasion of Czechoslovakia

Born in 1972, Jaromir Jagr chose a number symbolizing his country's struggle for freedom from communist repression. Ironically, his appearance on draft day in 1990 marked the first time a Czech player attended an NHL draft without having to defect.

18.14 D. Size 360

To cheer on the Red Wings during their 1997 Stanley Cup run, employees of East Side Team Sports in Warren, Michigan, dressed the muscular shoulders of the Spirit of Detroit statue in a giant Detroit jersey. The statue, outside the City County building, required a size 360. It's probably the largest hockey sweater ever made.

18.15 B. Gualazzi was already wearing the Greyhounds' No. 9 (Gretzky's favourite number)

As a kid, Wayne Gretzky's favourite jersey number, No. 9, was usually taken by an older player. When he joined the Sault Ste. Marie Greyhounds, the famous digit was worn by Brian Gualazzi. "No one ever asked me to give [No. 9] up," said Gualazzi in the *Hockey News*. "Not that I would have. It was no issue. I was a veteran and Wayne was a rookie." So Gretzky donned No. 14 in training camp and No. 19 to start the 1977–78 regular season. It didn't work out, though. "I tried 14 and 19 at first, but the ones didn't feel quite right on my back," said Gretzky. Then Greyhounds coach Muzz MacPherson and general manager Angelo Bumbacco suggested he wear two nines (No. 99), an idea borrowed from the New York Rangers'

Phil Esposito, who was using double sevens (No. 77). As Gretzky recalled, "At first I said, 'No, that's too hotdoggish.' But they convinced me to wear it." On his first night, No. 99 scored two goals. It was a lock. Gretzky played one season with Gualazzi on the Greyhounds before moving on to the WHA in 1978–79. Gualazzi never played in the NHL, but he will forever be the No. 9 who unintentionally gave hockey its greatest jersey number, 99.

18.16 A. Wayne Gretzky's close friend and agent, Mike Barnett

Gretzky gave the 801 jersey to Mike Barnett on March 20, 1994, the night he equalled Gordie Howe's famous goal total. According to witnesses, Barnett, who hadn't owned a Gretzky game-worn sweater to that point, was speechless. As thanks, Barnett purchased the Pacific Coliseum net in which his most famous client scored his 802nd goal and gave it to the Great One for his Toronto restaurant.

18.17 C. No. 97

Since the Great One quit hockey in 1999 and his famous No. 99 was retired league-wide, the next-highest jersey number donned by a player belongs to Philadelphia's Jeremy Roenick. He wore No. 27 in Chicago, but after his trade to Phoenix at the 1997 Entry Draft, Roenick picked No. 97. During 2002–03 there were less than a dozen players who sported sweater numbers in the nineties.

18.18 D. No. 95

Only a few goalies have broken with tradition and donned stratosphere-level sweater numbers. As of 2004–05, José Théodore sports a No. 60 on his Canadiens uniform, Kevin Weekes of Carolina wears No. 80 and Daren Puppa, when he played for Tampa Bay during the 1990s, donned No. 93. But Olivier Michaud hit the all-time high when he had No. 95 on his back for Montreal during 18 minutes of NHL action against Buffalo on October 26, 2001.

18.19 C. The Ottawa Senators

In September 1997, Ottawa general manager Pierre Gauthier ordered all his players with high jersey numbers to switch to numbers below 35. That left five players looking for new digits on their backs. Alexandre Daigle was forced to give up his familiar No. 91 in favour of No. 9; Radek Bonk switched from No. 76 to No. 14; Stan Neckar from No. 94 to No. 24; Denny Lambert from No. 42 to No. 28; and Radim Bicanek from No. 44 to No. 23. Gauthier said the move was taken to promote team unity. "To me big numbers singled out people from the rest of the team," Gauthier said. "This is a team sport and I think sometimes we forget that." When Gauthier left, the club rule seemed to soften, but only in a few cases. Goalie Patrick Lalime got No. 40, and Joé Juneau switched from No. 28 to No. 39 in 1999–2000. "You look at your jersey, and for some reason I just feel better about it. I always felt very bad about No. 28. Sometimes I felt like a defenseman with that number." Currently, Jason Spezza owns No. 39 and only four other players have numbers in the 40s.

18.20 A. Above the player nameplate

In a five-year U.S.$10-million deal, the NHL agreed to move the trademarks of Koho and CCM brands from the bottom right of the back of the sweaters to above the nameplate. Half of the 30 NHL teams would wear sweaters with the CCM logo; the other 15 would wear Koho. The new logo placement improved the visibility of the only non-NHL corporate trademark allowed on NHL jerseys.

18.21 B. Bryan Trottier's No. 19

On October 20, 2001, Trottier became the sixth Islander to have his number retired, joining Denis Potvin, Mike Bossy, Clark Gillies, Bob Nystrom and Billy Smith. Although long overdue, the occasion was handled with class. Trottier amassed a franchise-high 1,353 points in 15 seasons with the Islanders and won four Stanley Cups. He would add two more Cups with the Pittsburgh Penguins in 1991 and 1992. Few teams could contain the hard-driving centre during his prime, and the sight of all the Islander players circling the ice with Trottier's name and number made a vivid impression on visiting San Jose Sharks coach Darryl Sutter. "I told Trots that, if 20 years ago I'd seen 20 Bryan Trottiers skating around before a game, I would've just lain down at centre ice."

18.22 A. 1972–73

The last Canuck to wear No. 11 before Mark Messier was Wayne Maki, who joined Vancouver in its inaugural season (1970–71) and played with the club for three years before his untimely death from cancer in 1974. Afterwards, the number was "unofficially" retired and Vancouver's media guide listed No. 11 as "no longer worn." But when Messier signed with the Canucks in 1997, he took Maki's long-time playing number, much to the dismay of his widow, Beverly Maki. She wanted an acknowledgement that the number was retired and assurance that when Messier moved on No. 11 would be re-retired. The team offered to mount a plaque at GM Place in Maki's honour.

18.23 C. The Maple Leafs' Ace Bailey

Bailey is probably the first athlete to have his player number retired in North American professional sports, and certainly in hockey. On February 14, 1934, the Toronto Maple Leafs honoured their scoring champ by staging the NHL's inaugural benefit All-Star game and retiring his sweater, No. 6—a tribute that came just months after Bailey sustained a severe skull fracture in a sickening on-ice collision that left him near death. His forced retirement from hockey marked the first time the league's best players met in an All-Star contest. No pro sports figure had previously been so honoured. The Canadiens retired Morenz's No. 7 in 1937; the Yankees, Lou Gehrig's No. 4 in 1939; and the New York Giants, Ray Flaherty's No. 1 in 1935. Bailey was the first Maple Leaf to win the NHL scoring race.

18.24 D. Philadelphia's No. 1, Bernie Parent

Less than a dozen netminders have had their jerseys retired by NHL teams. Contrary to what one might expect, the first player distinguished wasn't an old-timer like Georges Vezina or Glenn Hall. In fact, the first retired goalie sweater belonged to a post-1967 expansion player. On October 11, 1979, the Philadelphia Flyers retired No. 1, honouring two-time Stanley Cup-winner Bernie Parent, who was forced to quit after being struck in the eye with a stick in 1979. In 486 games with the Flyers, Parent had a 232–141–104 record with a 2.42 GAA and 50 shutouts.

18.25 C. Dale Tallon

There was such bitterness in the Blackhawks' front office after Bobby Hull defected to the WHA that they had his team stats temporarily erased and his famous jersey No. 9 assigned to defenseman Dale Tallon. Tallon wore No. 9 for a week before handing it back, calling it a "sacrilege" for anyone but Hull to wear it.

18.26 B. Maurice Richard

When big stars are traded they often make a point of asking for the same number they wore before. But Pavel Bure broke with tradition after the Florida Panthers traded him to the New York Rangers on March 19, 2002. Instead of his customary No. 10, which was being worn by Rangers winger Sandy McCarthy, Bure asked for No. 9. The move was meant to honour his "namesake," Maurice "Rocket" Richard, who made the number famous with the Montreal Canadiens. As the Russian Rocket explained: "Rocket Richard wore No. 9 and it was available. I won his trophy (the Richard Trophy for top goal scorer in the league) twice. I think it's a good number." Prior to claiming the number, Bure placed a call to fan favourite Adam Graves, who wore No. 9 in Manhattan for a decade before being traded to the San Jose Sharks in the summer of 2001. Graves assured Bure there was no problem.

18.27 C. Bobby Orr's

A blood-spattered Boston Bruins jersey of Orr's and one of the hockey legend's Stanley Cup rings were among the mementoes that blasted off with Canadian astronaut Robert Thirsk on the space shuttle *Columbia* in June 1996. Although the two men had never met, Thirsk admitted that Orr had always been his hero. Shortly before embarking on his space adventure, "I finally got the nerve to call him up and ask him, out of respect, if I could fly something for him," said Thirsk. The astronaut, who assumed Orr's choice would be something of little value, was amazed when a package arrived containing Orr's diamond-studded 1970 Stanley Cup ring with the famous "No. 4" engraved on it. More surprising, it came via regular mail. A few days later, Thirsk received another parcel from Orr, containing one of his game-worn jerseys.

18.28 B. The Chicago Blackhawks

After wearing No. 9 for 13 NHL seasons with Los Angeles, New York, Edmonton and New Jersey, Nicholls chose No. 92 in Chicago to honour the memory of his son, Jack, who was born with Down's syndrome in 1992 (and died shortly after of spinal meningitis and pneumonia). Chicago great Bobby Hull was the Blackhawks' last No. 9.

18.29 C. He tried to set fire to an opponent's sweater

With Italian spectators screaming abuse, TV cameras caught Canadian Tony Job trying to set an opposition player's sweater on fire with a lighter taken from the debris thrown on the ice during a bench-clearing brawl. The bizarre incident occurred during Game 2 of the best-of-seven Italian League final series between Milan and Bolzano in April 1996. Fortunately, the jersey didn't ignite.

18.30 B. To honour a coach

Brett Hull, who wore No. 17 with Detroit, switched to No. 80 for the 2003–04 preseason to honour the late Herb Brooks, coach of the Miracle on Ice team that won the Olympic gold medal at Lake Placid in 1980. It is not without irony that Hull, known throughout his illustrious career as a coach killer, would pay tribute to Brooks. In fact, Brooks was the only coach Hull publicly admired, probably because both men wanted to give the game back to those who play it instead of to the technicians who overcoach it. Hull played for Brooks during the two-week period of the 2002 Olympics. Brooks died in August 2003 at age 66, after falling asleep behind the wheel of his van on a Minnesota highway.

18.31 D. Bailey wanted another Maple Leaf to wear No. 6

After 30 years, Toronto's No. 6 was unretired by Bailey himself, who offered it to Ron Ellis as a tribute to the winger's steady play. Ellis felt so honoured that he wore the famous No. 6 for the next 12 years. When Ellis quit in 1981, the Maple Leafs retired No. 6 again.

18.32 C. Because of the Lanny McDonald trade

Not only was McDonald the Toronto fans' most popular player, he and Darryl Sittler were linemates and best friends. In protest, Sittler renounced his captaincy by cutting the "C" off his jersey. Considered one of Punch Imlach's worst trades, the deal (McDonald and Joel Quenneville to the Rockies for Wilf Paiement and Pat Hickey) hurt Sittler personally and cut off his team support. Later, Leafs boss Harold Ballard made peace with his star captain, returning the "C" while Imlach was in hospital.

18.33 B. No. 17

Howe's career spanned an astonishing five decades, or 32 seasons, from 1946 to 1980. So incredible was his longevity that his totals, such as 2,421 NHL and WHA games played, are almost incomprehensible. Howe wore his famous No. 9 jersey in all but two seasons, 1946–47 and 1947–48. His only other sweater number was No. 17, which he wore when he scored his first goal in his first game on October 16, 1946. "It started in Omaha because I was 17 years of age, so I became No. 17 up here," Howe recalls. "But then the trainer came to me and said, '(Roy) Conacher just got traded to New York. No. 9 is open. Do you want it?' I said, 'No.' He said, 'It'll get you a lower berth on the train.' I said, 'I'll take it.'"

18.34 A. He defected in 1989

Considered the best young prospect in the Soviet system, Alexander Mogilny was the key to the Red Army team for three years. While attending the World Championships in Sweden, he met with Sabres officials, who spirited him out of the country. The cloak-and-dagger operation went more smoothly than expected, but the defection caused a major diplomatic flap. By fluke or by fate, Buffalo drafted Mogilny 89th overall in 1988.

18.35 B. Vladislav Tretiak

Like much of the former Soviet Union, the traditions of the Russian game are undergoing fundamental change, and a few new customs, such as retiring sweater numbers, are being embraced under the influence of the North American style of play. In 1993, before a sellout crowd at Moscow's Ice Palace hockey arena, Tretiak's No. 20 was raised to the rafters in a first-ever ceremony that saw one of hockey's greatest goalies honoured for his work backstopping the Central Red Army teams of the 1970s and early 1980s.

18.36 B. To make teams easier to distinguish on television

In the '30s, when Detroit played Montreal, the clubs' nearly identical red uniforms made it difficult to distinguish one team from the other, so the visitors wore white pullovers over their game sweaters. It wasn't until the advent of television that teams adopted two different sweaters: white for away games and coloured for home games. The contrasting uniforms made things easier for television viewers, as all TV sets were black-and-white. The policy was later reversed so that visiting clubs wore the coloured uniforms.

18.37 C. In 1981, in the QMJHL with the Laval Voisins

From age seven to 15, Lemieux played for a local team called the Ville Emard Hurricanes, in Mosquito, Atom, Pee Wee and Bantam division hockey. Usually, he wore No. 27, his big brother Alain's number. Then, in 1981, before joining Laval in major junior hockey, his co-agent Bob Perno suggested trying another number, one that would make Lemieux distinct from his brother yet would also be a comparison to Wayne Gretzky. They flipped Wayne's No. 99 around and Mario had his new sweater number, No. 66. It was special; no other hockey player in the world was using it. Lemieux wore it first with the Laval Voisins in 1981–82, when he scored 30 goals and, appropriately enough, 66 assists.

18.38 A. The Hamilton Tigers

During the early 1920s, long before it became cool to ice teams with the names and logos of vicious animals such as the Predators, Sharks and Panthers, the Hamilton Tigers sported a jersey with gold vertical stripes on a black background and the head of a fierce-looking tiger with long razor-like fangs.

18.39 C. A maple leaf

Talk about the unthinkable—a maple leaf on a Montreal Canadiens jersey! Say it ain't so. Hockey's most storied franchise, the Canadiens, not once but twice wore the emblem of their greatest rivals, the Maple Leafs. When George Kennedy purchased the Club Canadien in 1910, he had the new red uniform emblazoned with a green maple leaf and a gothic "C." A year later, the Canadiens got their new "barber pole" model with blue, white and red stripes. Again, the sweater had a small maple leaf crest (in white) with the letters "CAC," for Club Athletique Canadien. It was not until 1916 that the Canadiens' famous emblem—a large "C" surrounding a small "H"—was adopted. Toronto's familiar maple leaf crest was not worn until Conn Smythe bought the club in 1927.

— *GAME* 18

Rookie Wonders

ANDREW RAYCROFT'S CALDER TROPHY WIN in 2004 marked only the 15th occasion a netminder has been named top rookie. Find 12 rookie-of-the-year backstoppers by reading across, down or diagonally. Similar to Chicago's Mike K-A-R-A-K-A-S, the NHL's first Calder-winning goalie, connect the names using letters no more than once. Start with the letters printed in heavy type.

Solutions are on page 568

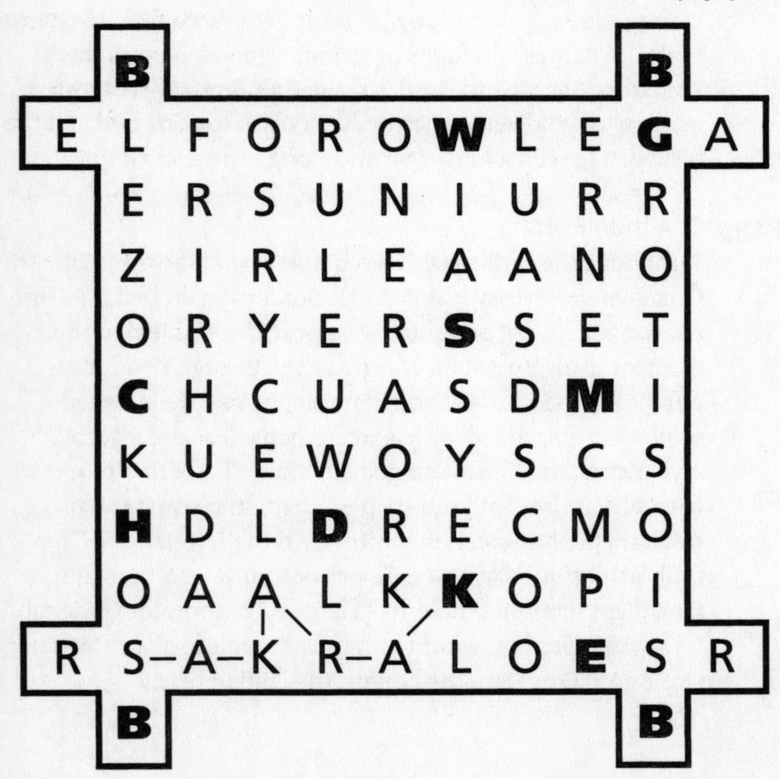

19

Susan Lucci and Other Trophy Winners

DESPITE NINE SEASONS of textbook netminding, his Stanley Cups and the distinction of being the only goalie in NHL history to record 40 wins in four seasons, Martin Brodeur could still laugh at his Vezina Trophy drought during 2002–03. "I'm the Susan Lucci of hockey," said Brodeur, referring to the soap opera star who finally won an Emmy after 18 years of nominations. Statistics may have been Brodeur's biggest problem in claiming the top goalie award, his first coming in 2003. New Jersey's defense is so tight he faces far fewer shots than most netminders; a fact that may work against him when general managers cast their Vezina votes.

Answers are on page 471

19.1 Who is the first player to win four major individual awards in one season?

A. Bobby Orr
B. Stan Mikita
C. Ed Belfour
D. Wayne Gretzky

19.2 How many times in NHL history has a player won MVP status with a cellar dweller?

A. It has never happened
B. Two times
C. 10 times
D. 20 times

19.3 Who was the first player to win the Hart Trophy as the NHL's most valuable player by a unanimous vote?

A. Maurice Richard
B. Gordie Howe
C. Bobby Orr
D. Wayne Gretzky

19.4 The Hart Trophy was first awarded in 1924. How many years elapsed before an American-born player won the Hart?

A. One year
B. 18 years
C. 36 years
D. An American has never won it

19.5 How many players have won the Hart Trophy but have not been elected to either the First or Second NHL All-Star team?

A. One player
B. Two players
C. Three players
D. It has never happened

19.6 Who is the only goal-scoring leader not elected to an All-Star team on two occasions?

A. Blaine Stoughton
B. Peter Bondra
C. Keith Tkachuk
D. Teemu Selanne

19.7 In 1999, the NHL created the Maurice Richard Trophy, an annual award to honour the NHL's leading goal scorer. How many times would Richard have owned the trophy if it had existed in his day?

A. Once
B. Three times
C. Five times
D. Seven times

19.8 When was the last time a scoring champion won the Art Ross Trophy with more goals than assists?

A. In 1941–42
B. In 1961–62
C. In 1981–82
D. In 2001–02

19.9 Which old-time sniper asked the league to take back a point from a January 1943 game total because he didn't believe he deserved it? At the end of the season, he missed winning the NHL scoring race by one point.

A. Lynn Patrick of the New York Rangers
B. Doug Bentley of the Chicago Blackhawks
C. Bill Cowley of the Boston Bruins
D. Billy Taylor of the Toronto Maple Leafs

19.10 Who was the oldest NHLer to win a scoring title?

A. Bill Cook
B. Elmer Lach
C. Gordie Howe
D. Phil Esposito

19.11 Among the four Norris Trophy winners below, who was the oldest player to win the NHL's top defenseman award?

A. Al MacInnis
B. Rob Blake
C. Ray Bourque
D. Chris Chelios

19.12 Which Original Six defenseman captured the Norris Trophy as the league's top rearguard while coaching an NHL team?

A. Carl Brewer
B. Doug Harvey
C. Bill Gadsby
D. Tom Johnson

19.13 Prior to Chris Pronger winning the Hart Trophy as league MVP in 2000, who was the last defenseman to capture the coveted award?

A. Ray Bourque in 1987
B. Rod Langway in 1984
C. Denis Potvin in 1976
D. Bobby Orr in 1972

19.14 Of the 1,508 voting points MVP candidates can share in, how many more votes did defenseman Chris Pronger receive than Jaromir Jagr to win 2000's Hart Trophy as the NHL's most valuable player?

A. One voting point
B. 10 voting points
C. 50 voting points
D. 100 voting points

19.15 If the most points for a Hart Trophy winner is Wayne Gretzky's 215 points in 1985–86, what is the lowest point total by a modern-day MVP (excluding goalies)?

A. 22 points
B. 52 points
C. 82 points
D. 112 points

19.16 Which player won the NHL scoring race while playing the lowest percentage of games in a season? (For example, if a player won the scoring race playing 70 games of an 82-game schedule, his percentage would be 85 per cent.)

A. Bobby Orr
B. Wayne Gretzky
C. Mario Lemieux
D. Jaromir Jagr

19.17 The original Lady Byng Trophy, honouring "sportsmanship, gentlemanly conduct and a high standard of playing ability," was given to which player to keep after he won the award seven times in eight years?

A. Syl Apps
B. Max Bentley
C. Frank Boucher
D. Howie Morenz

19.18 What is the most penalty minutes ever collected by a Lady Byng Trophy-winner?

A. 20 penalty minutes
B. 40 penalty minutes
C. 60 penalty minutes
D. 80 penalty minutes

19.19 Who racked up the most penalty minutes of any Art Ross Trophy-winner in league history?

A. Stan Mikita
B. Ted Lindsay
C. Gordie Howe
D. Bryan Trottier

19.20 The Frank Selke Trophy is awarded to the forward who best excels in the defensive aspects of the game. Who is the only four-time winner of the Selke?

A. Guy Carbonneau
B. Bob Gainey
C. Sergei Fedorov
D. Ron Francis

19.21 Which award is presented annually to the player judged to be the league's most outstanding player, as selected by the players themselves?

A. The Lester Patrick Trophy
B. The King Clancy Memorial Trophy
C. The Lester B. Pearson Award
D. The William M. Jennings Trophy

19.22 Which Vezina Trophy-winning goalie first requested that his partner's name also be inscribed on the award?

A. Glenn Hall
B. Don Simmons
C. Terry Sawchuk
D. Johnny Bower

19.23 Who was the first European goalie to win the Vezina Trophy as top NHL netminder?

A. Valdislav Tretiak
B. Pelle Lindbergh
C. Dominik Hasek
D. Arturs Irbe

19.24 Who was the first European-trained player to win the Art Ross Trophy as NHL scoring leader?

A. Teemu Selanne
B. Jaromir Jagr
C. Stan Mikita
D. Peter Stastny

19.25 Who owns the NHL record for both the highest and lowest plus-minus numbers by a scoring champion?

A. Bobby Orr
B. Guy Lafleur
C. Wayne Gretzky
D. Jaromir Jagr

19.26 Prior to Martin St. Louis and his league-leading 94 points in 2003–04, who was the last NHL scoring leader to record fewer points and win the title?

A. Gordie Howe in 1962–63
B. Stan Mikita in 1967–68
C. Jaromir Jagr in 1999–2000
D. Jarome Iginla in 2001–02

19.27 Of the players who have won the Norris Trophy as the NHL's top defenseman since expansion in 1967–68, which blueliner claimed the award with the fewest points?

A. Bobby Orr
B. Chris Chelios
C. Rod Langway
D. Larry Robinson

19.28 Who was the last defenseman to win the Norris Trophy before Bobby Orr took control for an unprecedented eight seasons?

A. Harry Howell
B. Tim Horton
C. Jacques Laperriere
D. Pierre Pilote

19.29 Who is the only defenseman to win the Hart Trophy as league MVP four times?

A. Eddie Shore
B. Bobby Orr
C. Red Kelly
D. Paul Coffey

19.30 What was the age of the NHL's oldest MVP winner?

A. 29 years old
B. 31 years old
C. 33 years old
D. 35 years old

19.31 Who was the first NHL goalie to be named league MVP since expansion in 1967?

A. Pete Peeters
B. Patrick Roy
C. Grant Fuhr
D. Dominik Hasek

19.32 Who has won the most Vezina Trophies as the NHL's most outstanding goalie?

A. Ken Dryden
B. Terry Sawchuk
C. Jacques Plante
D. Dominik Hasek

19.33 Since the Vezina Trophy was first awarded to the top goalie in 1927, how many winners wore their catching gloves on their right hands?

A. There has never been a right-handed-catching Vezina winner
B. Four goalies
C. Eight goalies
D. 12 goalies

19.34 Who was the first coach to win the Jack Adams Trophy as coach of the year with different teams?

A. Scotty Bowman
B. Pat Quinn
C. Pat Burns
D. Mike Keenan

19.35 Who holds the record for winning the Jack Adams Trophy with the most different teams?

A. Jacques Demers
B. Pat Burns
C. Mike Keenan
D. Roger Neilson

19.36 Which goalie owns the rare distinction of having been nominated for the rookie-of-the-year award in two different leagues in the same season?

A. Jim Carey
B. Mike Richter
C. Patrick Roy
D. Curtis Joseph

19.37 NHL rookie-of-the-year winners are not always first-round draft picks. Which Calder Trophy recipient was not picked until the 14th round of the draft, 241st overall?

A. Gary Suter
B. Steve Larmer
C. Luc Robitaille
D. Sergei Makarov

19.38 What is the shortest NHL career for a Calder Trophy winner as top rookie?

A. Fewer than 50 games
B. Between 50 and 100 games
C. Between 100 and 200 games
D. More than 200 games

19.39 After Wayne Gretzky, who is the next-youngest Hart Trophy winner as regular-season MVP in NHL history?

A. Bobby Orr
B. Bryan Trottier
C. Mario Lemieux
D. Eric Lindros

19.40 Who is the youngest player to win the Conn Smythe Trophy as playoff MVP?

A. Wayne Gretzky
B. Bryan Trottier
C. Patrick Roy
D. Bobby Orr

19.41 Who is the only player in NHL history to win both league MVP awards—the Hart Trophy (regular season) and the Conn Smythe (playoffs)—in the same season, and then later repeat the feat?

A. Bobby Orr
B. Guy Lafleur
C. Wayne Gretzky
D. Mario Lemieux

19.42 Who was the first recipient of the Conn Smythe Trophy awarded to the MVP of the playoffs?

A. Glenn Hall
B. Bobby Orr
C. Jean Béliveau
D. Serge Savard

19.43 Which goalie was the first to win the Conn Smythe Trophy as playoff MVP while playing for a losing team?

A. Roger Crozier
B. Ron Hextall
C. Bernie Parent
D. Glenn Hall

19.44 Who was the first player to play on a Stanley Cup-winning team before he won the Calder Trophy as rookie of the year?

A. Ken Dryden
B. Tony Esposito
C. Gaye Stewart
D. Danny Grant

Answers

19.1 A. Bobby Orr

"Bobby was a star from the moment they played the national anthem in his first NHL game," said Boston coach Harry Sinden. Few who had the pleasure of watching Orr in his prime would disagree. And Orr's star never shone brighter than in 1969–70, when the 22-year-old led the Bruins to the Stanley Cup and walked off with an unprecedented four major trophies. Orr won the Hart Trophy as league MVP, the Art Ross Trophy as top scorer, the Norris Trophy as top defenseman and the Conn Smythe Trophy as MVP of the playoffs.

19.2 B. Two times

Since the Hart Trophy was first awarded in 1924, only two players have won MVP honours on last-place teams: defenseman Tom Anderson, who earned a top-10 finish in the NHL scoring race while his Brooklyn Americans allowed the most goals in 1941–42; and Hart-winner Al Rollins, who kept most games close but backstopped the hapless Chicago Blackhawks in 66 contests to a disastrous 12–51–7 overall record in 1953–54.

19.3 D. Wayne Gretzky

In 1981–82, Gretzky was unstoppable. He set new NHL records for goals (92), assists (120) and points (212), and finished 65 points ahead of runner-up Mike Bossy in the scoring race. In recognition of his exploits, the 63 voting members of the Professional Hockey Writers' Association made the Great One a unanimous choice for the Hart Trophy, an NHL first.

19.4 A. One year

The Hart Trophy was awarded only once before an American nabbed it in 1925. The recipient was Billy Burch, who originally hailed from Yonkers, New York, but grew up in Toronto. At six feet, 200 pounds, Burch was a big man for his time and he had a big impact on the NHL, first during his MVP season in 1924–25 when his Hamilton Tigers finished first overall, and later, as a hometown boy, when the franchise was transferred to New York and renamed the Americans.

19.5 B. Two players

It's hard to imagine an MVP winner not being voted to either the First or Second All-Star teams, but that's exactly what occurred in 1954 and 1955. Chicago goalie Al Rollins got the nod as MVP in 1954 (with the worst goals-against average in the league), however, the voters selected Harry Lumley and Terry Sawchuk as the All-Star goalies that year. Centre Ted Kennedy of the Maple Leafs earned MVP honours the next year, despite counting only 10 goals and 52 points to finish 11th in the scoring race. Kennedy finished behind Jean Béliveau and Ken Mosdell in the All-Star balloting for his position.

19.6 B. Peter Bondra

Since 1930–31, when the NHL began voting for All-Star teams, six goal-scoring leaders have failed to make the grade on either the First or Second All-Star teams. Unlike his five colleagues, Bondra was burned twice: in 1994–95 and 1997–98, when the right-winger was upstaged by point-scoring leader and First All-Star Jaromir Jagr twice, and Second All-Stars Theo Fleury and Teemu Selanne.

19.7 C. Five times

Maurice Richard led the NHL in goal scoring in 1944–45, 1946–47, 1949–50, 1953–54 and 1954–55. Richard's five goal-scoring titles tied him with Charlie Conacher for top spot in the category. The mark was later erased by Bobby Hull, who led the league in goal scoring a record seven times.

19.8 D. In 2001–02

It's not easily accomplished, considering far more assists are recorded in a season than goals. Since 1965–66, when Bobby Hull notched 54 goals and 43 assists for a league-high 97 points, only one player has won the NHL scoring title with more goals than assists: Jarome Iginla, who enjoyed his breakout season of 2001–02, posting a 52–44–96 record to claim his Art Ross. In one offensive surge from October 18 to November 22, Iginla collected 18 goals and 13 assists in 15 straight games for the Calgary Flames.

19.9 C. Bill Cowley of the Boston Bruins

It might be the most costly gesture of sportsmanship in NHL play. After a game on January 16, 1943, between the Bruins and the Rangers, Cowley sent a letter to NHL president Red Dutton, explaining that he didn't feel he deserved an assist that he had been credited with during the game. Dutton granted Cowley's request and deleted the assist from his record. The Bruins centre finished the season second in the scoring race with 72 points (27 goals and 45 assists), one point behind Chicago's Doug Bentley. The point that was removed from Cowley's stats left him tied with his own NHL assist record and cost him the bonus the Bruins would have paid him for setting a new record. The extra point also cost Cowley perfect symmetry in his career stats. He finished with 548 points, one less than the number of games he had played—549.

19.10 A. Bill Cook

In 1932–33, the New York Rangers captain won the NHL scoring title with 50 points in 48 games. Cook was 36 years, five months old at the time, which makes him the oldest scoring champ in NHL annals. Gordie Howe, who ranks second on the greybeard list, won his last scoring title at age 34, in 1962–63.

The NHL's Oldest Scoring Champs*

PLAYER	AGE	YEAR	G	A	PTS
Bill Cook	36.5	1932–33	28	22	50
Gordie Howe	34.11	1962–63	38	48	86
Newsy Lalonde	33.5	1920–21	33	8	41
Wayne Gretzky	33.2	1993–94	38	92	130
Roy Conacher	32.5	1948–49	26	42	68

**Current to 2004–05*

19.11 A. Al MacInnis

Winning the Norris Trophy as the league's top rearguard in 1999 didn't bring MacInnis newfound respect as one of the game's finest defensemen. That reputation had already been well established during his distinguished 18-year career. So what took the St. Louis blueliner so long to garner the best D-man award? Overshadowed by the Bourques, Coffeys and Chelioses, MacInnis had twice been bridesmaid as the trophy's runner-up. When he finally won the Norris in 1998–99, he was almost 36, the most senior winner ever. MacInnis led all defensemen with 62 points and 314 shots on goal. Behind the blue line he was equally effective, ranking among the league leaders with a plus 33 rating.

19.12 B. Doug Harvey

Harvey won his seventh top defenseman award in 1961–62, the year he was player-coach of the Rangers. New York finished fourth in the standings and Harvey notched 30 points. It was Harvey's seventh and final trophy in an eight-year span.

19.13 D. Bobby Orr in 1972

Prior to 2000, no defenseman had been named Hart Trophy winner since Bobby Orr won MVP status in three consecutive years: 1970, 1971 and 1972. In fact, in that span of 28 years there were only four runner-up finishes by blueliners in MVP voting, including Denis Potvin (second to Bobby Clarke in 1976), Rod Langway (second to Wayne Gretzky in 1984) and Ray Bourque twice (second to Wayne Gretzky in 1987 and to Mark Messier in 1990). "I guess I have some pretty big standards to live up to," Chris Pronger said, upon receiving the Hart. Pronger was only the eighth D-man in NHL history to capture the MVP trophy.

19.14 A. One voting point

In the closest voting in Hart Trophy history to date, Chris Pronger received 396 votes to edge Jaromir Jagr, the league's scoring champion, by just one point in the 2000 MVP balloting. Pronger, the six-foot-five St. Louis rearguard, set career marks with a 14–48–62 record while leading the league with plus 52 and a monster 30:14 in ice time through 79 games during 1999–2000. Florida's Pavel Bure finished third with 346 points. The closest previous Hart vote came in 1990 when Mark Messier edged Ray Bourque by two points, 227 to 225.

19.15 B. 52 points

The mark for fewest regular-season points by an MVP is held by Herb Gardiner, a veteran defenseman of the disbanded western pro leagues who won the Hart in 1926–27. He scored just 12 points, but between 1925–26 and 1926–27, the year Gardiner arrived, Montreal shaved its goals-against from 108 to 67 goals and climbed from last place to second overall in just one season. Based on that single-season turnaround, Gardiner didn't need big points for his MVP award. The modern-day record after 1943–44 (when the red line at centre ice was introduced) of 52 points is held by Toronto's Ted Kennedy, who won it in his last full NHL season, 1954–55. Less deserving than perhaps other players that year (Kennedy didn't finish in the top-10 scorers), the gritty Toronto captain may have won based on his years of service as one of the club's greatest stars during a run of five Cups in seven seasons. To date, Kennedy is the last Maple Leaf to win the Hart.

19.16 C. Mario Lemieux

It might be the greatest comeback in hockey. During his 1992–93 bid to eclipse Wayne Gretzky's record 215-point total, Lemieux was diagnosed with Hodgkin's disease after doctors found a cancerous lymph node in his neck. Lemieux's recovery amazed even his doctors. After two months of midseason radiation therapy he was back playing hockey. During the last 20 games he scored 59 points, demolishing a 12-point lead by Pat LaFontaine to win the title with 160 points, 12 more than LaFontaine. Lemieux won the scoring title playing the lowest percentage of games ever, just 60 of 84 games, or 71 per cent. In 1999–2000, Pittsburgh's Jaromir Jagr chalked up the next-lowest percentage, 77 per cent, seeing action in 63 of 82 games while capturing his fourth scoring crown.

19.17 C. Frank Boucher

The classy New York Ranger centre claimed the Lady Byng Trophy seven times in eight years between 1928 and 1935. After Boucher's seventh win, the NHL gave him the award to keep; a new Lady Byng Trophy was presented in 1936.

19.18 B. 40 penalty minutes

Winners of the Lady Byng Trophy usually have low penalty-minute totals combined with a high scoring count. Only twice has the award gone to a player with 40 PIM—Frank Nighbor of the Ottawa Senators in 1925–26 and Billy Burch of the New York Americans in 1926–27, the second and third years the award was presented. In seasons of only 36 and 44 games, those were fairly high penalty-minute totals, an indication that the standards of gentlemanly conduct have changed over the years. In their respective trophy-winning seasons, Nighbor led the league in assists with 13, while Burch was a top-10 finisher.

19.19 A. Stan Mikita

Mikita set the standard for box time among all NHL scoring leaders, twice racking up more PIM than any other Art Ross winner: 146 penalty minutes in 1963–64 and 154 in 1964–65. Notorious for his chippy attitude, with opponents and officials alike, Mikita overcame his retaliatory streak to win two consecutive Lady Byng Trophies for sportsmanship and gentlemanly conduct with only 12 and 14 penalty-minute totals in 1966–67 and 1967–68, the same years he was awarded Art Ross Trophies as scoring leader and Hart Trophies as league MVP. In recent times, Mario Lemieux recorded one of the NHL's highest penalty-minute totals for a scoring leader, 100 PIM in 1988–89.

The NHL's Most Penalized Scoring Leaders

PLAYER	TEAM	SEASON	TP	PIM
S. Mikita	Chicago	1964–65	87	154
S. Mikita	Chicago	1963–64	89	146
J. Béliveau	Montreal	1955–56	88	143
T. Lindsay	Detroit	1949–50	78	141
B. Orr	Boston	1969–70	120	125

**Current to 2004–05*

19.20 B. Bob Gainey

Montreal fans asked "Bob who?" when the Canadiens used their first-round draft pick in 1973 to select Gainey from the OHL's Peterborough Petes. Gainey had struggled to score even 22 goals in the junior ranks; how could he possibly add to the Habs' attack? But general manager Sam Pollock wasn't looking for a scorer. He wanted a front-line checker. And Gainey filled that role to perfection, shutting down the opposition's top scoring threats and providing gritty team leadership for 16 years with Montreal. When the NHL created the Frank Selke Award to honour defensive play by a forward in 1978, it seemed tailor-made for Gainey. He won the first four Selkes, a total no other player has matched.

19.21 C. The Lester B. Pearson Award

Many mistakenly believe that the Hart Trophy is awarded to the NHL's outstanding player. But the Hart, which is voted on by the media, goes to the player judged to be most valuable to his team. It is the Pearson, which is voted on by the players themselves, that honours individual excellence. First presented in 1971, the Pearson winners list reveals some interesting anomalies. For example, Bobby Orr, who won three Hart Trophies, earned only one Pearson; Wayne Gretzky, a nine-time Hart winner, received just five Pearsons.

19.22 C. Terry Sawchuk

When Toronto finished 1964–65 with the best goals-against average in the NHL, Sawchuk was automatically awarded the Vezina Trophy because he had played 36 games compared to partner Johnny Bower's 34. In a gesture of true sportsmanship, Sawchuk pointed out that Bower deserved the Vezina, considering he had shut out Detroit 4–0 in the last game of the season to claim the award by a two-goal margin over Red Wing goalie Roger Crozier. As Sawchuk said, "There's the guy who won it. They can put Bower's name on it." In fact, Bower, with 2.38, had a better average than Sawchuk's 2.56. The league agreed, and for the first time the Vezina became a joint award. (Today, the best-average goalies are awarded the Jennings Trophy. The Vezina goes to the goalie considered best at his position as voted by the general managers of all clubs.)

19.23 B. Pelle Lindbergh

In his fourth NHL season, 1984–85, Swedish sensation Pelle Lindbergh blossomed into the league's top goalie, leading Philadelphia with a personal record of 40–17–7 to best the Edmonton Oilers in regular-season standings 113 to 109 points. Lindbergh also led the Flyers to the Stanley Cup finals. The Oilers won the Cup, but Lindbergh's mobility and lightning-quick reflexes proved his worth as he outballoted Buffalo's Tom Barrasso for the Vezina that year. Only months later, Lindbergh died in a high-speed, alcohol-related car crash. He was 26.

19.24 B. Jaromir Jagr

Although Czechoslovakian-born Stan Mikita won the NHL's scoring race four times in the 1960s, he never played professionally in Europe. One generation later, Mikita's fellow countryman, Jaromir Jagr, a Czech star in his native city, Kladno, defected to the NHL in 1990 and claimed the scoring title in 1995's 48-game season. Jagr netted 32 goals and 38 assists for 70 points to become the NHL's first European-trained Art Ross winner.

19.25 C. Wayne Gretzky

Since 1967–68, when plus-minus stats were recorded, most scoring champs have had superb plus-minus numbers; their prodigious goal totals are a considerable factor in their high plus-minus. Guy Lafleur amassed plus-minuses of plus 68, plus 89 and plus 73 during his three seasons as scoring leader between 1975–76 and 1977–78. Wayne Gretzky owns the highest plus-minus, a plus 98 in 1984–85, among all scoring leaders since 1968, but the Great One also has the worst plus-minus for a scoring champ, a minus 25 in 1993–94. Only one other player recorded a minus when he won the scoring race: Stan Mikita notched a minus three in 1967–68.

19.26 B. Stan Mikita in 1967–68

With his Art Ross Trophy win in 2003–04, Martin St. Louis may have single-handedly set hockey back a few decades. His league-high 94 points was the lowest point total since Mikita's 87 in 1967–68, when teams played 74-game schedules. St. Louis's height is another throwback to a bygone era. At five foot nine and 183 pounds he ranks as the smallest scoring leader since the five-foot-nine, 169-pound Mikita, if you believe the league and team media guides. Anyone who has stood next to St. Louis might think he was, at best, five foot seven, shorter than mighty mites Ted Lindsay and Marcel Dionne, who, at five foot eight, won the scoring crowns in 1950 and 1980, respectively.

19.27 A. Bobby Orr

Hockey's greatest offensive defenseman won the Norris Trophy with just 31 points in 1967–68, the lowest total of any D-man since expansion. Washington's Rod Langway is a close runner-up in the category, having won two Norris Trophies with 32 and 33 points respectively. Orr did have an excuse for his low point production—a knee injury sidelined him for 28 games during 1967–68. Still, in the 46 games he played, he impressed enough people to win the Norris, the first of eight straight that would end up on his mantelpiece. Actually, 31 points wasn't a bad total for a defenseman at the time. But Orr soon changed that with his off-the-chart numbers, making the Norris almost exclusively the domain of defensemen who generate goals rather than prevent them.

19.28 A. Harry Howell

Howell was the kind of player who improves with age. He toiled on the Rangers' blue line for 15 seasons before compiling his best offensive record of 40 points and landing an All-Star team appointment and the Norris as top defenseman in 1967. Of the 1,050 scheduled games during that stretch, Howell played in 1,030. Over the years, his blue line partners included greats such as Allan Stanley, Bill Gadsby and Doug Harvey. But no one impressed Howell like Bobby Orr, the 1966–67 rookie Howell paid tribute to in his Norris acceptance speech: "I am glad I won the Norris this year, because in 10 years it will be called the Bobby Orr Trophy."

19.29 A. Eddie Shore

Since its inception in 1924, the Hart Trophy has traditionally gone to the best offensive forwards of the game. Rarely has a defenseman been awarded league MVP honours. Even goalies have fared better than their defensive brethren in Hart voting—for example, Red Kelly's second-place finish to MVP-winning goalie Al Rollins in 1954, and Doug Harvey's loss to goalie Jacques Plante in 1962. Almost without exception, each generation of hockey writers has voted offense over defense and goalie over blueliner. Before Chris Pronger won the Hart in 2000, only Bobby Orr, who won three straight Harts (1970, 1971, 1972), could sway the polls. Even then, Orr's MVP success was rooted in his prodigious point scoring. There have been six other defensemen with regular-season MVP awards, but it is Eddie Shore's four Harts between 1933 and 1938 that stand apart. Interestingly, though Shore wasn't a strong point-earner, he attracted more MVP votes than scoring champs Charlie Conacher and Bill Cook. Shore, like Orr, had a riveting on-ice presence, controlling games and turning them in his team's favour with his headlong rushes and puckhandling virtuosity. And he always played for keeps. Hard, fast hockey was Shore's game. He steamrolled opponents; when they didn't go down he flattened them with his fists. A flying terror on the ice, Shore earned his MVPs as a character player with a heart the size of Boston Garden. He was the original Big Bad Bruin.

19.30 D. 35 years old

Although the average age of most Hart winners is 28, a few players have won an MVP title in their thirties. Dominik Hasek was 33.3 years when he captured his second Hart in 1998; Detroit's Gordie Howe was almost 35 (less a week) when he received his sixth award in 1963; and Eddie Shore of Boston was 35.4 years when he was honoured with his fourth trophy in 1938. The oldest MVP is Herb Gardiner, who joined the NHL at age 35 after playing for the Calgary Tigers in the rival

Western Canada Hockey League. The big blueliner was awarded the Hart at age 35.1 years, after leading Montreal to the best defensive record in the league in 1926–27. Born May 8, 1891, Gardiner is one of only two MVPs born in the 19th century (the other is Frank Nighbor).

19.31 D. Dominik Hasek

The Hart Trophy, awarded to the player most valuable to his team, has seldom gone to goaltenders. In fact, when Hasek won the Hart in 1997, he became the first goalie so honoured in 35 years, the longest drought between goalie winners in league history. During 1996–97 Hasek compiled the league's best save percentage (.930) and a 2.27 goals-against average to carry the struggling Buffalo Sabres to their first divisional championship in 16 years. When Hasek won the venerated trophy again in 1997–98, he became the first goalie ever awarded consecutive Harts and the first back-to-back winner since Wayne Gretzky, who won the trophy in 1986 and 1987.

19.32 C. Jacques Plante

Plante will always be remembered as the man who popularized the goalie mask, but he also left behind a legacy of other notable achievements, including his record seven Vezina Trophies. Plante collected the first six with Montreal between 1955–56 and 1961–62, equalling former Canadiens great Bill Durnan for the most in NHL history. Plante came out of retirement in 1968–69, and won his record-breaking seventh Vezina at age 40 with St. Louis. That season, he and 37-year-old Glenn Hall shared goaltending duties with the Blues and combined to record a league-high 13 shutouts and a sparkling 2.07 goals-against average.

19.33 C. Eight goalies

As of 2004–05, only eight netminders with a right-hand catching glove have won the Vezina Trophy. Why do so few goalies catch with their left hand? The simple explanation may be that the dominant hand is usually the right, and hockey players, goalies included, have greater control of their sticks with their right hand. Therefore, netminders tend to catch with their left hand. The first Vezina-winner to catch the puck with his right hand was Chicago's Charlie Gardiner. He won the award twice in 1932 and 1934. The NHL's other right-gloved Vezina-winners are Davey Kerr of the New York Rangers; Bill Durnan, Montreal's ambidextrous goalie; Tony Esposito of Chicago; Gilles Villemure of the New York Rangers; Tom Barrasso of Buffalo; Grant Fuhr of Edmonton; and, most recently, José Théodore of Montreal in 2002.

19.34 B. Pat Quinn

Few coaches have had as much success in as many cities as Quinn. He was voted the NHL's top bench boss in 1979–80 after piloting the Flyers to a record 35-game unbeaten streak and first-place overall. Twelve years later, Quinn won the award again when he led the formerly comatose Canucks to first place in the Smythe Division in 1991–92.

19.35 B. Pat Burns

Burns's feat indicates the perils of the profession. Being judged coach of the year in Montreal (1989), in Toronto (1993) and in Boston (1998) is impressive, but it also means he was fired three times.

19.36 A. Jim Carey

In 1994–95, the "Net Detective" was nominated for rookie-of-the-year honours in two different leagues in the same season. Carey's performance in 55 games with the AHL's Portland Pirates won him the Dudley "Red" Garrett Memorial Trophy as the league's top freshman. His sparkling netminding in 28 games, an 18–6–3 and a 2.13 goals-against after being called up by the Washington Capitals, also made him a finalist in the balloting for the NHL's Calder Trophy, which was won by high-scoring centre Peter Forsberg.

19.37 D. Sergei Makarov

There are always a few hidden gems each draft year; some even turn into Calder Trophy winners. Steve Larmer (120th), Luc Robitalle (171st) and Gary Suter (180th), all overlooked by scouts in their drafts, are prime examples of underrated juniors who later flourished as NHLers. But Sergei Makarov was different. When the Calgary Flames selected him in the last round (241st overall) at the 1983 Entry Draft, he was playing with the Central Army team in the Soviet Union's elite league. Makarov was already a multiple winner of the Izvestia Trophy as the USSR's leading scorer, an eight-time member of the USSR All-Star team and the USSR's player of the year in 1980, 1985 and 1989. His talent wasn't in question; it was Soviet politics that left many in doubt. But Calgary figured that Makarov was at least worth wasting a last-round pick on. Six years later, when the Soviets eased their grip and a few veterans, including Makarov, trickled into the NHL, Calgary had their man. At 31 years old, the 12-year international veteran of Olympic and world championships scored 86 points in the NHL and won the Calder Trophy. He is the lowest draft pick and the oldest player to win the Calder as rookie of the year.

19.38 B. Between 50 and 100 games

Old-time goalie Frank McCool owns hockey's greatest sophomore jinx story. After kicking around for years in western minor leagues, McCool was called up by Toronto in 1944–45 to replace star netminder Turk Broda, who was away on military duty. A less than ideal replacement, McCool was anything but cool under pressure. His nervousness earned him the nickname "Ulcers" and a reputation for regularly drinking milk before and during games to calm his upset stomach. But he survived the regular season with a 3.22 goals-against average, a statistic better than many expected, especially considering the third-rate Toronto team he backstopped into the playoffs. His league-high four shutouts in the 50-game schedule was equally impressive and won him a surprising Calder Trophy as

NHL rookie of the year. Despite his award, critics believed Toronto's "nervous Nellie" would be their downfall in the postseason, particularly as they faced the defending Stanley Cup champion Montreal Canadiens in the first round. But the Habs, a team that finished 28 points ahead of Toronto during the season, were shut out by McCool in the first playoff game. It proved to be no fluke as the Leafs went on to surprise the Canadiens in six. After the series, a nerve-racked McCool called out, "Somebody get me a glass of milk before I pass out." In the finals against Detroit, the rookie puck stopper notched an amazing three straight shutouts; then, just as quickly, dropped the next three in the best-of-seven format. In the seventh and final game, "Ulcers" chilled and held Detroit to one goal in a 2–1 Stanley Cup upset. It was quite a year for the rookie replacement, who faced as many pucks as doubters. The next season, McCool's sophomore year, Broda returned from the war and everything changed. Sharing the netminding duties, McCool played just 22 games but allowed 81 goals. After 1945–46, McCool never played pro hockey again. He just dropped off the radar after a 72-game NHL career, the shortest ever among Calder-winners.

19.39 A. Bobby Orr

Few players mature so quickly that they become MVP candidates early in their NHL careers. Wayne Gretzky was an exception, winning his first Hart in 1980 at age 19. The next-youngest MVP winner is Bobby Orr, who was 22.1 years old when he snagged his first of three straight awards beginning in 1970. Other young Hart winners include Eric Lindros (22.2 years), Mario Lemieux (22.6 years) and Bryan Trottier (22.9 years).

19.40 C. Patrick Roy

Roy was just 20 years old and an NHL rookie when he won the Conn Smythe in 1986. The Canadiens netminder posted a record-tying 15 wins and a 1.92 GAA in 20 postseason games.

Orr was 22 during his MVP playoff season in 1970. Who is the oldest playoff MVP? Goalie Glenn Hall, who, at age 37, won MVP honours for St. Louis in 1968.

19.41 A. Bobby Orr

The legendary Boston Bruins blueliner won Hart and Conn Smythe Trophies twice with matching MVP performances during the regular season and playoffs in 1970 and 1972. No other player has ever managed to win both MVP trophies on more than one occasion.

19.42 C. Jean Béliveau

The Conn Smythe Trophy was donated in 1964 by Maple Leaf Gardens Ltd. in honour of Conn Smythe, former Leafs coach, manager and owner as well as the driving force behind the building of Maple Leaf Gardens in 1931. The trophy was first presented during the 1965 Stanley Cup finals to Béliveau, who scored eight goals and collected 16 points in 13 playoff games. In Montreal's march to the Cup, the Habs captain had three game-winners. His most memorable goal came during the final's climactic seventh game, when he set the pace by scoring after only 14 seconds. The momentum catapulted Montreal past Chicago, who never got on the scoreboard during Montreal's 4–0 Cup-clinching victory. Only the Hawks' Bobby Hull scored more often than Béliveau that playoff year, collecting 10 goals and 17 points.

19.43 A. Roger Crozier

Although Detroit lost the 1966 Cup final to Montreal, Crozier had a sensational playoff series. Finishing the regular seasonin fourth place and 16 points behind the league-leading Canadiens, Detroit was hardly favoured. But the Wings surprised everyone by stealing two wins in Montreal on Crozier's brilliant netminding. Games 3 and 4 went to the fired-up Canadiens, with Detroit just holding its own after Crozier suffered a twisted ankle in a goal-crease crash with Bobby Rousseau. Crozier returned for the fifth game, but his injury was too much and the Wings lost 5–1. In Game 6, Detroit rebounded to outshoot the Habs 30–22 in a 2–2 tie after regulation time. In overtime, a controversial goal handed Montreal the Cup. As Henri Richard slid towards the net, he somehow redirected the puck past Crozier for the series-winner. The Wings were finished, but Crozier walked away with the Conn Smythe as playoff MVP, posting a 2.34 goals-against average and one shutout in 12 games. He was both the first member of alosing team and the first netminder to win MVP playoff honours.

19.44 C. Gaye Stewart

Ken Dryden, Danny Grant and Tony Esposito all played on Stanley Cup winners before copping rookie-of-the-year honours, but to find the first player to turn the trick you have to go back to the 1942 Cup finals between Toronto and Detroit. Trailing three games to none, the Leafs staged a miraculous rally to beat the Red Wings in seven games. Gaye Stewart, a rookie winger called up from the minors for Game 5, stayed in the Leafs' lineup for Games 6 and 7, thereby getting his name engraved on the Cup after playing only three NHL games. The next season, Stewart was voted the NHL's top rookie to complete the rare double.

GAME 19

Unusual Endings

WHEN GORDIE HOWE hung up his blades in 1980, it wasn't as a Detroit Red Wing—the team he set the NHL record with for most seasons played. No, Howe's 25-year career with the Red Wings ended in 1971, years before he finally retired from NHL play. So with which NHL franchise did Gordie play his last season? Below are other hockey greats who finished their careers with clubs they aren't widely associated with. Match the team with the player.

Solutions are on page 569

PART 1

1. _____ Detroit's Gordie Howe
2. _____ Montreal's Larry Robinson
3. _____ NYI/Buffalo's Pat LaFontaine
4. _____ Toronto's Darryl Sittler
5. _____ Chicago's Pierre Pilote
6. _____ Edmonton's Grant Fuhr
7. _____ St. L/Bos/Wash's Adam Oates
8. _____ Boston's Bobby Orr

A. Los Angeles Kings
B. Chicago Blackhawks
C. Calgary Flames
D. Hartford Whalers
E. Edmonton Oilers
F. New York Rangers
G. Detroit Red Wings
H. Toronto Maple Leafs

PART 2

1. _____ Montreal's Guy Lafleur
2. _____ Toronto's Borje Salming
3. _____ Chicago's Bobby Hull
4. _____ Washington's Dale Hunter
5. _____ New York's Andy Bathgate
6. _____ Quebec's Peter Stastny
7. _____ Buffalo's Rick Martin
8. _____ Edmonton's Paul Coffey

A. Hartford Whalers
B. Colorado Avalanche
C. Pittsburgh Penguins
D. St. Louis Blues
E. Quebec Nordiques
F. Detroit Red Wings
G. Boston Bruins
H. Los Angeles Kings

20

Cup Warriors

DURING THE 2003 PLAYOFFS, Philadelphia coach Ken Hitchcock was asked about fighting through the physical and psychological torture of playoff hockey. "It really comes down to how badly, as a group, you want to keep playing," Hitchcock said. "It's an awful price to pay to continue. I have seen things that I didn't think possible for athletes to do, but once you get to the point where you are willing to do it, anything is possible." In this chapter, we champion the indomitable spirit of the Stanley Cup warrior.

Answers are on page 498

20.1 What slogan did Colorado's Ray Bourque have written on his baseball cap during the 2001 playoffs?

A. Chase the Dream
B. True Believer
C. Mission 16W
D. The Last Dance

20.2 Which Toronto defenseman scored a crucial game-winner on a broken ankle in the 1964 playoffs?

A. Bobby Baun
B. Allan Stanley
C. Carl Brewer
D. Tim Horton

20.3 Which St. Louis defenseman tripped up Bobby Orr after Orr had scored the Stanley Cup-winning goal in 1970?

A. Jean-Guy Talbot
B. Barclay Plager
C. Bob Plager
D. Noel Picard

20.4 In 17 NHL seasons, defenseman and supreme shot-blocker Craig Ludwig scored just 38 goals. How many playoff goals did he amass during his career between 1982–83 and 1998–99?

A. None
B. Four goals
C. Eight goals
D. 16 goals

20.5 Which defenseman scored Toronto's 1951 Stanley Cup-winning goal?

A. Jim Thomson
B. Bill Barilko
C. Gus Mortson
D. Bill Juzda

20.6 Who was the first rookie defenseman to score a hat trick in the NHL playoffs?

A. Paul Reinhart
B. Denis Potvin
C. Al Iafrate
D. Andy Delmore

20.7 Which defenseman amassed the longest consecutive point-scoring streak in playoff action?

A. Colorado's Ray Bourque
B. Boston's Bobby Orr
C. Calgary's Al MacInnis
D. Edmonton's Paul Coffey

20.8 In which 1994 playoff round and before which game did New York Rangers captain Mark Messier make his famous prediction about winning the next crucial game?

A. Conference semifinals—Game 6 against the Capitals
B. Conference finals—Game 6 against the Devils
C. Cup finals—Game 6 against the Canucks
D. Cup finals—Game 7 against the Canucks

20.9 Which Calgary Flames player was credited with the goal that the Edmonton Oilers' Steve Smith scored on his own net in the 1986 playoffs?

A. John Tonelli
B. Perry Berezan
C. Paul Reinhart
D. Steve Bozek

20.10 Which former Edmonton Oiler holds the NHL record for the highest career plus-minus in the playoffs?

A. Charlie Huddy
B. Glenn Anderson
C. Jari Kurri
D. Wayne Gretzky

20.11 Who scored the greatest number of goals in one playoff series?

A. Jari Kurri
B. Tim Kerr
C. Reggie Leach
D. Wayne Gretzky

20.12 What is the highest goals-to-assists differential by a player in a playoff career?

A. A differential of 18
B. A differential of 28
C. A differential of 38
D. A differential of 48

20.13 Who shares the lead with Wayne Gretzky for most game-winning playoff goals in a career?

A. Claude Lemieux
B. Brett Hull
C. Maurice Richard
D. Mike Bossy

20.14 Who is the only player in NHL history to score every game-winning goal for his team in a best-of-seven playoff series?

A. Joe Sakic of the Colorado Avalanche
B. Mike Bossy of the New York Islanders
C. Mario Lemieux of the Pittsburgh Penguins
D. Jari Kurri of the Edmonton Oilers

20.15 What is the most consecutive game-winning goals scored by an NHLer in one playoff series?

A. Two consecutive winning goals
B. Three consecutive winning goals
C. Four consecutive winning goals
D. No player has ever scored consecutive winning goals

20.16 What is the most game-winners scored by a player in one playoff year?

A. Four goals
B. Five goals
C. Six goals
D. Seven goals

20.17 Who is the only player to score five game-winning goals in one playoff year and not win the Stanley Cup?

A. Bobby Smith
B. Joe Sakic
C. Joe Nieuwendyk
D. Mario Lemieux

20.18 Who was the first NHLer to score on a penalty shot in a playoff game?

A. Jim Roberts
B. Wayne Connelly
C. Frank Mahovlich
D. Bill Barber

20.19 Who owns the NHL record for scoring points in the most consecutive playoff games?

A. Al MacInnis
B. Bryan Trottier
C. Stan Mikita
D. Wayne Gretzky

20.20 Who holds the records for both goals and points by a rookie in one playoff year?

A. Chicago's Jeremy Roenick in 1990
B. Montreal's Claude Lemieux in 1986
C. The Islanders' Pat Flatley in 1984
D. Minnesota's Dino Ciccarelli in 1981

20.21 Who was the first player to break Maurice Richard's playoff career goal-scoring record?

A. Jari Kurri
B. Glenn Anderson
C. Mike Bossy
D. Wayne Gretzky

20.22 Which NHL player has won the most Stanley Cups?

A. Gordie Howe
B. Henri Richard
C. Mark Messier
D. Guy Lafleur

20.23 What is the greatest number of different teams with which a player has won the Stanley Cup?

A. Two teams
B. Three teams
C. Four teams
D. Five teams

20.24 What is the longest stretch between Stanley Cup wins by a player?

A. 11 years
B. 13 years
C. 16 years
D. 17 years

20.25 If the NHL mark for most Stanley Cups won by a skater is 11 championships, what is the Cup record for a goalie?

A. Five Stanley Cups
B. Six Stanley Cups
C. Seven Stanley Cups
D. Eight Stanley Cups

20.26 Which goalie faced the most shots in a Stanley Cup playoff year (since 1983–84, when shots on goal were first officially compiled)?

A. Philadelphia's Ron Hextall in 1987
B. Los Angeles' Kelly Hrudey in 1993
C. Vancouver's Kirk McLean in 1994
D. Washington's Olaf Kolzig in 1998

20.27 What is the oldest age at which a goalie made his first appearance in the NHL playoffs?

A. 37 years old
B. 39 years old
C. 41 years old
D. 43 years old

20.28 Who was the oldest goalie to win the Stanley Cup?

A. Johnny Bower
B. Glenn Hall
C. Patrick Roy
D. Mike Vernon

20.29 Which goalie has taken part in the longest two overtime playoff games in modern-day hockey?

A. Ron Tugnutt
B. Ed Belfour
C. Dominik Hasek
D. Patrick Roy

20.30 Which goalie recorded the most overtime wins in one playoff season?

A. Billy Smith of the Islanders in 1980
B. Grant Fuhr of Edmonton in 1985
C. Patrick Roy of Montreal in 1993
D. Kirk McLean of Vancouver in 1994

20.31 What is the NHL record for the most consecutive playoff wins by a goalie from the start of a career?

A. Five straight wins
B. Seven straight wins
C. Nine straight wins
D. 11 straight wins

20.32 Which goalie of the 1990s won the longest 1–0 game in the history of the Stanley Cup finals?

A. Florida's John Vanbiesbrouck
B. Detroit's Mike Vernon
C. New Jersey's Martin Brodeur
D. Colorado's Patrick Roy

20.33 Which two modern-day goalies allowed the most combined goals (15) in a Stanley Cup finals game?

A. The Islanders' Billy Smith and Edmonton's Grant Fuhr
B. Montreal's Ken Dryden and Chicago's Tony Esposito
C. Minnesota's Jon Casey and Pittsburgh's Tom Barrasso
D. Detroit's Mike Vernon and Philadelphia's Ron Hextall

20.34 What is the fewest goals allowed by a goalie in a best-of-seven Stanley Cup finals series?

A. No goals
B. Two goals
C. Four goals
D. Six goals

20.35 What is the greatest number of Cup-winning goals allowed by a goalie in a career?

A. Two goals
B. Four goals
C. Six goals
D. Eight goals

20.36 Who was the last maskless goalie to win a Stanley Cup?

A. The Canadiens' Gump Worsley
B. The Maple Leafs' Johnny Bower
C. The Maple Leafs' Terry Sawchuk
D. The Bruins' Gerry Cheevers

20.37 How many overtime goals did Mel "Sudden Death" Hill really score?

A. None—"Sudden Death" was a goalie
B. Two seventh-game winners
C. Three game-winners in a best-of-seven series
D. Three game-winners in three straight playoffs

20.38 Prior to brothers Rob and Scott Niedermayer playing opposite each other during the 2003 Stanley Cup finals, when was the last time siblings met during a final series?

A. 1946
B. 1966
C. 1986
D. It had never happened before

20.39 During the 1982 playoff games at Vancouver's Pacific Coliseum, how did fans mimic the Canucks coach?

A. Shook their fists at the referee
B. Waved white towels
C. Sang "Three Blind Mice"
D. Stood on their seats, waving their arms

20.40 What memento did each player on the first Stanley Cup-winning team, the 1893 Montreal AAA, receive along with the Cup?

A. A gold-and-silver pocket watch and chain
B. A miniature replica of the Cup
C. A silver-plated hockey stick
D. A gold ring

20.41 What is the longest suspension handed out during the playoffs?

A. Six games
B. 11 games
C. 16 games
D. 21 games

20.42 Who is considered to be the first NHLer to hold the Stanley Cup in the air and skate around the rink after winning the championship?

A. George Armstrong
B. Howie Morenz
C. Ted Lindsay
D. Howie Meeker

20.43 Who was the first individual to have his name on the Stanley Cup as a player, coach and general manager?

A. Toe Blake
B. Jack Adams
C. Al Arbour
D. Jacques Lemaire

Answers

20.1 C. Mission 16W

The most emotional moment of the 2001 postseason occurred when Colorado Avalanche captain Joe Sakic accepted the Stanley Cup from NHL commissioner Gary Bettman and handed the silverware to Ray Bourque. The 40-year-old defenseman had trouble holding back the tears. After 22 years, he had finally won hockey's ultimate prize. Throughout the playoffs, Bourque's teammates tried to downplay the media's persistent questions about winning the Cup for the future Hall of Famer, but when the mission was finally accomplished, they admitted it had been a rallying cry. "I talked to Ray before the year started and told him that we were going to win and that I wanted him to be the first one to lift it," said Sakic. "That was the goal from day one." Bourque called his championship chase Mission 16W—16 playoff wins to get the Cup—and had caps bearing the slogan made up to hand out in the dressing room.

20.2 A. Bobby Baun

In the annals of playoff hockey, the story of Baun's 1964 overtime winner is a testament to courage. With the score tied 3–3 in Game 6 and Toronto facing elimination, Baun takes a Gordie Howe slapper off the ankle. Carried away on a stretcher, the worst is expected. In overtime, out skates Baun on a frozen and taped ankle, and at the 2:43 mark lobs a shot that bounces past a maze of players and beyond a confused Terry Sawchuk. Baun's sudden-death goal propels the Leafs into Game 7. Baun goes into the final on crutches but plays without missing a shift as Toronto whips Detroit 4–0 to win another Stanley Cup. The next day, doctors examined Baun and confirmed what he already suspected: a bone fracture in his leg.

20.3 D. Noel Picard

Bobby Orr's "flying goal," which won Boston the 1970 Stanley Cup, is one of hockey's most enduring images. Photographer Ray Lussier froze the moment as Orr, with arms outstretched in celebration after scoring on Glenn Hall, was tripped by St. Louis defenseman Noel Picard. Orr is literally soaring through the air on the play. Interestingly, there were a number of "fours" associated with Orr's famous goal, which we originally discovered with the assistance of *Hockey Trivia* reader Rhys Richert, and Ted Wells, a Boston Garden tour guide. Of course, No. 4 was Bobby Orr's sweater number, but No. 4 was also on Picard's back. The historic goal was Orr's fourth of the playoffs and Boston's fourth of the game, coming in the fourth period (overtime) of a 4–3 score. Boston won the Cup in four straight final games. Orr captured four individual awards that year and the Bruins won 40 games during the season. Also, it was Orr's fourth NHL campaign. Most significantly, the goal was scored at 00:40, giving Boston its first Cup since 1941 and its fourth Cup in franchise history. Had Orr failed on his headlong rush and coughed up the puck in the Blues' zone, according to Orr's defensive partner, Dallas Smith, the result would have been a four-on-one break for St. Louis. But that never happened. Instead, Orr added another chapter to his legend. As Richert pointed out: "All those fours... it's kind of scary." Hockey trivia expert Liam Maguire once published his list and discovered 70 different "four" associations with Orr's goal.

20.4 B. Four goals

As one reporter observed, "It's not something you see every day." The phenomenon happened on June 10, 1999, when Dallas old-timer Craig Ludwig scored just his fourth playoff goal in his 173rd postseason match. "Wasn't that amazing?" said teammate Mike Keane. "He's playing like he's 36 again." Later, someone asked the 38-year-old Ludwig, "When was your last playoff goal?" Ludwig deadpanned: "It was just a few minutes ago, didn't you see it." Ludwig had last scored with Montreal during the 1987–88 playoffs, 11 years earlier.

20.5 B. Bill Barilko

Known as "Bashing Bill" for his punishing bodychecks, Barilko was a member of Conn Smythe's rugged defensive corps, which dominated the game for five years and propelled Toronto to four Stanley Cups between 1947 and 1951. But Barilko's Cup-winning goal in 1951 is probably Toronto's best-remembered goal, not just for the heroic manner in which he scored it but for the tragedy that followed. During overtime of Game 5 of the Cup finals against Montreal, Barilko charged in from the blue line and fired a puck from the faceoff circle at Montreal's Gerry McNeil. Barilko's windup was delivered with such momentum that he fell forward as the shot gunned past McNeil to win the Cup. The Maple Leafs were champions and Barilko the hero. But he would never play again. That summer, on a fishing trip in northern Ontario, his plane went down and vanished without a trace. Ominously, it marked the end of a championship era for the Leafs. Barilko's body was later found, but not until June 6, 1962, just weeks after Toronto ended its 11-year drought and captured its next Stanley Cup.

20.6 D. Andy Delmore

The playoffs have a way of making unlikely heroes. Little-known Andy Delmore, undrafted and signed as a free agent by Philadelphia in 1997, brought his hard shot and blazing speed into the 2000 playoffs and scored five flashy goals, including an overtime winner in Game 3 of the Flyers' Eastern Conference semifinals against Pittsburgh and a hat trick in Game 5 as Philadelphia won 6–3 on May 7, 2000. Delmore became the first rookie rearguard to notch a postseason hat trick and just the 11th NHL defenseman to accomplish the feat, joining the likes of Bobby Orr, Denis Potvin and Brian Leetch. Although Bobby Orr is often credited with the league's first playoff hat trick in 1971, that honour goes to Ottawa's Georges Boucher, who potted three goals a half-century earlier on March 10, 1921, in a 5–0 win against Toronto.

20.7 C. Calgary's Al MacInnis

No player in playoff annals has strung together a longer point-scoring streak than Bryan Trottier, who scored 29 points in 18 straight games in 1981. The next-best streak is 17 games, shared by Wayne Gretzky and defenseman Al MacInnis. With one of the game's hardest shots, MacInnis became a major factor in the Flames' Stanley Cup win of 1989. He led in playoff scoring with 31 points and amassed a 17-game point-scoring streak on seven goals and 19 assists. It's the second-longest streak in playoff history and the longest among all rearguards. MacInnis potted four game-winners of Calgary's 16 victories. He was awarded the Conn Smythe Trophy as playoff MVP, only the fourth blueliner so honoured.

20.8 B. Conference finals—Game 6 against the Devils

Perhaps the most prophetic fan signboard of the 1994 playoffs simply, but cleverly, read "MESSiah." And after guaranteeing "We'll win tonight" before Game 6 to stay alive in the Conference finals, then locking it with a natural hat trick, Messier proved once again that he could lead the faithful to the promised land of the Cup finals and hockey's holy grail. It was won in a classic seven-game final series by MESSiah's Stanley Cup-winning goal, ending 54 years of Ranger exile.

20.9 B. Perry Berezan

It was the seventh game of the Edmonton–Calgary divisional final. With the score tied early in the third period, Flames forward Perry Berezan dumped the puck into the Oilers' zone and headed to the Calgary bench for a line change. Rookie Steve Smith, being chased by Lanny McDonald, skated behind his own net and launched the puck towards teammate Glenn Anderson. But the cross-ice pass banked off the leg of Oilers goalie Grant Fuhr, parked at the edge of the crease and slid into the Edmonton net. Berezan, the last Flame to touch the puck, was credited with the goal—one he didn't even see go in. Smith, who was celebrating his 23rd birthday, fell to the ice in shame and utter disbelief. Calgary held the lead and scuttled the Oilers' dream of a third straight Stanley Cup. Wayne Gretzky, the consummate team player, remembered Smith's anguish the following year after Edmonton won its third Cup in 1987. The first player Gretzky handed the trophy to for the ceremonial skate around the rink was Smith.

20.10 A. Charlie Huddy

The dynasty years of the Edmonton Oilers spiked a lot of offensive records in the playoffs. Few categories had as many Oilers in the top spots as career plus-minus. Surprisingly, Charlie Huddy, Edmonton's steady blueliner, heads the list with a plus 93 in 183 playoff games with four teams between 1980–81 and 1996–97. The highest-ranking non-Oiler is Mark Howe with an eighth-place plus 51.

Highest Career Plus-Minus in the Playoffs*

PLAYER	GP	SEASONS	PLUS-MINUS
Charlie Huddy	183	1981–1997	plus 93
Jari Kurri	200	1981–1998	plus 88
Wayne Gretzky	208	1981–1999	plus 86
Randy Gregg	137	1982–1992	plus 84
Glenn Anderson	225	1981–1996	plus 67
Paul Coffey	194	1981–1999	plus 57
Mark Messier	236	1980–1996	plus 52
Mark Howe	101	1980–1995	plus 51

**Current to 2004–05*

20.11 A. Jari Kurri

No team has ever turned on red lights faster than the Wayne Gretzky-led Edmonton Oilers. And no Edmonton team has been more prodigious in any playoff series than the 1985 squad that averaged 7.3 goals per game against Chicago in the 1985 Western Conference finals. A multitude of records were set, including, first and foremost, Jari Kurri's 12-goal performance, the highest individual goal count in one postseason round. Kurri had two hat tricks and a four-goal game, another NHL mark. And Gretzky didn't come away empty-handed. As Kurri's set-up man, he notched a league-record 14 assists. Team and league records were also set in the wild, point-filled series. An NHL-record 69 goals were scored, with the Oilers outscoring the Hawks 44–25 in six games. Edmonton notched two double-digit games, an NHL first in modern history. Trying to stem the puck parade was Blackhawks goalie Murray Bannerman, who earned the distinction of allowing the most playoffs goals in one series in Chicago's 70-year history. The

Blackhawks, with Denis Savard, Steve Larmer and Doug Wilson, combined to average more than four goals per game. The goal gorge produced another NHL record: the highest scoring average by both teams in one playoff series—11.5 goals per game. General manager Glen Sather's brand of wide-open hockey worked to perfection: let them score, because we'll score more.

20.12 C. A differential of 38

Few players have ever matched Maurice Richard's intensity around the net. He lived to score goals. Between 1943 and 1960 he netted 82 and managed 44 assists, a differential of 38, the highest in playoff history.

Highest Goals-to-Assists Differential, Career*

PLAYER	GP	GOALS	ASSISTS	DIF
Maurice Richard	133	82	44	38
Dino Ciccarelli	141	73	45	28
Reggie Leach	94	47	22	25
Cam Neely	93	57	32	25

**Current to 2004–05*

20.13 B. Brett Hull

Brett Hull is no stranger to controversy. When his mouth's not getting him in trouble with the league, his game-winners are drawing fire from fans. Consider the noise Buffalo fans made over his foot-in-the-crease Cup-winner with Dallas in 1999; and, of course, there was his World Cup winner in 1996, a Hull deflection that was clearly above the crossbar. Hull plays his best in big games. And as of 2004–05, he had a record 24 game-winning playoff goals to prove it.

20.14 B. Mike Bossy of the New York Islanders

In the 1983 Conference finals between the Islanders and the Boston Bruins, Bossy established an NHL record by scoring all four game-winners against Boston. The Isles moved on to the Stanley Cup finals where they manhandled Edmonton in four straight. It was New York's fourth consecutive Cup.

20.15 B. Three consecutive winning goals

During the 2003 playoffs, Tampa Bay's Martin St. Louis proved that small players can still play huge roles in the NHL. Never drafted after a promising U.S. college career at the University of Vermont, the five-foot-nine 185-pound winger became just the fourth player in NHL annals to score three straight game-winners in one playoff series. After dropping the opening two games against Washington in the first round, the Lightning stormed back and won the next four as St. Louis notched winners in the last three games, including one in triple overtime that gave Tampa a 2–1 victory and its first playoff-series win in franchise history. He was also the Lightning's leading scorer in the series with five goals and four assists. "I would like to help out and open some eyes, that smaller players can still compete and play hard in this league and have success," said St. Louis. The other players with three straight playoff game-winners in a single series were all six foot two or taller: Boston's Roy Conacher in 1939, Clark Gillies of the Islanders in 1977 and Pittsburgh's Kevin Stevens in 1991.

20.16 D. Seven goals

It was a storybook season for Brad Richards. The PEI native from tiny Murray Harbour played clutch hockey in Tampa Bay's drive during the 2004 playoffs, scoring 12 goals and adding 14 assists for 26 points in 23 games to capture both the Stanley Cup and Conn Smythe Trophy as playoff MVP. In the process, Richards rewrote the NHL record book with seven game-winning goals, producing almost half of the Lightning's playoff wins. His heroics were greatest during the Cup finals against Calgary, when he notched four goals and nine points. Richards's seven game-winners broke the mark of six held by Joe Sakic and Joe Nieuwendyk.

20.17 A. Bobby Smith

As of 2005, seven players in NHL history have scored five or more game-winners in one postseason. Brad Richards (2004) leads the pack with seven game-winners, followed by Colorado's Joe Sakic (1996) and Dallas' Joe Nieuwendyk (1999) with six and Mike Bossy (1983), Jari Kurri (1987), Mario Lemieux (1992) and Bobby Smith (1991) each with five winners during their respective playoff years. Smith, however, is the only player among this group without a Cup to show for his efforts, as the Minnesota North Stars fell to the Pittsburgh Penguins in six games during the 1991 finals. (Smith did win a Cup in 1986 with Montreal.)

20.18 B. Wayne Connelly

Connelly became the first player to score on a penalty shot in playoff action on April 9, 1968, against the Kings' Terry Sawchuk. The shot was awarded after Dale Rolfe interfered with the North Star forward on a clean break. Connelly made no mistake, skating straight in and roofing it over Sawchuk's stick-side. Three previous penalty shots in playoff overtime—by Lionel Conacher in 1937, Alex Shibicky in 1937 and Virgil Johnson in 1944—all failed.

20.19 B. Bryan Trottier

The New York Islanders' championship squads of the 1980s boasted a host of talented performers, but none contributed more to the club's success than Trottier. The hard-driving centre counted a point in 27 consecutive playoff games between 1980 and 1982, setting a record that no other player has approached. Even Wayne Gretzky's point-scoring streak of 19 straight games in 1988 and 1989 is a distant second. Trottier logged 42 points (16 goals, 26 assists) in those 27 games, but he was especially impressive during the 1981 playoffs when he scored a point in all 18 games the Islanders played, setting the longest consecutive point-scoring streak in one postseason. Gretzky and Al MacInnis follow Trottier in this category, but just by one game. Trottier scored 29 points in 18 straight games; Gretzky tallied 41 points and MacInnis 26 points, each in 17 matches.

20.20 D. Minnesota's Dino Ciccarelli in 1981

A funny thing happened to the Minnesota North Stars on the way to the 1981 Stanley Cup finals: Dino Ciccarelli. The freshman who was never drafted amassed an astonishing 21 points on 14 goals and seven assists. His production brought the North Stars as close to the Cup as at any time in their history. Minnesota first signed Ciccarelli as a free agent in September 1979.

20.21 C. Mike Bossy

It took 26 years of postseason play before anyone toppled Maurice Richard's career record for most goals during the playoffs. The Rocket's 82-goal mark, set in 1960, was finally eclipsed during the 1986 playoffs by Bossy, who scored his 83rd career goal against the Washington Capitals' Pete Peeters on April 12, 1986. Bossy's career mark of 85 playoff goals was surpassed three years later by Wayne Gretzky during the 1989 postseason.

20.22 B. Henri Richard

Richard won a record 11 Stanley Cups during his 20-year tenure with the Montreal Canadiens. His first five Cups came in his first five NHL seasons, when the Canadiens went on a championship spree from 1956 to 1960. Richard never played more than four consecutive seasons without winning the Cup. In 180 playoff games, he scored 49 goals and 129 points. Two of those goals were Cup-winners: one in 1966 against Detroit and another versus Chicago in 1971. The only other individual to equal

Richard's 11 championships, either as a player or coach, is Toe Blake, who won three Cups as a player and eight as Montreal's bench boss between 1956 and 1968.

Most Stanley Cup Wins*

CUPS	PLAYER	TEAM	CUP YEARS
11	Henri Richard	Montreal	1956–1973
10	Jean Béliveau	Montreal	1956–1971
10	Yvan Cournoyer	Montreal	1965–1979
9	Claude Provost	Montreal	1956–1969
8	Red Kelly	Detroit/Toronto	1950–1967
8	Jacques Lemaire	Montreal	1968–1979
8	Maurice Richard	Montreal	1944–1960

**Current to 2004–05*

20.23 C. Four teams

He may not be a household name, but Jack Marshall's achievement—playing on four different Cup-winning teams prior to the formation of the NHL—has never been topped. His first championship came in 1901 with the Winnipeg Victorias; then, in 1902 and 1903, as a member of the Montreal AAA; in 1907 and 1910, with the Montreal Wanderers; and his final touch to a sterling career, in 1914, as the Toronto Blueshirts' player-manager. Marshall played on six league championship teams and five Stanley Cup winners, and led all playoff goal scorers twice. He was inducted into the Hockey Hall of Fame in 1965.

20.24 C. 16 years

Players who win a Stanley Cup early in their careers often say they never expected to wait so long for another chance to win it again. No one knows this better than the many rookies who claimed their first championship with Montreal in 1986. Brian Skrudland and Craig Ludwig waited 13 years for their next Cup (with Dallas), from 1986 to 1999. Still, they didn't top Mickey MacKay, who won the Cup in 1915 with the Vancouver Millionaires but waited another 14 years, until 1929, to win it again (with the Boston Bruins). Still another former Canadiens Cup-holder from 1986 established an even longer span between Cups: Chris Chelios went 16 years before he won it again, this time with Detroit, in 2002.

20.25 B. Six Stanley Cups

Toronto's Turk Broda won a record five Stanley Cups during the Maple Leafs' dynasty years of the 1940s, but he was eclipsed in the next decade by Jacques Plante, who won six championships with Montreal. That record was later tied by fellow Canadiens netminder and six-time Cup-winner Ken Dryden, during the 1970s. Interestingly, Broda probably would have captured a sixth Cup with Toronto in 1944–45 had he not served in World War II. But it was Plante who had the best chance of increasing his Cup count. Had Montreal not traded him for Gump Worsley in 1963, Plante could have played out the decade with the dynasty Canadiens and won another four Cups. This is a reasonable assumption, considering Plante was no older than Worsley and was still at the top of his game in 1969, the year he won his sixth Vezina Trophy—with Glenn Hall of St. Louis—and the same year Montreal, with Gump Worsley, won its fourth Stanley Cup of the 1960s.

20.26 C. Vancouver's Kirk McLean in 1994

In 1994, Kirk McLean became the busiest goalie in postseason action when he faced a record 820 shots while appearing in 24 playoff games—a 31.9 shots-per-game average. Yet despite his workload through 1,544 minutes, McLean still lost the championship. In Game 7, he bowed out in a 3–2 heartbreaker to the New York Rangers and goalie Mike Richter, who handled 623 shots in 23 postseason games for a 26.4 average. With the exception of McLean, no netminder in playoff history has ever topped the 800-shot mark. Still, McLean's shots-per-game average of 31.9 doesn't come close to the rubber count of John Vanbiesbrouck, who faced 33.1 shots in Florida's cage during his 22 games in 1996. Interestingly, six of the seven highest shots-against marks belong to goalies who did not win the Cup.

The NHL's Top Seven Most Shell-Shocked Playoff Goalies*

PLAYER	TEAM	SEASON	GP/MINS	SA	SAPG
Kirk McLean	Van	1994	24/1,544	820	31.9
Ron Hextall	Phi	1987	26/1,540	769	30.0
Olaf Kolzig	Wash	1998	21/1,351	740	32.9
John Vanbiesbrouck	Fla	1996	22/1,332	735	33.1
Miikka Kiprusoff	Cgy	2004	26/1,655	710	25.7
J.S. Giguère	Ana	2003	21/1,407	697	29.6
Bill Ranford	Edm	1990	22/1,401	672	28.8

**From 1983–84 to 2004–05*

20.27 C. 41 years old

You can't say that goalie Hugh Lehman lacked postseason experience before starting his first NHL playoff game in 1927. The 41-year-old had already made five appearances in the Stanley Cup finals with the Vancouver Millionaires of the Pacific Coast Hockey Association, and had actually won the Cup in 1915. Even so, when Lehman stepped between the pipes for the Chicago Blackhawks in the 1927 quarterfinals against Boston, technically speaking he became the oldest rookie to appear in an NHL playoff game. The Bruins gave Lehman a rough ride, beating the Hawks 6–1.

20.28 A. Johnny Bower

When playoff MVP Mike Vernon led Detroit to the 1997 Stanley Cup, the veteran netminder was 34 years old. Although he was considered in the twilight of his career, Vernon was still eight years younger than Bower, who won the 1967 Cup with Toronto at age 42. Remarkably, like many old-timers with lengthy careers, Bower didn't hang up the pads when he won the Cup. He played two more seasons, quitting in 1969 after playing his last postseason. He was 44. Although Lester Patrick, coach of the 1928 Cup-winning New York Rangers, was 45 years old when he stepped between the pipes for a half-game, he was not an active player. Bower is the oldest player with his name on the Cup.

20.29 A. Ron Tugnutt

The two longest games in NHL playoff history took place during the 1930s. On both occasions Lorne Chabot was between the pipes, in 1933 backstopping Toronto to a 1–0 win after 104:46 of overtime, and three years later as a Montreal Maroon in a 1–0 defeat that ended after 116:30 of extra time. Oddly, the two longest overtime games in modern times featured another netminder who dressed in both contests. Ron Tugnutt played in the third-longest overtime on May 4, 2000, as a member of the Pittsburgh Penguins, and three years later played backup to Marty Turco of the Dallas Stars during that marathon game on April 24, 2003.

Longest Overtime Games in the Playoffs*

TIME	WINNER/TEAM	LOSER/TEAM	SCORE	DATE
116:30	N. Smith/Det	L. Chabot/Mtl	1–0	03/24/1936
104:46	L. Chabot/Tor	C. Thompson/Bos	1–0	03/03/1933
92:01	B. Boucher/Phi	R. Tugnutt/Pit	2–1	05/04/2000
80:48	J.S. Giguère/Ana	M. Turco/Dal	4–3	04/24/2003
79:15	T. Barrasso/Pit	J. Carey/Wash	3–2	04/24/1996

**Current to 2004–05*

20.30 C. Patrick Roy of Montreal in 1993

Roy's prominence among his peers has been built on a number of defining moments. The Canadiens' unlikely run at the Stanley Cup in 1993 was one of Roy's finest hours. Back-stopping an almost-ordinary Habs team through 20 playoff games, Roy shut the door in 10 straight overtimes, giving Montreal skaters time to score the game-winner in sudden-death play. No team has ever won more than seven overtimes in one playoff year. Player for player, the Canadiens were in "the zone" behind Roy, literally chuckling to each other in the dressing room before overtime, trying to guess who would score the next winner.

20.31 B. Seven straight wins

While Tom Barrasso owns the NHL record for the most consecutive playoff wins (14 straight in the 1992 and 1993 playoffs), the leader in this category is Cecil "Tiny" Thompson, who earned five straight wins and the Stanley Cup in 1929 and another two wins to start the 1930 playoffs. During the 2003 playoffs, Jean-Sébastien Giguère came within a game of tying Thompson's mark after winning his first six playoff contests.

20.32 D. Colorado's Patrick Roy

On June 10, 1996, Patrick Roy and John Vanbiesbrouck met in Game 4 of the Stanley Cup finals. Both were absolutely brilliant, but Roy stopped all 63 shots before teammate Uwe Krupp scored the Cup-winner—after five gruelling periods of play—at 4:31 of triple overtime. The victory, the longest 1–0 game in finals history, capped an Avalanche four-game sweep over the Florida Panthers.

20.33 B. Montreal's Ken Dryden and Chicago's Tony Esposito

The 1973 Stanley Cup set a number of individual and team marks in finals action, including a record 56 goals by both Chicago and Montreal in the six-game round. It was a shooters' match as Dryden and Esposito performed like sieves in four double-digit scoring games. By far the worst night, Game 5 on May 8, 1973, saw the Blackhawks score eight times on Dryden. Esposito, no less embarrassing, walked away with a win after giving up seven Canadiens goals. The 15-goal count broke a 37-year record established in 1936, when Detroit and Toronto exploded for 13 goals in the Red Wings' 9–4 win. In the 1973 series, the lowest scores were Dryden's 4–0 and 4–1 wins. The other four contests were double-digit affairs of 10-, 11-, 11- and 15-goal games. Dryden allowed 23 goals and Esposito 33 as Montreal won the Cup. Eight months earlier Esposito and Dryden had been teammates for Canada in the 1972 Summit Series against the Soviet Union.

20.34 B. Two goals

The 1952 Stanley Cup finals may be old-time hockey's most convincing series of wins by an NHL champion. Detroit sophomore Terry Sawchuk established his playoff credentials, sweeping Toronto in the first series, then, in the finals, recorded two shutouts and held Montreal to just two goals in another four-game sweep. The Red Wings set an NHL benchmark by winning all eight postseason matches; Sawchuk, on five goals in eight playoff games, recorded a stingy 0.63, the lowest average in modern-day playoff history.

20.35 C. Six goals

Glenn Hall was such a good goalie that three teams put their faith in him despite his losing record in finals play. Hall lost with Detroit in 1956; Chicago in 1962 and 1965; and St. Louis in 1968, 1969 and 1970. The most memorable playoff goal he allowed was the 1970 Cup-winner by Boston's Bobby Orr. The goal produced hockey's most famous photograph: Orr sailing through the air, arms outstretched in celebration, and Hall picking himself up out of the net after being beaten by Orr. Hall did manage to get his name on one Cup, with Chicago in 1961.

20.36 A. The Canadiens' Gump Worsley

The Gumper played maskless when the Canadiens won back-to-back Stanley Cups in 1968 and 1969 (as did opposing goalie Glenn Hall for St. Louis). The next year, when Boston won the championship, Cheevers was sporting his famous white mask with the black stitch marks. After that, all Cup-winning goalies, including Ken Dryden, Bernie Parent and Billy Smith, wore face protection. Worsley, one of the last "old guard" goaltenders, played 21 seasons and waited until near-retirement, 1973–74, before reluctantly donning his first mask.

20.37 C. Three game-winners in a best-of-seven series

The Bruins' Mel Hill earned the handle "Sudden Death" the hard way. In the tough-fought Boston–New York semifinals of 1939, Hill scored three overtime goals in seven games. But even though "Sudden Death" would play on three Stanley Cup winners in his career, he never scored another overtime goal. His NHL record stands today.

20.38 A. 1946

The Niedermayers were the first brothers to battle in the Cup finals since Boston's Terry Reardon met Montreal's Ken Reardon during the 1946 Cup finals. Although the Niedermayers had gone head-to-head before in the playoffs (in 2000's first round), the family feud still proved a little tough on their mother, Carol. "[For] my mom, it might not be an easy situation for her," said Scott. "I guess she probably wishes we both could end up winning, but that's not the case." Ken Reardon won with Montreal in 1946; Scott won his third Cup in 2003 with the Devils.

20.39 B. Waved white towels

Vancouver's playoff towel-waving craze took inspiration from Game 2 of the 1982 Conference finals at Chicago Stadium. After referee Bob Myers disallowed a Canuck goal and called several Vancouver penalties, coach Roger Neilson stuck a white towel on a player's stick and began waving it in mock surrender. The entire bench got into it and the result cost the team $11,000 in fines. The Canucks returned home for Game 3 to a towel-waving frenzy at the Coliseum. Vancouver won the series 4–1 but was swept four straight by the mighty Islanders in the finals.

20.40 D. A gold ring

A championship ring was not always the reward for Cup champions. Gold watches, lapel pins and cash were often customary in early times. One exception came in 1893, the Cup's first year. In compliance with Lord Stanley's terms, the Montreal AAA were awarded the Stanley Cup after winning the AHA title. (No other team dared challenge Montreal, so the Cup was theirs without playing a single playoff game.) As thanks, each player was given a gold ring, a hockey tradition that was revived by Toronto's dynasty teams of the late 1940s.

20.41 D. 21 games

Washington's Dale Hunter was handed a 21-game suspension for hitting Pierre Turgeon into the boards after the Islander forward scored a series-winning goal on April 28, 1993. It was a cheap and senseless shot, but not the longest player-on-player suspension in NHL history. Marty McSorley earned 23 games during regular-season play in 1999–2000; Gord Dwyer, 23 games during an exhibition game in 2000–01; and Todd Bertuzzi could be handed an even stiffer sentence for his attack on Steve Moore in 2004, pending a league decision at the time of this writing.

20.42 C. Ted Lindsay

It might have been the climactic seventh-game overtime goal or it might have been the noise thundering down from the Detroit Olympia's rafters, but whatever inspired Ted Lindsay, hockey can thank him for one of its most enduring images. It happened during the Cup presentations of 1950. In a spontaneous act of sportsmanship, Lindsay grabbed the Cup from captain Sid Abel and hoisted it high above his head for a skate around the rink. Budd Lynch of Detroit television recalls: "In the excitement, he just picked up the Cup to get the crowd going. He moved right along the boards so the fans could see the Cup up close. I guess other people saw it because of TV, and it caught on." The "hoisting of the Cup" remains a venerated Stanley Cup tradition.

20.43 B. Jack Adams

Adams's success and longevity earned him the distinction of winning the Stanley Cup in each of the NHL's first five decades. He won two Cups as a player, one with the Toronto Arenas in 1918 and another as a member of the old Ottawa Senators in 1927; two as coach of the Detroit Red Wings in 1936 and 1937; and seven as manager of the Red Wings in 1936, 1937, 1943, 1950, 1952, 1954 and 1955.

GAME 20

Penalty-Shot History

WHO FIRST TOOK TWO PENALTY shots in one playoff year? Unscramble the players' names below by placing each letter in the correct order in the boxes. Each name starts with a bolded letter. Then unscramble the letters in the circled and diamond-shaped boxes. The circled boxes spell out the player's name, the diamond-shaped boxes, his NHL team name. To help you out, the two blackened circles are the first letters of his initials.

Solutions are on page 569

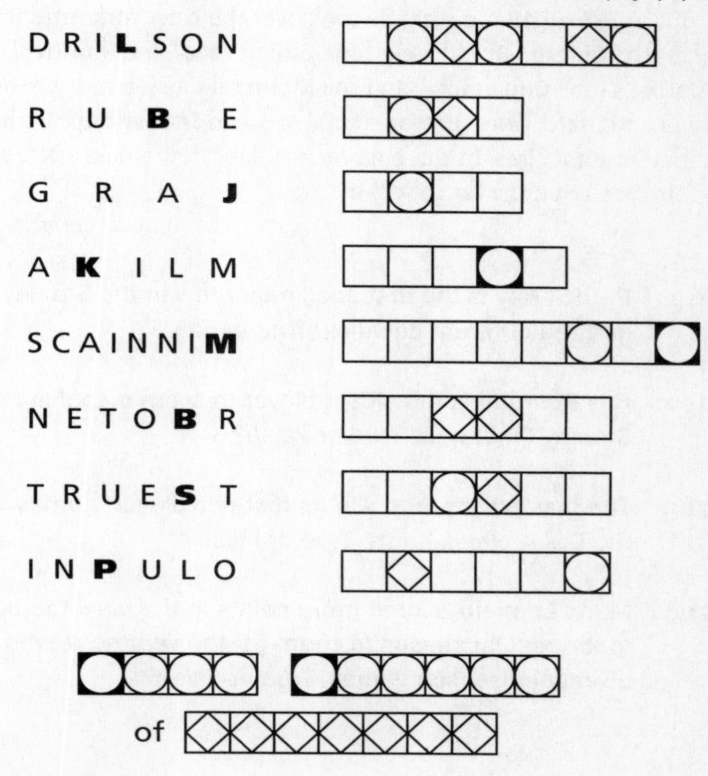

21

Stanley Cup Truths

TWO OF THE MAJOR FIGURES in Stanley Cup history are Conn Smythe and Jack Adams. But neither won as consistently with as many teams as Tommy Gorman. Tommy who? Gorman was one of the game's most extraordinary and successful individuals. Yet despite his triumphs, he still hasn't received his due among the pantheon of NHL builders. After turning Ottawa into the league's first dynasty with Cups in 1920, 1921 and 1923, he took over the New York Americans, then the Chicago Blackhawks (one Cup in 1934), the Montreal Maroons (one Cup in 1935) and the Montreal Canadiens (two Cups in 1944 and 1946). Gorman won a total of seven Stanley Cups with four different franchises. In this chapter, we slap a few true-or-false shots at the net and hope for the tip-in.

Answers are on page 522

21.1 Patrick Roy is the first goalkeeper to win the Stanley Cup in three different decades. True or False?

21.2 Ray Bourque is the oldest player to score a goal in a Stanley Cup finals. True or False?

21.3 The first NHL team to win its first two playoff games was the Los Angeles Kings. True or False?

21.4 Mario Lemieux scored more points in the playoffs than in the regular season in 1990–91, the year he played only 26 regular-season games. True or False?

21.5 Despite being donated by Maple Leaf Gardens in 1965 to honour the Maple Leafs' founder, the Conn Smythe Trophy for playoff MVP has never been won by a Toronto Maple Leaf. True or False?

21.6 Grant Fuhr was the first black player to have his name etched into the Stanley Cup. True or False?

21.7 Lord Stanley of Preston, donator of the Stanley Cup, is actually the only "Stanley" on hockey's championship trophy. True or False?

21.8 The distance between Quebec City and Denver is 1,996 miles. True or False?

21.9 No one who saw the New York Rangers win the Stanley Cup at Madison Square Garden in 1994 also witnessed the Rangers' previous Cup victory 54 years earlier in 1940. True or False?

21.10 Every time the New York Rangers captured the Stanley Cup, they won the Cup-clinching game by a one-goal margin. True or False?

21.11 The Detroit Red Wings have never won a Stanley Cup without a Howe in the team's organization. True or False?

21.12 No player has ever recorded 500 penalty minutes in a career during the playoffs. True or False?

21.13 Bobby Orr is the first defenseman to score more points than every playoff scorer in one season. True or False?

21.14 Wayne Gretzky and Mario Lemieux never met in a Stanley Cup playoff game. True or False?

21.15 **No NHL coach has ever been credited with a playoff tie.** True or False?

21.16 **Despite being fired with just eight games remaining in the 1999–2000 season, ex-Devils coach Robbie Ftorek still got his name on the Stanley Cup after New Jersey won the championship in June 2000.** True or False?

21.17 **The former home of the Quebec Nordiques, Colisée de Quebec has two Stanley Cup banners hanging from its rafters.** True or False?

21.18 **Colorado's Alex Tanguay became the youngest player to score a Cup-winning goal when he beat New Jersey's Martin Brodeur in Game 6 of the 2001 finals.** True or False?

21.19 **Patrick Roy is the only player to win the Conn Smythe Trophy as a playoff MVP with two different teams.** True or False?

21.20 **The St. Louis Blues are the only NHL team to lose three consecutive Stanley Cup finals.** True or False?

21.21 **Even though the 1995 Calgary Flames set the NHL record for most goals by one team in a playoff series that went seven games, they still lost that playoff round.** True or False?

21.22 **When the Pittsburgh Penguins won the Stanley Cup in 1990–91 and 1991–92, they finished exactly 18 points behind the regular-season league leaders in both years.** True or False?

21.23 **No goalie has ever recorded 100 playoff wins.** True or False?

21.24 **Only once since the formation of the NHL in 1917 has there been a year in which there was not a Canadian team involved in the Stanley Cup playoffs.** True or False?

21.25 **The Colorado Avalanche is the only team in NHL history to win the Stanley Cup in its first season in a new city.** True or False?

21.26 **Mark Messier never took the Vancouver Canucks to the playoffs.** True or False?

21.27 **Scott Stevens, with the New Jersey Devils at the time, won the Conn Smythe Trophy as MVP of the 2000 playoffs despite scoring fewer points than any other previous winner of the award (not including goalies).** True or False?

21.28 **Despite capturing the 2003 Stanley Cup with three shutouts in the finals, New Jersey's Martin Brodeur was not named playoff MVP.** True or False?

21.29 **As of 2005, the last four rookie coaches to win the Stanley Cup all coached the Montreal Canadiens to the championship.** True or False?

21.30 **No NHL coach has ever coached two Original Six teams to the Stanley Cup.** True or False?

21.31 **No team has won the Stanley Cup without having home-ice advantage in at least one playoff series.** True or False?

21.32 **The first NHLer awarded a penalty shot in a Stanley Cup finals was an American.** True or False?

21.33 **When Nicklas Lidstrom won the Conn Smythe Trophy as MVP of the 2002 Stanley Cup playoffs, he joined Bobby Orr**

and Scott Stevens as only the third defenseman to claim the coveted award. True or False?

21.34 **No team with a losing record in the regular season has ever won the Stanley Cup.** True or False?

21.35 **The Montreal Canadiens finished the regular season in first place for five consecutive years during their record five-in-a-row Stanley Cup streak from 1956 to 1960.** True or False?

21.36 **One individual won the Stanley Cup 11 times before his 10th birthday.** True or False?

21.37 **Theo Fleury was the last active Calgary player remaining from the Flames' Stanley Cup-winning team of 1998–99.** True or False?

21.38 **There has never been a penalty shot called in overtime of the Stanley Cup playoffs.** True or False?

21.39 **No team has ever swept all four playoff series en route to winning the Stanley Cup.** True or False?

Stanley Cup Truths

Answers

21.1 **True**

When Patrick Roy won the Cup in 2001, he entered uncharted territory. No netminder had ever won Cups in three different decades. Roy won one Cup during the 1980s (Montreal 1986), two during the 1990s (Montreal 1993 and Colorado 1996) and one in 2001 (Colorado).

21.2 False

Ray Bourque was 40 years, 154 days old when he scored a goal against New Jersey in a 3–1 Colorado win on May 31, 2001. A year later, Detroit's Igor Larionov bested Bourque to become the oldest greybeard, with a final series goal against Carolina at 14:47 of the third overtime period on June 9, 2002. Larionov, at 41 years, 188 days old, had just broken his own record, set hours earlier after scoring a second-period goal. Detroit won 3–2.

21.3 True

No club in NHL history had won its first two playoff matches until Los Angeles beat Minnesota April 4 and 6 by 2–1 and 2–0 scores during their 1968 quarterfinals. Unfortunately, the Kings couldn't sustain their luck and bowed to the Stars in seven games.

21.4 False

Chronic back problems limited Mario Lemieux to only 26 games and 45 points in 1990–91, but the Penguins sniper roared back in the postseason, scoring a personal best of 44 playoff points in 23 games to lead Pittsburgh to its first Stanley Cup. Lemieux tallied just one point more in regular-season action than in the playoffs.

21.5 False

Since the Conn Smythe was first awarded in 1965, only one Maple Leaf has won the trophy honouring that club's founder, the coach and builder of Maple Leaf Gardens. Toronto's Dave Keon was named playoff MVP of 1967 after a sensational post-season against Chicago and Montreal. Keon, a smooth-skating two-way centre, frustrated highly favoured Montreal in the Stanley Cup finals with his checking and defensive work. He also scored a goal and an assist as Toronto surprised the Canadiens to capture the Cup.

21.6 True

Grant Fuhr, the first black player to play for a Stanley Cup winner, claimed four championships with Edmonton—the first in 1983–84, when he backstopped the Oilers to 11 playoff victories.

21.7 False

Six Stanleys have had their names inscribed on the Cup since Lord Stanley first donated the trophy in 1892, including Barney Stanley of the Vancouver Millionaires (1915), Allan Stanley of the Toronto Maple Leafs (1962, 1963, 1964 and 1967) and executive Stanley Jaffe of the New York Rangers (1994).

21.8 True

Cue the *Twilight Zone* theme music. After 16 seasons without even a sniff of a championship, the Quebec Nordiques move to Denver and are renamed the Colorado Avalanche. The Avalanche promptly win the Cup in 1996. Denver is 1,996 miles from Quebec City.

21.9 False

Among a number of other long-time fans, New York hockey writer Norm MacLean and broadcaster Dick Irvin Jr. each witnessed both Ranger Cups, the first at Maple Leaf Gardens in 1940 and the next, 54 years later, at Madison Square Garden. MacLean, at age 10, travelled to Toronto with his father to see the deciding game in 1940; Irvin Jr., at age eight, was on hand as the son of Dick Irvin, coach of the losing Maple Leafs.

21.10 True

The Rangers have won four Stanley Cups, all by one-goal margins. Two goals of the series were pushed to the deciding match and the other two came in overtime victories. Similar to 1994's heart-stopping 3–2 victory over Vancouver in Game 7, in 1928, New York captured its first Cup in the fifth and final game of the best-of-five series with a close 2–1 win over the Montreal Maroons. In 1933 and 1940, the Rangers won the Cup again, edging their opponents by one-goal margins. On both occasions the Maple Leafs fell victim in 1–0 and 3–2 overtime losses.

21.11 True

As of 2005, the Red Wings had won nine Stanley Cups: three in 1935, 1936 and 1943 with Syd Howe (no relation to Gordie); four in 1950, 1952, 1954 and 1955 with Gordie Howe; and three in 1997, 1998 and 2002 with Mark Howe as a team scout.

21.12 False

The 500-minute plateau in the playoffs has been reached by only three players: Claude Lemieux with 529 minutes, Chris Nilan with 541 minutes and Dale Hunter (hockey's career playoff penalty leader) with a whopping 729 minutes. Hunter became the first 500-minute man during Washington's post-season drive in 1989–90, just one year ahead of Nilan, who hit 500 minutes in 1991.

21.13 False

Bobby Orr in 1972 and Pierre Pilote in 1961 each shared the playoff scoring lead during their respective years, but the first rearguard with more points than all scorers was Calgary's Al MacInnis in 1989. MacInnis amassed his league-leading 31 points on seven goals and 24 assists. Twenty-six points came during MacInnis's 17-game consecutive point-scoring streak, which equalled the second-longest in postseason play and the longest ever by a defenseman.

21.14 True

The NHL's two greatest scorers never opposed one another in a playoff game. Prior to Wayne Gretzky's move to the Rangers, the year they had the best chance of meeting was 1993, when

Gretzky led the Los Angeles Kings to the Cup finals. But Mario Lemieux's Penguins, the best-overall regular-season team, were upset by the Islanders in the Patrick Division finals.

21.15 False

Several old-time coaches have recorded playoff ties, all coming during an era when many series were decided by total goals (instead of most wins in a "best-of" format) and games could end in ties. Lester Patrick of the New York Rangers leads all NHL coaches with seven ties in postseason play between 1926 and 1939.

21.16 True

Robbie Ftorek's dismissal with just eight games remaining in the 1999–2000 regular season surprised a few people, though not those who knew of the problems between the coach and his players. Assistant coach Larry Robinson took over, pulled the team together and won the Stanley Cup. And Ftorek not only got his name on the Cup (as a coach) but also received a ring. His record with New Jersey was 88–49–19 in 156 games.

21.17 True

In pre-NHL days, the Quebec Bulldogs, with Hall-of-Famers Paddy Moran, Joe Hall and Joe Malone, were a force, winning back-to-back Cups in 1913 and 1914. Those two championship years are honoured with banners at La Colisée, hung by a hockey-starved city that will probably not see NHL action again for a long time.

21.18 False

Ted "Teeder" Kennedy (21.4 years old) was two months younger than Alex Tanguay (21.6 years) when he notched the Cup-winning goal for the Toronto Maple Leafs against Montreal Canadiens netminder Bill Durnan in Game 6 of the 1947 finals.

21.19 True

Five players have won the Conn Smythe Trophy more than once, but only Patrick Roy has done it with different teams. Roy bagged two Conn Smythes with Montreal in 1986 and 1993, then won the prestigious award a third time with the Colorado Avalanche in 2001.

21.20 False

St. Louis is not the only NHL franchise to go down in three straight Cup finals. The best of the NHL's six expansion teams in 1967, the Blues only reached the finals because the playoff format pitted them against the other fledgling franchises in earlier rounds. They had little chance of winning the Cup against Montreal in 1968 and 1969 and Boston in 1970. The only other team with a trio of consecutive defeats is the Toronto Maple Leafs. They lost the Cup finals in 1938 against Chicago, in 1939 against Boston and in 1940 against New York.

21.21 True

During the 1995 Conference quarterfinals against the San Jose Sharks, the Flames lost their seven-game series 4–3 despite outscoring the Sharks 35–26. Calgary's 35-goal performance in 1995 doesn't top Edmonton's record output of 44 goals and 35 goals during playoff rounds in 1985 and 1983, but neither of those Oilers teams lost, nor did those series hit the seven-game limit.

21.22 True

During their two Stanley Cup-winning seasons, the Penguins finished exactly 18 points back of the NHL's first-place teams. In 1990–91 Pittsburgh had 88 points compared to first-place Chicago's 106-point finish; in 1991–92 the Pens totalled 87 points, 18 less than the New York Rangers' 105.

21.23 False

Patrick Roy is the only netminder in league history to hit triple-digit numbers with 151 playoff wins. He passed the century plateau on April 24, 1999, in Colorado's 3–1 victory against San Jose. Grant Fuhr trails Roy with 92 career wins.

21.24 True

In 1969–70, New York and Montreal finished tied for fourth in the NHL's Eastern Division with identical win-loss-tie records, but the Rangers were awarded the final playoff berth because they had scored two goals more than the Canadiens. Montreal's elimination ended a 22-year string of consecutive playoff appearances. Coupled with Toronto's last-place finish, it marked the only time in league history that no Canadian team qualified for the playoffs.

21.25 True

After years of regular-season and playoff frustration, the Quebec Nordiques were sold to interests in Colorado and won the Stanley Cup as the Avalanche in 1996. It was the first time an NHL team captured the Cup in its first year in a new city. The Avalanche celebrated with two championship parades: the official celebration in Denver and another for tortured Nordiques fans when they paraded the Cup through Quebec City.

21.26 True

Despite a contract that paid him U.S.$6 million annually, Mark Messier never scored more than 22 goals during his three seasons for Vancouver and never led the Canucks into postseason play.

21.27 False

Although Scott Stevens compiled only 11 points during the 2000 playoffs, that was still one point better than the 10 points picked up by Montreal Canadiens defenseman Serge Savard, the Conn Smythe Trophy-winner in 1969. Still, considering that Stevens played 23 games as opposed to just 14 by Savard, it's safe to say that this was the first time the award was given to a player almost exclusively due to his defensive play.

21.28 True

Under most circumstances, notching three shutouts in the finals should be a lock for the Conn Smythe Trophy. But before the 2003 finals began, MVP voters were already picking their candidate: Jean-Sébastien Giguère. The Mighty Ducks netminder had carried Anaheim through three playoff rounds by defeating powerhouse teams Detroit and Dallas and then eliminating the upstart Minnesota Wild. In the final against New Jersey, Giguère pushed the Devils to the limit before losing Game 7. The Conn Smythe voters, professional hockey writers all, had their man—despite Brodeur's three 3–0 wins against Anaheim to capture the Cup. No goalie had accomplished such a feat since Frank McCool stunned Detroit with a trio of shutouts in 1945.

21.29 True

Although only 13 coaches have won the Stanley Cup in their inaugural season, the last four Cup-winning rookies have all come from behind the bench of the Canadiens. Toe Blake won in 1956, Claude Ruel in 1969, Al MacNeil in 1971 and Jean Perron in 1986. Jimmy Skinner was the last non-Montreal rookie coach to claim the trophy. Skinner led Detroit to the Cup in 1955. The league may be due for another rookie bench boss to win the championship: only one first-year coach—Jean Perron—has won a Cup since 1971.

21.30 False

Three coaches—Dick Irvin, Pat Burns and Mike Keenan—have coached three Original Six teams, but only Dick Irvin has won Cups with two different clubs from that famous hockey era between 1942 and 1967. Irvin coached Toronto to one Cup in 1932 and Montreal to three Cups in 1944, 1946 and 1953.

21.31 False

The New Jersey Devils won 1995's Stanley Cup despite not having home-ice advantage in any of the four series in which they played. The Devils posted a record 10 road victories, winning three times in Boston, twice in Pittsburgh, three times in Philadelphia and twice in Detroit.

21.32 True

The first penalty shot awarded in Cup finals action came on April 13, 1944, when Montreal's Bill Durnan stopped Chicago's Virgil Johnson. Johnson was one of several Americans in the NHL. Chicago dressed four other Yanks: Mike Karakas, Cully Dahlstrom, Fido Purpur and Vic Heyliger. Boston iced Irwin Boyd and Aldo Palazarri and New York had Bob Dill.

21.33 False

Nicklas Lidstrom was actually the seventh defenseman to win the Conn Smythe Trophy. The other blueliners to claim the hardware were Scott Stevens in 2000, Brian Leetch in 1994, Al MacInnis in 1989, Larry Robinson in 1978, Bobby Orr in 1970 and 1972 and Serge Savard in 1969.

21.34 False

Two teams have won the Cup after recording losing seasons—the 1938 Chicago Blackhawks and the 1949 Toronto Maple Leafs. The Hawks' triumph in 1938 was a real shocker. Chicago's win-loss-tie record was a pathetic 14–25–9.

21.35 False

The powerhouse Montreal Canadiens won five straight Stanley Cups between 1956 and 1960, missing only one league championship in 1956–57 when Detroit finished the regular season with 88 points, six better than Montreal's 82. Montreal finished in first place in each of the four remaining regular seasons during their Cup streak.

21.36 True

Born on February 29, 1936, Henri Richard celebrates his leap-year birthday once every four Gregorian calendar years. When he won his NHL-record 11th Stanley Cup in 1973 with Montreal, the Canadiens captain was technically just nine years old.

21.37 True

Theo Fleury became the last active member from the 1989 Stanley Cup-winning Calgary Flames when the second-to-last remaining Cup-winner, Gary Roberts, was traded to the Carolina Hurricanes on August 25, 1997. Calgary put its championship legacy to rest when Fleury was dealt to Colorado February 28, 1999.

21.38 False

Among the 45 penalty shots awarded in playoff action between 1937 and 2005, only two have come in overtime. Interestingly, neither shot resulted in a winning goal, but both involved the Pittsburgh Penguins in 3–2 scores. During a goal-mouth scramble in the second overtime period of Game 4 of the 1996 Pittsburgh–Washington quarterfinals, Pens defenseman Chris Tamer knocked the net off its moorings, an infraction that calls for an automatic penalty shot. The Caps selected Joé Juneau to take the shot but goalie Ken Wregget stopped him cold. The overtime lasted another 45 minutes before Petr Nedved scored to give Pittsburgh a 3–2 victory. In the only other playoff game with a penalty shot in an extra period, Montreal's Andy Moog stoned Aleksey Morozov of Pittsburgh, giving the Canadiens new life to score the winner in a 3–2 victory during the 1998 Conference quarterfinals.

21.39 True

Since 1987, when it became necessary to win four best-of-seven series to take the Cup, no team has swept all four playoff opponents. The 1988 Edmonton Oilers came the closest, winning 16 games and suffering only two losses.

GAME 21

Cup Quotes

IT WAS BRIAN LEETCH WHO ASKED, "Was that Dana Carvey?" after U.S. President Bill Clinton called to congratulate the New York Rangers for winning the Stanley Cup in 1994. Here are some other memorable champion quotes.

Solutions are on page 570

Wayne Gretzky	Gump Worsley	Mike Keenan	Olaf Kolzig
Mike Keane	Strip-club owner	Clark Gillies	Jeff Brown
Aerosmith's Steven Tyler			

1. _______ "This is the only thing that has seen more parties than us."
2. _______ "Tell him I can't hear a word he said. I've got a Stanley Cup ring in my ear." (On being criticized by a fellow player.)
3. _______ "Funny things happen when you've got a bunch of golf courses staring you in the face."
4. _______ "Why not? He's a good dog." (On his dog's behaviour with the Cup.)
5. _______ "If we do win this thing, that Cup's going to be beside me at the altar. I hope my wife doesn't get too mad."
6. _______ "You know you've come a long way when you look at the out-of-town scoreboards and there are no scores."
7. _______ "It was the first time I've seen our customers eager to touch something besides our dancers."
8. _______ "Tastes like horse pee from a tin cup."
9. _______ "I tell you it has its own personality. Like it's talking to you."

22

The Champions

WHAT CONSTITUTES A HOCKEY DYNASTY? There is no hard-and-fast rule, but many insist that a team has to capture three Stanley Cups in a row to qualify. As Steve Yzerman once noted: "Good teams win one, outstanding teams win two and a few truly great teams win three." Still, that definition would exclude the Edmonton Oilers, who won four Cups in five years in the 1980s, but not three in a row. While you consider that question, we'll fire some more your way on the subject of great teams.

Answers are on page 542

22.1 Which club holds the record for most consecutive first-place finishes?

A. The Montreal Canadiens
B. The Detroit Red Wings
C. The Edmonton Oilers
D. The New York Islanders

22.2 Regular-season champions don't always prevail in the playoffs. Of all the first-place finishers that failed to win the Cup, which team had the best regular-season winning percentage?

A. The 1929–30 Boston Bruins
B. The 1944–45 Montreal Canadiens
C. The 1970–71 Boston Bruins
D. The 1995–96 Detroit Red Wings

22.3 Which is the only NHL team to finish first in the regular season and yet fail to appear in the Stanley Cup playoffs?

A. The 1920–21 Ottawa Senators
B. The 1924–25 Hamilton Tigers
C. The 1929–30 Montreal Maroons
D. The 1941–42 New York Rangers

22.4 Which team beat the New Jersey Devils on the last weekend of the 1995–96 season to eliminate the defending Cup champions from playoff contention?

A. The Boston Bruins
B. The New York Islanders
C. The Ottawa Senators
D. The Tampa Bay Lightning

22.5 What is the greatest number of Canadian teams to qualify for the playoffs in one year?

A. Four teams
B. Five teams
C. Six teams
D. Seven teams

22.6 When the Boston Bruins failed to qualify for the playoffs in 1996–97, it ended a record streak of how many playoff appearances?

A. 20 consecutive postseasons
B. 23 consecutive postseasons
C. 26 consecutive postseasons
D. 29 consecutive postseasons

22.7 How many players from the Toronto Maple Leafs' 1966–67 Stanley Cup-winning squad finished in the top 20 regular-season scorers?

A. Two players
B. Four players
C. Six players
D. Eight players

22.8 Which dynasty holds the record for winning the most consecutive playoff series?

A. The 1950s Montreal Canadiens
B. The 1970s Montreal Canadiens
C. The 1980s New York Islanders
D. The 1980s Edmonton Oilers

22.9 Which team was the first to win 10 road games in one playoff year?

A. The 1993 Montreal Canadiens
B. The 1995 New Jersey Devils
C. The 1996 Colorado Avalanche
D. The 1998 Detroit Red Wings

22.10 Which NHL team was the first to win three consecutive Stanley Cups?

A. The Montreal Canadiens
B. The Detroit Red Wings
C. The Toronto Maple Leafs
D. The Boston Bruins

22.11 When the New Jersey Devils won the Stanley Cup in 1995, they broke a record for the most Americans on a Stanley Cup winner that dated back to which season?

A. 1937–38
B. 1957–58
C. 1977–78
D. 1987–88

22.12 Name the first American-based team to win the Stanley Cup.

A. The St. Louis Eagles
B. The Seattle Metropolitans
C. The New York Rangers
D. The Brooklyn Americans

22.13 Why were the New York Rangers forced to play every game of the 1950 Stanley Cup finals on the road?

A. The circus was using Madison Square Garden
B. Madison Square Garden was under renovation
C. Not enough tickets were sold in New York
D. The club couldn't pay its rent

22.14 How many years passed between the 1925 Victoria Cougars' Stanley Cup triumph and the next time a Western team won the Cup?

A. 10 to 20 years
B. 20 to 30 years
C. 30 to 40 years
D. More than 50 years

22.15 Which playoff upset is known as the "Miracle on Manchester"?

A. Chicago's upset of Toronto in the 1938 finals
B. Toronto's upset of Detroit in the 1949 finals
C. Los Angeles' upset of Edmonton in the 1982 division semifinals
D. The Islanders' upset of Pittsburgh in the 1993 division finals

22.16 Which underdog team from the 1986 playoffs is associated with the "Monday Night Miracle"?

A. The St. Louis Blues
B. The Montreal Canadiens
C. The Calgary Flames
D. The New York Rangers

22.17 Why will the Boston Bruins always remember the 1979 semifinals against Montreal?

A. It was the last time Boston made it to the semifinals
B. Boston lost the seventh game on a bad penalty
C. Boston coach Don Cherry was ejected from the game for fighting
D. Boston beat its long-time playoff adversary for the first time

22.18 In terms of total minutes played, which is the longest playoff series in NHL history?

A. New York Rangers vs. Boston 1939 semifinals
B. New Jersey vs. New York Rangers 1994 Conference finals
C. Colorado vs. Detroit 2002 Conference finals
D. Toronto vs. Philadelphia 2003 Conference quarterfinals

22.19 Which team made history by coming back from 3–1 series deficits twice in the same year?

A. The Anaheim Mighty Ducks
B. The Detroit Red Wings
C. The Minnesota Wild
D. The New York Islanders

22.20 The Detroit Red Wings' Russian unit played a key role in the team's march to the Stanley Cup in 1997. In how many of Detroit's 16 playoff wins did one of its five Russian players score a point?

A. In 13 wins
B. In 14 wins
C. In 15 wins
D. In all 16 wins

22.21 Which Stanley Cup champion of the 1990s featured a record six players who were former captains of other NHL clubs?

A. The 1992 Pittsburgh Penguins
B. The 1994 New York Rangers
C. The 1997 Detroit Red Wings
D. The 1999 Dallas Stars

22.22 How many formal challenges has the NHL received from non-NHL teams to play for the Cup since 1926?

A. Three challenges
B. Six challenges
C. Nine challenges
D. 12 challenges

22.23 Which was the first team to win the Stanley Cup in the Montreal Forum after it opened in 1924?

A. The Montreal Maroons
B. The Victoria Cougars
C. The New York Rangers
D. The Montreal Canadiens

22.24 Besides the Stanley Cup-champion New Jersey Devils in 1999–2000, how many other NHL clubs have defeated three 100-point teams en route to the title?

A. None
B. Only one other team
C. Three teams
D. Five teams

22.25 During one 1960 semifinals game between Toronto and Detroit, the Red Wings got some "extra help." What was it?

A. Players inhaled pure oxygen before hitting the ice
B. Jack Adams made a one-game coaching comeback
C. A sports psychologist sat on the bench
D. Three goalies were rotated during the game

22.26 Which team has won the Stanley Cup most often in overtime action in the Cup-winning game?

A. The Toronto Maple Leafs
B. The Detroit Red Wings
C. The Montreal Canadiens
D. The Philadelphia Flyers

22.27 Name the only team in NHL history to win the Stanley Cup in the seventh and deciding game in sudden-death overtime.

A. The Montreal Canadiens
B. The Edmonton Oilers
C. The Philadelphia Flyers
D. The Detroit Red Wings

22.28 To claim four Stanley Cups from 1976 to 1979, the Montreal Canadiens had to play between 16 final series games (four games per final to win four Cups) and 28 games in the four best-of-seven final series of 1976, 1977, 1978 and 1979. How many games did Montreal have to play in total during those four final rounds to win four Cups?

A. 16 games
B. 19 games
C. 22 games
D. 25 games

22.29 How many players from the 1995 Stanley Cup-winning New Jersey Devils played for the Colorado Rockies before that team moved its franchise to New Jersey in 1982?

A. None
B. One player
C. Two players
D. Three players

22.30 How many miles did the Pittsburgh Penguins travel during the 1992 playoffs to win the Stanley Cup?

A. 4,656 miles
B. 6,656 miles
C. 12,656 miles
D. 14,656 miles

22.31 During the NHL's six-team era from 1942–43 to 1966–67, what is the highest number of points a team finished out of first place in the regular season and went on to win the Stanley Cup?

A. Fewer than 15 points
B. Between 15 and 20 points
C. Between 20 and 25 points
D. More than 25 points

22.32 Which Stanley Cup-winning team finished the regular season with the highest number of points out of first place since NHL expansion in 1967?

A. The Montreal Canadiens of 1970–71
B. The New York Islanders of 1979–80
C. The Montreal Canadiens of 1985–86
D. The Colorado Avalanche of 1995–96

22.33 Since 1927, when competition for the Stanley Cup became limited to NHL teams, only one club that does not exist today has won the Cup. What was the name of the team?

A. The Hamilton Tigers
B. The Montreal Maroons
C. The Pittsburgh Pirates
D. The New York Americans

22.34 What made the 1951 Cup finals between Toronto and Montreal a "wild" series?

A. Every game went into overtime
B. Every game ended with a brawl
C. Every game had a penalty shot
D. Every game ended with the goalie pulled for an extra man

22.35 What made the 1954 Stanley Cup presentation ceremonies an historic occasion?

A. Both teams shook hands after the Cup ceremonies
B. A newly designed Cup was presented for the first time
C. The Cup was presented to a female owner
D. There was no Stanley Cup present

22.36 After the 1954 Cup finals, the Montreal Canadiens refused to participate in what long-standing tradition?

A. As winners, they didn't carry the Cup in the visitor's rink
B. As losers, they refused to shake hands with the winners
C. As losers, they gave no press conference
D. As winners, they celebrated with beer instead of champagne

22.37 In Stanley Cup finals action, what game had the most penalties by two teams?

A. Game 5 of the 1974 Philadelphia–Boston finals
B. Game 5 of the 1978 Montreal–Boston finals
C. Game 6 of the 1980 New York–Philadelphia finals
D. Game 4 of the 1986 Montreal–Calgary finals

22.38 What is the most penalty minutes amassed by two teams during a Stanley Cup finals?

A. 211 minutes
B. 311 minutes
C. 411 minutes
D. 511 minutes

22.39 Which was the last team composed entirely of Canadian-born players to win the Stanley Cup?

A. The 1975 Philadelphia Flyers
B. The 1977 Montreal Canadiens
C. The 1980 New York Islanders
D. The 1989 Calgary Flames

22.40 Which team iced the first Swedish-trained players to appear in a Stanley Cup finals?

A. The Detroit Red Wings
B. The Calgary Flames
C. The New York Rangers
D. The Toronto Maple Leafs

22.41 Of all the Stanley Cup-winning teams, which one had the most future Hall of Famers in its lineup?

A. The 1952 Detroit Red Wings
B. The 1956 Montreal Canadiens
C. The 1967 Toronto Maple Leafs
D. The 1973 Montreal Canadiens

Answers

22.1 B. The Detroit Red Wings

The Gordie Howe-led Detroit teams of the early 1950s were a formidable force. Detroit finished at the top of the NHL a record seven straight seasons from 1948–49 to 1954–55, winning four Stanley Cups. But as outstanding as these achievements are, had the Wings played up to their potential they could have won more. As the playoff favourites, the Motor City boys were upset in three separate series, each one costing them the championship. In the 1949 finals the Wings fell to the fourth-place Maple Leafs, a club that finished 18 points behind them in the standings. They were also surprised in the 1951 semifinals by the third-place Canadiens, who finished 36 points behind them, and in the 1953 semifinals by the third-place Bruins, who were 21 points back. The "what-ifs" are easy but count for nothing. On paper the Red Wings should have had seven Cups in a row.

22.2 A. The 1929–30 Boston Bruins

Based on regular-season performance, the 1929–30 Bruins rank as the biggest postseason flop in NHL history. Boston compiled a 38–5–1 win-loss-tie record, collecting 77 of a possible 88 points for a winning percentage of .875. Not even the 1995–96 Detroit Red Wings, who set a record for most regular-season wins, topped that. The Bruins' offense was led by the Dynamite Line of Cooney Weiland, Dit Clapper and Dutch Gainor; their defense was anchored by Hall of Famer Eddie Shore and Vezina Trophy-winning goalie Tiny Thompson. Few believed the Boston juggernaut could be stopped, but the Bruins proved unable to cope with the blinding speed of the Canadiens' Flying Frenchmen. They lost the best-of-three finals in two straight games. It was the first time that the Bruins lost back-to-back games all season.

Best Winning Percentages by Non-Cup Winners*

TEAM	GP	W	L	T	PCT
1929–30 Boston Bruins	44	38	5	1	.875
1944–45 Montreal Canadiens	50	38	8	4	.800
1995–96 Detroit Red Wings	82	62	13	7	.799
1970–71 Boston Bruins	78	57	14	7	.776
1985–86 Edmonton Oilers	80	56	17	7	.744

**Current to 2005*

22.3 B. The 1924–25 Hamilton Tigers

To accommodate two expansion teams in 1924–25, the NHL expanded its schedule from 24 to 30 games. The move sparked the league's first labour dispute. The first-place Hamilton Tigers refused to compete in the playoffs unless the team received a $200 raise per man as compensation for the six extra games it had played during the season. NHL president Frank Calder rejected the demand and the Hamilton players went on strike. Calder responded by suspending the striking players and fining them each $200. He also decreed that the second- and third-place teams, Montreal and Toronto, would meet to decide the NHL title. The next season, Hamilton's troublesome team was moved to New York, where it was renamed the Americans. Despite several bids, Hamilton has never made it back into the NHL.

22.4 C. The Ottawa Senators

Few defending Stanley Cup champions have ever plummeted in the ranks as quickly as the 1995–96 New Jersey Devils. The Devils' chances for a playoff berth went up in smoke as they crashed and burned on home ice in their final game of the regular season, losing 5–2 to the last-place Ottawa Senators. The anemic performance prompted coach Jacques Lemaire to declare, "There has to be a lack of leadership. You can't go out and play a game like that and say this team has leadership." Lemaire should know. He was a member of the 1969 Montreal Canadiens, the last team before New Jersey to suffer the indignity of failing to make the playoffs the year after winning the Stanley Cup.

22.5 D. Seven teams

In the days when one-third of NHL franchises had Canadian addresses and 16 clubs in the 21-team league qualified for postseason play, it wasn't unusual to see all or most of Canada's teams playoff bound. On two occasions—1982–83 and 1985–86—all seven Canadian teams earned a berth in the second season. In 1982–83, Edmonton and Montreal were the top teams north of the 49th parallel as Quebec, Calgary, Vancouver, Winnipeg and Toronto limped into the playoffs with .500 or worse. In 1985–86, Edmonton and Calgary were one-two in the Smythe Division and Quebec and Montreal were one-two in the Adams, while Winnipeg, Vancouver and Toronto won first-round dates due to their divisional rankings—despite finishing 16th, 17th and 18th overall.

22.6 D. 29 consecutive postseasons

The Bruins' streak of 29 straight playoff appearances is an NHL record, as is their string of 29 consecutive winning-regular-seasons, 1967–68 to 1995–96. The only team in North American pro sports to have a longer streak is baseball's New York Yankees, who had 39 winning seasons from 1926 to 1964. The Bruins missed the playoffs in 1966–67, the last year of the six-team era. Boston finished in the NHL cellar that season, but their future held great promise thanks to rookie-of-the-year Bobby Orr.

22.7 A. Two players

Common wisdom around the NHL in 1966–67 dictated that the Toronto Maple Leafs dynasty of the early 1960s was long over.

With an average age of 31, the Maple Leafs were considered too old to make another serious run at a championship. Toronto's offense certainly didn't scare anyone. Only two Leaf players—Dave Keon at 12th and Frank Mahovlich at 19th—placed among the top 20-point earners. Of the twenty 20-goal scorers in the league that season, just two were Leafs: Ron Ellis with 22 goals and Jim Pappin with 21. But Toronto's veteran crew could play solid defense, and with goalies Terry Sawchuk and Johnny Bower holding the fort, the club upset favourites Chicago and Montreal to capture the Stanley Cup.

22.8 C. The 1980s New York Islanders

During the Islanders' glory years, they captured four straight Stanley Cups and 19 straight playoff series. It's a record of sustained excellence that may never be broken. The closest contender is the Montreal Canadiens, who won 13 straight series from 1976 to 1980. The Isles' reign began in 1980, when they opened the playoffs with a three-games-to-one triumph over the Los Angeles Kings. The string continued until the 1984 finals when the Islanders were dethroned by the Edmonton Oilers, four games to one.

22.9 B. The 1995 New Jersey Devils

The Devils were one of the NHL's worst road teams during the 1994–95 lockout season, with an uninspired 8–14–2 mark. But New Jersey reversed the trend in the playoffs, going 10–1 on the road and defeating Boston, Pittsburgh, Philadelphia and Detroit to win its first Cup. As of 2004–05, two other teams have since hit double-digits in road wins: the Devils, again, in 2000, and the Calgary Flames in 2004, the only Cup-less team among the three.

22.10 C. The Toronto Maple Leafs

The real story of the NHL's first three-time Stanley Cup winner is the rebuilding job Conn Smythe and Hap Day performed after the Leafs failed to make the playoffs in 1946. And they did it almost overnight, starting on defense by recruiting big, tough talented rookies such as Garth Boesch, Gus Mortson, Jim Thomson and Bill Barilko. On offense, rookie-of-the-year Howie Meeker joined eight holdovers—Syl Apps, Ted Kennedy, Turk Broda, Don and Nick Metz, Bill Ezinicki, Gaye Stewart and Wally Stanowski—to form the nucleus of the Leafs' 1947 champions. Not satisfied, Smythe then engineered hockey's biggest trade up to that time, dealing five Leafs to Chicago for ace centre Max Bentley. Toronto now had Apps, Kennedy and Bentley, three of the top-six centres in the game, and enough firepower to drive three solid lines. The Leafs cruised through the 1948 playoffs, crushing the Wings in the Cup finals in four straight, then repeated the deed in 1949, victimizing Detroit and Howe's mighty Production Line. On their path to history the Leafs dominated three successive Cup finals, winning 12 of 14 games, with nine straight victories.

22.11 A. 1937–38

It's hard to imagine a Stanley Cup winner today without a small contingent of Americans, but 60 years ago, when the NHL was almost completely populated by Canadian players, it would have been unthinkable. In the old eight-team NHL, U.S.-born players were a rarity. So when Chicago Blackhawks owner Major Fredric McLaughlin seized upon the idea of an all-American team in 1936–37, it must have been thought of as lunacy. The following season, the patriotic McLaughlin even appointed an American, major-league baseball umpire Bill Stewart, as coach. McLaughlin's boys didn't disappoint the sceptics during the regular season, with Chicago posting a sub-.500 with a 14–25–9 record. But something unexpected happened in the playoffs. His name was Mike Karakas. The Chicago netminder from Aurora, Minnesota, stole the Cup in what is still regarded as one of hockey's greatest postseason upsets. In all, a record eight Americans suited up for the Hawks during that remarkable postseason, just four fewer than the 12 who helped New Jersey win the championship in 1995.

22.12 B. The Seattle Metropolitans

When the Metros defeated the Canadiens in 1917, Seattle became the first American city to claim the Cup. In those days, the Stanley Cup was a challenge trophy, disputed by pro teams from the eastern and western leagues. The first American-based NHL team to win the Cup, the New York Rangers, did so in 1928.

22.13 A. The circus was using Madison Square Garden

Logistical conflicts between Barnum & Bailey's circus and the Stanley Cup finals have a rich tradition at Madison Square Garden. Ever since the 1920s, if "the biggest show on earth" was at MSG, the Rangers were forced to play their home games on the road at a designated "home" site. In 1928, New York played the entire finals against the Maroons at the Montreal Forum. They won the Cup that year, but most other playoff seasons were more demanding. In 1950, the Rangers spent a lot of time riding trains between Detroit's Olympia and their "away-home" of Maple Leaf Gardens in Toronto. Going into Game 6 the Rangers were on a roll, ahead 3–2 in the series. But the next game, scheduled for Toronto, was moved to Detroit because an NHL rule required that a deciding Stanley Cup game could not be played at a neutral site. So Detroit became the home site for the visiting Rangers. And since Game 7 was also a deciding Cup-game, it was also played at the Olympia. In all, five games were played in Detroit and just two in Toronto (and obviously none in New York). In Game 7, the Red Wings prevailed in double overtime before a wild hometown crowd. The Rangers were crushed. A New York hockey crowd under similar circumstances may have helped the boys in blue. Today, things are different: MSG can accommodate both the circus and hockey. While the 1996 playoff games roared on, for example, not 50 feet from the penalty box, a backstage area was filled with elephants, lions and trapeze equipment.

22.14 D. More than 50 years

Before 1926, when the NHL assumed ownership of the Stanley Cup, the Cup was a challenge trophy awarded to the winners of a playoff series between the champions of Canada's eastern and western leagues. Although the Pacific Coast Hockey Association (PCHA) can be credited with expanding the interest and talent in hockey during its brief 15-year existence, it could do little to compete with the NHL once expansion into the United States raised the stakes and secured the best players during the 1920s. Attendance in the west fell and soon its two leagues collapsed, ending the annual east-west Cup-challenge and any further hopes of a western Cup-winner. After the Victoria Cougars' Cup-victory in 1925, the west waited more than a half-century for another Stanley Cup champion. The return of Lord Stanley's mug came in 1984 when the Edmonton Oilers defeated the New York Islanders.

22.15 C. Los Angeles' upset of Edmonton in the 1982 division semifinals

In 1981–82, the Edmonton Oilers emerged as a powerhouse, finishing second to the New York Islanders in the overall standings and claiming their first Smythe Division flag. Led by Wayne Gretzky, who rewrote the record book with a 92-goal, 212-point season, Edmonton became the first team in history to reach the 400-goal mark. But all that gaudy offense went to waste in the playoffs; the Oilers were ambushed by the fourth-place Los Angeles Kings in the best-of-five division semifinals. The turning point came on April 10, 1982, in Game 3, when the Kings rallied from a 5–0 deficit, forcing overtime on a goal by Steve Bozek at 19:55, then winning the game on a goal by rookie Daryl Evans at 2:25 of sudden death. The comeback became known as the "Miracle on Manchester," after the location of the Kings' arena on Manchester Boulevard in Inglewood, California. It is the greatest single-game playoff comeback in NHL history.

22.16 A. The St. Louis Blues

The Montreal Canadiens may have delivered the biggest surprise during the 1986 postseason, but their Stanley Cup championship was just one of the miracles performed that spring. After finishing the regular season just three games over .500, St. Louis fashioned its own string of playoff upsets, missing a trip to the Cup finals by just one game. The Blues first dropped heavily favoured Minnesota and then knocked off Toronto, both series going the distance. In the Conference finals against Calgary, they played underdogs again, inferior to the Flames in almost every position on the ice. Down 3–2 in the series and 5–2 in the score in Game 6, the Blues, just 12 minutes from elimination, pulled off their biggest shocker before 18,000 rabid fans at St. Louis Arena. They scored three times, the last goal with just 1:08 remaining, to tie the game 5–5 and force overtime. In the extra period, Doug Wickenheiser potted the winner against Mike Vernon. St. Louis lost a 2–1 soul destroyer to Calgary in Game 7, but the rally in Game 6 was unforgettable. For many Blues it was their proudest moment and will forever be remembered as the Monday Night Miracle.

22.17 B. Boston lost the seventh game on a bad penalty

Any Boston fan over the age of 35 remembers 1979. It was the year the Bruins bumbled the semifinals against Montreal and lost a Stanley Cup that was almost assuredly theirs. In Game 7 of the semis, with Boston leading 4–3 in the dying moments of regulation time, the Bruins got a bench penalty for too many men on the ice. On the ensuing power play, as the clock ticked down, the Canadiens' Jacques Lemaire streaked across Boston's blue line and dropped the puck to Guy Lafleur. The winger smoked a 30-footer into the low far corner past a startled Gilles Gilbert, who fell backwards in dramatic fashion, as if blown over by the puck's speed. In overtime, Yvon Lambert scored the winner, once more breaking Boston's spirit in the playoffs. The finals was played in anti-climactic fashion, as Montreal easily handled the New York Rangers to win their fourth straight Cup.

22.18 A. New York Rangers vs. Boston 1939 semifinals

New York and Boston battled through eight overtime periods in their seven-game death match in 1939. The series included a pair of triple-overtime marathons, the first occurring in Game 1 and the second in Game 7, which was won 2–1 by Boston on Mel Hill's goal at 48:00 of OT. The total series playing time was nine hours, 13 minutes, eight seconds. The Leafs–Flyers seven-game struggle in 2003 ranks second, clocking in at eight hours, 52 minutes, five seconds.

22.19 C. The Minnesota Wild

They were a team of castoffs who shocked not one, but two, star-filled clubs into elimination reality. The Wild had a bunch of no-names, but enough heart, character and audacity to come back from the brink twice—facing 3–1 deficits to 4–3 series wins against Colorado in the first round, followed by Vancouver in the second round during the 2003 playoffs. To say they did it with "the trap" would be unfair to coach Jacques Lemaire's mix-and-match lineup of muckers, grinders, role-players and one budding superstar in Marian Gaborik. There were no fancy-pants skaters on this blue-collar team, but in each game a different player stepped up, including goal-tenders Dwayne Roloson and Manny Fernandez. Minnesota ran out of gas during the Conference finals and was swept by the Anaheim Mighty Ducks.

22.20 C. In 15 wins

Detroit's talented Russian five—Sergei Fedorov, Slava Kozlov, Igor Larionov, Vladimir Konstantinov and Slava Fetisov—were criticized for not performing up to expectations in the club's disappointing playoff showing in 1996. But no one complained about the quintet's play in the 1997 playoffs. In Detroit's upset of the defending-champion Colorado Avalanche in the Western Conference finals, the Russians scored nine of the Wings' 16 goals. All told, Detroit's playoff record was a dazzling 15–0 when one of its Russian players registered a point. The only Detroit win they did not score in was the 2–1 Cup-clinching victory versus the Flyers. After the game, Larionov said, "I've been playing professional hockey for 20 years, and this is the happiest moment in my life. We've got five Russians and I've heard every player gets the Cup for two days. Five times two: 10 days. So we can take it to Russia for the Russian people to enjoy it, to touch it."

22.21 D. The 1999 Dallas Stars

The Stars' 1999 roster was laden with veteran leaders. In addition to captain Derian Hatcher, six other Dallas players had previously captained NHL teams. The list included Guy Carbonneau (Montreal, 1989–94), Mike Keane (Montreal, 1994–96), Joe Nieuwendyk (Calgary, 1991–95), Brett Hull (St. Louis, 1992–96), Pat Verbeek (Hartford, 1992–95) and Brian Skrudland (Florida, 1993–97).

22.22 A. Three challenges

If the original intentions of Lord Stanley were still being carried out as he had wished for his famous Cup, we might see a very different playoff format today. Rather than belonging to any one league, Stanley left specific instructions that his trophy was to be a challenge Cup. Under those guidelines, any beer league champions today could mount a challenge to get their names on the Stanley Cup. Although not an appealing prospect for hockey fans, it might make a great TV commercial. Nevertheless, since the NHL took control of the Cup in 1926, the league has had three formal challenges from non-NHL clubs: the 1931 Tulsa Oilers of the American Hockey Association, the 1932 Chicago Shamrocks of the AHA and the 1952 Cleveland Barons of the AHL. In each case, the NHL refused to meet in a showdown. A less serious challenge was mounted by the Lethbridge Community College Kodiaks during the 1992 player's lockout. Then, in April 2005, Toronto lawyer Tim Gilbert filed a claim in Ontario Superior Court, hoping to force the Cup's trustees to name a 2005 champion, even though the 2004–05 NHL season was cancelled due to a labour lockout.

22.23 A. The Montreal Maroons

Contrary to popular thought, the Forum was built for the Maroons, not the Canadiens. The famous arena was just two years old in 1926 when it hosted its first Stanley Cup celebration. The NHL sophomore Maroons challenged the Victoria Cougars, who came east after an exhausting 45-game season and a 3,000-mile train ride. But the cross-continent trip was in vain; the Maroons dispatched the Cougars in four games, three by shutouts. The New York Rangers won the next Cup on Forum ice in 1928. It wasn't until 1930 that the Canadiens won their first championship at the Forum, beating Boston in two straight games in the best-of-three final.

22.24 B. Only one other team

As of 2004–05, only two Stanley Cup champions have battled three 100-point regular-season teams during their playoff drive. In 1979–80, the 91-point New York Islanders won their first Stanley Cup after defeating three of the top four regular-season teams in their four playoff series. The Isles beat Los Angeles (74 points), Boston (105 points), Buffalo (110 points) and Philadelphia (116 points). It was an NHL first. New Jersey's championship in 2000 was just the second time three 100-point teams lost to the Stanley Cup winners. The Devils overcame Florida (98 points), Toronto (100 points), Philadelphia (105 points) and Dallas (102 points). The extra point for overtime regular-season losses accounted for some of the Leafs', Flyers' and Stars' team points. In fact, during 1999–2000, a record-tying seven NHL clubs recorded 100-points or more. In 1980, when the Islanders defeated three 100-point teams, four teams in regular-season action had 100 points or more.

22.25 A. Players inhaled pure oxygen before hitting the ice

Coaches carry an arsenal of tricks to motivate players; sometimes even the bizarre ones work. But strike the "wonders" of pure oxygen from that list. During the 1960 Detroit–Toronto semifinals, with the series deadlocked a game apiece, the Red Wings used pure oxygen to gain an edge in Game 3. Ahead 4–3 in the third, the strategy seemed to be working, when Wings rookie Gerry Melnyk tied the score. But, after 43 minutes of extra time, Leaf great Frank Mahovlich notched the winner, blowing the air (so to speak) out of the oxygen theory. Afterwards, Toronto coach Punch Imlach dismissed it as "a gimmick." Imlach should know. He had his own motivational scheme. Early in the series, Imlach had piled $1,250 worth of bills in the dressing room and scrawled on the blackboard: "Take a good look at the centre of the floor. This represents the difference between winning and losing." Imlach's Leafs won the series in six.

22.26 C. The Montreal Canadiens

As of 2004–05, the NHL has seen 15 Stanley Cup champions declared in overtime. Considering Montreal has won 23 championships in NHL history, it's a safe bet that the Habs would also lead in Cup-deciding overtime games. The Canadiens played in six sudden-death matches, winning four Cups (1944, 1953, 1966 and 1977) and losing two (1951 and 1954) in overtime decisions.

22.27 D. The Detroit Red Wings

It doesn't get any better than when one shot on net clinches the whole season and the Stanley Cup championship. And Detroit knows this better than any other team. In 1950, the Red Wings battled the Rangers into seventh-game overtime, winning at 8:31 of the second overtime period. Then, four years later, they pushed the envelope again, to a seventh-game overtime against the Canadiens. They won again, the only team ever to win the Stanley Cup in a seventh game overtime, and they did it twice. The heroes: Pete Babando in 1950 and Tony Leswick in 1954.

22.28 B. 19 games

During their four-in-a-row championship streak from 1976 to 1979, the dynasty Canadiens lost only three of 19 games played in four finals. In 1976, Montreal embarrassed the Flyers in four straight; in 1977, they swept Boston, winning Game 4 in overtime; in 1978, Boston came back and managed two victories; and in 1979, the Rangers went down in four straight after taking the first game of the series. Philadelphia's Reggie Leach may have said it best: "The Canadiens have one hell of a hockey team. They've got guys who skate 400 miles an hour and there was no way we could keep up with them." Eight players from that Canadiens team became Hall of Famers.

22.29 A. None

Ironically, the last Rockie to play with New Jersey was Aaron Broten, kid brother of 1995 Cup-winning Devil, Neal Broten. Aaron played one season with Colorado before the team moved to New Jersey, where he stayed seven years until his trade to the Minnesota North Stars on January 5, 1990. Brother Neal had better timing, coming to the Devils midseason from Minnesota's successor, the Dallas Stars, in 1995. The longest-surviving Devils to become 1995 Cup-champions are Ken Daneyko, Bruce Driver and John MacLean, who began their NHL careers in New Jersey in 1983–84, the Devils' second NHL season.

22.30 A. 4,656 miles

Considering that Cup finalists play best-of-seven series in four rounds while jetting between NHL buildings scattered across North America, it's amazing that the Penguins only travelled 4,656 miles to victory. Although the 1992 champs dispatched the Bruins and the Blackhawks in the minimum four games, geography played the biggest part in cutting down on their flyer miles. No league franchise is closer to more eastern and mid-western NHL cities than Pittsburgh.

22.31 D. More than 25 points

While the NHL was still reeling from Maurice Richard's stunning 50-goal season in 1944–45, another shocker came during the playoffs courtesy of third-place Toronto. In the first round, the spunky Maple Leafs defeated Richard's first-place Canadiens in six gruelling games and then pulled out a seven-game squeaker against Detroit to win the Stanley Cup. Toronto engineered the biggest upset of the six-team era, finishing the regular season with 52 points, 28 points behind league-leading Montreal (80 points). Interestingly, two other Toronto teams recorded the next-biggest upsets between 1942–43 and 1966–67. The 1948–49 Maple Leafs finished in fourth place and 18 points back of top spot to capture the Cup; and in 1966–67, Toronto's so-called "over-the-hill gang" surprised Montreal with a Stanley Cup championship after finishing 19 points out of first place.

22.32 C. The Montreal Canadiens of 1985–86

Six teams finished ahead of Montreal in the overall standings in 1985–86. Edmonton, with 119 points, held an astounding 32-point lead over the Canadiens, who struggled to finish with 87 points. By chance, during Montreal's four playoff rounds they faced only one club with a better regular-season record, the sixth-place Calgary Flames. That and a record number of Montreal rookies, including a new goaltender by the name of Patrick Roy, made history in the finals as Montreal defeated the Flames in five games to capture its 23rd Stanley Cup. Twenty-year-old Roy became the youngest player to win the Conn Smythe Trophy as playoff MVP.

Largest Point Spread Between First-Place Teams and Cup-Winners*

POINT-YEAR	FIRST-PLACE TEAM	POINTS	STANLEY CUP WINNER	POINTS	SPREAD
1985–86	Edmonton	119	Montreal	87	32
1995–96	Detroit	131	Colorado	104	27
1979–80	Philadelphia	116	NYI	91	25
1970–71	Boston	121	Montreal	97	24

**Since 1967–68; current to 2004–05*

22.33 B. The Montreal Maroons

In their brief 13-year history, the Maroons won the Stanley Cup twice. Their first triumph came in 1926, the last year that teams outside the NHL were able to compete for the Cup, when they beat the Western Hockey League champion Victoria Cougars in the finals. The Maroons won the Cup again in 1935, defeating Toronto in three straight games in the finals. They folded after the 1937–38 season but retain the distinction of being the last defunct NHL team to have won hockey's greatest prize.

22.34 A. Every game went into overtime

Even though the 1951 Toronto–Montreal best-of-seven Stanley Cup finals ended in just five games, every match was a thriller, requiring sudden-death overtime to settle each outcome. But all the overtimes ended quickly, in under six minutes, with the Maple Leafs summarily dispatching the Canadiens in all but Game 2. If there was a series star, it would have to be Toronto's Bill Barilko. During Game 1, he dove headfirst into the Leafs' open net to stop Maurice Richard's slap shot and preserve a 2–2 score in regulation time. In the series' final game, he whipped the puck past Montreal goalie Gerry McNeil for the overtime Cup-winner.

22.35 C. The Cup was presented to a female owner

Instead of the usual all-male gathering at centre ice for Cup presentations, the 1954 ceremonies at Detroit's Olympia featured Marguerite Norris, who received the Stanley Cup as Red Wing co-owner. Norris, upon the death of her father, James, became the NHL's first female executive and the first woman to have her name officially engraved on the Cup. It's an honour slightly tarnished by the legend of Lily Murphy, who allegedly had her name scratched into Lord Stanley's bowl at the request of her husband, Dennis Murphy, president of the Bank of Ottawa, after the original Ottawa Senators won the Cup in 1911. Since Norris broke the glass ceiling in 1954, several women are on the Cup's patina, including Sonia Scurfield, co-owner of the champion 1989 Calgary Flames; Marie-Denise DeBartolo York, president of the 1991 Pittsburgh Penguins; and Nancy Beard, executive assistant of the 2002 Detroit Red Wings.

22.36 B. As losers, they refused to shake hands with the winners

White-hot intensity is perhaps the best description for the Red Wings–Canadiens rivalry of the 1950s. Each game, regular or postseason, was a bitter contest between two teams that literally hated each other. Detroit had Gordie Howe, "Terrible" Ted Lindsay and shutout king Terry Sawchuk. Montreal had Maurice Richard, Jean Béliveau and defensive stalwart Doug Harvey. Their mutual hatred became legend during 1954's Cup finals in Game 7 when the two clubs tied 1–1 and headed into overtime. At 4:29 of the extra period, Harvey tried to glove a Tony Leswick shot and instead deflected the puck over Montreal goalie Gerry McNeil's shoulder. To have come so far and lose the Cup on such a bad goal to your worst enemy was too much for Montreal coach Dick Irvin. He led his team off the ice before the customary handshakes, later commenting: "If I had shaken hands, I wouldn't have meant it. I refuse to be a hypocrite."

22.37 A. Game 5 of the 1974 Philadelphia–Boston finals

It's to be expected that any 1970s playoff matchup between the Flyers and Bruins would spark a few NHL records in box time, especially in Cup finals action. In Game 5, with the Big Bad Bruins down 3–1 in games to the Broad Street Bullies, no-holds-barred hockey brought out the worst in the two clubs. A series record of 43 penalties were called in a procession of fights, high-stickings, spearings and butt-ending infractions. Boston won the May 16 mêlée 5–1 but crashed in Game 6 at the Philadelphia Spectrum, losing the Cup by a 1–0 decision to the Flyers. The six-game series produced a total of 142 penalties by both teams, an NHL record.

22.38 D. 511 minutes

Calgary and Montreal duelled in 1986's five-game final, accumulating a record 511 penalty minutes, split almost evenly between the Flames (256 minutes) and the Canadiens (255 minutes). Although the series is best remembered for rookie standouts Patrick Roy and Claude Lemieux, and the fastest goal in overtime playoff action by Brian Skrudland, a total of six NHL team penalty records for a finals were set. The record numbers were jacked up by a third-period brawl in Game 4, which accounted for 152 penalty minutes. A league-record 80 minutes went to the Canadiens with 25 minutes handed out to Claude Lemieux, who was assessed one minor, one major, one misconduct and one game misconduct.

22.39 A. The 1975 Philadelphia Flyers

The Broad Street Bullies was the last all-Canadian-born contingent of players to win the Stanley Cup. All of the other teams in our question had non-Canadians in their lineups. The 1977 Montreal Canadiens iced American-born Bill Nyrop and Mike Polich, and Venezuelan-born Rick Chartraw; the 1980 Islanders sported Stefan Persson, Bob Nystrom and Anders Kallur of Sweden; the 1989 Flames had Americans Joe Mullen and Gary Suter, and Swede Hakan Loob.

22.40 C. The New York Rangers

The first Swedes to skate in a Stanley Cup finals were Anders Hedberg and Ulf Nilsson of the Rangers. New York plucked the pair from the WHA Winnipeg Jets, where they starred with Bobby Hull for four seasons before their free-agent signings in June 1978. The Swedes brought the Rangers style and skill, and a chance, after a seven-year absence, at the Stanley Cup, in 1979. Unfortunately, New York, who had surprised everyone in the semifinals by beating the up-and-coming Islanders, met the reigning champion Montreal Canadiens. The Rangers took Game 1 but never won another match. Hedberg scored one goal in the Cup finals, an NHL first for a Swede, while Nilsson appeared in just two games.

22.41 D. The 1973 Montreal Canadiens

Although it's rarely cited as one of the greatest teams of all time, this Montreal Stanley Cup winner had a record 11 future Hall of Famers on its roster. The list includes Ken Dryden, Serge Savard, Larry Robinson, Guy Lapointe, Jacques Laperriere, Guy Lafleur, Steve Shutt, Henri Richard, Frank Mahovlich, Yvan Cournoyer and Jacques Lemaire.

Game 1: Strange Starts

PART 1

1. D. Brett Hull, Calgary Flames
2. G. Cam Neely, Vancouver Canucks
3. F. Reggie Leach, Boston Bruins
4. C. Billy Smith, Los Angeles Kings
5. B. Tony Esposito, Montreal Canadiens
6. A. Rick Middleton, New York Rangers
7. E. Randy Carlyle, Toronto Maple Leafs

PART 2

1. B. Dominik Hasek, Chicago Blackhawks
2. G. Eddie Shack, New York Rangers
3. E. Rick Kehoe, Toronto Maple Leafs
4. F. Bernie Parent, Boston Bruins
5. A. Mats Sundin, Quebec Nordiques
6. D. Teemu Selanne, Winnipeg Jets
7. C. Marcel Dionne, Detroit Red Wings

Game 2: Hockey Crossword

Game 3: Captains of Time

1. K. Johnny Bucyk, 11 seasons with Boston
2. D. George Armstrong, 12 seasons with Toronto
3. J. Pierre Pilote, seven seasons with Chicago
4. I. Alex Delvecchio, 11 seasons with Detroit
5. B. Jean Béliveau, 10 seasons with Montreal
6. H. Bob Gainey, eight seasons with Montreal
7. E. Bill Cook, 11 seasons with New York
8. F. Brian Sutter, seasons years with St. Louis
9. G. Hap Day, 10 seasons with Toronto
10. L. Stan Smyl, nine seasons with Vancouver
11. A. Rod Langway, 11 seasons with Washington
12. C. Ray Bourque, 11 seasons with Boston

Game 4: Bloodlines

Pavel/Valeri Bure
Frank/Pete Mahovlich
Bobby/Brett Hull
Max/Doug Bentley
Phil/Tony Esposito
Gordie/Mark Howe
Kevin/Derian Hatcher
Scott/Rob Niedermayer
Geoff/Russ Courtnall
Maurice/Henri Richard
Dale/Dave Hunter
Brian/Brent Sutter
Eric/Brett Lindros
Pierre/Sylvain Turgeon
Neal/Aaron Broten
Ken/Dave Dryden
Daniel/Henrik Sedin
Wayne/Brent Gretzky
Joe/Brian Mullen
Peter/Anton Stastny
Marcel/Gilbert Dionne
Chris/Sean Pronger

Game 5: What's in a Name?

1. Dany Heatley
2. Nashville
3. Run the goalie
4. Punch Imlach
5. Ron Hextall
6. Nikolai Khabibulin
7. Bench-clearing brawl
8. Bernie Nicholls
9. Punch Line
10. Frank Mahovlich
11. Sudden-death goal
12. Glenn Healey
13. Jocelyn Thibault
14. Pinch the play

Game 6: Stanley's MVPs

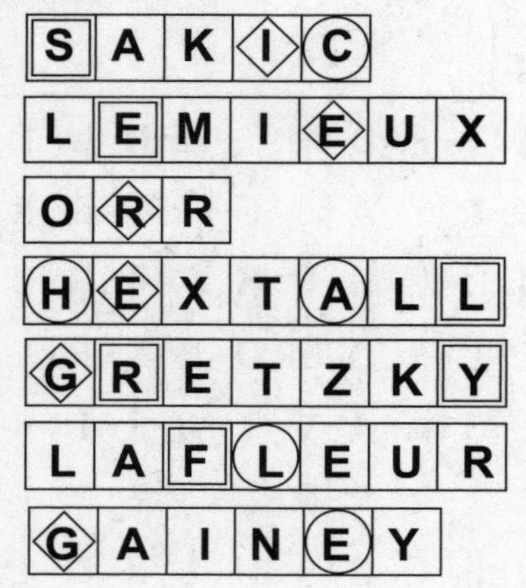

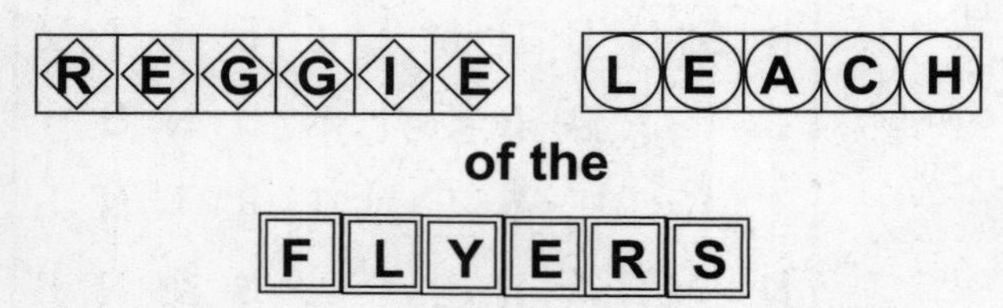

As of 2005, only one forward from a losing team has won MVP status in the postseason. It was **REGGIE LEACH** of the **FLYERS** in 1976.

Game 7: *Frère Jacques* (French 101)

1. E. Patrick Roy, King
2. J. Pat LaFontaine, The Fountain
3. L. Simon Gagné, Win
4. G. Eric Desjardins, The Gardens
5. B. Michel Petit, Small
6. A. Guy Lafleur, The Flower
7. D. Jacques Lemaire, The Mayor
8. C. Vincent Lecavalier, The Knight
9. K. Wilf Paiement, Payment
10. H. Sylvain Côté, Side
11. I. Rod Brind'Amour, Little Bit of Love
12. F. Mario Lemieux, The Best

Game 8: Puck Crossword

Game 9: The First Time

1. Paul Coffey became the first rearguard to score 100 points for two teams on March 20, 1989, after campaigns with Edmonton and Pittsburgh.
2. Red Kelly won the first Norris Trophy on May 10, 1954.
3. Babe Pratt notched six assists on January 8, 1944. No other defenseman had accomplished the feat before.
4. Bill Gadsby scored his 500th career point on November 4, 1962, becoming the first NHL rearguard to reach the number.
5. Paul Reinhart was the NHL's first defenseman to score two playoff hat tricks. The mark was set on April 8, 1984.
6. Mark Howe became the first D-man to score a pair of shorthanded goals in one game, on October 9, 1980.
7. Ian Turnbull scored five times on February 2, 1977, to become the first five-goal blueliner.
8. Denis Potvin was the first D-man to net 1,000 points in a career. It happened on April 4, 1987.
9. Bobby Orr became the first modern-day defenseman to score a hat trick in the playoffs, on April 11, 1971.

Game 10: The Player's Choice

O	R	R	E	L	L	E	T	A	R
L	T	D	V	O	R	O	D	E	F
E	A	I	O	D	I	O	N	N	E
I	K	F	S	M	I	N	N	I	G
X	G	R	L	O	R	G	A	J	R
U	R	I	A	E	P	K	M	H	E
E	E	A	N	L	U	S	R	S	T
I	I	E	L	L	C	R	E	K	Z
M	S	C	I	K	A	S	Z	B	K
E	S	H	U	L	L	U	Y	F	Y
L	E	F	T	D	R	A	W	A	A
L	M	O	S	O	R	D	N	I	L

In descending order, the 19 remaining circled letters spell out: **DOMINIK HASEK BUFFALO**. Hasek is the only goalie since Mike Liut to win the Pearson. He did it in back-to-back years, 1997 and 1998.

Game 11: Big Trades

1.	G. Patrick Roy, Mike Keane Montreal	for	Andrei Kovalenko, Martin Rucinsky, Jocelyn Thibault Colorado
2.	D. Ray Bourque, Dave Andreychuk Boston	for	Brian Rolston, Martin Grenier Colorado
3.	E. Todd Bertuzzi, Bryan McCabe The New York Islanders	for	Trevor Linden Vancouver
4.	A. Mats Sundin, Garth Butcher Quebec	for	Wendel Clark, Todd Warriner, Sylvain Lefebvre Toronto
5.	C. Brett Hull Calgary	for	Rob Ramage, Rick Green St. Louis
6.	B. John LeClair, Eric Desjardins Montreal	for	Mark Recchi Philadelphia
7.	F. Wayne Gretzky, Marty McSorley, Mike Krushelnyski Edmonton	for	Jimmy Carson, Martin Gelinas, with draft picks/cash Los Angeles

Game 12: Backup to the Greats

PART 1

1. D. Manny Legace backed up Dominik Hasek/Detroit 2002
2. E. Charlie Hodge backed up Gump Worsley/Montreal 1966
3. B. Rick Wamsley backed up Mike Vernon/Calgary 1989
4. F. Wayne Stephenson backed up Bernie Parent/Philadelphia 1975
5. C. Roman Turek backed up Ed Belfour/Dallas 1999
6. G. Eddie Johnston backed up Gerry Cheevers/Boston 1970
7. A. David Aebischer backed up Patrick Roy/Colorado 2001

PART 2

1. E. Corey Schwab backed up Martin Brodeur/New Jersey 2003
2. G. Grant Fuhr backed up Bill Ranford/Edmonton 1990
3. F. Michel Larocque backed up Ken Dryden/Montreal 1978
4. D. Glenn Healy backed up Mike Richter/NY Rangers 1994
5. C. Don Simmons backed up Johnny Bower/Toronto 1964
6. A. Ken Wregget backed up Tom Barrasso/Pittsburgh 1992
7. B. Roland Melanson backed up Billy Smith/NY Islanders 1983

Game 13: Rearguard Records

Nicklas Lidstrom
Paul Coffey
Ray Bourque
Al MacInnis
Doug Wilson
Chris Pronger
Rob Blake
Bobby Orr
Phil Housley
Denis Potvin
Larry Robinson
Larry Murphy
Gary Suter
Ian Turnbull
Brian Leetch
Chris Chelios
Steve Duchesne
Tom Bladon
Serge Savard
Doug Harvey
Rod Langway
Eddie Shore

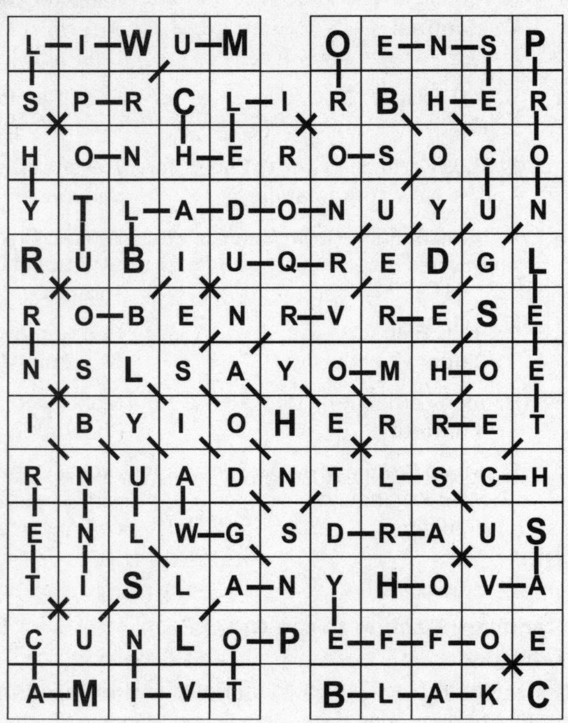

Game 14: The Ultimate 30-Goal Man

MIKE GARTNER is the only NHLer to score 30 goals in a season with five different teams: the Washington Capitals, Minnesota North Stars, New York Rangers, Toronto Maple Leafs and Phoenix Coyotes.

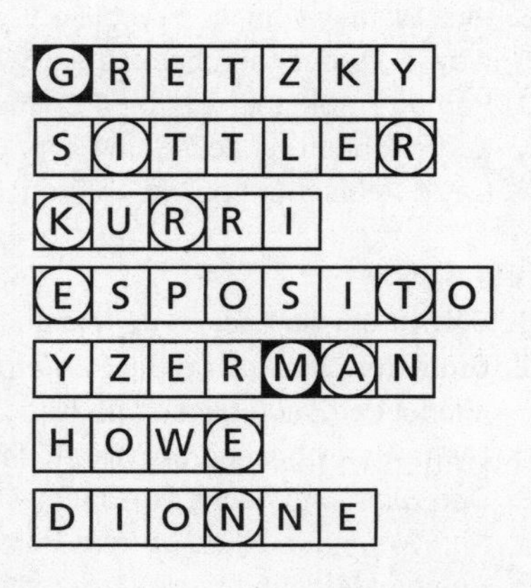

Game 15: Goalie Gunners

1. First goalie to score a goal: Billy Smith, the New York Islanders, November 28, 1979
2. First goalie to shoot and score a goal: Ron Hextall, Philadelphia, December 8, 1987
3. First goalie to score a game-winner: Martin Brodeur, New Jersey, February 15, 2000
4. First goalie to score a goal and record a shutout in the same game: Damian Rhodes, Ottawa, January 2, 1999
5. First goalie to shoot and score a goal and record a shutout in the same game: José Théodore, Montreal, January 2, 2001
6. First goalie to score a power-play goal: Evgeni Nabokov, San Jose, March 10, 2002
7. First goalie to receive credit for an assist: Tiny Thompson, Boston, January 14, 1936
8. First goalie to score 10 points in one season: Grant Fuhr, Edmonton, 1983–84
9. First goalie to score three points in one game: Jeff Reese, Calgary, February 10, 1993

Game 16: Stanley Cup Captains

In descending order the 12 remaining letters spell out: **CHUCK GARDINER,** the only goalie to captain an NHL team to Stanley Cup greatness. Gardiner was the key to Chicago's success in 1933–34. While his Blackhawks sputtered on offense and scored a league-low 88 goals during the regular season, Gardiner sparkled, leading all other netminders that year with just 83 goals-against. In the best-of-five finals against Detroit, he limited the Red Wings to two goals in his club's three victories. The Blackhawks were repeat Cup-winners in 1938, again managing the lowest regular-season goal-count. Chicago's goalie that year was Mike Karakas.

S	H	U	P	U	A	E	V	I	L	E	B
C	T	A	O	H	Y	A	S	D	N	I	L
G	R	E	T	Z	K	Y	R	E	M	U	Y
E	E	N	V	C	L	A	R	K	E	C	O
R	P	N	I	E	H	K	L	A	S	D	U
A	P	O	N	C	N	E	G	L	S	A	N
R	A	B	I	A	B	S	R	B	I	Y	G
D	L	R	G	A	I	N	E	Y	E	Z	N
Y	C	A	H	T	N	A	M	R	R	E	R
D	L	C	O	U	R	N	O	Y	E	R	O
E	K	D	D	L	A	N	O	D	C	M	H
N	A	G	N	O	R	T	S	M	R	A	G
N	S	I	H	I	T	C	H	M	A	N	E
E	S	P	P	A	X	U	E	I	M	E	L
K	N	E	D	N	A	L	E	I	W	R	C

Game 17: Mario's Big Comeback

1. Jaromir Jagr on the Penguins' captaincy issue.
2. Luc Robitaille, who played with Pittsburgh in 1994–95, the only full season Mario Lemieux missed during his career.
3. New Jersey goalie Martin Brodeur.
4. NHL spokesman Frank Brown, who, prior to the big announcement, would not confirm Mario Lemieux's plans to resume his hockey career.
5. NHL commissioner Gary Bettman.
6. Dallas sniper Brett Hull.
7. Pittsburgh Penguins coach Ivan Hlinka.
8. Wayne Gretzky, after being asked about his future plans.
9. Mario Lemieux, after being asked if he would defer some of his salary. He made the comment with a big grin.
10. Phoenix centre Jeremy Roenick.

Game 18: Rookie Wonders

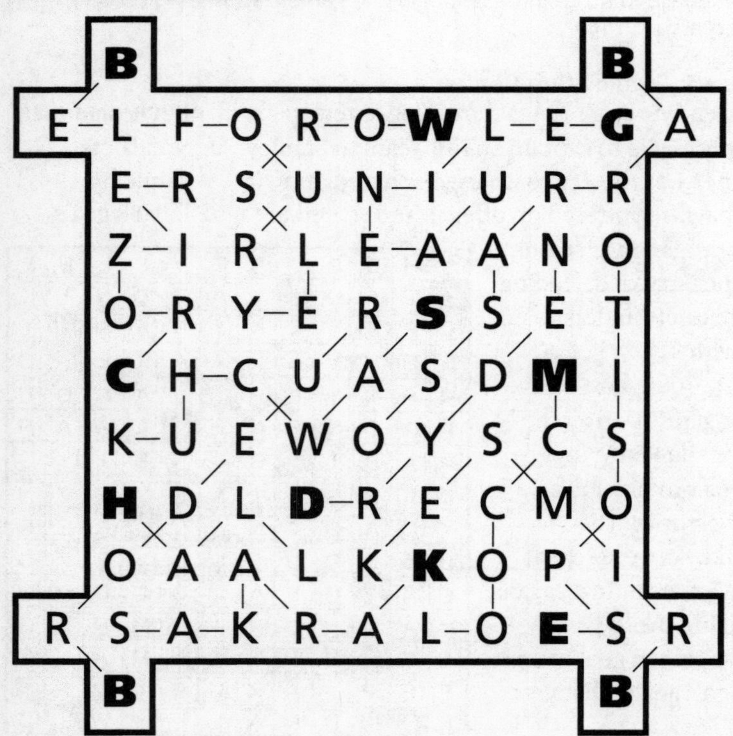

Game 19: Unusual Endings

PART 1

1. D. Gordie Howe, Hartford Whalers
2. A. Larry Robinson, Los Angeles Kings
3. F. Pat LaFontaine, New York Rangers
4. G. Darryl Sittler, Detroit Red Wings
5. H. Pierre Pilote, Toronto Maple Leafs
6. C. Grant Fuhr, Calgary Flames
7. E. Adam Oates, Edmonton Oilers
8. B. Bobby Orr, Chicago Blackhawks

PART 2

1. E. Guy Lafleur, Quebec Nordiques
2. F. Borje Salming, Detroit Red Wings
3. A. Bobby Hull, Hartford Whalers
4. A. Dale Hunter, Colorado Avalanche
5. C. Andy Bathgate, Pittsburgh Penguins
6. D. Peter Stastny, St. Louis Blues
7. H. Rick Martin, Los Angeles Kings
8. G. Paul Coffey, Boston Bruins

Game 20: Penalty-Shot History

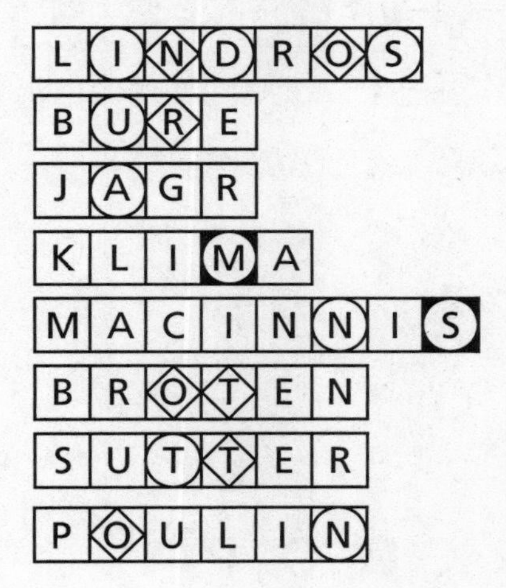

During the 1999 playoffs, **MATS SUNDIN** of **TORONTO** became the first NHLer to take two penalty shots in one postseason. He was stopped by John Vanbiesbrouck, but scored against Dominik Hasek.

Game 21: Cup Quotes

1. Aerosmith's Steven Tyler, comparing the Cup's many celebrations to his band's legendary reputation for partying.
2. Mike Keane, after being told that Al Iafrate didn't like his playing style.
3. Jeff Brown, St. Louis defenseman, before Game 7 against Toronto during the 1993 playoffs.
4. Clark Gillies, New York Islanders forward, responding to comments concerning his dog drinking from the Cup's bowl.
5. Olaf Kolzig, Washington goalie, on his tentative plans to include Stanley at his upcoming wedding.
6. Wayne Gretzky, on making it to the Cup finals.
7. Strip-club owner Lonnie Hanover, on Mark Messier bringing the Cup to his nightclub after the Rangers won in 1994.
8. Gump Worsley, Hall of Fame goalie, on what it's really like to drink champagne from the Cup.
9. Mike Keenan, 1994 Cup-winning coach, on the silverware's mesmerizing effect.

Acknowledgements

Thanks to the following publishers and organizations for the use of quoted and statistical material:

- The *Hockey News*, various excerpts. Reprinted with the permission of the *Hockey News*, a division of GTC Transcontinental Publishing, Inc.
- *The Official NHL Guide and Record Book*. Published by Total Sports Canada.
- *Total Hockey*, second edition; *Total Stanley Cup* (1998, 2000); and *Total NHL* (2003) by Dan Diamond and Associates Inc. Published by Total Sports. 1998, 2000.
- *In The Crease* by Dick Irvin. Published by McClelland & Stewart, Inc. 1995.
- *Boom-Boom: The Life and Times of Bernard Geoffrion* by Bernard Geoffrion and Stan Fischler. Published by McGraw-Hill Ryerson. 1997.
- *The Game I'll Never Forget: 100 Hockey Stars' Stories* by Chris McDonell. Published by Firefly Books Ltd. 2002.
- *The Hockey Handbook* by Lloyd Percival. Published by McClelland & Stewart. 1992.
- *20th Century Hockey Chronicle* by Stan and Shirley Fischler, Morgan Hughes, Joseph Romain and James Duplacey. 1994.
- *Same Game, Different Name: The History of the World Hockey Association* by Jack Lautier and Frank Polnaszek. 1996.
- The *National Post*; the *Montreal Gazette*; the *Globe and Mail*; the *Edmonton Journal*; the *Calgary Herald*; the *Vancouver Sun*; *Sports Illustrated*; the *Dallas Morning News*; the *Miami Herald*; the *Associated Press*; the *Late Show with David Letterman*; *Too Colourful for the League*; and numerous other books, publications and radio and TV programs that both guided and corroborated our research.

The author gratefully acknowledges all the help throughout the years from Jason Kay and everyone at the *Hockey News;* Gary Meagher and Benny Ercolani of the NHL; Phil Pritchard and Craig Campbell at The Hockey Hall of Fame; the staff at the McLellan-Redpath Library at McGill University; Rob Sanders, Susan Rana and Chris Labonté at Greystone Books; designers Peter Cocking, Jessica Sullivan and Lisa Hemingway; Bruce Bennett and the photographers at Bruce Bennett Studios; the many hockey writers, broadcast journalists, media and Internet publishers who have made the game better through their own work; statistical resources such as the Elias Sports Bureau, hockeydb.com, faceoff.com, hhof.com and shrpsports.com; and inputter Bev Jang, editor Anne Rose and puzzle designer Adrian van Vlaardingen for their dedication, expertise and creativity.

Finally, special thanks to sportswriter and author Kerry Banks for his contributions, from research to writing; and for being my "second pair of eyes" on the facts.